THE LIFE RECORDS OF
John Milton

RUTGERS STUDIES IN ENGLISH

NUMBER 7

MILTON AT THE AGE OF 21

From a copy of Houbraken's engraving in the possession of the editor

THE LIFE RECORDS OF

John Milton

VOLUME II

1639-1651

EDITED BY J. MILTON FRENCH

GORDIAN PRESS, INC.

NEW YORK

1966

Published by Gordian Press, Inc. 1966 by
arrangement with Rutgers, The State University

Printed in U.S.A. by
EDWARDS BROTHERS, INC.
Ann Arbor, Michigan

PREFACE

THE present volume continues the records of Milton's life from the point where Volume I ended, namely his arrival back in England in 1639 after his journey to Italy. This date opens a distinct new epoch of his life, in which he turns from the cultivation of poetry and scholarship to a public and frequently controversial career. The present volume ends with the appearance of the book which he considered the crown of that career, his first *Defense of the English People* in 1651. Though his appointment as Latin Secretary in 1649 might possibly have been a more appropriate date to end, the demands of space have forced me to choose the later date in order not to leave too heavy a burden for Volume III, in which I hope it may be possible to carry the story of Milton's life through to 1660.

The same abbreviations and references used in Volume I are followed here.

A preface, written after a book is substantially complete and after the author has therefore committed himself irrevocably, recalls the poignant words of the litany in which we confess our awareness of having done the things we should not have done and left undone the things which we should have done. But it also offers him the somewhat compensating pleasure of acknowledging his indebtedness to many people whose co-operation often appears all too dimly in the book itself.

It is a pleasure and an honor to be able to continue my thanks to those whom I named in the preface to Volume I and, in addition, to express my grateful appreciation of many new favors from others. Some of the latter I should have thanked more conspicuously in Volume I, and to them I hereby express my regret for not having done so. If still others should be included here but are not, I beg their forgiveness for my inadequate memory, but I hope that they will be reassured to find their names in the notes in the proper places.

Lord Delamere and his agent, W. Cullimore, Esq., Dr. John Fulton, and Miss Dorothy M. Stuart have graciously allowed me to reprint manuscript materials in their possession. The late

Professor Wilbur Cortez Abbott, Noel Blakiston, Esq., Professor Donald C. Dorian, G. R. Hughes, Esq., Professor William A. Jackson, Professor Maurice Kelley, Professor Thomas Ollive Mabbott, Professor Remigio U. Pane, Professor Dora Neill Raymond, and Professor G. H. Turnbull have given me information and advice most generously. Mr. William D. Morley, Messrs. Maggs Brothers, and Mr. George Smith have courteously assisted me in tracing books and manuscripts which have passed through their hands. Mr. Harold N. Munger, Jr., who has succeeded Mr. Earl S. Miers as Director of the Rutgers University Press, has found many ways to speed up and improve this book. The Bibliothèque Nationale, the Sutro Library, and the libraries of Columbia University, Trinity College, Cambridge, and the Union Theological Seminary have provided photostats and microfilms and have granted me permission to reprint them. Finally, the Goldsmiths' Company, the Guildhall, the Historical Society of Pennsylvania, the National Portrait Gallery, and the Prerogative Court of Canterbury have assisted my search for biographical information.

In conclusion, may I repeat my appeal in Volume I to all readers and reviewers to call to my attention any corrections and additions which should be gathered in Volume IV? Though I am not so naïve as to suppose that I can make this work complete or definitive, I hope to load every possible rift with ore. My hope is to follow, even if at a great distance, the practice which Milton himself described in the preface to his *Brief History of Moscovia*: *What was scatter'd in many Volumes, and observ'd at several times by Eye-witnesses, with no cursory pains I laid together, to save the Reader a far longer travaile of wandring through so many desert Authours; who yet with some delight drew me after them, from the eastern Bounds of Russia, to the Walls of Cathay. . . ."*

J. MILTON FRENCH

Rutgers University
June, 1950

THE LIFE RECORDS OF
John Milton

The Life Records of John Milton

1639
continued

SEPTEMBER (?). BUYS A BIBLE IN CANTERBURY (?).

1639—J. Milton, A.M. . . . .

1639, at Canterbury city—Jn° Milton, son of Jn° Milton, born in Oxford, late of Christ College, Cantabridd. This year of very dreadful commotion, and I weene will ensue murderous times of conflicting fight. . . .

> When that day of Death shall come,
> then shall nightly shades prevaile—
> soone shall Love & Music faile—
> soone the fresh turfes tender Blade
> shall florish ore my sleeping shade.

These notes purport to have been written in Milton's autograph in a copy of the 1637 edition of the Bible. It is described at some length in the *Gentleman's Magazine*, LXII (1792), 612, 615, 789, 900, 1102; *ibid.*, LXIII (1793), 106; *ibid.*, LXX (1800), 199-200; French, "The Autographs of John Milton," # 82; CM, XVIII, 562, 599. Other entries are noticed below under date of October 2, 1640. The Bible is said to contain also signatures of a number of people of the seventeenth and later centuries, as well as several sketches of Milton. No trace of the volume has been found since the bookseller Thomas Kerslake sold it about 1884 (*Athenæum*, I [1884], 19-20, 56). Its genuineness is open to grave question. The editors of Volume XVIII of the Columbia Milton questioned whether the entries were possibly a forgery by Thomas Chatterton.

SEPTEMBER (?). ACQUIRES A BIBLE AND OTHER BOOKS (?).

The evidence of the genuineness of these volumes as having been part of Milton's library is of the slenderest. They were first mentioned in public in the Los Angeles *Examiner* of January 20, 1929, in a story in which they were described by Professor J. Tarbotton Armstrong of the University of Southern California. The books comprised (1) a

Bible of 1599 bound with a Book of Psalms of 1639, (2) a concordance of 1599, (3) a French prayer book, and (4) a volume of sermons. Professor Armstrong conjectured that a manuscript prayer in the Bible and some notes in the concordance were in the hand of the poet Milton. The books were described as having been kept for a long time in a wrapper marked, "The Milton Books." See French, "The Autographs of John Milton," # 69, 94, 95; CM, XVIII, 564, 580. Inquiries to California have failed to elicit any information about the present whereabouts of these books.

VISITS WITH FATHER AND OTHER FRIENDS.

Soon after his return [from Italy], and visits paid to his Father and other Friends. . . .

Phillips, p. xvi; Darbishire, p. 62.

NOVEMBER 3. RECEIVES INTEREST ON COPE BOND (?).

. . . neyther ye s'd principall debt of 150^ll nor any pte thereof nor any Jnterest due for ye forbearance of the same since November 1641 hath been paid or satisfied. . . .

Milton's bill against Lady Elizabeth Cope and Sir Anthony Cope, June 16, 1654, *q.v.*; see entry under May 3, 1638.

DECEMBER 12. RECEIVES INTEREST PAYMENT FROM RICHARD POWELL.

. . . the growing Jnterest for the forbearance of the said Principall debt was for some yeares then following likewise payd And soe continued to bee paid vntill June Jn the yeare of our Lord One Thousand six hundred ffortie and ffower. . . .

From Milton's answer to Elizabeth Ashworth, February 22, 1653/4, *q.v.*

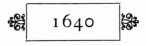

1640

GROWING CONFIDENCE IN HIS OWN GENIUS.

I began thus farre to assent both to them and divers of my friends here at home, and not lesse to an inward prompting which now grew daily upon me, that by labour and intent study (which I take to be my portion in this life) joyn'd with the strong propensity of nature, I might perhaps leave something so written to aftertimes, as they should not willingly let it die.

Milton, *The Reason of Church Government*, 1641, p. 37; cm, iii, 236. Though incapable of precise dating, this state of mind seems to fit the year 1640 as well as any time. This passage follows directly after Milton's description of the enthusiastic reception of his writings by his friends in Italy.

KEEPS POETIC NOTEBOOK WITH PLANS FOR POEMS AND OTHER WRITINGS.

The so-called Trinity or Cambridge Manuscript, which was probably used by Milton over a considerable period of years (perhaps 1630-1658), contains a number of his poems, sketches for other poems, and miscellaneous notes on his reading. Given to Trinity College, Cambridge, in 1691 by Sir Henry Newton Puckering, it has remained there ever since. It has often been reproduced, completely or partially, the standard facsimile being that edited by W. A. Wright in 1899 and reproduced in Fletcher's facsimile, I, 384. Sotheby reproduces a considerable number of pages. Todd (iii [1826], 515), Masson (ii, 102), cm (xviii, 228), and many other editions and commentaries print most of the entries. Though it cannot be assigned to any one year in respect to the time of composition, it seems convenient to mention it at the time when Milton returned from Italy and settled down to concentrated study. For a study of the stylistic problems involved in it, see French, "Chips from Milton's Workshop," *E L H*, x (1943), 230.

This manuscript contains the following material:

I   Poems.
  1. "Arcades."
  2. "At a solemn Musick" (3 drafts).
  3. "How soone hath Time the suttle theefe of Youth."
  4. "On Time."
  5. "Upon the Circumcision."
  6. "When the assault was intended to ye Citty."
  7. "Ladie, that in ye prime of Earliest youth."
  8. "To ye Lady Margaret Ley."
  9. "A maske" ["Comus"].
  10. "Lycidas."
  11. "To my freind Mr Hen. Laws Feb. 9. 1645" (3 drafts).
  12. "On the detraction wch follow'd upon my writing certain treatises" (2 drafts).
  13. "On ye religious memorie of Mrs Catharine Thomason" (3 drafts).
  14. "A booke was writ of late call'd Tetrachordon" (2 drafts).
  15. "On ye Lord Gen. Fairfax at ye seige of Colchester."

16. "To the Lord Generall Cromwell May 1652."
17. "To Sr Henry Vane the younger."
18. "On the forcers of Conscience."
19. "To day deep thoughts resolve with me to drench."
20. "Cyriack, this three years day these eys, though clear."
21. "Mee thought J saw my late espoused saint."

II Plans for dramas and poems.
  1. Sketches for *Paradise Lost.*
  2. "Abram from Morea."
  3. "Baptistes."
  4. "Sodom Burning."
  5. "Moabitides or Phineas."
  6. "Christus patiens."

III Miscellaneous entries.
  1. A letter to an unknown addressee (2 drafts).
  2. Notes from Old Testament history.
  3. Notes from early English history.
  4. "Scotch Stories."

See also CM, XVIII, 511, 654; French, "The Autographs of John Milton," # 2.

BEGINS TO KEEP A COMMONPLACE BOOK.

Similarly incapable of exact dating with the Trinity Manuscript is the very important Commonplace Book of Milton. It is a collection of jottings by Milton himself and by several amanuenses, arranged under numerous headings and dealing with many topics. Discovered in 1874 by Alfred J. Horwood among the papers of Sir Frederick Graham, it is now Additional Manuscript 36,354 in the British Museum.

The Commonplace Book is divided by Milton into three sections: (1) Index Ethicus, (2) Index Œconomicus, (3) Index Politicus. The first section comprises entries on moral evil, on the good man, on virtue, on lust, on poetry, and on numerous other rather widely varied subjects. The second section deals with food, with matrimony, with divorce, with usury, and with various other subjects. The third section covers the commonwealth, the king, the subject, the courtiers, property and taxes, spectacles, war, and the like. Written largely in Latin, it gathers quotations and ideas from a good many writers.

Several references in the Commonplace Book show that Milton also kept other books of a similar nature which are now lost. Half a dozen allusions to subjects treated in a "Theological Index" are collected in CM, XVIII, 227. A somewhat similar set of notes from the so-called Columbia Manuscript is printed in CM, XVIII, 221.

For further information see Horwood's facsimile edition of the Commonplace Book, 1876, and his printed texts in the publications of the Camden Society, 1876 and 1877; J. H. Hanford, "The Chronology of Milton's Private Studies," *PMLA*, XXXVI (1921), 251; French, "The Autographs of John Milton," #9; CM, XVIII, 128, 505.

BEGINS A BOOK ON CHRISTIAN DOCTRINE.

The inception of Milton's *De Doctrina Christiana*, first published posthumously in 1825, has been placed at various points in his life from 1640 to 1655. Arthur Sewell (*A Study in Milton's Christian Doctrine*, 1939, p. 3) says: "In 1640, then, it is likely that he was already occupied with the first stage, 'the dictation of a tractate from the ablest of divines.'" Hilaire Belloc (*Milton*, 1935, p. 305) thinks the bulk of the work on it was done from 1642 to 1649. Hanford believes (*Studies in Philology*, XVII [1920], 309) that it was begun soon after his return from Italy. Edward Phillips mentions it among the other items in his description of the scholastic regime under which he and others studied from Milton (Darbishire, p. 61): "The next work after this, was the writing from his own dictation, some part, from time to time, of a Tractate which he thought fit to collect from the ablest of Divines, who had written of that Subject; *Amesius*, *Wollebius*, &c. viz. A perfect System of Divinity, of which more hereafter." Further references to this work will be found under the year 1655, when he very likely resumed work on it more actively than for some years previously.

LETTERS TO MONKS AT VALLOMBROSA (?).

James Dixon asserted in 1873 that he had heard of some letters written to the fathers at Vallombrosa by Milton after his return to England, but that he was unable to find any of them himself. A correspondent signing himself C. J. H. wrote in 1877 that he had been shown two of these letters, written to the convent, and still in excellent preservation. Aldo Sorani wrote in 1925 that though he could then find no trace of any Miltonic letters, he had evidence that two written in Latin had still been extant a century or so earlier. See *Notes and Queries*, IV, xi (1873), 62; *ibid.*, v, viii (1877), 117; *Saturday Review of Literature*, II (1925), 318; French, "The Autographs of John Milton," #8; CM, XII, 413; CM, XVIII, 528.

DATI AND FRANCINI WRITE COMMENDATORY POEMS ABOUT HIM.

> Quin & nostra suas docuerunt nomina fagos
> Et Datis, & Francinus, erant & vocibus ambo
> Et studiis noti, Lydorum sanguinis ambo.

Milton, "Epitaphium Damonis," lines 136-138; CM, I, 308. Though the poems cannot be exactly dated, they are obviously earlier than the poem in which they are cited, which seems to belong about in the summer of 1640. It may be that these are the same poems which were later used among the prefatory matter to the *Poems* of 1645.

[Indeed, Dati and Francini, who were both famous for their studies and their publications, both of Lydian blood, taught my name to their beech-trees.]

MOVES TO ST. BRIDE'S CHURCHYARD AND BEGINS TUTORING.

Soon after his return [from Italy], and visits paid to his Father and other Friends, he took him a Lodging in St. *Brides* Church-yard, at the House of one *Russel* a Taylor, where he first undertook the Education and Instruction of his Sister's two Sons, the Younger whereof had been wholly Committed to his Charge and Care. And here by the way, I judge it not impertinent to mention the many Authors both of the Latin and Greek, which through his excellent judgment and way of Teaching, far above the Pedantry of common publick Schools (where such Authors are scarce ever heard of) were run over within no greater compass of time, then from Ten to Fifteen or Sixteen Years of Age. Of the Latin the four Grand Authors, *De Re Rustica, Cato, Varro, Columella, and Palladius; Cornelius Celsus,* an Ancient Physician of the *Romans*; a great part of *Pliny's* Natural History, *Vitruvius* his Architecture, *Frontinus* his Stratagems, with the two Egregious Poets, *Lucretius,* and *Manilius.* Of the Greek; *Hesiod,* a Poet equal with *Homer; Aratus* his *Phænomena,* and *Diosemeia, Dionysius Afer de situ Orbis, Oppian's Cynegeticks & Halieuticks. Quintus Calaber* his Poem of the *Trojan* War, continued from *Homer; Apollonius, Rhodius* his *Argonuticks,* and in Prose, *Plutarch's Placita Philosophorum &* Περι Παιδων 'Αγογιας, *Geminus's* Astronomy; *Xenophon's Cyri Institutio & Anabasis; Aelians Tacticks,* and *Polyænus* his Warlike Stratagems; thus by teaching he in some measure increased his own knowledge, having the reading of all these Authors as it were by Proxy; and all this might possibly have conduced to the preserving of his Eyesight, had he not, moreover, been perpetually busied in his own Laborious Undertakings of the Book or Pen. Nor did the time thus Studiously imployed in conquering the *Greek* and *Latin*

Tongues, hinder the attaining to the chief Oriental Languages, *viz.* The *Hebrew*, *Caldee* and *Syriac*, so far as to go through the *Pentateuch*, or Five Books of *Moses* in *Hebrew*, to make a good entrance into the *Targum* or *Chaldee* Paraphrase, and to understand several Chapters of St. *Matthew* in the *Syriac* Testament, besides an Introduction into several Arts and Sciences, by Reading *Urstisius* his Arithmetick, *Riffs* Geometry, *Petiscus* his Trigonometry, *Joannes de Sacro Bosco de Sphæra*; and into the *Italian* and *French* Tongues, by reading in *Italian*, *Giovan Villani's* History of the Transactions between several petty States of *Italy*; and in *French* a great part of *Pierre Davity*, the famous Geographer of *France* in his time. The *Sunday's* work was for the most part the Reading each day a Chapter of the *Greek* Testament, and hearing his Learned Exposition upon the same, (and how this savoured of Atheism in him, I leave to the courteous Backbiter to judge). The next work after this, was the writing from his own dictation, some part, from time to time, of a Tractate which he thought fit to collect from the ablest of Divines, who had written of that Subject; *Amesius*, *Wollebius*, &c. *viz.* A perfect System of Divinity, of which more hereafter. Now persons so far Manuducted into the highest paths of Literature both Divine and Human, had they received his documents with the same Acuteness of Wit and Apprehension, the same Industry, Alacrity, and Thirst after Knowledge, as the Instructor was indued with, what Prodigies of Wit and Learning might they have proved! the Scholars might in some degree have come near to the equalling of the Master, or at least have in some sort made good what he seems to predict in the close of an Elegy he made in the Seventeenth Year of his Age, upon the Death of one of his Sister's Children (a Daughter) who died in her Infancy.

Phillips, pp. xvi-xix; Darbishire, pp. 60-62. The process here described must have continued throughout the period in which Milton was teaching his nephews, but since it is impossible to break it up and distribute it over the years, it is here given as a whole. On Milton's house in St. Bride's see Masson, II, 102; London *Times*, December 8, 1908,

p. 10; *The Complete Poetical Works of John Milton*, ed. H. H. Fletcher, 1941, p. 10.

Hee had from his first settling taken care of instructing his two Nephews by his Sister Phillips, and, as it happen'd, the Sonn of some friend.

The "earliest" biography, fol. 142; Darbishire, p. 24.

im̄ediately after his return he took a lodging at Mr Russell's a Taylour in St Brides church yard & took into his tuition his sisters two sons Edw: & John Philips ye first 10 the other 9 years of age & in a years time made them capable of interpreting a Latin authour at sight & within 3 years they went through ye best of Latin & Greec Poetts Lucretius & *Manilius* of ye Latins & wth him the use of the Globes and some Rudim^ts of Arithm: & Geom: Hesiod Aratus Dionysius Afer. Oppian Apollonij, Argonautica & Quintus Calaber. Cato Varro & Columella de Re rusticâ were the very first Authors they learn't.

As he was severe on one hand, so he was most familiar and free in his conversation to those to whome most severe in his way of education.—NB. He made his Nephews Songsters, and sing from the time they were with him.

Aubrey, fol. 64v; Darbishire, p. 12, with facsimile facing p. 12. Miss Darbishire identifies the handwriting of the first paragraph of this passage as that of Edward Phillips, with the exception of a few passages added in Aubrey's hand. The phrase "& wth him the use of the Globes" is added above the line, and "and some Rudim^ts of Arithm: & Geom:" in the margin. Before "Cato" comes a cancelled "Colo," probably the beginning of "Columella," later pushed along to follow "Varro." The "Apollonij, Argonautica" may be a later addition.

(12) That soon after he setled in an house in S. *Brides* Churchyard, near *Fleetstreet* in *London*, where he instructed in the Lat. Tongue two Youths named *John* and *Edw. Philips*, the Sons of his Sister *Anne* by her Husband *Edward Philips*: both which were afterwards Writers, and the eldest principl'd as his Uncle.

Wood, I, 881; Darbishire, p. 38.

. . . neither his Converse, nor his Writings, nor his manner of Teaching ever savour'd in the least any thing of Pedantry.

Phillips, p. xxviii; Darbishire, pp. 67-68; CM, XVIII, 377.

John Milton · 1640

EDWARD PHILLIPS . . . educated in Grammar Learning under his Uncle *J. Milt.* before-mention'd. . . .

This *Edw. Phillips* hath a Brother called *Joh. Phillips*, who having early imbib'd in a most plentiful manner the rankest Antimonarchical Principles, from that villanous leading incendiary *Joh. Milton* his Uncle, but not in any University. . . .

Wood, *Athenæ Oxonienses*, 1721, II, 1116, 1118, *s.v.* Edward Phillips and John Phillips.

MOVES TO ALDERSGATE; STUDYING AND TUTORING; HOLIDAYS.

Ipse, sicubi possem, tam rebus turbatis & fluctuantibus, locum consistendi circumspiciens, mihi librísque meis, sat amplam in urbe domum conduxi; ibi ad intermissa studia beatulus me recepi; rerum exitu Deo imprimis, & quibus id muneris populus dabat, facilè permisso.

Milton, *Defensio Secunda*, 1654, pp. 87-88; CM, VIII, 126-128. The phrase "sat amplam . . . domum" seems to refer to the Aldersgate house rather than to that in St. Bride's; compare the wording of the accompanying selections. For details of this house of Milton's, see Masson, II (1894), 208n.; Masson, "Local Memories of Milton," *Good Words*, XXXIV (1893), 130-134; *Notes and Queries*, x, x (1908), 404. In the first of these references Masson quotes a letter from a person who remembered having seen the house before its demolition, and places its main entrance as on the present Shaftesbury Place, with a side entrance on Maidenhead Court.

[I myself, looking about wherever I could amid so disturbed and fluctuating affairs for a place of residence for myself and my books, took a rather large house in the city. There I betook myself blissfully to my interrupted studies, willingly leaving the outcome of affairs first to God and then to those to whom the people gave that duty.]

Now hee took a large house, where the Earle of Barrimore, sent by his Aunt the Lady Ranalagh, Sʳ Thomas Gardiner of Essex, and others were under his Tuition: But whether it were that the tempers of our Gentry would not beare the strictness of his Discipline, or for what other reason, hee continud that course but a while.

The "earliest" biography, fol. 142; Darbishire, pp. 24-25.

. . . he made no long stay in his Lodgings in St. *Brides* Church-yard; necessity of having a place to dispose his Books in, and other Goods fit for the furnishing of a good handsome House, hastning him to take one; and accordingly a pretty Garden-House he took in *Aldersgate*-Street, at the end of an Entry; and therefore the fitter for his turn, by the reason of the Privacy, besides that there are few Streets in *London* more free from Noise then that.

Here first it was that his Academick Erudition was put in practice, and Vigorously proceeded, he himself giving an Example to those under him, (for it was not long after taking this House, e're his Elder Nephew was put to Board with him also) of hard Study, and spare Diet; only this advantage he had, that once in three weeks or a Month, he would drop into the Society of some Young Sparks of his Acquaintance, the chief whereof were Mr. *Alphry*, and Mr. *Miller*, two Gentlemen of *Gray's*-Inn, the *Beau's* of those Times, but nothing near so bad as those now-a-days; with these Gentlemen he would so far make bold with his Body, as now and then to keep a Gawdy-day.

In this House he continued several Years. . . .

Phillips, pp. xx-xxi; Darbishire, p. 62; CM, XVIII, 377. One may perhaps be allowed to speculate that he made the acquaintance of Alphry and Miller through his brother Christopher, who was now studying law. As to the identity of the two young sparks, *The Register of Admissions to Gray's Inn, 1521-1889*, ed. Joseph Foster, 1889, lists several possibilities. John Miller, Knight, was admitted to Gray's Inn on August 1, 1624 (p. 173), and John Miller, gentleman, son and heir of Richard Miller of Liston, Middlesex, on August 5, 1628 (p. 185). Richard Alfrey of Catsfield, Sussex, gentleman, was admitted on November 22, 1602 (p. 104), and Thomas Alfray, his son and heir, on July 20, 1633 (p. 200). If any of these were Milton's friends, the second in each case is the more likely.

And to this end that he might put it [the philosophy of his tractate on education] in practice, he took a larger house, where the Earl of *Barrimore* sent by his Aunt the Lady *Rannelagh*, Sir *Thomas Gardiner* of *Essex*, to be there with others (besides his two Nephews) under his Tuition. But whether it were that the tempers of our Gentry would not bear the strictness of his discipline, or for what other reasons I cannot tell, he continued that course but a while.

Wood, I, 882; Darbishire, p. 42.

Those morning haunts are where they should be, at home, not sleeping, or concocting the surfets of an irregular feast, but up, and stirring, in winter often ere the sound of any bell awake men to labour, or to devotion; in Summer as oft with the Bird that first rouses, or not much tardier, to reade good Authors, or cause them to be read, till the attention bee weary, or memory have his full fraught. Then with usefull and generous labours preserving the bodies health, and hardinesse; to render lightsome, cleare, and not lumpish obedience to the minde, to the cause of religion, and our Countries liberty, when it shall require firme hearts in sound bodies to stand and cover their stations, rather then to see the ruine of our Protestation, and the inforcement of a slavish life. These are the morning practises. . . .

Milton, *An Apology for Smectymnuus*, 1642, p. 13; CM, III, 298-299. The passage is Milton's answer to Hall's accusation that he spends his mornings and afternoons in idleness and immorality.

LINES ON SHAKESPEARE REPRINTED.

An Epitaph on the admirable Dramaticke Poet, William Shakespeare.

What neede my *Shakespeare* for his honoured bones,
· · · · · · · ·

That Kings for such a Tombe would wish to die.

I. M.

William Shakespeare, *Poems: Written by Wil. Shake-speare. Gent.*, 1640, sigs. K8-K8v; H. W. Garrod, "Milton's Lines on Shakespeare," *Essays and Studies by Members of the English Association*, XII (1926), 7-23. Collated in CM, I, 429. Reproduced in facsimile in Fletcher, I, 366.

POEM (OR POEMS) ON HOBSON PRINTED.

Here Hobson *lyes, who did most truely prove.* . . .

A Banquet of Jests, 1640, pp. 129-131; William R. Parker, "Milton's Hobson Poems: Some Neglected Early Texts," *Modern Lan-*

guage Review, XXXI (1936), 395-402; CM, XVIII, 349, 584. Facsimile in Fletcher, I, 370.

Here *Hobson* lyes amongst his many debters. . . .

A Banquet of Jests, 1640, pp. 131-132; William R. Parker, "Milton's Hobson Poems: Some Neglected Early Texts," *Modern Language Review*, XXXI (1936), 395-402; CM, XVIII, 359, 590. The authorship of this poem is by no means certain, but it may be by Milton. The notes in CM, XVIII, 591, give variant readings from *Wit Restor'd*, 1658, and from three manuscripts in which this poem appears: Bodleian MS. Tanner 465, pp. 235-236; British Museum MS. Add. 15,227, fol. 74; and British Museum MS. Sloane 542, fol. 52.

POEM ON LAVINIA PUBLISHED (?).

LAVINIA WALKING IN A FROSTY MORNING.

I' the non-age of a winter's day. . . .

William Shakespeare, *Poems: Written by Wil. Shake-speare, Gent.*, 1640, sig. L6v; CM, XVIII, 360, 592. This poem, attributed in Henry Lawes's *Second Book of Ayres*, 1655, in which it was reprinted, to "Mr. I. M.," was ascribed to Milton by Todd (Milton's *Works*, I, 1800, lxxxix-xci. Todd notes that Milton's verses on Shakespeare in the same volume are also subscribed with the initials I.M.

JANUARY 26. BROTHER CHRISTOPHER CALLED TO BAR OF INNER TEMPLE.

Christopher Milton . . . called to the bar.

A Calendar of the Inner Temple Records, ed. F. A. Inderwick, 1896 ff., II, 254; Masson, II, 488; Stern, I, ii, 161, 464; Brennecke, p. 144.

FEBRUARY 10. JOSEPH HALL'S *EPISCOPACY BY DIVINE RIGHT* REGISTERED.

10° ffebruarij 1639 . . . .

Master Butter   Entered for his Copie vnder the hands of Doctor BRAY and Master **Bourne** warden a booke called. *Episcopacy by diuine right asserted* by JOSEPH [HALL]: EXON [*i.e.* Bishop of EXETER]. . . . vj^d

The Stationers' Registers, ed. Arber, IV, 472; Masson, II, 126. Although not by Milton, of course, this book was virtually the opening gun in the long war of the books over episcopacy, to which Milton contributed several volumes. For a bibliography of the controversy, see Parker, *Milton's Contemporary Reputation*, pp. 263 ff.

APRIL (?). HALL'S *EPISCOPACY BY DIVINE RIGHT* PUBLISHED.

Episcopacie by Divine Right. Asserted, by Jos. Hall, B. of Exon. London . . . 1640.

Title page of the first edition. For the entry of this volume in the Stationers' Registers, see above under date of February 10, 1640. Though the copy in the Thomason collection in the British Museum is not dated, the editor of the Thomason catalogue dates the book in April, 1640. As much as any other single volume, this probably was responsible for the Smectymnuus controversy in which Milton was involved during the years 1641 and 1642.

APRIL 14. BROTHER CHRISTOPHER VICTIM OF RIOTS (?).

In J. C. Jeaffreson's *Middlesex County Records*, III (1888), 144, there is a summary of an entry from the Middlesex Sessions Rolls, the original of which I have not seen. It is to the effect that at a General Sessions of the Peace held at Westminster on April 14, 16 Charles I [1640], John Caster *alias* Carter, Harbert Caster, and Sylvester Caster, all of Heston, yeomen, were to be indicted for riot against Christopher Milton Esq. It is not certain that this Christopher Milton was the brother of the poet, and I have no further information about the incident.

MAY 3. RECEIVES INTEREST ON COPE BOND (?).

. . . neyther ye s'd principall debt of 150^{li} nor any pte thereof nor any Jnterest due for ye forbearance of the same since November 1641 hath been paid or satisfied. . . .

Milton's bill against Lady Elizabeth Cope and Sir Anthony Cope, June 16, 1654, *q.v.*; see entry under May 3, 1638.

JUNE 12. FATHER'S SUIT AGAINST DUCK AND CHILD DEFEATED.

M Johem Milton et Thomam Lune xij° Junij
L Bower q' Arthurum Ducke Vpon openinge of the matter
   in Legib$_3$ Dctor et Wm' this p^{r}sent Day by M^r ffoun-
   Childe Deft taine of Co: with the Deft
   vpon theire Demurrer put
   into the pt' Bill

Jt was alleadged that the pt' by theire Bill sett forth that one Mathew Evans being indebted vnto Rose Downer vpon a bond

[13]

for 50ˡˡ the pt paid the same to Mʳ. Downer and Had the Bond assigned to them but before any satisfaccōn hereof made Mathew Ewens Died and left Mathew Ewens his sonne his heire & extōr whoe to satisfie his ffathers Debtᵱ made sale of his ffathers Lands to the Deft Dʳ Ducke for a greate some of monie which hee received all to twoe or three thousand pound which was left in the Deft hands to satisfie amongst others the said 50ˡˡ out of which monie to haue satisfaccōn of the said 50ˡˡ from the Deft is the scope of the p't Bill to which the Deft have Demurred and say that the said p't have in their Bill set forth that Allexander Ewens one of the Deft was by the said Mathew Ewens Deceased appointed extor of his will whoe proved the will and tooke vpon him thexecucon thereof and possed himselfe of the monie remaininge in theire hands whereby the Deft alleadge they are acquited of the same and the p't are to Demaund satisfaccōn from the said Allexander Ewens Jt is herevpon ordered that vnles the said p't shall by thend of this Terme shew good cause to the contrary then the said Bill shall stand clearelie Defaulted out of this Courte & the p't payinge the Deft the ordinary Costᵱ./

Public Record Office, C 33/173, f. 349; French, *Milton in Chancery*, 290.

JUNE 30. FUTURE FATHER-IN-LAW, RICHARD POWELL, TRANSFERS REAL ESTATE IN FOREST HILL TO SIR ROBERT PYE.

That the said Richard Powell by his Indenture beareing date the 30°. Iune 1640. In consideracon of 1400ˡˡ. therein alleaged to bee paid, did graunt bargaine sell assigne and sett ouer to Sr. Robert Py knᵗ. the said Mannor of forresthill and other the premisses, for the whole tearme therein then to come, and unexpired: Vnder this prouiso to bee voyd vpon payment of the somme of 1510ˡⁱ the first of Iuly 1641. As by the said deed now produced vnder the hand and seale of the said Richard Powell. The sealeing and deliuery whereof is proved by Richard Sherwyn gent. . . . And I finde by an affidauit of the said Sʳ Robert

[14]

Py, here taken, That before the 30°. June 1640 hee redeemed a
lease forfeited by Richard Powell Esqz to George ffursman
by payinge 1000^{li}. to the said ffursman for the said Richard
Powell. And that hee lent the said Richard Powell before the
tyme aboue mentioned 300^{li} more in mony, both which sommes
togeather with 100^{li} for consideraćon amounted to 1400^{li}. for
security whereof the said Richard Powell did Convey by his
owne desire vnto the deponent the premisses by the deed before
mentioned, which debt is still vnpaid. . . .

From Reading's report of January 1, 1650/1, Public Record Office,
State Papers Domestic, 23/109, pp. 517-518; Hamilton, pp. 55-56.
For the story of Powell's financial affairs and their connection with
Milton, see French, *Milton in Chancery*, pp. 71 ff. Though the original
document of this Powell-Pye transfer has not been found, it is mentioned
often; see Hamilton, pp. 85, 89, 90, 106, 122. See also the entry following the present one.

JUNE 30 (?). TAKES POWELL'S LANDS IN WHEATLEY BY MORTGAGE.

The Petićon [of Anne Powell] further setts forth, That y^e
Lands belonging to y^e s^d. Richard Powell deceased, lying in y^e
County of Oxford, were mortgaged before y^e late Warres, vizt.
in y^e Yeare, 1640, The Freehold land to M^r. John Milton; & y^e
Lease Land, being a Lease for 31. Yeares, at, 272^{li} = 15^s = 8^d.
p annum, was mortgaged to S^r. Robert Pye, & by him assigned
to his Second Sonne M^r. John Pye.

Public Record Office, State Papers Domestic, 23/110, p. 529;
Hamilton, p. 122. Though the month and date are not mentioned in
this reference, it seems likely that this transaction is closely connected
with the preceding action between Powell and Pye; it is therefore tentatively given the same date here. That Milton's holdings were in Wheatley is specified in the following document. The excerpt is from the commissioners' report of 1653.

The Lands belonging to ye s^d Richard Powell lying in y^e
County of Oxford, were mortgaged before ye late vnhappy
warres: The Freehold lying in Wheatley in ye s^d County, to M^r.
John Milton; who hath payed ye Composićon for ye same. . . .
The Lease lands lying in Forresthill in ye s^d County, (being a
Lease for 31: yeares of ye yearely value of 272^{li}.-15^s.-8^d. over

& above 20^li. issuing out of it to a Curate, & 5^s. for Chiefe Rent) was mortgaged to S^r. Robert Pye, & by him assigned to his 2^d. Sonne M^r. John Pye.

Public Record Office, State Papers Domestic, 23/110, p. 525; Hamilton, p. 112. This excerpt is from Anne Powell's petition of October 20, 1652.

SUMMER (?). *EPITAPHIUM DAMONIS* PRINTED; GRIEF FOR DIODATI'S DEATH AND MEMORIES OF THEIR FRIEND-SHIP; PLANS FOR FUTURE POETRY.

EPITAPHIUM DAMONIS.

ARGUMENTUM.

Thyrsis & Damon ejusdem viciniæ Pastores, eadem studia sequuti a pueritiâ amici erant, ut qui plurimùm. Thyrsis animi causâ profectus peregrè de obitu Damonis nuncium accepit. Domum postea reversus, & rem ita esse comperto, se, suamque solitudinem hoc carmine deplorat. Damonis autem sub personâ hîc intelligitur Carolus Deodatus ex urbe Hetruriæ Luca Paterno genere oriundus, cætera Anglus; ingenio, doctrina, clarissimisque cæteris virtutibus, dum viveret, juvenis egregius. . . .

Et jam bis viridi surgebat culmus arista,
Et totidem flavas numerabant horrea messes,
Ex quo summa dies tulerat Damona sub umbras,
Nec dum aderat Thyrsis; pastorem scilicet illum
Dulcis amor Musæ Thusca retinebat in urbe.
Ast ubi mens expleta domum, pecorisque relicti
Cura vocat, simul assuetâ sedítque sub ulmo,
Tum vero amissum tum denique sentit amicum,
Cœpit & immensum sic exonerare dolorem.
　　Ite domum impasti, domino jam non vacat, agni. . . .
At mihi quid tandem fiet modò? quis mihi fidus
Hærebit lateri comes, ut tu sæpe solebas
Frigoribus duris, & per loca fœta pruinis,
Aut rapido sub sole, siti morientibus herbis?
Sive opus in magnos fuit eminùs ire leones
Aut avidos terrere lupos præsepibus altis;

Quis fando sopire diem, cantuque solebit? . . .
    Ite domum impasti, domino jam non vacat, agni.
Tityrus ad corylos vocat, Alphesibœus ad ornos,
Ad salices Aegon, ad flumina pulcher Amyntas,
Hîc gelidi fontes, hîc illita gramina musco,
Hîc Zephiri, hîc placidas interstrepit arbutus undas;
Ista canunt surdo, frutices ego nactus abibam.
    Ite domum impasti, domino jam non vacat, agni.
Mopsus ad hæc, nam me redeuntem forte notârat
(Et callebat avium linguas, & sydera Mopsus)
Thyrsi quid hoc? dixit, quæ te coquit improba bilis?
Aut te perdit amor, aut te malè fascinat astrum,
Saturni grave sæpe fuit pastoribus astrum,
Intimaque obliquo figit præcordia plumbo.
    Ite domum impasti, domino jam non vacat, agni.
Mirantur nymphæ, & quid te Thyrsi futurum est?
Quid tibi vis? aiunt, non hæc solet esse juventæ
Nubila frons, oculique truces, vultusque severi,
Illa choros, lususque leves, & semper amorem
Jure petit, bis ille miser qui serus amavit.
    Ite domum impasti, domino jam non vacat, agni.
Venit Hyas, Dryopéque, & filia Baucidis Aegle
Docta modos, citharæque sciens, sed perdita fastu,
Venit Idumanii Chloris vicina fluenti;
Nil me blanditiæ, nil me solantia verba,
Nil me, si quid adest, movet, aut spes ulla futuri. . . .
Heu quis me ignotas traxit vagus error in oras
Ire per aëreas rupes, Alpemque nivosam!
Ecquid erat tanti Romam vidisse sepultam?
Quamvis illa foret, qualem dum viseret olim,
Tityrus ipse suas & oves & rura reliquit;
Ut te tam dulci possem caruisse sodale,
Possem tot maria alta, tot interponere montes,
Tot sylvas, tot saxa tibi, fluviosque sonantes. . . .
Ah quoties dixi, cùm te cinis ater habebat,
Nunc canit, aut lepori nunc tendit retia Damon,

Vimina nunc texit, varios sibi quod sit in usus;
Et quæ tum facili sperabam mente futura
Arripui voto levis, & præsentia finxi,
Heus bone numquid agis? nisi te quid forte retardat,
Imus? & argutâ paulùm recubamus in umbra,
Aut ad aquas Colni, aut ubi jugera Cassibelauni?
Tu mihi percurres medicos, tua gramina, succos,
Helleborúmque, humilésque crocos, foliúmque hyacinthi,
Quasque habet ista palus herbas, artesque medentûm,
Ah pereant herbæ, pereant artesque medentûm,
Gramina, postquam ipsi nil profecere magistro.
Ipse etiam, nam nescio quid mihi grande sonabat
Fistula, ab undecimâ jam lux est altera nocte,
Et tum forte novis admôram labra cicutis,
Dissiluere tamen rupta compage, nec ultra
Ferre graves potuere sonos, dubito quoque ne sim
Turgidulus, tamen & referam, vos cedite silvæ.
    Ite domum impasti, domino jam non vacat, agni.
Ipse ego Dardanias Rutupina per æquora puppes
Dicam, & Pandrasidos regnum vetus Inogeniæ,
Brennúmque Arviragúmque duces, priscúmque Belinum,
Et tandem Armoricos Britonum sub lege colonos;
Tum gravidam Arturo fatali fraude Jögernen
Mendaces vultus, assumptáque Gorlöis arma,
Merlini dolus. O mihi tum si vita supersit,
Tu procul annosa pendebis fistula pinu
Multùm oblita mihi, aut patriis mutata camœnis
Brittonicum strides, quid enim? omnia non licet uni
Non sperasse uni licet omnia, mi satis ampla
Merces, & mihi grande decus (sim ignotus in ævum
Tum licet, externo penitúsque inglorius orbi)
Si me flava comas legat Usa, & potor Alauni,
Vorticibúsque frequens Abra, & nemus omne Treantæ,
Et Thamesis meus ante omnes, & fusca metallis
Tamara, & extremis me discant Orcades undis. . . .

Milton, "Epitaphium Damonis," *Poems*, 1645, Part II, pp. 77-87;
CM, I, 294-317. What appears to be the only extant copy of an undated

[18]

edition of about this time is in the British Museum, catalogued as C.57.d.48. It is an octavo pamphlet of four leaves, unnumbered, without title page or date, but with the word "Londini" at the end of the last page. It is described as the first edition by Leicester Bradner in the London *Times Literary Supplement*, August 18, 1932, p. 581. It was published with a verse translation by Walter W. Skeat in 1933, and was included in *Milton's Lament for Damon and his Other Latin Poems*, ed. E. H. Visiak, Oxford, 1935. The differences between this edition and that of 1645 used in the above selection are almost entirely in spelling and punctuation. It is reproduced in facsimile in Fletcher, I, 355ff. Full collation is given in CM, XVIII, 641-642.

The date is open to some question. Mackellar (*The Latin Poems of John Milton*, 1930, p. 61) dates it "a few months after his return from Italy," and Hughes gives it to 1639 with a question mark. On the other hand, Milton says quite specifically in the first three lines of the quoted passage that two springs and two autumns have passed since Diodati's death. If Milton intended his words to be taken at their face value, the date of the poem would then necessarily be the summer of 1640, since Diodati had died in August of 1638. It is therefore so dated in the present work.

[ON THE DEATH OF DAMON.

THE ARGUMENT.

Thyrsis and Damon, shepherds of the same neighbourhood, following the same pursuits, were friends from their boyhood, in the highest degree of mutual attachment. Thyrsis, having set out to travel for mental improvement, received news when abroad of Damon's death. Afterwards at length returning, and finding the matter to be so, he deplores himself and his solitary condition in the following poem. Under the guise of Damon, however, is here understood Charles Diodati, tracing his descent on the father's side from the Tuscan city of Lucca, but otherwise English,—a youth remarkable, while he lived, for his genius, his learning, and other most shining virtues. . . .

> Twice had the ears in the wheatfields shot through the
>   green of their sheathing,
> As many crops of pale gold were the reapers counting as
>   garnered,
> Since the last day that had taken Damon down from the
>   living,

Thyrsis not being by; for then that shepherd was absent,

Kept by the Muse's sweet love in the far-famed town of the
   Tuscan.

But, when his satiate mind, and the care of his flock recol-
   lected,

Brought him back to his home, and he sat, as of old, 'neath
   the elm-tree,

Then at last, O then, as the sense of his loss comes upon him,

Thus he begins to disburthen all his measureless sorrow:—

   "Go unpastured, my lambs: your master now heeds not
   your bleating. . . .

But for myself what remains? For me what faithful companion

Now will cling to my side, in the place of the one so familiar,

All through the season harsh when the grounds are crisp
   with the snow-crust,

Or 'neath the blazing sun when the herbage is dying for
   moisture?

Were it the task to go forth in the track of the ravaging
   lions,

Or to drive back from the folds the wolf-packs boldened by
   hunger,

Who would now lighten the day with the sound of his talk
   or his singing? . . .

   "Go unpastured, my lambs: your master now heeds not
   your bleating.

Tityrus calls to the hazels; to the ash-trees Alphesibœus;

Ægon suggests the willows: 'The streams,' says lovely
   Amyntas;

'Here are the cool springs, here the moss-broidered grass
   and the hillocks;

'Here are the zephyrs, and here the arbutus whispers the
   ripple.'

These things they sing to the deaf; so I took to the thickets
   and left them.

"Go unpastured, my lambs: your master now heeds not
  your bleating.
Mopsus addressed me next, for he had espied me returning
(Wise in the language of birds, and wise in the stars too,
  is Mopsus):
'Thyrsis,' he said, 'what is this? what bilious humour afflicts
  thee?
'Either love is the cause, or the blast of some star inaus-
  picious;
'Saturn's star is of all the oftenest deadly to shepherds,
'Fixing deep in the breast his slant leaden shaft of sick-
  ness.'
  "Go unpastured, my lambs: your master now heeds not
  your bleating.
Round me fair maids wonder. 'What will come of thee,
  Thyrsis?
'What wouldst thou have?' they say: 'not commonly see we
  the young men
'Wearing that cloud on the brow, the eyes thus stern and
  the visage:
'Youth seeks the dance and sports, and in all will tend to
  be wooing:
'Rightfully so: twice wretched is he who is late in his
  loving.'
  "Go unpastured, my lambs: your master now heeds not
  your bleating.
Dryope came, and Hyas, and Ægle, the daughter of Baucis
(Learned is she in the song and the lute, but O what a
  proud one!);
Came to me Chloris also, the maid from the banks of the
  Chelmer.
Nothing their blandishments move me, nothing their prattle
  of comfort;
Nothing the present can move me, nor any hope of the
  future. . . .

Ah! what roaming whimsy drew my steps to a distance,
Over the rocks hung in air and the Alpine passes and
glaciers!
Was it so needful for me to have seen old Rome in her
ruins—
Even though Rome had been such as, erst in the days of her
greatness,
Tityrus, only to visit, forsook both his flocks and his coun-
try—
That but for this I consented to lack the dear use of thy
presence,
Placing so many seas and so many mountains between us,
So many woods and rocks and so many murmuring riv-
ers? . . .
Ah! how often I said, when already the black mould be-
rapt thee,
'Now my Damon is singing, or spreading his snares for the
leveret;
'Now he is weaving his twig-net for some of his various
uses.'
What with my easy mind I hoped as then in the future
Lightly I seized with the wish and fancied as present before
me.
'Ho, my friend!' I would cry: 'art busy? If nothing prevent
thee,
'Shall we go rest somewhere in some talk-favouring covert,
'Or to the waters of Colne, or the fields of Cassibelaunus?
'There thou shalt run me over the list of thy herbs and
their juices,
'Foxglove, and crocuses lowly, and hyacinth-leaf with its
blossom,
'Marsh-plants also that grow for use in the art of the
healer.'
Perish the plants each one, and perish all arts of the healer
Gotten of herbs, since nothing served they even their mas-
ter!

I too—for strangely my pipe for some time past had been
  sounding
Strains of an unknown strength—'tis one day more than
  eleven since
Thus it befell—and perchance the reeds I was trying were
  new ones:
Bursting their fastenings, they flew apart when touched,
  and no farther
Dared to endure the grave sounds: I am haply in this over-
  boastful;
Yet I will tell out the tale. Ye woods, yield your honours
  and listen!
  "Go unpastured, my lambs: your master now heeds not
  your bleating.
I have a theme of the Trojans cruising our southern head-
  lands
Shaping to song, and the realm of Imogen, daughter of
  Pandras,
Brennus and Arvirach, dukes, and Bren's bold brother,
  Belinus;
Then the Armorican settlers under the laws of the Britons,
Ay, and the womb of Igraine fatally pregnant with Arthur,
Uther's son, whom he got disguised in Gorlois' likeness,
All by Merlin's craft. O then, if life shall be spared me,
Thou shalt be hung, my pipe, far off on some brown dying
  pine-tree,
Much forgotten of me; or else your Latian music
Changed for the British war-screech! What then? For one
  to do all things,
One to hope all things, fits not! Prize sufficiently ample
Mine, and distinction great (unheard of ever thereafter
Though I should be, and inglorious, all through the world
  of the stranger),
If but yellow-haired Ouse shall read me, the drinker of
  Alan,
Humber, which whirls as it flows, and Trent's whole valley
  of orchards,

Thames, my own Thames, above all, and Tamar's western
   waters,
Tawny with ores, and where the white waves swinge the
   far Orkneys.]

Masson, II, 85-94. Though the proper names mentioned as associates
of the poet probably refer to actual persons, no identification of them has
been offered. Milton's reference to the eleven days of high poetic ex-
citement, probably in some new kind of verse, is also tantalizing. It may
possibly have some connection with the early work on *Paradise Lost*
mentioned by Edward Phillips, who asserted that not far from this time
he saw a draft of the first speech of Satan for a poem on the fall of Adam.
There is also undoubtedly some relation between this experience and
the keeping of the poetic notebook mentioned above. At any rate, the
poem is certainly a farewell of some sort to pastoral poetry.

Testor illum mihi semper sacrum & solenne futurum Damonis
tumulum; in cujus funere ornando cum luctu & mœrore oppressus, ad ea quæ potui solatia confugere, & respirare paulisper
cupiebam. . . .

From Milton's letter to Dati, April 21, 1647, in his *Epistolarum
Familiarium Liber Unus*, 1674, p. 30; CM, XII, 48.

[I call to witness the tomb of Damon, which shall always be
sacred and solemn to me. When I was overcome with grief and
sadness in adorning his funeral rites, and sought whatever ways
I could to achieve consolation and to find a little breathing
space. . . .]

SUMMER (?). SENDS COPIES OF *EPITAPHIUM DAMONIS* TO FRIENDS IN ITALY.

Id quod ipse jamdiu legisse debes, siquidem ad vos carmen
illud pervenit, quod ex te nunc primum audio. Mittendum ego
sane sedulo curaveram. . . .

Milton, letter to Carlo Dati in Florence, April 21, 1647, *q.v.* Although Dati did not acknowledge the gift until 1647, and although the
date on which Milton sent him a copy cannot be dogmatically pro-
nounced, it seems likely that it was shortly after its first publication.
The tone of Milton's letter indicates that the lapse of time between the
gift of the poem and the letter was considerable. On the other hand, the
reference may be to Milton's *Poems* of 1645.

[This you must have read for yourself long ere now, if that

poem reached you, as now first I hear from you it did. I had carefully caused it to be sent. . . .]

Masson, III, 653.

AUGUST 11. BROTHER CHRISTOPHER'S DAUGHTER SARAH BAPTIZED.

1640. . . . Sarah yᵉ Daughter of Christopher & Thomazin Milton Bap: Aug: 11ᵗʰ.

Parish Register, Horton; Masson, II, 488; Brennecke, p. 144.

OCTOBER 2. ENTRIES IN BIBLE (?).

Mr. Hartlibe to Mr. Miltone sendeth the 12 booke of the Greciane volumes, and is obliged to hime—Octbre 2nd 1640/ Londone. . . . Johne Miltone, 16. A.M. 40. . . . J. Miltonius, M.A.C. Coll. . . . Myself, 1640.

These entries are found at different places in the Canterbury Bible noted above under date of September, 1639. For further information the reader is referred to that entry.

NOVEMBER. ATTRIBUTED WORK ABOUT BISHOPS.

Lord Bishops none of the Lords Bishops.

Attributed dubiously to Milton in Maggs Brothers' Catalogue 620, 1936, item 126; CM, XVIII, 639. The catalogue goes on to state that the work is generally assumed to be the work of William Prynne.

NOVEMBER 3. RECEIVES INTEREST ON COPE BOND (?).

. . . neyther yᵉ s'd principall debt of 150ˡˡ nor any pte thereof nor any Jnterest due for yᵉ forbearance of the same since November 1641 hath been paid or satisfied. . . .

Milton's bill against Lady Elizabeth Cope and Sir Anthony Cope, June 16, 1654, *q.v.*; see entry under May 3, 1638.

DECEMBER 12. RECEIVES INTEREST PAYMENT FROM RICHARD POWELL.

. . . the growing Jnterest for the forbearance of the said Principall debt was for some yeares then following likewise payd And soe continued to bee paid vntill June Jn the yeare of our Lord One Thousand six hundred ffortie and ffower. . . .

From Milton's reply to Elizabeth Ashworth, February 22, 1653/4, *q.v.*

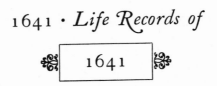

RELUCTANT CHANGE FROM PRIVATE STUDIES TO PUB-
LIC CONTROVERSY.

... if I hunted after praise by the ostentation of wit and learning, I should not write thus out of mine own season, when I have
neither yet compleated to my minde the full circle of my private
studies, although I complain not of any insufficiency to the
matter in hand, or were I ready to my wishes, it were a folly to
coṁit any thing elaborately compos'd to the carelesse and interrupted listening of these tumultuous times. . . . Lastly, I
should not chuse this manner of writing wherin knowing my
self inferior to my self, led by the genial power of nature to
another task, I have the use, as I may account it, but of my left
hand. . . . For although a Poet soaring in the high region of his
fancies with his garland and singing robes about him might
without apology speak more of himself then I mean to do, yet
for me sitting here below in the cool element of prose, a mortall
thing among many readers of no Empyreall conceit, to venture
and divulge unusual things of my selfe, I shall petition to the
gentler sort, it may not be envy to me. . . . I trust hereby to
make it manifest with what small willingnesse I endure to inter-
rupt the pursuit of no lesse hopes then these, and leave a calme
and pleasing solitarynes fed with cherful and confident thoughts,
to imbark in a troubl'd sea of noises and hoars disputes, put from
beholding the bright countenance of truth in the quiet and still
air of delightfull studies to come into the dim reflexion of hol-
low antiquities sold by the seeming bulk, and there be fain to
club quotations with men whose learning and beleif lies in
marginal stuffings . . . hors load of citations and fathers. . . .

Milton, *The Reason of Church Government*, 1641, pp. 36-41; CM,
III, 234 ff. Probably the change in Milton's thinking, study, and writing
here described was a somewhat gradual process, beginning perhaps as
soon as he returned to England, perhaps even earlier. But it is convenient to place it in the year 1641, since this is the first year in which he
produced a work specifically known to be his and in this new vein.

Quanquam fateor accessisse ad illam silentii causam, turbulentissimus iste, ex quo domum reversus sum, Britanniæ nostræ status, qui animum meum paulo post ab studiis excolendis, ad vitam & fortunas quoquo modo tuendas necessario convertit. Ecquem tu inter tot Civium commissa prælia, cædes, fugas, bonorum direptiones, recessum otio Literario tutum dari putes posse? Nos tamen etiam inter hæc mala, quoniam de studiis meis certior fieri postulas, sermone patrio haud pauca in lucem dedimus. . . .

Milton, letter to Carlo Dati, April 21, 1647, *q.v.*

[There was, I confess, an additional cause for my silence in that most turbulent state of our Britain, subsequent to my return home, which obliged me to divert my mind shortly afterwards from the prosecution of my studies to the defence anyhow of life and fortune. What safe retirement for literary leisure could you suppose given one among so many battles of a civil war, slaughters, flights, seizures of goods? Yet, even in the midst of these evils, since you desire to be informed about my studies, know that we have published not a few things in our native tongue. . . .]

Masson, III, 653.

CHOICE OF ENGLISH RATHER THAN LATIN AS LITERARY MEDIUM.

These thoughts at once possest me . . . there ought no regard be sooner had, then to Gods glory by the honour and instruction of my country. For which cause, and not only for that I knew it would be hard to arrive at the second rank among the Latines, *I* apply'd my selfe to that resolution which *Ariosto* follow'd against the perswasions of *Bembo*, to fix all the industry and art I could unite to the adorning of my native tongue; not to make verbal curiosities the end, that were a toylsom vanity, but to be an interpreter & relater of the best and sagest things among mine own Citizens throughout this Iland in the mother dialect. That what the greatest and choycest wits of *Athens*, *Rome*, or modern *Italy*, and those Hebrews of old did for their country,

I in my proportion with this over and above of being a Christian, might doe for mine: not caring to be once nam'd abroad, though perhaps I could attaine to that, but content with these British Ilands as my world. . . .

Milton, *The Reason of Church Government*, 1641, pp. 2, 14; CM, III, 236. The mental experience described here, which is of course not susceptible of exact dating, closely coincides with the tenor of some of his early writing, as for example the "Vacation Exercise" of 1629. Milton must, however, have made a somewhat similar decision some time between the writing of his "Epitaphium Damonis" and the opening of his series of anti-episcopal tracts in 1641. The quotation is therefore here placed in the year 1641.

APPEARANCE OF ROYALIST TREATISES ON CHURCH GOVERNMENT.

Certaine Briefe Treatises, written by Diverse Learned Men, concerning the ancient and Moderne government of the Church . . . Oxford . . . 1641.

From the title page of the first edition. This work, to which Milton's *Reason of Church Government*, 1641, is in part a reply, is an anthology of selections from Hooker, Andrews, Bucer, Rainoldes, Usher, Brerewood, and others.

. . . whilst other profound Clerks of late greatly, as they conceive, to the advancement of Prelaty, are so earnestly meting out the Lydian proconsular Asia, to make good the prime metropolis of Ephesus, as if some of our Prelates in all haste meant to change their soile, and become neighbors to the English Bishop of Chalcedon; and whilest good *Breerwood* as busily bestirres himselfe in our vulgar tongue to divide precisely the three Patriarchats, of Rome, Alexandria, and Antioch and whether to any of these England doth belong. . . . [Milton's Chapter V is an answer to Andrewes and the Primate in] a little treatise lately printed among others of like sort at *Oxford*, and in the title said to be out of the rude draughts of Bishop *Andrews*.

Milton, *The Reason of Church Government*, 1641, pp. 2, 14; CM, III, 182-183, 201. The reference to Lydia is to Usher's essay, "A Geographicall and Historicall disquisition, touching the *Lydian* or *Proconsular Asia*," part 4, pp. 76 ff. The Brerewood reference is to Edward Brerewood's "The Patriarchicall Government of the ancient

John Milton · 1641

Church. . . . *The first Question. Whether every Church or Bishop, at the time of the* Nicene *Councell, were subject to the three Patriarchs, of* Rome, *of* Alexandria, *and of* Antiochia." The contribution of Andrewes was *A Summary view of the Government both of the Old and New Testament: by* Lancelot Andrewes. See also Masson, ii, 363, and ii (1894), 367-368.

Father and brother Christopher move to Reading.

Though there is no record of the move, the fact that Christopher's child was baptized in Reading on August 27 of this year places the change previous to that date. It is here tentatively dated as simply in the year 1641.

Acquires Farnaby's book on grammar.

Systema Grammaticum . . . Ii Milton.

This book, published in 1641, is now in the Harvard College Library. See French, "The Autographs of John Milton," #83; cm, xviii, 346, 573. Milton's name is inscribed on the title page, but probably not in his handwriting. If "Ii" is the correct reading, it probably is an abbreviation for some form of "Johannes." But it is not certain; it may possibly be "li," which would probably mean "liber," or the book of Milton. The name is followed by some figures, the significance of which is not clear. First written of in 1858 by Washington Moon (*Notes and Queries,* ii, vi, 39), it has never been seriously questioned as a volume from Milton's library, though there is little tangible proof of his ownership. It contains a few unimportant notes.

Heavily taxed.

St Buttolphes Parish . . . The Second Precinct . . . Jo: Milton —03.04.00.

Fragment of a tax list of St. Botolph's Parish, undated, Guildhall Library MS. 1503/7; *Modern Language Review,* xxvi (1931), 179. In the manuscript the original amount of the tax, £2-8-0, which preceded Milton's name, has been crossed out and the higher amount, £3-4-0, added after his name. Similar raises occur in the names of some of his neighbors. Dr. Gill, for example, is increased from £1-12-0 to £2-2-0. The list, for the benefit of anyone interested in Milton's neighbors, reads in the following order: Loring, Gill, Botsford, Corker, Pearse, Woodington, Brownbakers Hall, Tudman, Cragg, Hopper (lodger), Clarke, Beamont, Dawson (lodger), Muscle, Pallavicine, Milton, Wilsford, Mathews, etc. Since Hopper's name as a lodger has been crossed off the similar list of April 29, 1641 (*q.v.*), it seems likely that the present list precedes that one. The taxes levied in this neighborhood range from ten shillings to six pounds, indicating that Milton was in fairly comfortable circumstances comparatively.

... domi fere me continebam, meis ipse facultatibus, tametsi hoc civili tumultu magna ex parte sæpe detentis, & census ferè iniquiùs mihi impositum, & vitam utcunque frugi tolerabam.

Milton, *Defensio Secunda*, 1654, p. 94; CM, VIII, 136.

[I usually stayed at home and supported myself, however frugally, with my own means, though these were often in large part detained during this civil tumult, and a rather unjust tax was laid on me.]

JANUARY. WORK SOMETIMES ATTRIBUTED TO MILTON.

A short view of the Prælatical Church of England.

See CM, XVIII, 636. The author was probably John Barnard or Richard Bernard. There is no likelihood whatever that it was written by Milton. The January dating is from the Thomason Catalogue (I, 7).

JANUARY 13. JOSEPH HALL'S *HUMBLE REMONSTRANCE* ENTERED FOR PUBLICATION.

13° Januarii 1640

... Master Butter. Entred ... vnder the hands of Doctor WYKES, and both the wardens, a booke called, *An humble remonstrance to the High Co^{rt} of parliam^t by a dutifull sonne of the church* ... vj^d.

The Stationers' Registers (ed. Eyre and Rivington), I, 9. For a summary of the Smectymnuus controversy, of which this title is a most important part, see Masson, II, *passim*; Parker, *Milton's Contemporary Reputation*, pp. 263-265; C. Looten, "Les débuts de Milton pamphletaire," *Études Anglaises*, I (1937), 297-313.

ABOUT JANUARY 25. HALL'S *HUMBLE REMONSTRANCE* PUBLISHED.

An Humble Remonstrance to the High Covrt of Parliament, By A dutifull Sonne of the Chvrch. London, Printed for Nathaniel Butter ... 1640.

Title page of the first edition. Though the editor of the Thomason Catalogue dates it merely January, 1641, Robert Baillie's letter quoted below places it somewhat more precisely. The date 1640, as it appears on the title page, means 1640/1.

Bishop Hall. . . . This week he has put out a remonstrance to the parliament, for keeping up of bishops and liturgies. . . .

Robert Baillie, letter from London to the Presbytery of Irvine, dated January 29, printed in his *Letters and Journals*, I (Edinburgh, 1775), 237. Parker, p. 263, dates the appearance of Hall's book January 26-29.

MARCH 20. SMECTYMNUUS'S *ANSWER TO THE HUMBLE REMONSTRANCE* ENTERED FOR PUBLICATION.

20° Martii 1640

. . . Master Rothwell, Junr. Entred . . . under the hands of Sr EDWARD DEERING (appointed at a Committee of the Comons house of parliam^t for licensing of bookes) and Master DOWNES warden, *An Answere to a booke entituled An humble remonstrance in wch the originall of Liturgy & Episcopacy is discussed & Queries propounded concerning both*, &c. . . . vj^d.

The Stationers' Registers (ed. Eyre and Rivington), I, 16; Masson, II, 219. Masson thinks that Milton contributed materials for some twenty pages of this volume; *ibid.*, II, 239. For further discussion, see CM, XVIII, 629-630.

MARCH (?). SMECTYMNUUS'S *ANSWER* TO HALL PUBLISHED.

An Answer to a Booke entitvled, An Hvmble Remonstrance. In which, The Originall of $\begin{Bmatrix} \text{Liturgy} \\ \text{Episcopacy} \end{Bmatrix}$ is discussed. . . . Written by Smectymnvvs. London, Printed for I. Rothwell . . . 1641.

From the title page of the first edition. The date given in the Thomason Catalogue is February (1, 8), but since the volume was not registered until March 20, it is more likely that it appeared toward the end of March.

APRIL 12. HALL'S *DEFENCE* LICENSED FOR PUBLICATION.

12° Aprilis 1641

. . . Master Butter. Entred for his copie under the hands of Master HANSLEY and both wardens, *A defence of the humble Remonstrance against the frivolous & false exceptions of Smectimnius* . . . vj^d.

The Stationers' Registers (ed. Eyre and Rivington), I, 20.

April (?). Hall's *Defence* Published.

A Defence of the Humble Remonstrance, Against the frivolous and false exceptions of Smectymnvvs . . . By the Author of the said Humble Remonstrance. . . . London, Printed for Nathaniel Butter . . . 1641.

From the title page of the first edition. See also Masson, II, 253. Though the Thomason Catalogue does not list this volume, it is likely that it appeared some time during the month of April, since it was entered in the Stationers' Registers on April 12.

April 29. Taxed in Aldersgate.

Aldersgate ward. the lowe bookes for the subsedyes seased the XXIXth of Aprill 1641. . . . St Butholphes parrish. . . . The Second Precinct. . . . John Milton gentleman—04-00-00.

Guildhall Library, London, MS 1503/5; *Modern Language Review*, XXVI (1931), 178. The text of the entry is not given in the latter article. The taxes levied in Milton's immediate neighborhood range from three pounds to eight pounds. His neighbors include Thomas Warcutt (or Warrutt), William Horing, Dr. Gill, William Bottsford, Robert Corker, Edward Pearson, John Woodrington, Brownebakers Hall, John Trobridge, Auditor Worffeild, John Cragg, Mr. Hoppe, lodger (his name later crossed through), Sir Nicholas Rowe, John Starke, Stephen Beaumont, Richard Masked, Mr. Lawson, lodger, Mr. Pallavicine, and John Wilford. The entry means that Milton was taxed four pounds for the period covered, which probably was six months; see the entry given later under date of September 21, 1641.

May (?). *Of Reformation* Published.

Of Reformation Touching Chvrch-Discipline in England: And the Cavses that hitherto have hindred it. Two Bookes, written to a Freind. . . . Printed, for Thomas Vnderhill 1641.

From the title page of the first edition, reproduced in facsimile in CM, III, facing p. 1; the text begins on p. 1. The "friend" addressed in the title page may have been Milton's former schoolmaster Thomas Young; see A. Barker, "Milton's Schoolmaster," *Modern Language Review*, XXXII (1937), 517 ff.; CM, XVIII, 533. The date is uncertain. The Thomason Catalogue dates it in June; Masson (II, 239) in May or June; Parker (*Milton's Contemporary Reputation*, p. 263) May 12-31. The earliest of these choices would seem to be the least troublesome, partly because the speech of Digby in the House of Commons, to which it was in part an answer (see George W. Whiting, London *Times Literary Supplement*, September 5, 1935, p. 552), dates back to February 9 of this year, and partly because it is mentioned by title in Almoni's *Compendious Discourse*, dated by Thomason May 31. Heinrich Mutschmann has developed the somewhat fantastic theory (in his *Milton's Projected Epic on the Rise and Future Greatness of the Britannic Nation*, Tartu, 1936) that *Of Reformation* and the anonymous *Great Britain's Ruin Plotted by Seven Sects*, 1641, were twin writings by Milton, that both either now contain or originally contained much epic material which Milton intended for use in a heroic poem, and that much of the left-over material was later incorporated in *Paradise Lost*. See CM, XVIII, 533, 538.

Interea Parlamento rem strenuè gerente, Episcoporum fastus detumuit. . . . Ad hæc sanè experrectus, cùm veram affectari viam ad libertatem cernerem, ab his initiis, his passibus, ad liberandam servitute vitam omnem mortalium, rectissimè procedi, si ab religione disciplina orta, ad mores & instituta reipublicæ emanaret, cùm etiam me ita ab adolescentia parâssem, ut quid divini, quid humani esset juris, ante omnia possem non ignorare, méque consuluissem ecquando ullius usus essem futurus, si nunc patriæ, immo verò ecclesiæ tótque fratribus evangelii causâ, periculo sese objicientibus deessem, statui, etsi tunc alia quædam meditabar, huc omne ingenium, omnes industriæ vires transferre. Primùm itaque de reformanda ecclesia Anglicana, duos ad amicum quendam libros conscripsi. . . .

Milton, *Defensio Secunda*, 1654, pp. 88-89; CM, VIII, 128.

[Meanwhile, as Parliament was doing business strenuously, the pride of the bishops collapsed. . . . When I really awakened to this situation and perceived that men were searching for the right way to liberty, and that, if the discipline arising from religion should spread to the customs and institutions of the state, men were heading as directly as possible toward delivering the whole life of mortals from slavery; and also because I had prepared myself from youth to be able before all else to know what belonged to divine and to human law; and when it came to me that I, who had meditated how I might be of some use, might now fail my country or indeed my church and so many brothers who were exposing themselves to peril for the sake of the gospel—then I decided, though I was then planning other work, to transfer all my ability and energy to this pursuit.

So first I wrote to a certain friend two books about reforming the Church of England.]

Hee had by this time laid in a large stock of knowlege; which as he design'd not for the purchase of Wealth, so neither intended hee it, as a Misers hoard, to ly useless: Having therefore taken a house, to bee at full ease and quiet, & gotten his books about him, hee sett himselfe upon Compositions, tending either to the public benefit of Mankind, and especially his Countrymen, or to the advancement of the Commonwealth of Learning. And his first labours were very happily dedicated to, what had the chiefest place in his affections, and had bin no small part of his Study, the service of Religion.

It was now the Year 1640: And the Nation was much divided upon the Controversies about Church Government, between the Prelatical party, & the Dissenters, or, as they were commonly then calld, Puritans. Hee had study'd Religion in the Bible and the best Authors, had strictly livd up to it's Rules, and had no temporal concern depending upon any Hierarchy, to render him suspected, either to himselfe, or others, as one that writt for Interest; and therefore with great boldness, and Zeal offer'd his Iudgment, first in *two Books of Reformation* by way of address to a friend. . . .

The "earliest" biography, fol. 141; Darbishire, pp. 21-22. Italics here represent underlining in the manuscript. Miss Darbishire gives alterations in the manuscript.

In this House [Aldersgate] he continued several Years, in the one or two first whereof, he set out several Treatises, *viz.* That of *Reformation*. . . .

Phillips, p. xxi; Darbishire, pp. 62-63.

Of Reformation touching Church-Discipline in *England*, and the Causes that hitherto have hindred it. Two Books written to a Friend. 4*to.*

Phillips, p. [1]; not in Darbishire.

But the times soon after [his return from Italy] changing, and the Rebellion thereupon breaking forth, *Milton* sided with the Faction, and being a man of parts, was therefore more capable than another of doing mischief, especially by his pen, as by those books which I shall anon mention, will appear. (13) That at first we find him a Presbyterian and a most sharp and violent opposer of Prelacy, the established ecclesiastical Discipline and the orthodox Clergy. . . . As for the things which he hath published, are these, (1) *Of Reformation, touching Church Discipline in England, and the causes that hitherto have hindred it*, &c. Lond. 1641. qu. At which time, as before, the Nation was much divided upon the Controversies about Church Government between the prelatical party, and Puritans, and therefore *Milton* did with great boldness and zeal offer his judgment as to those matters in his said book of Reformation.

Wood, I, 881; Darbishire, pp. 38-39.

Whatever he wrote against Monarchie was out of no animosity to the King's person, or out of any faction, or Interest but out of a pure zeall to the Liberty Mankind, wch he thought would be greater under a free state than under a Monarchall government. His being so conversant in Livy and the Rom: authors, and the greatnes he saw donne by the Rom: comonwealth & the virtue of their great Comanders (Captaines), induc't him to.

Aubrey, fol. 65v; Darbishire, pp. 13-14. In the manuscript "Captaines" is written above "Comanders."

Of Reformation.

Aubrey, fol. 64; Darbishire, p. 11.

MAY (?). AUTHOR OF "THE FABLE OF THE HEAD AND THE WEN"?

Francis Peck (*New Memoirs*, 1740, p. 431) mentions this as the title of a work by Milton, but no such book has been found. It is possible that Peck had seen some separate publication of the story which is found in *Of Reformation* (CM, III, 47-49), but it is now known only as part of that book and is accordingly here filed with it. See also CM, XVIII, 638.

MAY (?). PRESENTS COPIES OF *OF REFORMATION*.

By, m^r: John. Milton Ex Dono. Authoris.

Inscription on the title page of the Thomason copy, British Museum, shelf-mark E. 208. (3); French, "The Autographs of John Milton,"

#10; Stern, I, ii, 457. The writing is pretty certainly Thomason's. There are several manuscript corrections in a hand which may be Milton's (according to Stern) or that of some employe of the printer. Since these are not gathered in the notes of the Columbia Milton, they may be mentioned here. P. 6, third line from the end, "we" is crossed out and "she" written in the margin. P. 7, line 9, "the" is crossed out and "discipline which is the" written in the margin. P. 70, line 6, "all" is crossed out. P. 72, line 5, the "s" of "others" is crossed out.

[Nine short lines in Latin.]

The Archivist, VII (1894), 8-9. This reference is pretty surely to the collection of tracts presented to Patrick Young and now in the Library of Trinity College, Dublin. See French, "The Autographs of John Milton," # 11, 21. In the Latin catalogue of the library, *Catalogus Librorum . . . Collegii . . . Trinitatis . . . Dublin*, v (1879), 583, it is entered as a copy of *Of Reformation*, but the shelf-number, R.dd.39, makes it clear that the same volume is intended. For the main entry of this volume, see the year 1645.

MAY 3. RECEIVES INTEREST ON COPE BOND (?).

. . . neyther ye s'd principall debt of 150^{li} nor any pte thereof nor any Jnterest due for ye forbearance of the same since November 1641 hath been paid or satisfied . . . .

Milton's bill against Lady Elizabeth Cope and Sir Anthony Cope, June 16, 1654, *q.v.*; see entry under May 3, 1638.

MAY 14. PUBLICATION OF WORK ATTRIBUTED TO MILTON.

Canterbvries Dreame: in which The Apparition of Cardinall Wolsey did present himselfe unto him on the fourteenth of May last past . . . 1641.

From the title page of the first edition in the Harvard College Library. The date is from the Thomason Catalogue. See Francis Peck, *New Memoirs*, 1740, p. 431; CM, XVIII, 636. Though Halkett and Laing follow Peck's attribution, I see no particular reason for attributing this work to Milton. It is a soliloquy spoken by Archbishop Laud, to whom the ghost of Wolsey appears as a warning. Though sober in tone, with a slightly satirical tinge, it can equally credibly be assigned to any one of dozens of other writers. It is highly unlikely that Milton would have written it without some more specific indication of having done so.

MAY 21. A FURTHER BOOK IN THE EPISCOPAL QUARREL
ENTERED FOR PUBLICATION.

21ᵐᵒ die Maij 1641

Master Downes warden. Entred for his copie under the hands
of Doctor WYKES and Master MAN warden, a booke called
*The Judgment of Dʳ Reynolds touching the originall of Epis-
copacy, more largely confirmed out of antiquity,* by the now
Bishop of Armagh . . . vjᵈ.

The Stationers' Registers, ed. Eyre and Rivington, I, 24. This book,
written by James Usher, was as important as any writing of the time
in provoking Milton to write his *Of Prelatical Episcopacy.*

MAY (?). USHER'S *JUDGMENT OF DR. REYNOLDS* PUB-
LISHED.

The Ivdgement of Doctor Reignolds Concerning Episcopacy,
Whether it be Gods Ordinance. Expressed in a Letter to Sir
Francis Knovvls, Concerning Doctor Bancrofts Sermon at Pauls-
Crosse, the ninth of February, 1588. In the Parliament time.
London, Printed by Thomas Paine, 1641.

From the title page of the first edition; Masson, II, 248 ff. The
Thomason Catalogue dates the book simply in May, but since it was
entered in the Stationers' Registers on May 21, it is likely that it was
not out till the end of the month. On the other hand, if Almoni's *Compendious Discourse* (see May 31) is an answer to Milton's *Of Prelatical
Episcopacy* (see late May), and if the latter is in turn an answer to Usher's book, the whole question of dates becomes extremely difficult. One
can always fall back on the old explanation that manuscript copies circu-
lated before actual publication, but I can offer no convincing chronology.

MAY (?). *OF PRELATICAL EPISCOPACY* PUBLISHED.

Of Prelatical Episcopacy, and VVhither it may be deduc'd
from the Apostolical times by vertue of those Testimonies which
are alledg'd to that purpose in some late Treatises: One whereof
goes under the Name of Iames Arch-Bishop of Armagh. . . .
London, Printed by R.O. and G.D. for Thomas Vnderhill, and
are to be sold at the signe of the Bible, in Wood-Street, 1641.

From the title page of the first edition, which is reproduced in facsimile
in CM, III, facing p. 81. The date is not at all certain. It has usually
been given as June or July, and the Thomason Catalogue dates the

book in July. But if Professor Whiting is correct in asserting (*PMLA*, LI [1936], 430-435) that Milton's book is quoted and discussed in Almoni's *Compendious Discourse*, and if the dating of that book on May 31 is correct, then Milton's book must have been out before the end of the month of May. It may be that the Thomason copy [British Museum, shelf-mark E.164. (19)] was a presentation from Milton, who gave his bookseller-friend copies of several others of his books; but the only notation on the title page is the non-committal "By John Milton." See French, "The Autographs of John Milton," # 12; CM, XVIII, 551; Masson, II, 251; Stern, I, ii, 458. The Armagh title referred to is *The Judgment of Doctor Reynolds*, noticed above.

. . . deinde, cum duo præ cæteris magni nominis Episcopi suum jus contra Ministros quosdam primarios assererent, ratus de iis rebus, quas amore solo veritatis, & ex officii Christiani ratione didiceram haud pejùs me dicturum quàm qui de suo quæstu & injustissimo dominatu contendebant, ad hunc libris duobus, quorum unus de Episcopatu prælatico, alter de ratione Disciplinæ ecclesiasticæ inscribitur, ad illum, scriptis quibusdam animadversionibus, & mox Apologia, respondi.

Milton, *Defensio Secunda*, 1654, p. 89; CM, VIII, 128-130.

[. . . then, when two bishops of high name above others asserted their cause against certain leading ministers, I, convinced that on those subjects which I had studied for the pure love of truth and by way of Christian duty I should hardly write worse than those who were contending for their own profit and for a most unjust domination over others, replied to one of them in two books, of which one is entitled *Of Prelatical Episcopacy* and the other *Of the Reason of Church Government*; to the other in certain *Animadversions* and presently in an *Apology*.]

And then in answer to a Bishop hee writt of *Prelatical Episcopacy*. . . .

The "earliest" biography, fol. 141; Darbishire, p. 22.

In this House . . . he set out . . . that against *Prelatical Episcopacy*. . . .

Phillips, p. xxi; Darbishire, pp. 62-63.

Of Prelatical Episcopacy, and whether it may be deduc'd from the Apostolical times by vertue of those Testimonies which are alledged to that purpose in some late Treatises; one whereof goes under the name of *James* Archbishop of *Armagh*. 4*to.*

> Phillips, p. [1]; not in Darbishire.

Against prelatical Episcopacy.

> Aubrey, fol. 64; Darbishire, p. 11.

Against prelatical Episcopacy. This I have not yet seen.

> Wood, I, 881; Darbishire, p. 40.

MAY 31. *OF REFORMATION* AND *OF PRELATICAL EPIS-COPACY* ATTACKED.

A Compendious Discourse, Proving Episcopacy To Be Of Apostolicall, And Conseqvently Of Divine Institution . . . By Peloni Almoni, Cosmopolites. London, Printed by E. G. for Richard Whitaker . . . 1641. . . .

The late unworthy Authour of a booke intituled, *Of Reformation*, &c. hath found some quarrell against him [Irenaeus]: but *Fevardentius*, in his apologeticall preface (in the defence of *Irenæus*) hath well answered such exceptions.

From the title page of the first edition and from sig. A4. Parker (*Milton's Contemporary Reputation*, p. 71) quotes this allusion, and argues (*ibid.*, p. 15n) that it is to *Of Reformation* only. It is true that there is no direct mention of Milton's other writings in the book. But Whiting [*PMLA*, LI (1936), 430-435] has argued very convincingly that the whole construction of the book is like that of *Of Prelatical Episcopacy*, and that many of the arguments are nearly word for word as Milton expresses them. It is indisputable at least that Almoni's book is concerned chiefly with the ideas of Irenaeus, who also occupies a prominent position in *Of Prelatical Episcopacy*, whereas he is merely mentioned once in passing in *Of Reformation*.

JUNE (?). SIR EDWARD DERING HAS A COPY OF *OF PRE-LATICAL EPISCOPACY* (?).

I have seen a copy of Milton's *Of Prelatical Episcopacy* in the Yale University Library (shelf-mark Z77.147d) which is said to have belonged to Dering and which contains many manuscript notes said to be in his hand. It belonged formerly to Wynne E. Baxter and was number 10 in the catalogue of the sale of his library: *A Catalogue of the Milton Collection of the late Wynne E. Baxter, Esq. To be Sold . . . July 12th, 1921.* Dering's name is not in the book; the ascription appears in the sale catalogue.

JUNE (?). SMECTYMNUUS'S *VINDICATION* PUBLISHED.

A Vindication of the Ansvver to the Hvmble Remonstrance . . . By The Same Smectymnvvs. London, Printed for Iohn Rothwell . . . 1641.

From the title page of the first edition. The Thomason Catalogue (I, 19) dates simply June, but it is likely that its appearance was later than June 26, the date of entry in the Stationers' Registers. See Masson, II, 255.

JULY. TRACT ATTRIBUTED TO MILTON.

A Discourse Shewing in what State the three Kingdoms are in at this Present . . . 1641.

This anonymous eight-page tract has been attributed to Milton by Halkett and Laing (with a question mark) and by a note on the Gay copy in the Harvard College Library (shelf-mark Gay 641.338.786). In the Thomason Catalogue, from which the date is taken, it is anonymous (I, 22). See also CM, XVIII, 636. The substance of the pamphlet is an attack against the Earl of Strafford. But the style is so wandering, so euphuistic and vulgar, somewhat like that of John Taylor, that it seems incredible that it could have been written by Milton.

JULY. TAXED IN ALDERSGATE.

St Buttolphes Parishe . . . The Second Precinct . . . Jo: Milton . . . gent   Jaine Yates servant.

Public Record Office, E179/252/1(A), a list of the inhabitants of the ward of Aldersgate in July, 1641; see also Hunter, pp. 24-26; British Museum Add. MS. 24, 501, fol. 26; Masson, II, 357. Masson explains the list as a survey of inhabitants of London subject to a poll-tax to be levied in support of the Scotch War.

JULY (?). *ANIMADVERSIONS* PUBLISHED.

Animadversions upon The Remonstrants Defence, against Smectymnvvs. London, Printed for Thomas Vnderhill, and are to be sold at the Signe of the Bible in Woodstreet, 1641.

From the title page of the first edition, which is reproduced in facsimile in CM, III, facing p. 105. The book is reprinted in CM, III, 105 ff. The Thomason copy in the British Museum [shelf-mark E.166. (11)] bears the manuscript note on the title page: "written by m^r John Milton," but no date. The Thomason Catalogue dates it in September, which seems too late. On the other hand, there is a possibility that the publication originally occurred in, or was planned for, about the time here indicated, but that the need for revision caused a postponement of most if not all of the published copies. Professor Parker has pointed out (*Library*, 4th Series, xv, 1934, 243-246, and *Milton's Contemporary Reputation*, p. 266) that all known copies of the first edition show signs of the cancellation of a passage of some 1500-2000 words in length. In all copies consulted, pp. 45-48 are missing, and Sections 6-12 of Hall's *Defence* are omitted from consideration, though all other sections are taken up. Toland's reprint in 1698 exhibits similar difficulties. What reason may have prompted the cancellation of this passage remains unexplained. For further discussion, see Masson, II, 257; CM, XVIII, 540. In the absence of further definite information about this bibliographical peculiarity, the main entry of the book is placed under the present date even though the book as we have it after cancellation may not have appeared until September.

. . . deinde, cum duo præ cæteris magni nominis Episcopi suum jus contra Ministros quosdam primarios assererent . . . ad hunc libris duobus . . . ad illum, scriptis quibusdam animadversionibus . . . respondi.

Milton, *Defensio Secunda*, 1654, p. 89; CM, VIII, 128-130. The bishop to whom this is an answer is Joseph Hall.

[. . . then, when two bishops of high name above others asserted their cause against certain leading ministers, . . . I replied to one of them in two books . . . to the other in certain *Animadversions*.]

After that *Animadversions upon the Remonstrants defense* (the work of Bishop Hall) *against Smectymnyus.*

The "earliest" biography, fol. 141v; Darbishire, p. 22.

Animadversions upon the Remonstrants defence against *Smectymnuus. 4to.*

Phillips, p. [1]; not in Darbishire.

(2) *Animadversions upon the Remonstrants defence against Smectymnus.* Lond. 1641. qu. Which *Rem. Defence* was written (as 'tis said) by Dr. *Jos. Hall* Bishop of *Exeter*.

Wood, I, 881; Darbishire, pp. 39-40.

JULY (?). DEFENDS HIS SATIRICAL COARSENESS.

I shall adresse my selfe in few words to give notice before hand of something in this booke, which to some men perhaps

may seeme offensive, that when J have render'd a lawfull rea-
son of what is done, J may trust to have sav'd the labour of
defending or excusing hereafter . . . in the detecting, and con-
vincing of any notorious enimie to truth . . . it will be nothing
disagreeing from Christian meeknesse to handle such a one in
a rougher accent, and to send home his haughtinesse well be-
spurted with his owne holy-water. . . . And . . . such a grim
laughter . . . hath oft-times a strong and sinewy force in teach-
ing and confuting; nor can there be a more proper object of in-
dignation and scorne together then a false Prophet taken in the
greatest dearest and most dangerous cheat, the cheat of soules:
in the disclosing whereof if it be harmfull to be angry, and
withall to cast a lowring smile, when the properest object calls
for both, it will be long enough ere any be able to say why those
two most rationall faculties of humane intellect anger and laugh-
ter were first seated in the brest of man.

Milton, *Animadversions*, 1641, pp. 1-4; CM, III, 105-108.

JULY (?). PLANNING GREAT POETRY.

And he that now for haste snatches up a plain ungarnish't
present as a thanke-offering to thee, which could not bee deferr'd
in regard of thy so many late deliverances wrought for us one
upon another, may then [when peace comes to the church]
perhaps take up a Harp, and sing thee an elaborate Song to Gen-
erations.

Milton, *Animadversions*, 1641, p. 38; CM, III, 148.

JULY 28. HALL'S *SHORT ANSWER* TO SMECTYMNUUS REGISTERED.

28° Julii 1641 Master Butter. Entred for his copie under the
hands of Master HANSLEY and Master PARKER warden, a
booke called *A short answeare to the tedious vindica͡con of*
Smectymnius, by the author of the humble remonstrance . . .vjᵈ.

The Stationers' Registers, ed. Eyre and Rivington, I, 30.

AUGUST 3. TAX STILL UNPAID.

The Names of those that have not payd vs, of yᵉ gentrie, in
yᵉ 2̄ precȳct . . . .

Munies colected for the 2 precynt of the parish of Sct buttals wthout ālldersgat by bengemyn Ely &. Christopher Nettleton. colectors. for ye pole munies of the sayd precynt. . . .

Mr Milton gentellman. . . .

M^r mylton serv̄—0-0-6.

Public Record Office, E179/252/1(F); British Museum Add. MS. 24,501, fol. 25; Hunter, p. 26; Masson, II, 357. This manuscript document is part of a group of returns for the four precincts of St. Botolph's without Aldersgate. On the outside cover of one of them [E179/252/1(E)] is the date August 3, 1641, so that the actual information must date from some time before that time. Neither the amount of Milton's tax nor the name of his servant who was rated at sixpence is given. The total amount for the whole precinct, however, is given as £5-10-0.

AUGUST 27. BROTHER CHRISTOPHER'S DAUGHTER ANNE BAPTIZED.

August 1641 . . . 27 Anne Daughter of——Milton Esq.

Parish register, St. Laurence, Reading; *Notes and Queries*, XI, vii (1913), 21; Masson, II, 489. Brennecke (p. 144) incorrectly dates this event August 27, 1640.

SEPTEMBER (?). PUBLICATION OF ATTRIBUTED WORK.

A True Description or rather a Parallel between Cardinall Wolsey, Archbishop of York, and William Laud, Archbishop of Canterbury.

Attributed to Milton by Francis Peck; CM, XVIII, 636. The Thomason Catalogue (1, 33) dates the book September, 1641, but gives no author's name. It seems most unlikely that Milton was the author.

SEPTEMBER (?). PUBLICATION OF ATTRIBUTED WORK.

Newes from Hell. Rome. and the Inns of Court. Wherein Is sett forth The Coppy of a letter written from the Diuell to the Pope. . . . By J M. Printed in the yeare of grace and reformation. 1641.

From the title page of the first edition in the British Museum; reprinted in *The Harleian Miscellany*, IV (1809), 387 ff., and *ibid.*, VII (1811), 212 ff. There was another edition dated 1642, of which there is a copy in the British Museum [E.133. (13)]. This pamphlet, attributed with a question mark to Milton by Halkett and Laing (1928), is a slangy, vulgar, badly printed hodgepodge, so utterly unlike any

known production of Milton that it seems wholly impossible that it could
have been written by him. On p. 24 of the British Museum copy (shelf-
mark 4105. aa.60) is the entertaining note in what appears to be seventeenth-century handwriting: "Receaued by me, fountaine of iniquity
this 22ᵗʰ of Septemb 1641." The work is described in the *Catalogue of
Prints and Drawings in the British Museum Division I. Political and
Personal Satires*, 1 (1870), 238-239, #327.

SEPTEMBER (?). PUBLICATION OF ATTRIBUTED WORK.

The Plot Discovered and Counterplotted. . . .
J . . . Milton Gent'.

This work was first attributed to Milton by E. H. Gillette in "Newly
Discovered Prose Writings of John Milton," *Hours at Home*, IX
(1869), 532-536. See also London *Times Literary Supplement*, 1936,
pp. 868, 1056; C. Looten, "Les Debuts de Milton Pamphletaire,"
Études Anglaises, I, #4 (1937), 298; CM, XVIII, 533, 580, 635. The
"J . . . Milton Gent' " is written in a seventeenth-century hand on the
copy of this work now in the General Theological Seminary in New
York, where it forms one of eleven tracts all bound together and all,
except the present, dated 1641. The present bears no date, but has been
dated September, 1641, in the Thomason Catalogue. Though it seems
highly unlikely that Milton was either the author or the owner of this
work, it is possible that Milton may have been, or have been considered,
the person addressed in the letter-like pamphlet. The work, it should be
pointed out, is an earlier edition of *Great Britain's Ruin Plotted*, filed
below under date of January, 1642.

SEPTEMBER (?). PUBLICATION OF JOSEPH HALL'S
SHORT ANSWER.

A Short Answer to the Tedious Vindication of Smectymnvvs.
By the Avthor of the Humble Remonstrance. . . . London,
Printed for Nathaniel Butter . . . 1641.

From the title page of the first edition; Masson, II, 391. The month
is that of the Thomason Catalogue. Though this work is not directly
related to Milton, it is definitely a step in the Smectymnuan controversy,
in which Milton played a considerable part.

SEPTEMBER 1-21. TAXED IN ALDERSGATE.

1641 Aldersgate Ward 1° Septembris A° 1641 / Seased the
21ᵗʰ of September. 1641. . . . Sᵗ Buttolphes Parish. . . . The
Second Precinct. . . . Jo: Milton gent—06-00-00.

Guildhall Library MS. 1503/6; *Modern Language Review*, XXVI
(1931), 179. The meaning of the entry is that in a tax levied between

September 1 and 21, 1641, Milton's tax amounted to £6. Those of his neighbors in Aldersgate run from £3 to £8.

OCTOBER. ATTRIBUTED WORK.

The True Character of an Untrue Bishop.

Occasionally attributed to Milton, but without any reasons for the attribution; CM, XVIII, 639. The date is from the Thomason Catalogue, in which no author is named.

OCTOBER 29. RICHARD POWELL OBTAINS A NEW LEASE OF WHEATLEY.

The said *Richard Powell* afterwards in the yeare 1641. repaires to the Colledge, and concealing from them his said assignment to *Bateman*, and his said grant to *Herne*, without the privity or concurrents of the said *Bateman* and *Herne*, by their joyning with him in their making of an actuall surrender of their, or either of their estates to the said Colledge, upon his giving in of the said old Lease made in the yeare of our Lord, 1626. obtaines a new Lease from the said Colledge to begin immediately. . . . The Colledge new Lease to *Richard Powell* in the year 1641. was void, for that the Lease to *Bateman* was then in being for many yeares then to come, and that Lease not then surrendred. . . . *Richard Powell* upon such his renewing in 1641. did pay to the Colledge 26.li. 13.s. 4.d. for a Fine.

Bodleian MS. Wood 515 (William Powell *alias* Hinson *versus* All Souls' College, 1656), p. 3; Stevens, *Milton Papers*, p. 10; French, *Milton in Chancery*, p. 82. The exact date, October 29, not found in the passage quoted above, is given in a Chancery bill of Sir Edward Powell filed in 1648 (Public Record Office, C5/2/65).

NOVEMBER. *OF PRELATICAL EPISCOPACY* PARAPHRASED BY LORD BROOKE.

The Authority of *Tertullian* also, is of the same credit: Hee tels us that *Polycarpus* was placed by St. *John* at *Smyrna*; and at *Rome Clement* by St. *Peter*. This no body will dispute; (though I am not bound to beleeve it.) But where is the stresse of this Argument?

Robert Greville, second Lord Brooke, *A Discourse Opening the Nature of That Episcopacie*, 1641, p. 68. The corresponding passage in Milton's *Of Prelatical Episcopacy* (CM, III, 96-97) reads as follows:

[45]

"*Tertullian* accosts us next . . . whose testimony, state but the question right, is of no more force to deduce *Episcopacy*, then the two former. He saies that the Church of *Smirna* had *Polycarpus* plac't there by *John*, and the Church of *Rome Clement* ordain'd by *Peter*. . . . None of this will be contradicted . . . it remaines yet to be evinc't out of this and the like places, which will never be, that the word Bishop is otherwise taken, then in the language of Saint *Paul*, and the *Acts*, for an order above *Presbyters*."

This borrowing from Milton was first pointed out by George W. Whiting in *Modern Language Notes*, LI (1936), 161-166, who gives numerous other similar passages. It seems unnecessary to quote here more than one example of the influence on Lord Brooke, since there seems to be no possible doubt of the facts.

The Thomason Catalogue dates Brooke's work November, 1641. The author himself says in his address to Parliament that it was written in "the *Retirements* of Your Humble Servant in the Last *Recese*," which Whiting points out would be between September 9 and October 20, 1641.

NOVEMBER 3. RECEIVES INTEREST ON COPE BOND (?).

. . . neyther ye s'd principall debt of 150^{li} nor any pte thereof nor any Jnterest due for ye forbearance of the same since November 1641 hath been paid or satisfied . . . .

Milton's bill against Lady Elizabeth Cope and Sir Anthony Cope, June 16, 1654, *q.v.*; see entry under May 3, 1638. The present payment was evidently the last made, but from Milton's statement there must almost surely have been a payment on this date.

DECEMBER 12. RECEIVES INTEREST PAYMENT FROM RICHARD POWELL.

. . . the growing Jnterest for the forbearance of the said Principall debt was for some yeares then following likewise payd And soe continued to bee paid vntill June Jn the yeare of our Lord One Thousand six hundred ffortie and ffower. . . .

From Milton's answer to Elizabeth Ashworth, February 22, 1653/4, *q.v.*

DECEMBER 18. RICHARD POWELL SUBLETS WHEATLEY TO SIR EDWARD POWELL.

[Sir Edward Powell] Sheweth That about the 18° Decemb 1641 Richard Powell of fforrest Hill in Com. Oxoñ, Esqz deceased did assigne vnto him All that Tenem[t] & one hundred acres of Land meadow & pasture, in Whately in the County of Oxon aforesd held by lease from the Colledge of all Soules to have & hold the same for the terme of one & twenty yeares from thence next ensueing Vpon condicon that if the said Richard Powell should repay the some of 300[li] wth interest at the end of six monthes then the said Assignem[t] to be void as apps by the same.

Sir Edward Powell's petition of August 28, 1650, Public Record Office, SP 23/110, p. 587; Hamilton, pp. 86-87; French, *Milton in Chancery*, pp. 82-83. There is no record of Richard Powell's having repaid the amount indicated.

[Richard Powell obtained a lease of Wheatley in 1641 from All Souls' College] which he afterwards mortgaged to Sir *Edward Powell*. . . . All the pretence for the Plaintiff [William Powell], is, because his testator bought the last lease made in 1641. This in truth was no Lease . . . which was unknown to the Colledge, but well known to *Richard Powell* the Lessee, who wittingly deceived himselfe, that he might cozen Sir *Edward Powell*, the Plaintiffs testator.

Bodleian Library MS. Wood 515, pp. 3, 5 (William Powell *alias* Hinson *versus* All Souls' College, 1656); Stevens, *Milton Papers*, p. 10. Mentioned also in Sir Edward Powell's Chancery suit, Public Record Office, C5/2/65.

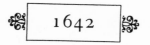

1642

NOT IN MILITARY SERVICE.

Nam cùm ab adolescentulo humanioribus essem studiis, ut qui maximè deditus, & ingenio semper quàm corpore validior, posthabitâ castrensi operâ, quâ me gregarius quilibet robustior facilè superâsset, ad ea me contuli, quibus plus potui.

Milton, *Defensio Secunda*, 1654, p. 7; CM, VIII, 10-11. For some discussion of the possibilities of Milton's having been in the army, see Masson, II (1894), 481 ff.; J. W. Hales, *Folia Litteraria*, New York, 1893, pp. 243-245 (from an article published in *Academy*, October 31, 1876).

[For since I had been devoted in the highest degree from my youth to the more humane studies and was always stronger in mind than in body, and since I esteemed less highly the work of the camp, in which any ordinary stronger man would easily have surpassed me, I betook myself to those pursuits in which I could be more effective.]

MAKES AMBITIOUS PLANS FOR WRITING POETRY.

Time servs not now, and perhaps I might seem too profuse to give any certain account of what the mind at home in the spacious circuits of her musing hath liberty to propose to her self, though of highest hope, and hardest attempting, whether that Epick form whereof the two poems of *Homer*, and those other two of *Virgil* and *Tasso* are a diffuse, and the book of *Iob* a brief model: or whether the rules of *Aristotle* herein are strictly to be kept, or nature to be follow'd, which in them that know art, and use judgement is no transgression, but an inriching of art. And lastly, what K. or Knight before the conquest might be chosen in whom to lay the pattern of a Christian *Heroe*. And as *Tasso* gave to a Prince of *Italy* his chois whether he would command him to write of *Godfreys* expedition against the infidels, or *Belisarius* against the Gothes, or *Charlemain* against the Lombards; if to the instinct of nature and the imboldning of art ought may be trusted, and that there be nothing advers in our climate, or the fate of this age, it haply would be no rashnesse from an equal diligence and inclination to present the like offer in our own ancient stories. Or whether those Dramatick constitutions, wherein *Sophocles* and *Euripides* raigne shall be found more doctrinal and exemplary to a Nation, the Scripture also affords us a divine pastoral Drama in the Song of *Salomon* consisting of two persons and a double *Chorus*, as *Origen* rightly judges. And the Apocalyps of Saint *Iohn* is the majestick image of a high and stately Tragedy, shutting up and intermingling her solemn Scenes and Acts with a sevenfold *Chorus* of halleluja's and harping symphonies: and this my opinion the grave authority of *Pareus* commenting that booke is sufficient to confirm. Or if occasion shall lead to imitat those magnifick Odes and Hymns wherein *Pindarus* and *Callimachus* are in most things worthy, some others in their frame judicious, in their matter most an end faulty: But those frequent songs throughout the law and prophets beyond all these, not in their divine argument alone, but in the very critical art of composition may be easily made appear over all the kinds of Lyrick poesy, to be incomparable. These abilities, wheresoever they be found, are the inspired guift of God rarely bestow'd, but yet to some (though most abuse) in every Nation. . . . And what a benefit this would be to our youth and gentry, may be soon guest by what we know of the corruption and bane which they suck in dayly from the writings and interludes of libidinous and ignorant Poetasters. . . . The thing which I had to say, and those intentions which have liv'd within me ever since I could conceiv my self any thing worth to my Countrie, I return to crave excuse that urgent reason hath pluckt from me by an abortive and foredated discovery. . . . Neither doe I think it shame to covnant with any knowing reader, that for some few yeers yet I may go on trust with him toward the payment of what I am now indebted, as being a work not to be rays'd from the heat of youth, or the vapours of wine, like that which flows at wast from the pen of some vulgar Amorist, or the trencher fury of a riming parasite, nor to be obtain'd by the invocation of Dame Memory and her Siren daughters, but by devout prayer to that eternall Spirit who can enrich with all utterance and knowledge, and sends out his Seraphim with the hallow'd fire of his Altar to touch and purify the lips of whom he pleases: to this must be added industrious and select reading, steddy observation, insight into all seemly and generous arts and affaires, till which in some measure be compast, at mine own peril and cost I refuse not to sustain this expectation from as many as are not loath to hazard so much credulity upon the best pledges that I can give them.

Milton, *The Reason of Church Government*, 1641 [*i.e.*, 1642], pp. 38-41; cm, iii, 237-241. The date is of course impossible to place exactly, but the state of mind in which the poet found himself as described in this book must have been as true of 1642 as of any other year, and the language suggests that he felt in this way and had these plans at the time of writing, which must have been early in 1642. This passage is discussed by W. R. Parker in *Modern Philology*, XXXIII (1935), 49-53. Professor Parker points out that it lays down no hard and fixed timetable of proposed poetic composition, but rather shows considerable uncertainty on Milton's part.

... with such abstracted sublimities as these, it might be worth your listning, Readers, as I may one day hope to have ye in a still time, when there shall be no chiding . . . if hereafter it befall me to attempt something more answerable to their great merits. . . .

Milton, *An Apology for Smectymnuus*, 1642, pp. 17, 37; CM, III, 305, 334-335.

COMPOSES SOME VERSES FOR DRAMATIC VERSION OF *PARADISE LOST*.

Paradise Lost . . . was first designed a Tragedy, and in the Fourth Book of the Poem there are Six Verses, which several Years before the Poem was begun, were shewn to me, and some others, as designed for the very beginning of the said Tragedy. The Verses are these;

> O Thou that with surpassing Glory Crown'd!
> Look'st from thy sole Dominion, like the God
> Of this New World; at whose sight all the Stars
> Hide their diminish'd Heads; to thee I call,
> But with no friendly Voice; and add thy Name,
> O Sun! to tell thee how I hate thy Beams
> That bring to my remembrance, from what State
> I fell; how Glorious once above thy Sphere;
> Till Pride and worse Ambition threw me down,
> Warring in Heaven, against Heaven's Glorious King.

Phillips, pp. xxxiv-xxxv; Darbishire, pp. 72-73; CM, XVIII, 266, 536. Though the date is uncertain, the passage is placed here since it is so closely connected with the quotations from *The Reason of Church Government* and elsewhere on Milton's poetic plans at this time. In "Milton's Lost Tragedy," *Philological Quarterly*, XVIII (1939), 78-83, Grant McColley thinks that this drama was composed about 1648-1652. But any such statement can be hardly more than a guess.

It may be mentioned here that according to Francis Peck (*New Memoirs*, 1740, p. 86; see also CM, XVIII, 266, 536) Milton is supposed to have planned "two large heroic poems; the one entitled, ARTHUR, in imitation of the ILIAD; the other, ALFRED, in imitation of the ODYSSEY." Though there is some general suggestion for Peck's theory in the quotation from *The Reason of Church Government*, there seems to be no definite record.

In the 4th Booke of Paradise lost, there are about 6 Vses of Satan's exclamation to the Sun, wch Mr. E. Ph. remembers, about 15 or 16 yeares before ever his Poem was thought of, wch Vses were intended for the Beginning of a Tragœdie wch he had designed, but was diverted from it by other businesse.

Aubrey, fol. 65; Darbishire, p. 13. In the first line quoted Aubrey first wrote "2d or 3d," then crossed it out and substituted "4th." The date is given in such a way as to be obviously approximate, coming from Phillips's memory, rather than mathematically exact. But it fits this present location well enough.

Milton, voyageant en Italie dans sa jeunesse, vit représenter à Milan une comédie intitulée Adam ou le Péché originel, écrite par un certain Andreino. . . . Milton conçut le dessein de faire une tragédie de la farce d'Andreino: il en composa même un acte et demi. Ce fait m'a été assuré par des gens de lettres qui le tenaient de sa fille, laquelle est morte lorsque j'étais à Londres.

Voltaire, "Essai sur la Poésie Épique," *Œuvres Complètes de Voltaire*, Paris, VII (1817), 263 ff. This essay was first composed by Voltaire in English and published under the title of *The Epick Poetry of the European Nations* in 1726. However, only the first part of the above quotation is found in the English version; the rest was added in some later French version. It is likely that Voltaire, though calling the composition an imitation of Andreini, had in mind the dramatic form of *Paradise Lost* to which Phillips and Aubrey referred. No other commentator speaks of so considerable an amount of composition as the act and a half specified here by Voltaire.

[Milton, traveling in Italy in his youth, saw acted at Milan a comedy entitled *Adam, or Original Sin*, written by a certain Andreini. . . . Milton conceived the plan of making a tragedy of Andreini's farce; he even composed an act and a half of it. This fact was vouched for to me by literary people who got it from his daughter, who died while I was in London.]

READS AND ANNOTATES MALVEZZI'S *DISCOURSES UPON TACITUS* (?).

Discourses upon Cornelius Tacitus. Written in Italian by the Learned Marquesse Virgilio Malvezzi . . . And Translated into English, by Sir Richard Baker, 1642.

A copy of this book containing numerous notes thought to be in Milton's hand belonged formerly to Wynne Baxter and is now in the collection of Professor Thomas O. Mabbott. The annotations are reprinted and discussed in CM, XVIII, 493, 574-575; see also French, "The Autographs of Milton," #84. There is no definite proof of Miltonic authorship or ownership beyond the opinions of several previous owners of the book and the resemblance in handwriting. On the other hand, Milton's allusion in *Of Reformation* to "*Malvezzi* that can cut *Tacitus* into slivers and steaks" (CM, III, 39) proves that Milton had at least some acquaintance with the author at about this same period. In a collection of miscellaneous manuscript material relating to Milton in the Manuscript Room of the New York Public Library is a clipping from an undated catalogue of Tregaskis in London, reproducing pp. 199 and 201 of the Malvezzi volume with Milton's notes.

OF REFORMATION CRITICIZED BY THOMAS FULLER.

One lately hath traduced them [the bishops] with such language, as neither beseemed his parts (whosoever he was) that spake it, nor their piety of whom it was spoken. If pious Latimer, whose bluntnesse was incapable of flattery, had his simplicity abused with false informations, he is called *another Doctour Shaw, to divulge in his Sermon forged accusations*. Cranmer and Ridley for some failings styled, *the common stales to countenance with their prostituted gravities every politick fetch which was then on foot, as oft as the potent Statists pleased to employ them*. And, as it follows not farre after, *Bishop Cranmer, one of King Henries Executours, and the other Bishops, none refusing (lest they should resist the Duke of Northumberland) could find in their consciences to set their hands to the disenabling and defeating of the Princesse Marie, &c*. Where Christian ingenuity might have prompted unto him to have made an intimation, that Cranmer (with pious Justice Hales in Kent) was last and least guilty, much refusing to subscribe; and his long resisting deserved as well to be mentioned, as his yielding at

last. Yea, that very Verse, which Doctour Smith at the burning
of Ridley used against him, is by the foresaid Authour (though
not with so full a blow, with a slenting stroke) applyed to those
Martyrs, *A man may give his body to be burnt, and yet have
not charity.*

Thomas Fuller, *The Holy State*, 1642, pp. 291-292; Masson, II,
359-360; Stern, I, ii, 464; Parker, *Milton's Contemporary Reputation*,
p. 72. According to the article on Fuller in the *DNB*, this book was written, or at least finished, toward the beginning of 1641.

There is a marginal note opposite the beginning of the quotation:
"*Authour of the book lately printed of Causes hindring Reformation in
England, lib.* I. *pag;* 10." The quotations from *Of Reformation* may be
found in CM, III, 8-9.

Other editions of this book during Milton's lifetime appeared in 1648,
1652, and 1663.

POSSIBLE ALLUSION BY PETER HEYLYN TO MILTON'S EPISCOPAL TRACTS.

[Bishop Joseph Hall's] Reverend Pen grew wearied not with
the *strength* or *number* of his Adversaries, but their *importuni-
tie*, who were resolved *to have the last words*, as himselfe ob-
serveth.

From Theophilus Churchman's (i.e., Peter Heylyn's) *The Historie of
Episcopacie*, 1642, sig. a verso. This work of about 400 pages is an elaborate defense of episcopacy against Smectymnuus, to whose writings and
to Hall's the author constantly refers, giving many side notes specifying
the titles and pages of the books. Though the chief books mentioned are
the *Defense of the Humble Remonstrance*, the *Vindication of the Answer*, and the *Answer to the Vindication*, and though Milton is nowhere
named, the whole book is an attack on the ideas which Milton had been
and was championing, and Heylyn's statement quoted above could
hardly, it seems, have failed to include Milton's early tracts in its general condemnation.

FRIEND OF CHARLES FLEETWOOD.

. . . te primum, Fletuode, quem ego ab ipsis tyrociniis ad hos
usque militiæ honores, quos nunc obtines à summis proximos,
humanitate, mansuetudine, benignitate animi eundem novi; hostis fortem & imperterritum, sed & mitissimum quoque victorem
sensit. . . .

Milton, *Defensio Secunda*, 1654, pp. 157-158; CM, VIII, 232. The
date of Milton's first acquaintance with Fleetwood is purely conjectural,

but 1642, in which the Civil War began, is as good a year as any to use when none can be certain. He entered the army in 1642.

[And first you, Fleetwood, whom from your very first attempts to these last military honors which you now receive from our greatest ones I have known to be always the same in humanity, mildness, and kindness of spirit. The enemy has felt you to be strong and fearless, but also the mildest of victors.]

The Bohn edition translates "ab ipsis tyrociniis . . . novi" as "I have known from a boy" (1, 292), but it seems more likely that, as the Columbia translation suggests ("from the time you first entered upon the profession of a soldier") it refers to Fleetwood's beginnings in military activity rather than to Milton's.

FRIEND OF RICHARD OVERTON.

Te, Overtone, mihi multis abhinc annis, & studiorum similitudine, & morum suavitate, concordiâ plusquam fraternâ conjunctissime. . . .

Milton, *Defensio Secunda*, 1654, p. 158; CM, VIII, 232. The date is of course only a guess, since we have no source of exact knowledge other than the vague "multis abhinc annis" of Milton's language. But 1642 is as good a guess as any.

[You, Overton, most intimately joined with me now for many years in a more than brotherly union, both by the similarity of our studies and by the charm of your manners. . . .]

JANUARY (?). WORK ATTRIBUTED TO MILTON.

Nevvs from Hell, Rome, and Innes of Court. Wherein is set forth the coppy of a Letter written from the Devill to the Pope. . . . By J.M. . . . Printed in the yeare of Grace and Reformation. 1642.

CM, XVIII, 636; Stevens, *Reference Guide*, #2650. See above under date of September, 1641 (?), for first edition. The present date is from the Thomason Catalogue (1, 72).

JANUARY (?). JOSEPH HALL'S (?) CONFUTATION OF SMECTYMNUUS PUBLISHED.

A Modest Confutation of A Slanderous and Scurrilous Libell, entitvled, Animadversions vpon the Remonstrants Defense against Smectymnuus. . . . Printed in the yeer M.DC.XLII.

The title is from the Thomason copy in the British Museum (E 134). The dating is that of the Thomason Catalogue. Parker (*Milton's Contemporary Reputation*, p. 268) dates it after March 26, 1642, and questions Hall's authorship. Unlike many other volumes in the Thomason collection, this bears no date of receipt by Thomason. It does, however, bear on the title page the manuscript comment: "against Mr Milton." See also Masson, II, 394. Reprinted in facsimile in Parker, pp. [123]-[168].

[Milton is] *a scurrilous* Mime, *a personated, and (as himself thinks) a grim, lowring, bitter fool . . . it is like hee spent his youth, in loytering, bezelling, and harlotting. Thus being grown to an Imposthume in the brest of the* University, *he was at length vomited out thence into a Suburbe sinke about* London; *which, since his comming up, hath groaned under two ills,* Him, *and the* Plague. *Where his morning haunts are I wist not; but he that would finde him after dinner, must search the* Play-Houses, *or the* Bordelli, *for there I have traced him. . . . Many of late, since he was out of Wit and Cloaths, as* Stilpo *merrily jeered the poor Starveling* Crates, *he is new clothed in Serge, and confined to a Parlour; where he blasphemes God and the* King, *as ordinarily as erewhile he drank Sack or swore.*

Hall, *A Modest Confutation*, 1642, sigs. A3-A3v; Parker, pp. 125-126. This is the chief passage in the book which refers to Milton, though to some extent Milton is of course involved in the whole book.

JANUARY 24. JOSEPH HALL ALLUDES TO MILTON.

Can any man pretend to a ground of taxing me (as I perceive one of late hath most unjustly done) of too much worldlinesse?

Joseph Hall, *A Letter lately sent by a Reverend Bishop from the Tovver, to A private Friend*, 1642. I owe this reference to Stern, I, ii, 461. The letter is dated at the end: *"From the Tower, Ian. 24. 1641."* The accusation of worldliness is very much in evidence in Milton's allusions to Bishop Hall.

FEBRUARY (?). PUBLISHES *THE REASON OF CHURCH GOVERNMENT*.

The Reason Of Church-governement Urg'd against Prelaty By Mr. John Milton. In two Books. [Ornament] London, Printed by E. G. for Iohn Rothwell, and are to be sold at the Sunne in Pauls Church-yard. 1641.

From the title page of the Thomason copy in the British Museum (E.137.9); CM, I, 130 ff. The date is that of the Thomason Catalogue.

cum duo præ cæteris magni nominis Episcopi suum jus contra Ministros quosdam primarios assererent . . . ad hunc libris duobus, quorum unus de Episcopatu prælatico, alter de ratione Disciplinæ ecclesiasticæ inscribitur . . . respondi.

Milton, *Defensio Secunda*, 1654, p. 89; CM, I, 128-130.

[. . . when two bishops of high name above others asserted their cause against certain leading ministers, I . . . replied to one of them in two books, of which one is entitled *Of Prelatical Episcopacy* and the other *Of the Reason of Church Government*.]

And then in answer to a Bishop hee writt of *Prelatical Episcopacy* & *The Reason of Church Governm^t*.

The "earliest" biography, fol. 141; Darbishire, p. 22.

(4) *Against prelatical Episcopacy*. This I have not yet seen. (5) *The reason of Church Government*; nor this.

Wood, I, 881; Darbishire, p. 40.

In this House [Aldersgate] . . . he set out . . . The *Reason of Church-Government*.

Phillips, p. xxi; Darbishire, pp. 62-63.

The reason of church goverment.

Aubrey, fol. 64; Darbishire, p. 11.

FEBRUARY (?). PRESENTS A COPY OF *THE REASON OF CHURCH GOVERNMENT* TO GEORGE THOMASON.

Ex Dono Authoris.

This inscription, presumably in Thomason's hand, appears on the title page of Thomason's copy of *The Reason of Church-Government*, 1641 (British Museum, shelf-mark E.137.9); Masson, II, 361; Stern, I, ii, 460; French, "The Autographs of John Milton," #13; CM, XVIII, 551.

MARCH 30. LETTER TO MOLIÈRE (?).

Ce 30 mars.

Monsieur,

Je suis bien aise vous scavoir en possession tous les papiers de feu M. Rotrou. . . . Or par ce moyen vous estes aussy devenu

possesseur d'un nombre d'escrits du très illustre Galilée. . . .
les jésuites . . . disant qu'il était maudit de Dieu, qui lui avoit
enlevé la lumière par punition . . . mais il n'a jamais cessé de
voir. . . . *A monsieur Molière.*   John Milton.

   This is one of a series of letters purporting to have been written to or
from Milton, and first described in the French journal, *Comptes Rendus
hebdomadaires des sceances de l'academie des sciences* (Paris), LXVIII
(1869), 745 ff. The texts of the letters are there given in full. They
are described as having then been owned by a Monsieur Chasles, but
they have never come to light. There seems to be little doubt that they
are a forgery, designed to fill the void in our knowledge of Milton's
visit to Galileo during his Italian visit. The other letters in the series,
each of which will be noticed in its chronological place, are as follows:

May 3	Milton to Voiture
May 29	Milton to Voiture
June 24	Milton to Voltaire
Aug. 23	Milton to King Louis XIV
Sept. 2	King Louis XIV to Milton.

The subject of all the letters is chiefly Galileo, though some other details of Milton's foreign travels, undoubtedly taken chiefly from his own
account in his *Defensio Secunda*, are interspersed. The reasons for con-
sidering them spurious, and hence for giving only a few representative
sentences from them here, are as follows: (1) if Milton had written
letters to these famous people, he would probably have published at least
some of them with his other letters; (2) there is a vast amount of repetition among the letters, too much to accord with Milton's habits of
writing; (3) he would probably have written in Latin, not in French;
(4) if he had been in touch with these men, he would probably have
mentioned them in his own autobiographical account; (5) his insist-
ence that Galileo was not entirely blind when Milton saw him does not
square well with other accounts; (6) there is nothing distinctive of
Milton's style anywhere in the letters; (7) they have been rejected by
almost every Milton scholar who has noticed them. See Fletcher, p. 50;
CM, XVIII, 535.

   For lack of a better date these letters, undated as Chasles gives them,
are here assigned to the year 1642 since that is the year in which Galileo
died.

                    [This March 30.
Dear Sir:

   I am very glad to know that you have all the papers of the
late M. Rotrou. . . . Now you have thus also became the pos-
sessor of a number of the writings of the very famous Galileo.
. . . the Jesuits . . . saying that he was cursed by God, who had

taken his eyesight away as punishment . . . but he never ceased
to see. . . .

To M. Molière.   John Milton.]

MAY (?). FINANCIALLY IN COMFORTABLE CIRCUMSTANCES: THE "RICH WIDOW."

For this I cannot omit without ingratitude to that providence
above, who hath ever bred me up in plenty, although my life
hath not bin unexpensive in learning, and voyaging about, so
long as it shall please him to lend mee what hee hath hitherto
thought good, which is anough to serve me in all honest and
liberall occasions, and something over besides. . . . I think with
them who both in prudence and elegance of spirit would choose
a virgin of mean fortunes honestly bred, before the wealthiest
widow.

> Milton, *An Apology Against . . . A Modest Confutation*, 1642, p.
> 42; CM, III, 342. The original reference in *A Modest Confutation* is
> very brief and seems like a merely impersonal gibe: "A rich Widow, or
> a Lecture, or both, contents you" (*op. cit.*, p. 22; Parker, *Milton's
> Contemporary Reputation*, p. 150). No elaboration of the point is given,
> and there is no hint in the context that the writer really knows anything
> about Milton's circumstances or hopes or plans. The date is uncertain;
> see the note to the entry of the publication of Milton's *Apology*. The
> date of the *Confutation* is similarly uncertain.

MAY (?). FIRST MEETS FUTURE MOTHER-IN-LAW ANNE POWELL.

[Anne Powell testified on June 4, 1656, that] for about
fourteene yeares [she] hath knowne the dēft John Milton
Es^{qr}. . . .

> From Anne Powell's deposition in the Ashworth-Milton suit, June 4,
> 1656, *q.v.* If the time given had been exactly fourteen years instead of
> "about," the acquaintance would have come about after the marriage of
> John Milton and Mary Powell; but we may interpret the statement,
> I believe, as meaning that Milton met Mrs. Powell during his courtship
> of her daughter.

MAY (?). PUBLICATION OF MILTON'S *APOLOGY AGAINST . . . A MODEST CONFUTATION*.

An Apology Against a Pamphlet call'd A Modest Confutation of the Animadversions upon the Remonstrant against

Smectymnuus. London, Printed by E.G. for Iohn Rothwell,
and are to be sold at the signe of the Sunne in Pauls Church-
yard. 1642.

Title page of the first edition; CM, III, 281. The date, which is uncertain, is that of the Thomason Catalogue. Masson (II, 398) assigned
it to February or March of this year. A title page combining *The Reason of Church Government* and *An Apology* has been recorded; see
Maggs Brothers' *Mercurius Britannicus*, number 105, November, 1947,
item 754. As given there the title reads: "An Apology for Smectymnuus.
With the Reason of Church-Government. By John Milton, Gent. London: for John Rothwell [1642]. The Reason of Church-Government
ur'd [*sic*] against Prelaty. By Mr. John Milton. In two Books. London:
E. G. for John Rothwell, 1641." The explanation of this volume given
by Maggs is that "unsold copies [of the *Reason*] were appended to the
'Apology,' a special title-page embracing both works."

cum duo præ cæteris magni nominis Episcopi suum jus contra
Ministros quosdam primarios assererent . . . ad illum, scriptis
quibusdam animadversionibus, & mox Apologia, respondi.

Milton, *Defensio Secunda*, 1654, p. 89; CM, VIII, 128-130.

[. . . when two bishops of high name above others asserted
their cause against certain leading ministers, I . . . replied to the
second in some written *Animadversions* and soon after in an
Apology.]

And then in answer to a Bishop hee writt . . . *Animadversions
upon the Remonstrants defense* (the work of Bishop Hall)
against Smectymnyus and *Apology for those Animadversions.*

The "earliest" biography, ff. 141-141v; Darbishire, p. 22.

Apology against the humble Remonstrant. This was written
in vindication of his *Animadversions.*

Wood, I, 881; Darbishire, p. 40.

An Apology for *Smectymnuus*, with the Reason of Church-
Government. 4*to.*

Phillips, sig. [b4v].

3. *A defence of Smectymnuus.*

Aubrey, fol. 64; Darbishire, p. 11.

MAY (?). PRESENTS COPY OF *APOLOGY* TO GEORGE
THOMASON.

by m^r Milton Ex dono Authoris.

This inscription, presumably in Thomason's hand, appears on his copy of *An Apology*, 1642 (British Museum, shelf-mark E.147.22); Stern, I, ii, 461; French, "The Autographs of John Milton," #14; CM, XVIII, 551.

MAY 3. LETTER TO VOITURE (?).

Ce 3 may

Monsieur,

Lors de mon séjour à Paris, je me rappelle que vous me dites avoir un bon nombre de lettres du célèbre Galilée. . . . Pourriez-vous scavoir ce que sont devenus ces précieux documents. . . .

A monsieur Voiture. John Milton

Comptes Rendus, LXVIII (1869), 747-748. For comment on this almost certainly spurious letter, see above under date of March 30, 1642.

[This May 3.

Dear Sir:

From the time of my stay in Paris, I remember that you told me you had a good number of letters of the famous Galileo. . . . Do you know what has become of these precious documents? To M. Voiture. John Milton.]

MAY 28. FUTURE FATHER-IN-LAW RICHARD POWELL PAYS SIR ROBERT PYE £110 INTEREST.

S^r. Robert Pye paid him by M^r. Powell in May. 1642— 110:00:00.

Public Record Office, London, SP Dom 23/109, p. 521; Hamilton, p. 106; French, *Milton in Chancery*, p. 83. This entry occurs in a list of Powell's debts and credits dated July 4, 1651. A similar entry is found in Pye's account dated April 8, 1651, in Hamilton, p. 101.

MAY 29. LETTER TO VOITURE (?).

Ce 29 may.

Je vous mandois, monsieur, dan une précédente lettre, que j'estois fort estonné des persécutions et humiliations de toute sorte qu'on avoit fait supporter au très célèbre Galilée pendant sa vie, et des moyens qu'on cherche, maintenant qu'il n'est plus, pour ensevelir sa mémoire avec ses cendres. . . . Et ce que je trouve estrange, c'est que messieurs Torricelli, Viviani et autres encore, qui scavent le contraire, c'est-à-dire qui scavent parfaitement que la cécité ne fut complette que les derniers mois de son existence, laissent propager de pareilles erreurs. . . .

A monsieur Voiture. John Milton.

Comptes Rendus, LXVIII (1869), 748. For comment on this almost certainly spurious letter, see above under date of March 30, 1642.

[This May 29.

I informed you, sir, in a previous letter, that I was much surprised at the persecutions and humiliations of all kinds which the very famous Galileo had had to undergo during his life, and at the means by which people try, now that he is no more, to bury his memory with his ashes. . . . And what I find strange is that Messrs. Torricelli, Viviani, and still others who know the contrary, namely who know perfectly that the blindness was not complete till the last months of his life, let such errors be propagated. . . .

To M. Voiture. John Milton.]

MAY 29 (?). MARRIES MARY POWELL.

In this while, his manner of Settlement fitting him for the reception of a Wife, hee in a moneths time (according to his practice of not wasting that precious Talent) courted, marryed, & brought home from Forrest-hall near Oxford a Daughter of Mr Powell. But shee, that was very Yong, & had bin bred in a family of plenty and freedom, beeing not well pleas'd with his reserv'd manner of life, within a few days left him, and went back into the Country with her Mother: Nor though hee sent severall pressing invitations could hee prevayl wth her to return, till about foure yeers after, when Oxford was surrendr'd (the nighness of her Fathers house to that Garrison having for the most part of the mean time hindred any communication between them) shee of her own accord came, & submitted to him; pleading that her Mother had bin the inciter of her to that frowardness. Hee in this Interval, who had entred into that State for the end design'd by God & Nature, and was then in the full vigor of his Manhood, could ill bear the disappointment hee mett with by her obstinate absenting: And therefore thought upon a Divorce, that hee might bee free to marry another; concerning which hee also was in treaty.

The "earliest" biography, fol. 141v; Darbishire, pp. 22-23. There are a few revisions in the manuscript, but they in no wise affect the sense of the passage.

The date and circumstances of Milton's marriage to Mary Powell are still hazy. In spite of diligent search among village and parish records by numerous investigators, including the present editor, no record of the wedding has been found. Though it is not impossible that it may yet appear, the chief likely sources have been rather thoroughly searched. It used to be taken for granted that the year of the marriage was 1643, but it now seems more likely that 1642 is the correct year. On this point the reader may be referred to Burns Martin, "The Date of Milton's First Marriage," *Studies in Philology*, xxv (1928), 457-461; B. A. Wright, "Milton's First Marriage," *Modern Language Review*, xxvi (1931), 383-400, and *ibid.*, xxvii (1932), 6-23. For the older interpretation, see Masson, II, 491 ff. For some additional details of the Powell family, see French, *Milton in Chancery*, chapter VI. The specific date of May 29 comes from Phillips's statement that Milton took this action about Whitsuntide; and Whitsunday in 1642 fell on May 29. It must not be supposed, however, that May 29 is anything more than an approximation. For that matter, as these biographers tell us, the process of courtship and marriage occupied a month or more; but since the date is so vague, one entry here will suffice for the whole process. It should, however, be borne in mind that Milton must have had the matter on his mind for a considerable length of time, and that our limitation of the entry about it to one day is so misleading that it must be interpreted very broadly.

For some interesting details and pictures about Forest Hill, see *Forest Hill with Shotover 1933 The Village Book*, edited by Ella Miller and printed by Hall in Oxford.

Though some of the material quoted above and in the succeeding passages will be repeated later under suitable dates, it seemed advisable to quote the complete passages about the marriage here in order to give a more or less complete picture even at the risk of repetition.

Though it is not likely that Milton spent much time at Forest Hill, tradition still connects several items there with him. It is of course assumed, and with reason, that he was married in the parish church, which is just across the fields from the site of the manor-house; and on the way are still standing the "Milton gateway," through which the bride and groom presumably passed on the way to the wedding ceremony in the chapel, and the "Milton stone," said to have been removed from the room in the house which Milton used as a study. Though the last section of the old manor house was torn down in 1854, a drawing of it as it appeared somewhat earlier is reproduced in French, *Milton in Chancery*, facing p. 100; on the same page is also reproduced an old illustration of the church and the gateway. Joseph Hunter visited Forest Hill on June 20, 1850, and found the manor house "pretty much in the state in which it was when they lived in it, except that portions of it have been taken down" (*Chorus Vatum*, IV, 183 (otherwise numbered 331). The daughter of the farmer-inhabitant showed him the hedgerow elms and eglantine of "L'Allegro"!

One further tradition may be added in this place. According to Sir William Jones in a letter to Lady Spencer written in 1769, "several papers in Milton's own hand, were found by the gentleman who was last in possession of the estate." See Lord Teignmouth, *Memoirs of . . . Sir William Jones*, London, 1804, pp. 66 ff.; Todd, 1826, I, 23, 25, 365; French, "The Autographs of John Milton," #129a; CM, XVIII, 546. Though there is every likelihood that some papers of Milton's might have remained in the house at Forest Hill, no further information about any such has come to light.

About *Whitsuntide* it was, or a little after, that he took a Journey into the Country; no body about him certainly knowing the Reason, or that it was any more than a Journey of Recreation: after a Month's stay, home he returns a Married-man, that went out a Batchelor; his Wife being *Mary* the Eldest Daughter of Mr. *Richard Powell*, then a Justice of Peace, of *Forresthil*, near *Shotover* in *Oxfordshire*; some few of her nearest Relations accompanying the Bride to her new Habitation; which by reason the Father nor any body else were yet come, was able to receive them; where the Feasting held for some days in Celebration of the Nuptials, and for entertainment of the Bride's Friends. At length they took their leave, and returning to *Forresthill*, left the Sister behind; probably not much to her satisfaction; as appeared by the Sequel; by that time she had for a Month or thereabout led a Philosophical Life (after having been used to a great House, and much Company and Joviality) Her Friends, possibly incited by her own desire, made earnest suit by Letter, to have her Company the remaining part of the Summer; which was granted, on condition of her return at the time appointed, *Michalemas*, or thereabout: In the mean time came his Father, and some of the forementiond Disciples.

Phillips, pp. xxii-xxiii; Darbishire, pp. 63-64.

He married his first wife . . . Powell of Fosthill at Shotover in Oxoñshire A°. Dnī . . . she was a zealous Royalist. She went from him to her Mother at . . . in yᵉ Kings quarters neer Oxförd. and [he] wrote the triple chord, about Divorce. and went wᵗʰout her husbands consent to her mother in the Kings quarters. by whom he had 4 children: hath two daughters living; Deborah was his Amanuensis, he taught her Latin, & to read Greeke to him, when he had lost his eie sight, wᶜʰ was A°. Dni. . . .

Aubrey, fol. 63; Darbishire, pp. 2-3. Though Aubrey's writing is like a patchwork quilt, the order of sentences used above seems as near like what he intended as any. Preceding the phrase "and wrote the triple chord" are the canceled words "He parted from her A°. Dnī." After "Greeke" is the canceled "& Hebrew."

Two different Rell: opinions doe not well on the same Boulster. She was a . . . Royalist, & went to hr mother neer the K's Quarters Oxford. I have so much charity ꝑ hac for her yᵗ she might not wrong his bed: but what man (especally 9templative) wold like to have a young wife environ'd & storm'd by the sons of [Mars] and those of the enemi partie?

Aubrey, fol. 68; Darbishire, p. 14. Aubrey uses for "Mars" its astronomical sign, an arrow attached to a circle.

His first wife (Mʳˢ Powell a Royalist) was brought up & lived where there was a great deale of company & dancing merriment &c, and when she came to live wᵗʰ her husband at Mʳ Russells in Sᵗ Brides ch:yd, she found it very solitary: no company came to her, often-times heard his Nephews beaten, and cry. This life was irkesome to her; & so she went to her Parents at Fosthill: he sent for her (after some time) and I thenke his servant was evilly entreated. but, as for wronging his bed, I never heard the least suspicion: nor had he of that, any Jealousie.

Aubrey, fol. 66; Darbishire, pp. 3-4. Aubrey originally wrote "cry, and beaten," but later changed the order by placing a figure 1 over "beaten" and 2 over "cry."

It must be now known, that after his settlement, upon his return from his Travels, he in a months time courted, married, and brought home to his house in *London*, a Wife from *Forsthill* lying between *Halton* and *Oxford,* named *Mary* the daughter of Mr. - - - *Powell* of that place Gent. But she, who was very young, and had been bred in a family of plenty and freedom, being not well pleas'd with her Husbands retired manner of life, did shortly after leave him and went back in the Country with her Mother. Whereupon, tho he sent divers pressing invitations, yet he could not prevail with her to come back, till about 4 years after when the Garrison of *Oxon* was surrendred (the nighness of her Father's house to which having for the most part of the mean time hindred any communication between them) she of her own accord returned and submitted to him, pleading that her Mother had been the chief promoter of her frowardness. But he being not able to bear this abuse, did therefore upon consideration, after he had consulted many eminent Authors, write the said book of Divorce, with intentions to be separated from her, but by the compromising of her Relations the matter did not take effect: so that she continuing with him ever after till her death, he had several Children by her, of whom *Deborah* was the third daughter, trained up by the Father in Lat. and Greek, and made by him his *Amanuensis.*

Wood, I, 881; Darbishire, pp. 40-41.

JUNE (?). THE MILTON-POWELL FAMILY BIBLES.
John Milton was born the 9th of December 1608. . . .

This entry, already quoted above, is taken from the best known of the Milton Bibles, now Add. MS. 32,310 in the British Museum. Though Milton may have acquired it much earlier than 1642, this reference to it is made for the sake of consistency, since it is at the time of marriage that people are likely to think of such objects. See French, "The Autographs of John Milton," #71; CM, XVIII, 274, 559 ff. This Bible was printed for R. Barker, London, 1612. It contains numerous entries and marks.

I am the book of Mary Milton.

This Bible, published in either 1636 or 1638, seems to have come to him through his wife, Mary Powell. In addition to the above inscription, probably in the hand of his wife, it contained notices of the births of their children, said to be in Milton's hand, and a Latin note also by him. Thomas Birch saw it on January 6, 1750, when it was in the possession of Milton's granddaughter Elizabeth Foster, and copied the entries.

Since then it has disappeared. See French, "The Autographs of John Milton," #86; CM, XVIII, 275, 561. Birch's transcripts are now in the British Museum, Add. MS. 4,244, fols. 53-54.

JUNE (?). MRS. MILTON'S FRIENDS AND RELATIVES RETURN HOME.

. . . some few of her nearest Relations accompanying the Bride to her new Habitation; which by reason the Father nor any body else were yet come, was able to receive them; where the Feasting held for some days in Celebration of the Nuptials, and for entertainment of the Bride's Friends. At length they took their leave, and returning to *Forresthill*, left the Sister behind; probably not much to her satisfaction; as appeared by the Sequel; by that time she had for a Month or thereabout led a Philosophical Life.

Phillips, p. xxii; Darbishire, pp. 63-64.

JUNE 2. CONTRIBUTES FOR RELIEF OF IRISH PROTESTANTS.

The authority for this assertion is tantalizingly missing. Masson (II, 358) says that in January, 1641/2, Milton contributed four pounds for a collection for Ireland. This is said to be a greater amount than most of his neighbors in St. Botolph's Street gave. Masson's authority is Hunter, who gives the information on pp. 26-27 of his printed pamphlet and on f. 22 of his manuscript, British Museum Add. MS. 24,501. Masson never saw the original records, since Hunter gave no references. Hunter himself admitted that Milton's name was missing in the list, but he assumed that since the list was so like others of about this time in the years 1641-1642, and since some names are gone from about the place in the list where Milton's should be, his name was undoubtedly there originally.

After considerable effort in looking through Exchequer papers in the Public Record Office, I have found a document which is probably the one to which Hunter referred. Its number is E179/252/14, and it gives the list of those in the second precinct of St. Botolph's Parish who contributed to Irish relief on June 2, 1642. Perhaps Hunter mistakenly read June as "Jan.," or he may possibly have been using another document. But at least this paper gives the familiar list of residents similar to that already met with under date of April 29, 1641. There is a similar list in E179/252/1A. In all three cases the name of Povey is preceded by that of Mathews; and in two that of Mathews is preceded by that of Milton. So it is a reasonable guess that Milton's similarly preceded that of Mathews here. If so, Masson is right as to the amount of the contribution, since Povey is down for one pound, Mathews for two, and his predecessor for four. The page is badly damaged.

JUNE 24. LETTER TO MOLIÈRE (?).

Ce 24 juin.

Monsieur, ye crois vous avoir dit que les jésuites ont esté et sont peut estre encore les plus grands ennemis de Galilée. . . . Lorsque je vis Galilée en 1639, je passay plusieurs semaines près de luy. . . . Je tiens de luy quelques escrits fort précieux, et j'ay aussi des lettres que je conserve comme souvenirs qui me sont chers. . . .

A monsieur Moliere.   John Milton

Comptes Rendus, LXVIII (1869), 749. For comment on this almost certainly spurious letter, see above under date of March 30, 1642.

[This June 30.

Sir, I think I told you that the Jesuits have been and may still be the greatest enemies of Galileo. . . . When I saw Galileo in 1639, I spent several weeks near him. . . . I got from him several very precious writings and I also have some letters which I keep as souvenirs which are dear to me. . . .

To M. Molière.   John Milton.]

JULY (?). MRS. MILTON'S FRIENDS INVITE HER HOME TO FOREST HILL.

Her Friends, possibly incited by her own desire, made earnest suit by Letter, to have her Company the remaining part of the Summer; which was granted, on condition of her return at the time appointed, *Michalemas*, or thereabout.

Phillips, pp. xxii-xxiii; Darbishire, p. 64. The date is necessarily only an approximation. See also CM, XVIII, 528.

JULY (?). MARY MILTON RETURNS TO HER HOME.

[Mrs. Milton] within a few days left him, and went back into the Country with her Mother.

The "earliest" biography, fol. 141v; Darbishire, p. 22.

Her Friends, possibly incited by her own desire, made earnest suit by Letter, to have her Company the remaining part of the

Summer; which was granted, on condition of her return at the time appointed, *Michalemas*, or thereabout.

Phillips, pp. xxii-xxiii; Darbishire, p. 64.

she went from him to her Mother at . . . yᵉ Kings quarters neer Oxford. . . . and went wᵗʰout her husbands consent to her mother in the Kings quarters. . . . This life was irkesome to her; & so she went to her Parents at Fosthill.

Aubrey, fols. 63, 66, 68; Darbishire, pp. 2-4, 14.

But she, who was very young, and had been bred in a family of plenty and freedom, being not well pleas'd with her Husbands retired manner of life, did shortly after leave him and went back in the Country with her Mother.

Wood, I, 881; Darbishire, p. 40.

Ejusdem porro hominis est, uxorem suam post annum nuptiarum, nescio quas ob causas, quas ipse noverit, repudiare, & repudium omne quacunque de causa factum legitimum esse tradere, & alienarum uxorum famam calumniosis dictis lacerare.

Salmasius, *Ad Johannem Miltonum Responsio, Opus Posthumum*, London, 1660, p. 3. We should not expect accuracy in such a source as this, because Salmasius is of course merely trying to discomfit and disgrace Milton, at whatever cost to truth or decency. It is interesting to notice, however, that the interval of time is here placed at a year, and that the decision for the separation is attributed to Milton rather than to his wife.

[The same gentleman has the additional distinction of having repudiated his wife after a year of marriage, for certain or uncertain reasons known to himself, and of propounding the lawfulness of divorce for any cause whatsoever, and wounding the reputation of the wives of others by calumnious insinuations.]

Masson, VI, 206.

Sed Miltonus hanc Theologiam non didicit, qui uxorem suam post annum à nuptiis dicitur res suas sibi habere jussisse, ob graves tantum mores; cum Christus ob solam adulterii causam id fieri permiserit.

Salmasius, *Ad Johannem Miltonum Responsio*, 1660, p. 253.

[But Milton doesn't teach this theology, who is said to have ordered his wife, a year after their marriage, to take her things home on account of her troublesome behavior, although Christ permitted this to be done only because of adultery.]

July 2. Attributed work published.

Observations upon His Majesties late Answers and Expresses, 1642.

Though sometimes attributed to Milton, this title is more probably from the pen of Henry Parker, to whom it is attributed by the Thomason Catalogue, the Harvard College Library, and Halkett and Laing. The date is from the Thomason Catalogue, though there were two editions in the same year. See cm, xviii, 636.

August (?). Receives additional students (?).

In the mean time came his Father, and some of the fore-mention'd Disciples.

Phillips, p. xxiii; Darbishire, p. 64. The "mean time" here is the interval between Mrs. Milton's returning to her parents at Forest Hill (about July, 1642) and Michaelmas (September 29), when it was agreed that she should return to her husband. But the dating is undependable, since it seems much more likely that the elder Milton arrived on April 27, 1643 (*q.v.*) rather than at this time.

His first wife . . . often-times heard his Nephews beaten, and cry.

Aubrey, fol. 66; Darbishire, p. 14. Although without date, this entry is placed here to be with the preceding reference to Milton's students.

August and later. Visits lady margaret ley.

Our Author, now as it were a single man again, made it his chief diversion now and then in an Evening to visit the Lady *Margaret Lee*, Daughter to the——*Lee*, Earl of *Marlborough*, Lord High Treasurer of *England*, and President of the Privy Councel to King *James* the First. This Lady being a Woman of great Wit and Ingenuity, had a particular Honour for him, and took much delight in his Company, as likewise her Husband Captain *Hobson*, a very Accomplish'd Gentleman; and what Esteem he at the same time had for Her, appears by a Sonnet he made in praise of her, to be seen among his other Sonnets in his Extant Poems.

Phillips, p. xxiii; Darbishire, p. 64. This lady's father must have been James Ley, first Earl of Marlborough (1550-1629), created Earl of Marlborough in 1626 (*D.N.B.*). He died on March 14, 1628/9. John Aubrey gives the epitaphs of both the Earl and his wife, Mary, daughter of John Petty of Stock Talmadge, Oxon., from monuments in the church at Westbury, Wilts., in his *Wiltshire. The Topographical Collections* (ed. Jackson, Devizes, 1862), pp. 404-405. She married John Hobson, a captain in the Parliamentary forces, in December, 1641 (Milton, *Paradise Regained* etc., ed. Merritt Y. Hughes, New York, 1937, p. 343). Although Milton's friendship with this couple cannot be exactly dated and must have extended for several years, it would seem to have begun about the time indicated here since Phillips mentions it just after he records the return of Milton's first wife to Forest Hill. Milton's sonnet to Lady Ley will be entered below under 1645. Toland (p. 18) and Newton (p. xv) repeat the statements of Phillips in substance. See also CM, XVIII, 380, 389.

AUGUST 23. LETTER TO KING LOUIS XIV (?), DESCRIBING HIS ITALIAN JOURNEY AND ESPECIALLY HIS VISIT TO GALILEO.

Ce 23 août.

Au Roy.

Sire,

Selon le désir que me tesmoigne Vostre Majesté, je luy feray le récit de mon voyage en Italie, et en mesme tems je luy feray part de mon appréciation touchant le très illustre Galilée.

Je diray d'abord à Vostre Majesté que ce fut au commencement du printemps de l'année 1638 que j'entrepris ce voyage. Je me rendis d'abord en France: je fus reçu amicalement chez monsieur Grotius, à Paris, à qui j'estois recommandé, et qui m'introduisit dans toutes les bonnes sociétés. Bientost je connus tous les scavans et les lettrés, et j'acquis leur estime. Il n'est pas nécessaire que j'entre ici dans des détails; j'informeray seulement Vostre Majesté que ayant sceu de moy que j'avois dessein de me rendre à Florence pour y voir l'illustre Galilée duquel j'avois entendu faire si bel éloge à Paris, chascun m'encouragea à faire ce voyage, et tout un chascun aussi me donna une lettre de recommandation pour luy. J'en emportay pour le moins une vingtaine, sinon plus, ce qui tesmoigne que l'illustre astronome florentin avoit beaucoup d'amis et de partisans en france. En quittant Paris je me rendis donc à Florence et de là à Arcetri, non loin de cette ville, où Galilée avoit fixé sa demeure. Je le trouvay chez luy occupé à travailler un télescope qu'il vouloit perfectionner pour étudier Saturne et son entourage, me dit-il. Je luy remis toutes les missives dont j'estois chargé, desquelles il prit connaissance, et dont la lecture le rendit joyeux. Aussi m'en témoigna-t-il grande satisfaction, me questionnant sur un chascun de ceux que je venois de quitter, et cela de telle manière qui prouvoit qu'il les avoit en grande estime. Il me retint à dîner avec luy, et m'engagea à revenir le voir souvent pendant tout le temps que je resterois à Florence. Ce que je fis. Et une fois que je fus le voir, estant sur mon départ, il me retint mesme plusieurs jours chez luy, pendant lesquels il me fit connoistre ses précieux escrits et une infinité de lettres quil avoit reçues de ses amis. Il m'entretint non-seulement d'astronomie, mais aussy de littérature dont il avoit fait une bonne estude. Avant que de le quitter il me fit faire la promesse de ne point quitter l'Italie sans retourner le voir. Je quittay donc Florence pour de là me rendre à Sienne où je restay peu. De là j'allay à Rome, où je fus parfaitement accueilli de tous les scavans et principalement de monseigneur le cardinal Barberin, qui me présenta au saint père qui luy aussy me questionna beaucoup sur chascun des scavans de France, et principalement des poëtes; car il se piquoit d'avoir certaines connoissances en cet art. il me donna plusieurs fois audience, ainsi que le cardinal Barberini qui m'admettoit à ses concerts. Ce fut là que j'entendis la fameuse musicienne Leonora. Je fus tellement charmé de ses chants et de sa beauté, que je n'ay pu m'empêcher de faire ses louanges dans un sonnet. Après un séjour assez long dans la capitale du monde chrétien, je m'en allay à Naples, où je fus parfaitement reçu aussi par les scavans. j'y fis connoissance du très illustre marquis de Villa, vieillard plein d'esprit, ingénieux et enthousiaste, qui avoit esté l'amy et l'admirateur du Tasse, et qui parloit de luy avec cette abondance de souvenirs que laisse ordinairement dans la mémoire l'intimité d'un homme illustre et malheureux. Je me sentis comme inspiré en escoutants les beaux récits de cet amy du Tasse: et il me retint plusieurs jours en sa villa où j'eus le tems de compulser plusieurs escrits de ce poëte infortuné. De Naples j'avois le dessein de me rendre en Sicile et en Grèce; mais ayant appris la triste nouvelle des troubles survenus dans ma patrie, cela arresta mes pérégrinations. Je résolus donc de quitter l'Italie, mais non pas sans revoir l'illustre Galilée. Je quittai Naples et me rendis à Florence par Rome et Milan. Je revis donc le très illustre Galilée. Je le retrouvay quelque peu changé, c'est à dire que la trop grande application qu'il avoit portée à l'estude des astres et de Saturne en particulier, luy avoit tellement fatigué la vue, qu'il fust obligé de suspendre cette estude, à son grand déplaisir, ainsy qu'il me l'avoua. Car, me dit-il, il y a du costé de Saturne des choses extraordinaires, qu'il avoit déja entrevu, mais qu'il ne pouvoit encore bien démontrer. C'estoit donc pour luy une grande privation de ne pouvoir plus se livrer à son estude favorite; car ses yeux s'estoient tellement affoiblis, qu'il ne voyoit plus le ciel. Aussy en estoit-il très affecté. Lorsque je le revis il s'occupoit à mettre de l'ordre dans ses papiers, c'est à dire à les classer par catégories pour les partager entre ses amis; car, ainsy quil me l'avoua, il prévoyoit quaprès sa mort, si ces papiers restoient entre les mains de ses ennemis ils courroient risque d'estre anéantis. Aussi prit-il des mesures pour éviter cette catastrophe; et bien lui en prit; car nous avons un tesmoignage du sort qui les attendoit. Mais je reviens à mon sujet. A mon retour à Florence je restay encore une quainzaine de jours en cette ville; et j'allay souvent, mesme presque chaque jour, présenter mes hommages au très illustre astronome qui m'invita plusieurs fois à partager son souper. Il y avoit parfois nombreuse société, composée soit d'amis, soit d'estrangers. Nostre hote y estoit on ne peut plus aimable: car malgré ses indispositions et toutes les vicissitudes qu'il a eu à supporter dans sa vie, sa gayeté ne fut jamais altérée. Je tiens mesme pour certain quil la conserva jusqu'à la fin de ses jours. Ce qui suppose en luy l'organisation la plus heureuse. Il estoit d'un temperamment sanguin, flegmatique et très robuste. Sa taille estoit ordinaire, et sa stature carrée.

Les traits de sa figure annonçoient le calme de son esprit, su-
périeur aux revers de la fortune. Il estoit très éloquent, et ce
ton d'éloquence le rendoit imposant dans ses entretiens. Mais ce
qu'il y avoit surtout de remarquable en luy, c'est qu'il saississoit
de suite tout ce qu'il vouloit scavoir. Il avoit beaucoup de mémoire et d'imagination, et il avoit une abondante dose de littérature, et la meilleure. Non-seulement il connoissoit tous les
anciens auteurs, mais il estoit aussi très familiarisé avec les mo-
dernes. Il estimoit beaucoup le Dante, Petrarque, Boccace,
l'Arioste et le Tasse en littérature. Mais dans les sciences ce fust
Pythagore, Archimède, Anthemius qu'il estudioit. Pendant que
j'estois avec luy il me montra une infinité des notes quil avoit
extrait d'un manuscrit de ce dernier, sur les paradoxes de mé-
chanique, lequel manuscrit se trouve au Vatican. Ce manuscrit
d'Anthemius n'a, à ce qu'il paroist, jamais vu la lumière, et il
avoit dessein de luy donner le jour, ou du moins de le retirer de
l'oubli où il sembloit estre enséveli. Mais je vois que je m'es-
loigne du sujet. Je disois donc à Vostre Majesté qu'à force d'ob-
server les astres, la vue de Galilée s'estoit considérablement
affoiblie depuis que je l'avois vu pour la première fois, c'est-à-
dire dans l'espace de 1638 à la fin de 1639 où nous étions alors.
Et toutefois, quoique ce fut pour luy une grande privation de
ne pouvoir plus voir le ciel, néanmoins il trouvoit encore à se
consoler dans l'estude des belles lettres. Il lisoit beaucoup, com-
pulsoit, résolvoit mesme des problesmes nouveaux; et c'est alors
enfin qu'il s'occupa de réunir ensemble une grande quantité de
remarques faites et recuillies depuis longtemps, touchant divers
auteurs et divers ouvrages. Il se remit donc de nouveau a lestude
de la littérature et des beaux arts, qui avoit fait la charme de
sa jeunesse. Il faisoit des vers, composoit des canevas de comé-
dies, et faisoit des commentaires sur Dante, l'Arioste et le Tasse.
Telles estoient ses occupations alors que je le quittay; et ce fut
à mon grand regret que je quittay un homme si affable, si aimable, et qui estoit doué de cette faculté qui anime et embellit les
pensées les plus sévères et les plus difficiles à bien exprimer; cet
homme enfin qu'on peut considérer comme ayant esté un des

plus vastes génies du monde. En le quittant il me chargea de remettre à ses amis de France un bon nombre de lettres. Je fus mesme chargé de remettre à messieurs Rotrou, Pascal et à madamoiselle de Gournay, de petits paquets qui devoient renfermer des documents. Mais je m'arreste. Ce récit est assez long et je serois heureux s'il peut estre agréable à vostre Majesté. Je suis, sire, de Vostre Majesté le très-humble et très obéissant serviteur.

John Milton.

Comptes Rendus, LXVIII (Paris, 1869), 745-747. For comment on this almost certainly spurious letter, see above under date of March 30, 1642. Despite its probable spuriousness, however, it is given in full because of the elaborate detail which it furnishes. Even though not genuine and in places certainly contradicting the known facts of Milton's itinerary (e.g., visiting Galileo "à la fin de 1639") and his religious ideas (referring to the feared and hated Pope as "saint père"), it is an interesting fiction.

[August 23.

To the King. Sire:

According to the desire which Your Majesty intimated to me, I will describe my visit to Italy and at the same time acquaint you with my appreciation of the very illustrious Galileo. First, I will tell Your Majesty that it was at the beginning of the spring of the year 1638 that I undertook this voyage. I went first to France. I was received cordially at Paris by M. Grotius, to whom I was recommended, and who introduced me into all the best circles. I soon knew all the savants and men of letters and earned their esteem. I do not need here to go into details; I will merely inform Your Majesty that, having learned that I was planning to go to Florence to see the illustrious Galileo, of whom I had heard so high praise in Paris, everyone encouraged me to make this journey, and every single one also gave me a letter of recommendation to him. I carried away at least a score of them, if not more, which proves that the illustrious Florentine astronomer had many friends and supporters in France. After leaving Paris, then, I went to Florence and from there to Arcetri, not far from that city, where Galileo had taken up residence. I found him at home busy at work on a telescope which he told me he wished to perfect in order to study Saturn and its satellites. I gave him all the letters which I had for him; and he looked at them and enjoyed reading them. He also seemed to take great pleasure in them, questioning me about each one of the men whom I had just left, and in a way which proved that he esteemed them highly. He kept me to dine with him and made me promise to return to see him often during the time I stayed in Florence. I did so. And once when I was calling on him and was ready to leave, he kept me even several days at his home, during which he acquainted me with his precious writings and an infinity of letters which he had received from his friends. He entertained me not only with astronomy but also with literature, of which he had made a considerable study. Before I left, he made me promise not to leave Italy without returning to see him. So I left Florence to go to Siena, where I stayed a short time. Thence I went to Rome, where I was perfectly received by all the scholars and principally by Cardinal Barberini, who presented me to the Holy Father, who also asked me many questions about every one of the scholars of France, and principally the poets; for he piqued himself on having some knowledge of that art. He gave me audience several times, as did Cardinal Barberini, who admitted me to his concerts. It was there that I heard the famous musician Leonora. I was so charmed by her songs and her beauty that I could not help praising her in a sonnet. After a fairly long stay in the capital of the Christian world I went to Naples, where I was perfectly received by the scholars. There I made the acquaintance of the very illustrious Marquis of Villa, an old man but full of vigor, witty, and enthusiastic, who had been the friend and admirer of Tasso, and who spoke of him with that wealth of recollections which intimacy with an illustrious and unfortunate man ordinarily leaves in the memory. I felt as if inspired while listening to the wonderful stories of this friend of Tasso; and he kept me several days at his villa, where I had the time to examine several writings of that unfortunate poet. From Naples I planned to go to Sicily and Greece; but my learning the sad news of the troubles which had come on my country stopped my travels. So

I resolved to leave Italy, but not without seeing the illustrious Galileo again. I left Naples and went to Florence by way of Rome and Milan. So I saw the very illustrious Galileo again. I found him a little changed; that is, the too great intensity with which he had studied the stars and particularly Saturn had so tired his eyesight that he had to give up this study, to his great displeasure as he confessed to me. For, as he told me, there are near Saturn wonderful things of which he had already caught glimpses but which he could not yet demonstrate. So it was a great privation for him not to be able to devote himself to his favorite study; for his eyes were so weakened that he could no longer see the sky. He was much affected about it. When I visited him, he was busy putting his papers in order; that is, classifying them by subjects to share them among his friends; for, as he confessed to me, he foresaw that after his death, if these papers remained in the hands of his enemies, they would run the risk of being destroyed. So he took steps to prevent that catastrophe; and it was well that he did so, for we have evidence of the fate that awaited them. But I return to my subject. On my return to Florence I stayed another fortnight in that city; and I went often, even almost every day, to pay my compliments to the very illustrious astronomer, who invited me several times to share his supper. There was sometimes a considerable group, composed partly of friends and partly of strangers. Our host was most gracious: for despite his illness and all the vicissitudes which he had had to endure through his life his gayety was never changed. I even feel certain that he retained it to the end of his days. This implies in him the most fortunate constitution. He was of a sanguine, phlegmatic, and most robust temperament. His figure was average, and his bearing erect. The features of his face expressed the calm of his mind, above the reverses of fortune. He was very eloquent, and this tone of eloquence made him impressive in his entertainments. But what was especially remarkable in him was that he grasped at once whatever he wanted to know. He had excellent memory and imagination, and he had an abundant dose of literature, and that the best. He not only knew all the ancient writers, but was also very familiar with the moderns. He highly esteemed Dante, Petrarch, Boccaccio, Ariosto, and Tasso in literature. But in the sciences it was Pythagoras, Archimedes, and Anthemius whom he studied. While I was with him, he showed me an infinity of notes which he had extracted from a manuscript of this last, on the paradoxes of mechanics, a manuscript located in the Vatican. This manuscript of Anthemius, it appears, has never seen the light, and he planned to publish it, or at least to lift it from the oblivion in which it seemed to be buried. But I see that I wander from my subject. I told Your Majesty that by his looking closely at the stars Galileo's eyesight had become much weakened since I first saw him, that is, between 1638 and the end of 1639, in which we then were. And yet, although it was for him a great privation no longer to be able to see the heavens, nevertheless he still found consolation in the study of literature. He read a good deal, examined documents, even solved new problems; and it was then that he busied himself with gathering a great many notes made or taken long before, concerning various authors and writings. He turned anew to the study of literature and fine arts, which had captivated him in youth. He wrote verses, made sketches of comedies, and wrote commentaries on Dante, Ariosto, and Tasso. Such were his occupations when I left him; and it was with deep regret that I left a man so affable and lovable, endowed with that faculty which invigorates and adorns the severest thoughts and those most difficult to express well; a man, in short, whom one may consider to have been one of the greatest geniuses of the world. When I left, he asked me to return a number of letters to his friends in France. I was even asked to return to M. Rotrou, M. Pascal, and Mlle. de Gournay some little packets which must have contained documents. But I stop. This account is long enough, and I should be happy if it could please Your Majesty. I am, Sire, Your Majesty's very humble and very obedient servant.

John Milton.]

I have tried to make the translation sound like fairly idiomatic English but have made no attempt to disguise or conceal the wearisome repetitions and the formless wandering of the original. Two further factors add to the unlikeliness of Miltonic authenticity: the fact that the original language is French, whereas Milton usually wrote to foreigners in Latin; and the preoccupation with Galileo, whom Milton scarcely mentions elsewhere in his writings. It would seem that the man who actually wrote it, probably in the nineteenth century, had taken a bare skeleton from Milton's *Defensio Secunda*, embroidered on it a fanciful description of Galileo, and then inserted numerous hints of lost manuscripts, which might serve to lend an air of authenticity to supposedly recovered manuscripts when they later appeared. It reads like the groundwork of a gigantic literary hoax which never quite came off.

SEPTEMBER 2. LOUIS XIV REPLIES TO MILTON'S LETTER (?).

Monsieur Milton, vostre lettre par laquelle vous me faites le récit de vostre voyage en Italie et particulierement de vos entretiens avec le très illustre Galilée, m'a fait grand plaisir. . . . Serais-je indiscret en vous demandant communication de ces lettres, sinon les originales au moins des copies fidèles. Un de mes bons serviteurs qui est en ce moment en Angleterre pourra se charger de cette mission, si vous le permettez. . . .

Ce 2 septembre.   Louis.

Comptes Rendus, LXVIII (1869), 747. For comment on this almost certainly spurious letter, see above under date of March 30, 1642.

[M. Milton, Your letter in which you give me the account of your travel to Italy and particularly of your visits with the very illustrious Galileo has given me great pleasure. . . . Should I be indiscreet in asking you to let me have those letters, if not the originals at least faithful copies? One of my trusty servants who is now in England can undertake this mission if you will allow him. . . .

This September 2.   Louis.]

SEPTEMBER 21. FINISHES SECOND READING OF HARINGTON'S ARIOSTO.

Questro libro due volte Io letto, Sept. 21. 1642.

A marginal note in Milton's hand in his copy of Sir John Harington's translation of Ariosto's *Orlando Furioso*, 1591, p. 405. The book is now in the possession of Miss M. K. Surridge, whose father, Rev. H. A. D. Surridge, first discovered it as a Milton item. The annotations are recorded in CM, XVIII, 330-336, with a note on pp. 569-570. See also French, "The Autographs of John Milton," #63; Ralph A. Haug, "Milton and Sir John Harington," *Modern Language Quarterly*, IV (1943), 291. Haug notes that Milton takes some material from Harington in his *Of Reformation*, 1641.

[I have read this book twice, September 21, 1642.]

SEPTEMBER 30. PUBLICATION OF ATTRIBUTED WORK ON THE MILITIA.

An Argument Or, Debate in Lavv: of the Great Question concerning the Militia; As it is now settled by Ordinance of both the Houses of Parliament. . . . By J.M.C.L. London . . . 1642.

According to Todd (*Poetical Works of John Milton*, 1826, I, 223) the second Earl of Bridgewater, who acted the elder brother in *Comus*, wrote Milton's name on the title page of his copy of this pamphlet, which at least as late as 1908 was still at Bridgewater House, according to the Grolier Catalogue. Todd also describes (*ibid.*, 224) a copy in the Archiepiscopal Library at Lambeth, bound with several other tracts, and described in contemporary handwriting in the book as containing among other titles: "John Milton's Speech for unlicensd Printing . . . *His Argument concerning y*e *Militia*." Todd also mentions (*ibid.*, 223-224) a copy of Phillips's life of Milton annotated by William Oldys, in which Oldys added this title as by Milton.

Nevertheless, the likelihood is rather that the author was John Marsh. In the Thomason copy in the British Museum the "J.M.C.L." is expanded, probably in Thomason's hand, to "J. Marsh Canc. Lincolns Jnne." The same attribution is made by Halkett and Laing, the Harvard College Library, and Alfred Stern (I, ii, 144, 462-463). See CM, XVIII, 637.

The date is from the Thomason copy, on which is written in ink on the title page: "Sep: 30."

OCTOBER (?). SENDS FOR WIFE TO RETURN.

Nor though hee sent severall pressing invitations could hee prevayl wth her to return, till about foure yeers after.

The "earliest" biography, fol. 141v; Darbishire, p. 22. The dates of his letters of invitation are entirely a matter of conjecture, since none of them is known to have survived. But since the agreement is said to have been that Mrs. Milton should return to her husband at Michaelmas (September 29), it is reasonable to assume that Milton may have written at least the first letter in October. Others may have stretched out over the months or years following. It may also be possible that the auto-graph letters of Milton referred to above as having been found at Forest Hill may have been, at least in part, these letters to his wife. See also CM, XII, 413; XVIII, 528.

. . . he sent for her (after some time) and I thenke his servant was evilly entreated.

Aubrey, fol. 66; Darbishire, p. 14.

Whereupon, tho he sent divers pressing invitations, yet he could not prevail with her to come back, till about 4 years after.

Wood, I, 881; Darbishire, p. 40.

Michalemas being come, and no news of his Wife's return, he sent for her by Letter; and receiving no answer, sent several other Letters, which were also unanswered; so that at last he dispatch'd down a Foot-Messenger with a Letter, desiring her return.

Phillips, pp. xxiii-xxiv; Darbishire, p. 64; See also CM, XVIII, 528.

OCTOBER (?). THE POWELLS REBUFF MILTON'S DE-MANDS FOR HIS WIFE'S RETURN.

[The letters which Milton wrote remained unanswered, and the messenger which he sent] came back not only without an answer, at least a satisfactory one, but to the best of my remem-brance, reported that he was dismissed with some sort of Con-tempt; this proceeding, in all probability, was grounded upon no other Cause but this, namely, That the Family being generally addicted to the Cavalier Party, as they called it, and some of them possibly ingaged in the King's Service, who by this time had his Head Quarters at *Oxford*, and was in some Prospect of Success, they began to repent them of having Matched the Eld-est Daughter of the Family to a Person so contrary to them in Opinion; and thought it would be a blot in their Escutcheon, when ever that Court should come to Flourish again; however, it so incensed our Author, that he thought it would be dis-honourable ever to receive her again, after such a repulse; so that he forthwith prepared to Fortify himself with Arguments for such a Resolution, and accordingly wrote two Treatises.

Phillips, p. xxiv; Darbishire, pp. 64-65. Several briefer notes to the same effect are included in the accounts, quoted above, of Milton's attempts to induce his wife to return.

OCTOBER 21. BROTHER CHRISTOPHER IN READING SUPPORTS ROYAL CAUSE.

Boroughe
of   ss M^r. Thomas Thackam Mayor 21 Octobris
Readinge   Ao—1642/

Richard Edmundę

....Serieantę

Henry Ayres

. . .

S^t. Lawrence parishe

. . .

Corslettę-Muscottę-Menn

X M^r. Milton ....

X D^{tor} ffloyde ....

X M^r. Page ....

. . .

From the Muster Roll of Reading, among the manuscripts of the Corporation of Reading kept in the Town Hall; abstracted in the Eleventh Report of the Commission on Historical Manuscripts, appendix, part 7 (1888), p. 209. I wish to acknowledge the kindness of Mr. C. S. Johnson, Town Clerk of Reading, who generously sent me photographic copies of these entries. The "X" probably indicates compliance.

The editor of the HMC report interprets this entry as meaning that Christopher Milton was bound to furnish arms or supplies and not personal services to the royal army. From the length of the lines drawn after the names given above, I venture to guess that Milton was asked to provide muskets whereas Dr. Floyd and Mr. Page were called on for corslets. It is evident that Milton must have been a settled resident in St. Lawrence parish at this period.

Christopher . . . in the time of the Civil Wars of *England* . . . being a great favourer and assertor of the King's Cause, and Obnoxious to the Parliament's side, by acting to his utmost power against them, so long as he kept his Station at *Reading*. . . .

Phillips, pp. v-vi; Darbishire pp. 52-53. Though undated, this item may well be included with the document from Reading.

NOVEMBER 13 (?). SONNET ON ASSAULT OF THE CITY.

Captain or Colonel, or Knight in Arms. . . .

Poems, 1645, pp. 49-50; CM, I, 60. In the Trinity Manuscript this appears on p. 9 with the original title: "On his dore when ye Citty expected an assault." This was later scored through and a new title substituted: "When the assault was intended to ye Citty." Most editors agree on a date in October or November of 1642 for this sonnet, but Hughes (p. 340) dates it about November 13, when the Royalists had reached London but were turned back at Turnham Green. Smart (p. 56) dates it "before the retreat from Turnham Green on November 13."

DECEMBER 12. RECEIVES INTEREST PAYMENT FROM RICHARD POWELL.

. . . the growing Jnterest for the forbearance of the said Princivall debt was for some yeares then following likewise payd And soe continued to bee paid vntill June Jn the yeare of our Lord One Thousand six hundred ffortie and fflower. . . .

From Milton's answer to Elizabeth Ashworth, February 22, 1653/4, *q.v.*

SAMUEL HARTLIB REFERS TO MILTON WITH HIGH PRAISE.

Mr Milton in Aldersgate Street hase written many good books a great traveller and full of piects and inuentions.

[Marginal entry:] Milton.

From Hartlib's "Ephemerides," or notebook for 1643, in the collection of Lord Delamere, by whose kind permission this and numerous subsequent items from these papers are taken; printed in G. H. Turnbull's *Hartlib, Dury and Comenius*, Liverpool, 1947, p. 40. The words "piects" (i.e., projects) and "inuentions" are difficult to read and may not be correct.

John Milton · 1643

OF REFORMATION ATTACKED BY JOHN BRAMHALL.

With what indignation doe all good Protestants see those blessed Men, stiled now in Print by a younge novice, *halting and time-serving Prelates,* and *common stales to countenance with their prostituted gravities every Politick fetch.* It was truely said by *Seneca,* that the most contemptible Persons ever have the loosest tongues.

[Marginal note:] *Two Books of Reformation.*

John Bramhall, *The Serpent Salve, Or, A Remedie For the Biting of an Aspe . . . Printed in the year 1643,* p. 212; Parker, *Milton's Contemporary Reputation,* p. 73; Masson, II, 361; Stern, I, ii, 464. The "blessed Men" refers to Cranmer, Latimer, Ridley, and Hooker. Bramhall's name does not appear on the title page, but the work is generally attributed to him, and is included in his *Works,* Dublin, 1676, p. 598.

ATTRIBUTED SHARE IN TRANSLATING DIODATI'S *ANNOTATIONS.*

Piovs Annotations Vpon the Holy Bible . . . By . . . M^r. Iohn Diodati . . . London . . . 1643.

The copy of this work in the possession of the present editor bears a paragraph of pencilled comment on the front flyleaf signed "H.C.H.C.," presumably Hugh C. H. Candy. It reads in part: "It seems not unlikely that the present translation from the Italian original was made, or supervised, by Milton. The Preface is not uncharacteristic and in the present copy two small omissions (on a3) have been supplied in a Script which might easily have passed for Milton's."

It seems highly unlikely to me, however, that Milton had any hand in this work. One sentence in the preface (sig. a4v) alone would almost preclude any such possibility: "Now stand and admire our carefull mother the Church of *England.*" This surely was not the tone of Milton's writing and thinking in 1643. The corrections mentioned (the insertion of "by" in line 12 and of "truth" seven lines from the bottom) are in a hand not unlike Milton's, but the amount of writing involved is too limited to allow of much opinion either way.

FATHER'S MUSICAL COMPOSITION PUBLISHED.

I trust in God then to my soule . . . I. Milton.

This is Psalm 11 in William Slatyer's *The Psalmes of David,* 1643. See CM, XVIII, 538. It has sometimes been wrongly stated that the younger Milton composed the words of the Psalm, but this idea evidently comes from mistaking the name of the composer, the elder Milton, for that of the poet.

[83]

BROTHER-IN-LAW RICHARD POWELL SUPPORTS ROYAL
CAUSE.

May it please yor. Hono^r.

To remember that vpon his late Ma^{ts}. Returne to Oxon, after
Brainford Fight. J did present His Ma^{ty}. 50^{ll}. in Gould, w^{ch}.
He was pleased to deliver to yor. hands. And likewise that I did
often send Jnteligence to yor. Hono^r. at Oxon. by the hands of
M^r: Richard Powell now Bencher of the Temple. . . .

May 29th. 1667./   William Garret

Mr Powell Live^d at forrest-hill neare Oxōn./

British Museum Eg. MS. 2539, fol. 101; Edward Scott in the
Athenaeum, 1879, II, 337. Though the name of the addressee is not
given, it was probably Sir Edward Nicholas, since it occurs among his
papers. The endorsement at the bottom is said by Scott to be in the
hand of Sir Joseph Williamson, but the writing does not resemble that
of Williamson. The date of the intelligence work here referred to is
not definite, but since the King retired to Oxford soon after the battle of
Brentford (Brainford here), which occurred on November 12, 1642,
we may date it some time in 1643. It must have been a fairly lengthy
process. Scott interprets it as a process by which Mary Powell, Delilah-
like, stole Milton's secrets and slipped them to her brother Richard;
but such an explanation seems far-fetched. Young Richard Powell, who
was born in 1621 and later became a Bencher, was about 22 years old
at this time.

FEBRUARY 3. PUBLICATION OF ATTRIBUTED WORK.

A Reply to the Answer (Printed by His Majesties Command
at Oxford) to a Printed Booke Intituled Observations upon
some of his Maiesties late Answers and Expresses. By J. M.
London, Printed for Matthew Walbancke, Anno Dom. 1642.

Mentioned as possibly by Milton in Todd, 1 (1826), 222-223, but
immediately rejected because of royalist leanings. Attributed to Milton
also by E. H. Gillette in *Hours at Home*, IX (1869), 532-536; by
Halkett and Laing; and by the Harvard University Library. Rejected
as not by Milton in CM, XVIII, 636. The date is from Thomason.

FEBRUARY 9. PUBLICATION OF ATTRIBUTED TRANSLA-
TION OF *BAPTISTES*.

Tyrannicall-Government Anatomized: or, A Discovrse Concerning Evil-Councellors. Being the Life and Death of John

the Baptist And Presented to the Kings most Excellent Majesty by the Author. Die Martis, 30. Januarii, 1642. It is Ordered by the Committee of the House of Commons concerning Printing, That this Book be forthwith printed and published: Iohn VVhite. London, Printed for John Field, 1642.

Translated from George Buchanan's *Baptistes, sive Calumnia, tragoedia,* 1578. Attributed to Milton by Francis Peck, in *New Memoirs,* 1740, and by Halkett and Laing. But it has generally been rejected as by Milton; see CM, XVIII, 602. The date is from the Thomason copy, which bears a manuscript notation on the title page: "feb: 9."

APRIL 27. PUBLICATION OF ATTRIBUTED WORK.

A Soveraigne Salve to Cvre the Blind. . . . By J.M. Esquire . . . 1643.

Attributed to Milton by E. H. Gillette in *Hours at Home,* IX (1869), 532-536; by Halkett and Laing, on Gillette's authority; and by Sotheby's in a sale in 1901, *Book Prices Current,* XV (1901), 588. Todd notes (1826 ed., I, 224) that a copy in the Archiepiscopal Library in Lambeth Palace, numbered I. 5. 23, is endorsed in an old hand as by Milton. Though the work is a vigorous defense of the supremacy of the Parliament, it is highly unlikely that Milton is the author. Any work omitted from lists like those of Phillips is automatically suspect; and the author of this work describes himself on the first page as "a pen ever before still." Such a characterization would in no sense fit Milton. The date is that of the Thomason copy.

APRIL 27. BROTHER CHRISTOPHER FORCED TO LEAVE READING.

. . . and after that Town [Reading] was taken by the Parliament Forces, being forced to quit his House there, he [Christopher Milton] steer'd his course according to the Motion of the King's Army.

Phillips, p. vi; Darbishire, pp. 52-53. According to Masson (II, 465) Reading capitulated to the Parliamentary forces on April 27, 1643.

APRIL 27. FATHER LEAVES READING AND COMES TO LIVE WITH POET.

His Father, who till the taking of *Reading* by the Earl of *Essex* his Forces, had lived with his other Son at his House there, was upon that Son's dissettlement necessitated to betake himself to this his Eldest Son, with whom he lived for some Years, even to his Dying Day.

Phillips, p. xxi; Darbishire, p. 63; Brennecke, p. 145. The Earl of Essex took Reading on April 27, 1643.

In the mean time came his Father, and some of the foremention'd Disciples.

Phillips, p. xxiii; Darbishire, p. 64. The date of this entry seems to contradict that of the previous one. The phrase "In the mean time" seems to refer to the interval between Mrs. Milton's returning to her parents at Forest Hill (about July, 1642) and Michaelmas of that year (September 29), when it was agreed that she should return to her husband. But the first statement is so much more circumstantial than the second that it seems almost certain to be right and the second wrong.

MAY 2. A NAMESAKE INVOLVED IN ACTION BY HOUSE OF LORDS.

Die Martis, *videlicet*, 2° Maii [1643]. . . .

This House entered into Consideration of the Charge brought up from the House of Commons, against *Will. Cooper*, Parson of *St. Thomas Apostles*.

The said *Cooper* not appearing according to the Order of this House, Affidavit was made, by *Philip Adams* and *Anthony Brooks*, "that the Order was left at his House:" Upon this Contempt, the House proceeded to hear the Evidence, to prove the Particulars of the Charge. . . .

John Mylton, "To prove his vexatious Suits against his Parishioners, and excommunicated him."

Journals of the House of Lords, VI, 25. There is no reason to assume that the Milton here mentioned is the poet, but the item is here included for completeness.

MAY 24. ATTRIBUTED WORK ON MONARCHY.

A Treatise of Monarchy . . . 1643.

CM, XVIII, 636. Now generally attributed to Philip Hunton. The date is from Thomason (I, 262).

JUNE 19. DANIEL OXENBRIDGE (OR FRANCIS GHERARD) SENDS MILTON A COPY OF BOIARDO.

Orlando Innamorato del S. Matteo Maria Boiardo [Venice, 1608].

John Milton · AUGUST 1643

Bought at Venyce by Mr. Francis Gherard for Daniel Oxenbridge and by hym sent to his good Freynd Mr. John Milton, in London, p ye Golden Lyon, Thomas Whiteing, Mr., ye 19th June, 1643, in Lyvorne.

From the description in Catalogue 123 (1930) of Bernard Halliday of Leicester; repeated in Catalogue 182; CM, XVIII, 577. The book is said to contain no marginalia. It is not clear from the ambiguous wording of the inscription whether the "his" in the phrase "his good Freynd" refers to Oxenbridge or to Gherard; either interpretation could be sustained. Milton had visited Lyvorne (i.e., Leghorn) in his continental travels and may have met the Gherard family. He later sent one of his books to a member of the Oxenbridge family, as we learn from Marvell's letter to Milton in 1654. Milton included several quotations from Boiardo's book in his own Commonplace Book. I have not seen the Boiardo book myself.

AUGUST 1. PUBLICATION OF FIRST EDITION OF *THE DOCTRINE AND DISCIPLINE OF DIVORCE*.

The Doctrine and Discipline of Divorce: Restor'd to the Good of Both Sexes, From the bondage of Canon Law, and other mistakes, to Christian freedom, guided by the Rule of Charity. Wherein also many places of Scripture, have recover'd their long-lost meaning. Seasonable to be now thought on in the Reformation intended. Matth. 13. 52. Every Scribe instructed to the Kingdome of Heav'n, is like the Maister of a house which bringeth out of his treasurie things old and new. London, Printed by T.P. and M.S. In Goldsmiths Alley. 1643.

From the title page of the Thomason copy of the first edition, which bears the manuscript notations on the title page: "Written by J: Milton" and "Aug: 1st." On the various issues and states and editions of this work, see Parker, *Milton's Contemporary Reputation*, pp. 270 ff.; CM, III, 367-511; facsimile of title page facing p. 367.

... in the doctrine and discipline of divorce ... [I] *had only the infallible grounds of Scripture to be my guide. ... When I had almost finisht the first edition, I chanc't to read in the notes of* Hugo Grotius *upon the 5. of Matth. ... Glad therfore of such an able assistant, however at much distance, I resolv'd at length to put off into this wild and calumnious world. For God, it seems, intended to prove me, whether I durst alone take up a*

*rightful cause against a world of disesteem, & found I durst.
My name I did not publish, as not willing it should sway the
reader either for me or against me. But when I was told, that
the stile, which what it ailes to be so soon distinguishable I cannot tell, was known by most men. . . .*

    Milton, *The Judgement of Martin Bucer*, 1644, sig. B2; CM, IV, 11.

Reversus *Librum de Divortiis* conscripsit, quo conjugia quæ-
vis ritè sociata pro alterutrius conjugum arbitrio solvi posse contendit; Idque impune illi fuit, in ea scilicet Republica, in qua
Domini licentiam scelerum injuriâ sibi vindicarent, nisi eam
quoque partium suarum hominibus tribuerent.

    [Peter du Moulin], *Regii Sanguinis Clamor*, Vlacq, The Hague,
1652, pp. 8-9.

[After his return he wrote a *Book on Divorce*, in which he
contended that marriages, however solemnized, might be dis-
solved at the pleasure of either of the married persons; and he
could do this with impunity, of course, in a Republic in which
the masters could hardly claim the license of crimes for themselves unless they allowed it also to the men of their party.]

    Masson, IV, 456.

Non aliud scripsi atque ante me Bucerus de regno Christi
copiosè, Fagius in Deuteronomium, Erasmus in Epistolam primam ad Corinthios dedita operâ in Anglorum gratiam, aliíque
multi percelebres viri, in commune bonum scripserunt. Quod in
illis nemo reprehendit, cur id mihi præ cæteris fraudi esset, non
intelligo: vellem hoc tantùm, sermone vernaculo me non scrip-
sisse; non enim in vernas lectores incidissem; quibus solëne est
sua bona ignorare, aliorum mala irridere.

    Milton, *Defensio Secunda*, 1654, pp. 78-79; CM, VIII, 114-115.

[I wrote nothing but what Bucer before me, writing about
the kingdom of Christ, Fagius on Deuteronomy, Erasmus on
the first Epistle to the Corinthians, a work done for the benefit
of the English, and many other very celebrated men had written at length for the common good. I do not understand why an
act which no one blamed in them should be counted a fault in
me more than others. I can only wish this one thing, that I had

not written in the vernacular; for then I should not have fallen on immature readers, with whom it is customary to be ignorant of their own good fortune and to laugh at the misfortunes of others.]

Cùm petiti omnium telis Episcopi tandem cecedissent, otiúmque ab illis esset, verti aliò cogitationes; si qua in re possem libertatis veræ ac solidæ rationem promovere; quæ non forìs, sed intus quærenda, non pugnando, sed vitam rectè instituendo, rectéque administrando adipiscenda potissimùm est. Cùm itaque tres omnino animadverterem libertatis esse species, quæ nisi adsint, vita ulla transigi commodè vix possit, Ecclesiasticam, domesticam seu privatam, atque civilem, déque prima jam scripsissem, déque tertia Magistratum sedulò agere viderem, quæ reliqua secunda erat, domesticam mihi desumpsi; ea quoque tripartita, cùm videretur esse, si res conjugalis, si liberorum institutio rectè se haberet, si denique liberè philosophandi potestas esset, de conjugio non solùm ritè contrahendo, verùm etiam, si necesse esset, dissolvendo, quid sentirem explicui; ídque ex divina lege, quam Christus non sustulit, nedum aliam, tota lege Mosäica graviorem civiliter sanxit; quid item de excepta solùm fornicatione sentiendum sit, & meam aliorúmque sententiam exprompsi, & clarissimus vir Seldenus noster, in Uxore Hebræâ plùs minùs biennio pòst editâ, uberiùs demonstrâvit. Frustrà enim libertatem in comitiis & foro crepat, qui domi servitutem viro indignissimam, inferiori etiam servit; ea igitur de re aliquot libros edidi; eo præsertim tempore cùm vir sæpè & conjux hostes inter se acerrimi, hic domi cum liberis, illa in castris hostium materfamilias versaretur, viro cædem atque perniciem minitans.

Milton, *Defensio Secunda*, 1654, pp. 89-91; CM, VIII, 130-133.

[When the Bishops, the targets of everyone's weapons, had fallen and there was leisure to turn our thoughts from them elsewhere, (I decided) to advance the cause of true and sound liberty in any way I could; which is most to be sought for, not without but within, and which is to be obtained, not by fighting but by rightly ordering and rightly adjusting life. Since therefore I noticed that there are three kinds of liberty—religious, domestic or private, and civil—and that unless they are present hardly any life can be decently lived, and since I had already written about the first, and since I saw that the magistrate was busily working on the third, I took on myself the second which remained, the domestic. When this too appeared to be three-fold, depending on whether it was a conjugal matter, or the right bringing up of children, or finally there was the power of free investigation, I set forth what I thought not only about the right contracting of marriage but also about its dissolution if necessary. This was based on divine law, which Christ never overthrew, nor did he sanction any other law for civil use of higher authority than the whole Mosaic law. And I set forth my opinion and that of others about what we should think of the sole exception of fornication. And our most famous man Selden demonstrated this point more at length in his *Hebrew Wife* published two years later, more or less. For a man shouts in vain about liberty in meetings and in court who at home suffers a servitude most unworthy of a man, and to an inferior too. About this matter I therefore published several books; especially at that time, when often man and wife were most bitter enemies to each other, when he was at home with the children and she, the mother of the family, had turned to the camp of the enemy, threatening her husband with death and destruction.]

The lawfulness and expedience of this [divorce], duly regulat in order to all those purposes, for which Marriage was at first instituted; had upon full consideration & reading good Authors bin formerly his Opinion: And the necessity of justifying himselfe now concurring with the opportunity, acceptable to him, of instructing others in a point of so great concern to the peace & preservation of Families; and so likely to prevent temptations as well as mischiefs, hee first writt *The Doctrine and Discipline of Divorce*, then *Colasterion*, and after *Tetrachordon*: In these hee taught the right use and design of Marriage; then the Original and practise of Divorces amongst the Iews, and show'd that our Savior, in those foure places of the Evangelists, meant not the abrogating, but rectifying the abuses of it; rendring to that purpose another Sense of the word Fornication (and wch is also the Opinion, amongst others, of Mr Selden in his Uxor Hebræa) then what is commonly received. Martin Bucers Iudgment in this matter hee likewise translated into English.

The "earliest" biography, fol. 141v; Darbishire, pp. 23-24.

[Upon his wife's failure to return when sent for, Milton] forthwith prepared to Fortify himself with Arguments for such a Resolution [divorce], and accordingly wrote two Treatises, by which he undertook to maintain, That it was against Reason (and the enjoynment of it not proveable by Scripture) for any Married Couple disagreeable in Humour and Temper, or having an aversion to each, to be forc'd to live yok'd together all their Days. The first was, His Doctrine and Discipline of Divorce; of which there was Printed a Second Edition, with some Additions.

Phillips, pp. xxiv-xxv; Darbishire, pp. 65-66.

The Doctrin & disciplin of divorce.

[Marginal note:] All these in prosecution of ye same subject.

Aubrey, fol. 64; Darbishire, p. 11. The marginal note covers the titles of all Milton's books on divorce.

(14) That shortly after [his books on episcopacy] he did set on foot and maintained very odd and novel Positions concerning Divorce. . . . (6) *The doctrine and discipline of divorce*, &c. in two books. Lond. 1644-45, qu. To which is added in some Copies a translation of *The judgment of Mart. Bucer concerning divorce*, &c. . . . But he being not able to bear this abuse [*i.e.*, his wife's desertion], did therefore upon consideration, after he had consulted many eminent Authors, write the said book of Divorce, with intentions to be separated from her, but by the compromising of her Relations the matter did not take effect.

Wood, I, 881; Darbishire, pp. 38-41.

AFTER AUGUST 1. DIVORCE BOOK ATTACKED AND EVEN CENSORED.

[Milton complains of] *this wild and calumnious world . . . a world of disesteem . . . some of the Clergie began to inveigh*

and exclaim . . . such an indiscreet kind of censure . . . rayling . . .
lavishly traduc't . . . esteem'd the deviser of a new and per-
nicious paradox . . . thir virulence. . . . I would ask now the fore-
most of my profound accusers, whether they dare affirm that to
be licentious, new and dangerous, which Martin Bucer *so often,*
and so urgently avoucht to be most lawfull, most necessary, and
most Christian. . . . [If the books of Bucer and Erasmus are allowed to appear without censorship] *and mine containing but*
the same thing, shall in a time of reformation, a time of free
speaking, free writing, not find a permission to the Presse, I re-
ferre me to wisest men, whether truth be suffer'd to be truth,
or liberty to be liberty now among us, and be not again in danger
of new fetters and captivity after all our hopes and labours lost.

Milton, *The Judgement of Martin Bucer*, 1644, sigs. B2-Fv; CM,
IV, 11-20, 61. The date of these criticisms is vague. No further information about them is known. The attacks on Milton by Herbert Palmer
and others, recorded below, appeared after Milton's book had been published.

NOVEMBER 22. BROTHER CHRISTOPHER'S GOODS SEIZED AS DELINQUENT.

Mr Milton & Mr Brown John of Reading A Warrant to
Carswell to seize goods of theirs in a Barge at Brookes Wharfe
in —44.10.11.

From a note by Joseph Hunter, British Museum MS. Add. 24,501,
fol. 11, said to be taken from the Account of the Committee for Sequestration, fol. 34. I have not found the original, and Hunter's handwriting
is so difficult to read that I am not entirely sure of the text as quoted.
The section here quoted from is, however, an account of the estates of
delinquents and papists as described in the warrant given to the collec-
tors employed in that service from the first time of their sitting until
November 22, 1643.

DECEMBER 9 (?). PORTRAIT BY JEAN PETITOT (?).

Alfred Stern reported that he saw a portrait of Milton by Petitot on
exhibit in the South Kensington Museum in the summer of 1871; see
Stern I, i, 317, and *Notes and Queries*, IV, viii (1871), 46. He describes
it as a miniature by Petitot, "brustbild, ziemlich jung, etwa 35 Jahre,
aber mit *blonden* herabwallenden Haaren, *blauen* Augen" (half-length,
fairly young, some 35 years old, but with blond low-hanging hair, blue
eyes). There is no longer any trace of it in the Museum, and its later

history is unknown. This is probably the same item as that described by Dr. Williamson (*Milton Tercentenary*, p. 23). Williamson states that there was exhibited at South Kensington in 1865 an enamel on gold of the poet when young. It was attributed to Petitot and was lent for the exhibition by T. M. Whitehead.

Jean Petitot was a French-Swiss enamel painter, born in the same year as Milton, who spent a number of years in England prior to the execution of Charles I. During this time he made many portraits. See the article on him by G. C. Williamson in the *Encyclopaedia Britannica*, 11th edition, *s.v.* "Petitot, Jean."

DECEMBER 12. RECEIVES INTEREST PAYMENT FROM RICHARD POWELL.

... the growing Jnterest for the forbearance of the said Principall debt was for some yeares then following likewise payd And soe continued to bee paid vntill June Jn the yeare of our Lord One Thousand six hundred ffortie and ffower. ...

From Milton's answer to Elizabeth Ashworth, February 22, 1653/4, *q.v.*

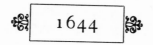

WIDE READING CONCERNING DIVORCE.

Who among the fathers have interpreted the words of Christ concerning divorce, as is heer interpreted; and what the civil law of Christian Emperors in the primitive Church determined. ...

Iustin Martyr in his first Apology . . . *Eusebius* . . . *Tertullian* . . . writing his 4 book against *Marcion* . . . *Origen* . . . his 7. homily on *Matthew* . . . *Lactantius* . . . in the 6. of his *institutions* . . . the Councel of *Eliberis* in *Spain* . . . The council of *Neocæsarea* in the year 314 . . . The council of *Nantes* . . . *Basil* in his 73. rule, as *Chamier* numbers it . . . *Epiphanius* . . . in his second book, *Tom.* 1 . . . *Ambrose* on the 16. of *Luke* . . . *Jerom* on the 19. of *Matthew* . . . *Austin* . . . in his books to *Pollentius* . . . And in the first book of his *retractations*, chap. 16 . . . the council of *Agatha* in the year 506, can. 25 . . . *Theodosius*

and *Valentinian* . . . the edict of *Constantine* to *Dalmatius, Co.
1.5. tit.* 17 . . . and *Authent. collat.* 4. *tit.* 1. *Novell.* 22 . . . In
the 117. *Novell* . . . *Justinian* . . . *Procopius* a good historian . . .
Photius the patriarch, with the avertiments of *Balsamon* and
Matthœus Monachus thereon . . . *Leo* the son of *Basilius,
Macedo* . . . *Constitut. Leon.* 111.112 . . . *Agathias* the historian . . . *Ambrose* upon *Luke* . . . *Gregory* the pope, writing to
Theoctista . . . *decret. Gregor.* 1. 4. *tit.* 14 . . . *Wicklef* . . . *Arnisœus* of *Halberstad on the right of mariage*, who cites it from
Corasius of *Tolouse c.* 4. *Cent. Sct.* . . . *Luther* . . . in his book of
conjugal life quoted by *Gerard* out of the Dutch . . . *Melanchton,*
the third great luminary of reformation in his book, *concerning
marriage* . . . *Erasmus,* who for learning was the wonder of his
age, both in his *notes* on *Matthew,* and on the first to the
Corinthians . . . and in his answer to *Phimostomus* . . . *Bucer,*
whom our famous Dᵣ *Rainolds* was wont to preferr before
Calvin . . . *Fagius* . . . The whole Church of *Strasburgh.* in her
most flourishing time, when *Zellius, Hedio, Capito,* and other
great Divines taught there, and those two renouned magistrates
Farrerus and *Sturmius* . . . *Peter Martyr* . . . *Musculus* . . .
Gualter of Zuric . . . in his Homilies on *Matthew* . . . *Hemingius*
. . . *Hunnius* . . . on the 19. of *Matt.* . . . *Felix Bidenbachius* . . .
Gerard cites *Harbardus* . . . *Arnisœus* cites *Wigandus* . . . *Beza*
. . . *Aretius* . . . in his *Problemes* . . . *Alciat* of *Millain* . . . in the
sixt book of his *Parerga* . . . *Corasius* . . . *Wesembechius* . . .
Grotius . . . On the fifth of *Matt.* . . .

These authorities, without long search I had to produce, all
excellent men, some of them such as many ages had brought
forth none greater. . . . But God, I solemnly attest him, withheld from my knowledge the consenting judgment of these men
so late, untill they could not be my instructers, but only my unexpected witnesses to partial men, that in this work I had not
given the worst experiment of an industry joyn'd with integrity
and the free utterance though of an unpopular truth.

Tetrachordon, 1645, pp. 81-96; CM, IV, 206-229. Though the time
of Milton's reading here itemized cannot be closely dated, it evidently
fell between the date of the first publication of *The Doctrine and Dis-*

cipline of Divorce (August 1, 1643), and that of *Tetrachordon* (March 4, 1645). It is therefore here placed for convenience as simply 1644.

OWNS AND ANNOTATES LETTERS OF POLYCARP AND IGNATIUS (?).

Polycarpi et Ignatii Epistolæ, Oxford, 1644.

[On title page:] pretium 8^d.

[p. iv] Vide q$^{\overline{ae}}$ Author subjunxerit Prolegomenis, In fine libri. p. 243. [See what the author subjoins in the prolegomena at the end of the book, p. 243.]

[p. xxvii] quanquam & has etiam &c. vide Errata. [Although and these also etc., see the errata.]

[p. lxxxix] ex posteriore &c. vide Emendanda. [From the later etc., see the emendations.]

From the copy of this work now in the library of Ely Cathedral; CM, XVIII, 346, 574. Details of this book were first published in the Columbia Milton from notes furnished by Professor Maurice Kelley of Princeton. Through the courtesy of the present librarian of Ely, I am able to quote the following excerpts from notes written in the flyleaf of this volume by Frederick W. Joy, a former librarian, and dated 1882:

"I do not doubt that this book was, like its companion Dion Chrysostom, once the property of the poet, John Milton. It does not bear his *name*, but the 'pretium' is certainly in my opinion in his handwriting. [Here follow facsimiles of Milton's entries on the flyleaves of his copies of Aratus, Euripides, della Casa, and Heraclides Ponticus.] The latter half of the word 'pretium' is exactly similar to Milton's letters—and especially the 't'."

None of the entries is dated; the volume is therefore entered under the year of its publication. A few other slight entries, given in the Columbia Milton, are here omitted.

ALLEGED APPEARANCE OF ATTRIBUTED WORK (?).

The Rights of the People over Tyrants, 1644.

Attributed to Milton by Wood but without date as having been published "lately"; added by William Oldys to the bibliography of Milton in his copy of Phillips's edition of Milton's *Letters of State*, 1694 (see *Notes and Queries*, III, ii [1862], 382); CM, XVIII, 637. Actually, as William R. Parker has shown in a careful study ("Milton on King James the Second," *Modern Language Quarterly*, III [1942], 41-44), a work of similar title appeared in 1689 and was almost a reprint of Milton's *Tenure of Kings and Magistrates*. Its title, in somewhat more complete form, is *Pro Populo Adversus Tyrannos: Or The Sovereign Right and Power of the People Over Tyrants*. The editors of the Columbia

Milton, who had not seen this work, were not sure that it was not the same with *Jus Populi*, 1644. Actually there is no connection.

HOBSON VERSES QUOTED IN MANUSCRIPT ANTHOLOGY.

Here Hobson lies who did most truly prove. . . .

Bodleian Library MS. Malone 21, fol. 69; discussed by William R. Parker in *Modern Language Review*, XXXI (1936), 395 ff.; CM, XVIII, 349, 584-585. Malone's manuscript note on the front flyleaf says this anthology was written on or after 1644.

JANUARY 19. PARTLY RESPONSIBLE FOR *MANS MORTALLITIE* (?).

Denis Saurat (*Milton Man and Thinker*, 1935, first published 1925) spends a number of pages in trying to prove that Milton was one of the group who were responsible for the publication of this book, which Thomason dated January 19, 1644. Saurat states that "Milton, who was 'among the sectaries and in a world of discontent' in 1643-1644, must have known the Mortalists then" (p. 311); that "Whoever held the pen, Overton or Wrighter, he was secretary to a group, and Milton was in the group when the London edition came out" (p. 312); and that in the later edition of 1655 a "Miltonic passage, in an addition which is in the Miltonic spirit, seems to me to leave no room for doubt" that Milton's hand was in the book (p. 321). On the other hand, William Haller (*Tracts on Liberty*, I, 1934, 134n.) finds Saurat's assumption "untenable." Most Milton scholars follow Haller rather than Saurat.

FEBRUARY 2. SECOND EDITION OF *THE DOCTRINE AND DISCIPLINE OF DIVORCE* IS PUBLISHED.

The Doctrine & Discipline of Divorce: Restor'd to the good of both Sexes, From the bondage of Canon Law, and other mistakes, to the true meaning of Scrip-ture in the Law and Gospel compar'd. Wherin also are set down the bad consequences of abolishing or condemning of Sin, that which the Law of God allowes, and Christ abolisht not. Now the second time revis'd and much augmented, In Two Books: To the Parlament of England with the Assembly. The Author J. M. Matth. 13. 52. Every Scribe instructed to the Kingdome of Heav'n, is like the Maister of a house which bringeth out of his treasury things new and old. Prov. 18. 13. He that answereth a matter before he heareth it, is folly and shame unto him. London, Imprinted in the yeare 1644.

John Milton · FEBRUARY 1644

From the title page of this edition. CM, III, 367 ff.; Masson, III, 65. There is a facsimile of the title page in CM, III, 512. Thomason's copy in the British Museum is dated February 2, with the year changed in ink from 1644 to 1643 (i.e., 1643/4).

The bibliography of this book is confused. The Columbia editors distinguish five printings of the second edition in 1644 and 1645; Parker (p. 271) says: "Actually, there are *four* editions of *The Doctrine and Discipline*, representing a variety of 'states' or issues." It is, however, safe to say that all the editions except the first are substantially alike, being considerably augmented over the first.

I seek not to seduce the simple and illiterat; my errand is to find out the choisest and the learnedest, who have this high gift of wisdom to answer solidly, or to be convinc't. I crave it from the piety, the learning and the prudence which is hous'd in this place [i.e., Parliament]. It might perhaps more fitly have bin writt'n in another tongue; and I had don so, but that the esteem I have of my Countries judgement, and the love I beare to my native language to serv it first with what I endeavour, made me speak it thus, ere I assay the verdit of outlandish readers. And perhaps also heer I might have ended nameles, but that the addresse of these lines chiefly to the Parlament of *England* might have seem'd ingratefull not to acknowledge by whose Religious care, unwearied watchfulnes, couragious and heroick resolutions, I enjoy the peace and studious leisure to remain . . . Iohn Milton.

Milton, *The Doctrine and Discipline of Divorce*, second edition, 1644, "To the Parlament of England," sig. A4v; CM, III, 378-379.

My name I did not publish [in the first edition], *as not willing it should sway the reader either for me or against me. But when I was told, that the stile, which what it ailes to be so soon distinguishable, I cannot tell, was known by most men . . . I took it then for my proper season both to shew them a name that could easily contemn such an indiscreet kind of censure, and to reinforce the question with a more accurat diligence. . . . And having now perfected a second edition, I referr'd the judging therof to your high and impartial sentence, honour'd Lords and Commons. . . . the book hath bin twice printed, twice bought up.*

Milton, *The Judgement of Martin Bucer*, 1644, sigs. B2-B3; CM, IV, 12-15.

... there was Printed a Second Edition, with some Additions.
Phillips, p. xxv; Darbishire, p. 65.

The Doctrine and Discipline of Divorce, restored, to the
Good of both Sexes, from the Bondage of Canon Law and other
mistakes, to the true meaning of Scripture in the Law and
Gospel compared. Wherein also are set down the bad conse-
quences of Abolishing, or Condemning of Sin, that which the
Law of God allows, and Christ abolisht not. Now the second
time Revised, and much Augmented in Two Books. To the
Parliament of *England*, with the Assembly. In 4*to*.

Phillips, p. [li]; not in Darbishire.

Doctrina & Disciplina divortii . . . bis editus est, & posteriori
editione multo auctius.

Milton, letter to Leo Aizema, February 5, 1655; CM, XII, 72.

[*The Doctrine and Discipline of Divorce* was twice issued,
and in the later edition much enlarged.]

FEBRUARY 2. MAKES MANUSCRIPT CORRECTIONS IN COPIES OF *THE DOCTRINE AND DISCIPLINE OF DIVORCE* (?).

Several copies of the second edition of this book have manuscript corrections which have been attributed to Milton, but which may of course
have been made by someone in the printer's office. The chief changes are:
(1) on sig. A3, the first two letters of "from," line 30, are in ink; (2)
on sig. A3v, an "e" has been added over a caret after the "c" in "fierc-
nes"; (3) on p. 38, "contriving" has been changed to "conniving" by
the erasure of the "tr" and the addition of "n" above; (4) on p. 65, "in-
dicental" has been changed to "incidental"; (5) on p. 67, "conniving"
has been changed to "contriving"; and (6) on p. 73 "selues" has been
written in the margin to replace "seves" in the text. Volumes which
show these or similar changes are: (1) the Thomason copy in the British
Museum, shelf-number E.31.(5.), which may have been a presentation
copy, and from which the date above is taken; (2) another copy, also in
the British Museum; (3) the Van Sinderen copy in New York; (4) a
copy listed in Lowndes' *Bibliographer's Manual*, London, 1900, III,
1565, said to be "ex dono authoris"; (5) a copy which in 1942 was in
the collection of the Rosenbach Company in New York, which also bore
"ex dono authoris" on the title page; and (6) the copy in the Yale University Library acquired from Dr. John Fulton. It is impossible to be
sure that there is not some duplication among items 3, 4, and 5 in this
list. A copy described in the *Catalogue of . . . Books the Property of the*

John *Milton* · MAY 1644

Rt. Hon. the Earl of Ashburnham . . . which will be sold by auction . . .
June 1897, item 2584, which is said to have contained the autograph
signature "JO. MILTON" on the title page, may be identical with one
of these. For information on these volumes, see CM, XVIII, 551; French,
"The Autographs of John Milton," nos. 15, 16; Stern, I, ii, 466; BPC,
XII (1898), 79.

FEBRUARY 2 (?). PRESENTS COPY OF *DOCTRINE AND DISCIPLINE* TO HENRY JACKSON.

H. Jackson   Ex dono Authoris.

Written on the title page of a copy of Milton's *Doctrine and Discipline
of Divorce*, 1644, which for some years was [and may still be] in the
possession of the Rosenbach Company in New York. Through the courtesy of Dr. Rosenbach the present editor was allowed to examine it in
1942. The name "H. Jackson" is written above "The Author J.M." of
the title in a slanting hand wholly unlike Milton's. The words "Ex
dono" are written at the left of "The Author J.M." and "Authoris" at
the right, both in a hand which closely resembles Milton's. It seems likely
that he may have written the "Ex dono Authoris" himself, whereas the
recipient added his own name. The manuscript corrections already described as being in several copies are also found in this one. This volume
is described and offered for sale in the Rosenbach Company's "English
Poetry to 1700," 1941, item 498, priced at $1850. In this catalogue both
the inscriptions on the title page and the corrections in the text are said
to be in Milton's hand. Henry Jackson (1586-1662) was a friend
and kinsman of Anthony Wood, rector of Meysey Hampton, Gloucestershire, from 1630 to 1662, and the editor of various works of Richard
Hooker.

MARCH 28. BROTHER CHRISTOPHER PAYS FINE.

Chris Milton: Rec. of Arthur Mansfield 28 Mar 1644 for
. . . £10.

British Museum Add. MS. 24,501, fol. 56. This is Joseph Hunter's
transcript of records of sequestrations of delinquents in 1643 and 1644.
Like all his manuscripts it is virtually illegible, so that the present transcript may not be entirely correct. But it seems to mean that Christopher
Milton paid ten pounds as a holder of Royalist property on this date.

MAY (?). CONVERSATIONS WITH SAMUEL HARTLIB ABOUT EDUCATION.

. . . to write now the reforming of Education . . . I had not yet
at this time been induc't, but by your earnest entreaties, and
serious conjurements . . . the satisfaction which you professe to

have receiv'd from those incidentall discourses which we have wander'd into. . . . I . . . will forthwith set down in writing, as you request me, that voluntary *Idea* . . . of a better Education.

Milton, *Of Education. To Master Hartlib*, 1644, pp. 1-3; CM, IV, 275-277. The date is, of course, only approximate; but since the book was published on June 5, it is likely that the conversations took place a short time before. It is, however, likely that they may have reached back considerably further, as most certainly did Milton's "many studious and contemplative yeers altogether spent in the search of religious and civil knowledge" (*Of Education*, p. 3). It may be noted that Hartlib apparently inspired educational ideas in several people, since not only Milton's tract but also Sir William Petty's *The Advice to Mr. S. Hartlib for the Advancement of some Parts of Learning* (1648) was addressed to him. Anthony Wood mentions an edition of this book in 1647 or another similar title.

MAY 2. FIRST READS WRITINGS OF MARTIN BUCER.

When the book [*The Doctrine and Discipline of Divorce*] *had bin now the second time set forth wel-nigh three months, as I best remember, I then first came to hear that* Martin Bucer *had writt'n much concerning divorce: whom earnestly turning over.* . . .

Milton, *The Judgement of Martin Bucer*, 1644, sig. B2v; CM, IV, 13. Three months from the date of the second edition of Milton's book, February 2, would be May 2.

JUNE (?). SAMUEL HARTLIB MAKES MANUSCRIPT COPY OF TITLE PAGE OF MILTON'S *OF EDUCATION*.

Of Education. To Master Samuel Hartlib. by John Milton. in qto. Paj. 8.

Written on a single sheet among Hartlib's papers in the collection of Lord Delamere; printed in G. H. Turnbull's *Hartlib, Dury and Comenius*, p. 91. In Hartlib's handwriting, this page looks as if it had been made for a manuscript copy of the whole book, but only this one sheet has been found in the collection. The references to the size and pagination of the book seem to indicate that it followed the appearance of the printed work. A last line, not reproduced here, consists of several short-hand characters.

JUNE 4. BOOK ON EDUCATION REGISTERED FOR PUBLICATION.

4° Junii 1644

Tho. Underhill. Entred for his copie under the hands of Master CRANFORD and Master MAN warden, a litle tract touching *Education of Youth*, &c. ....vj^d.

Stationers' Registers, ed. Eyre and Rivington, I, 117.

JUNE 5. PUBLICATION OF TRACT ON EDUCATION.

Of Education. To Master Samuel Hartlib.

This little eight-page pamphlet has no separate title page but simply the above heading at the top of page 1. Under it is written in the Thomason copy in the British Museum, presumably in Thomason's hand, "By m^r John Milton 5 June 1644."

. . . to write now the reforming of Education, though it be one of the greatest and noblest designes, that can be thought on, and for the want whereof this nation perishes, I had not yet at this time been induc't, but by your earnest entreaties, and serious conjurements . . . the satisfaction which you professe to have receiv'd from those incidentall discourses which we have wander'd into, hath prest and almost constrain'd you. . . . I . . . will forthwith set down in writing, as you request me, that voluntary *Idea*, which hath long in silence presented it self to me, of a better Education . . . as it were the burnishing of many studious and contemplative yeers altogether spent in the search of religious and civil knowledge. . . .

Milton, *Of Education*, 1644, pp. 1-3; CM, IV, 275-277. Milton's words are of course addressed to Samuel Hartlib.

Institutionem deinde liberorum uno opusculo breviùs quidem tractatam; sed quod satis arbitrabar iis fore, qui ad eam rem, quâ par esset diligentiâ, incumberent; quâ quidem re, nihil ad imbuendas, unde vera atque interna oritur libertas, virtute hominum mentes, nihil ad rempublicam bene gerendam, & quam diutissimè conservandam majus momentum potest afferre.

Milton, *Defensio Secunda*, 1654, p. 91; CM, VIII, 132-133.

[Then I treated the education of children rather briefly in a little book, but I thought it would be enough for those who would devote themselves to the subject with the diligence which it demanded; a subject than which nothing can be of greater force in imbuing the minds of men with virtue, from which arises true and inner freedom, nothing of greater force in guiding the state wisely and preserving it as long as possible.]

His small treatise *of Education*, address'd to Mr Hartlib, was the laying a Foundation also of Public Weale: Jn it hee prescrib'd an easy and delightful method for training up Gentry in such a manner to all sorts of Literature, as that they might at the same time by like degrees advance in Virtue, and Abilities to serve their Country; subjoyning directions for their attayning other necessary, or Ornamental accomplishments: And it seem'd hee design'd in some measure to put this in practise.

The "earliest" biography, fol. 142; Darbishire, p. 24.

[In Aldersgate he wrote] one Sheet of Education, which he Dedicated to Mr. *Samuel Hartlib*, he that wrote so much of Husbandry; this Sheet is Printed at the end of the Second Edition of his Poems.

Phillips, p. xxi; Darbishire, p. 63.

Of Education.

Aubrey, fol. 64; Darbishire, p. 11.

(9) *Of Education*, written or addressed to Mr. *Sam. Hartlib*. In this Treatise he prescrib'd an easie and delightful method for the training up of Gentry to all sorts of Literature, that they might at the same time by like degrees advance in virtue and abilities to serve their Country, subjoyning directions for their obtaining other necessary or ornamental Accomplishments.

Wood, 1, 882; Darbishire, pp. 41-42.

JUNE 5. POSSIBLE PRESENTATION COPY OF TRACT *OF EDUCATION* (?).

A copy of Milton's *Of Education* was recently advertised (Robinson's 56th Catalogue, item 133, price £300) as containing a manuscript entry on page 1, "by m^r John Milton." The handwriting is said to be that of Milton, and the implication is that it was a presentation copy. But it is unlikely that Milton would have written these particular words. See French, "The Autographs of John Milton," no. 17a; CM, XVIII, 551.

JUNE 11. RICHARD POWELL FAILS TO PAY INTEREST DUE.

... June Jn the yeare of our Lord One Thousand six hundred ffortie and ffower Att What time the said Richard Powell failed ... in the payment of the Jnterest then due and payable and from thence growing due and payable. ...

The date of this event has been placed by the present editor as June 11 since that was the date of the bond, given in 1627. From Milton's own account the interest had been faithfully paid up to this time. The source is Milton's answer to Elizabeth Ashworth, February 22, 1653/4, *q.v.*; see French, *Milton in Chancery*, p. 305.

JUNE 21. BROTHER CHRISTOPHER TAXED ON HOUSE IN LONDON (?).

9 Oct 44 for 2 quarters at Midsummer last a house Ludgate Hill 7.10.0.

From Hunter's manuscript extracts from the records of the sequestrations of delinquents, British Museum Add. MS. 24,501, fol. 56. The exact purport of the entry is not clear, but it seems to mean that a payment of £7-10-0 became due from Christopher Milton at Midsummer (June 21) for a house in Ludgate Hill in London and that the payment was received on October 9, 1644.

AFTER JUNE. ATTEMPTS TO SEIZE POWELL'S PROPERTY FOR DEBT.

... June Jn the yeare of our Lord One Thousand six hundred ffortie and ffower. ... Wherevpon this Def^t Did take out severall Extents vpon the said Statute before hee could gett any of the Lands and Tenements of the said Richard Powell duely extended Butt this Def^t saith that after the death of the said Richard Powell. ...

Milton's answer to Elizabeth Ashworth, February 22, 1653/4; French, *Milton in Chancery*, p. 305. An extent is a writ by means of which a creditor can secure temporary possession of the lands of a debtor. It was not until July 16, 1647 (*q.v.*), that Milton finally succeeded in obtaining the writ which he sought. The date is vague, but at least it is later than June 21, 1644, when Powell first failed to pay the interest due. Between this date and July 16, 1647, Milton took further steps, including negotiations with Sir Robert Pye, who was also financially interested in Powell's property. For lack of a more definite date, these undated transactions are entered under the year 1647, since some of them must have followed the death of Richard Powell, which occurred on January 1 of that year. As clear a story of these transactions as I can make out is given in chapters VII and VIII of *Milton in Chancery*.

JULY (?). SECOND EDITION OF *THE DOCTRINE AND DISCIPLINE OF DIVORCE* SOLD OUT.

. . . the book [The Doctrine and Discipline of Divorce] hath bin twice printed, twice bought up. . . .

Milton, *The Judgement of Martin Bucer*, 1644, sig. B3; CM, IV, 15. The Bucer book, though published in August, was registered in July; hence that date is here adopted for the time Milton had in mind.

JULY 1. ALLOWANCE TO BROTHER CHRISTOPHER FOR MAINTAINING CHILDREN.

[July 1, 1644. Paid to Mrs. Elijah Webster for keeping Mr. Milton's children—£2-14-0.]

Account book of William Williamson or William Fox of the Committee of Sequestrations in London, fol. 50, as summarized in Hunter's manuscript, British Museum Add. MS. 24,501, fol. 23. I have not found the original, and the text quoted above is not reliable since I have only hasty notes of it. The entry occurs among the items entered under the name of Christopher Milton, delinquent. Hunter quotes (fol. 56) a similar entry from the Sequestration of Delinquents' Books, January 1643—December 1644, in which the amount is given as two pounds exactly instead of two pounds fourteen shillings as above.

JULY 11. POSSIBLE ALLUSION TO *OF EDUCATION* BY JOHN DURY.

Deare freind

. . . The discourse of education wch you sent me is brief & generall, & hath many requisits wch J doubt will hardly bee obtained in a tyme of Peace   it is wisdome to doe what may bee done in an easie waye; but more of this in due tyme. . . .

Hague this 21/11 July   Your Most affectionat & Faithfull
1644.   freind & servant in Chr.
                                                         John Durey.

[Addressed outside:] A Monsieur Monsieur Hartlib at his house in Dukes place neer Algate a Londres.

From a letter from John Dury to Samuel Hartlib in the collection of Lord Delamere; printed in G. H. Turnbull, *Hartlib, Dury and*

Comenius, pp. 39, 242. Although the allusion here is not specifically to Milton, both the date and the interest which both Hartlib and Dury took in Milton's book make it highly likely.

JULY 15. TRANSLATION OF BUCER REGISTERED FOR PUBLICATION.

15° Julii 1644...

Math. Symmons.   Entred . . . under the hand of Master DOWNEHAM and Master PARKER warden, *The Judgment of Martin Bucer concerning divorse written to King Edw. yᵉ 6ᵗʰ, in his second booke of the kingdome Christ, englished by Mʳ* **Milton** . . . vjᵈ.

The Stationers' Registers, ed. Eyre and Rivington, I, 122.

AUGUST 6. TRANSLATION OF BUCER PUBLISHED.

The Ivdgement of Martin Bucer, Concerning Divorce. Writt'n to Edward the sixt, in his second Book of the Kingdom of Christ. And now Englisht. Wherin a late Book restoring the Doctrine and Discipline of Divorce, is heer confirm'd and justify'd by the authoritie of Martin Bucer. To the Parlament of England. John 3. 10. Art thou a teacher of Israel, and know'st not these things? Publisht by Authoritie. London, Printed by Matthew Simmons, 1644.

From the title page of the first edition; CM, IV, 1 ff. (facsimile of title page facing p. 1). The date is from the Thomason catalogue.

. . . *a printed Calumny . . . It was preacht before ye, Lords and Commons, in August last upon a special day of humiliation, that* there was a wicked Book abroad, *and ye were taxt of sin that it was yet* uncensur'd, the book deserving to be burnt . . . *and with the same censure condemns of wickednesse not onely* Martin Bucer . . . *whom also I had publisht in English by a good providence, about a week before this calumnious digression was preach'd.* . . .

Milton, *Tetrachordon*, 1645, sig. A2v; CM, IV, 65-66. Milton here refers to Herbert Palmer's sermon of August 13 (*q.v.*).

Then the better to confirm his own Opinion, by the attestation of others, he set out a Piece called the Judgement of *Martin Bucer*, a Protestant Minister, being a Translation, out of that Reverend Divine, of some part of his Works, exactly agreeing with him in Sentiment.

Phillips, p. xxv; Darbishire, p. 65.

The Judgment of *Martin Bucer* concerning Divorce, written to *Edward* the Sixth, in his second Book of the Kingdom of Christ, and now *Englished*; wherein a late Book restoring the Doctrine and Discipline of Divorce is here Confirmed and Justified by the Authority of *Martin Bucer*. To the Parliament of *England*. 4*to*.

Phillips, p. [lii]; not in Darbishire.

AUGUST 13. DIVORCE BOOKS ATTACKED IN SERMON BEFORE PARLIAMENT.

If any plead Conscience for the Lawfulnesse of *Polygamy*; (or for divorce for other causes then Christ and His Apostles mention; Of which a *wicked booke* is abroad and *uncensured*, though *deserving to be burnt*, whose *Author* hath been so *impudent* as to *set his Name* to it, and *dedicate it to your selves*,) or for Liberty to *marry incestuously*, will you grant a *Toleration* for all *this*?

Herbert Palmer, *The Glasse of Gods Providence towards his Faithfvll Ones. Held forth in a Sermon preached to the two Houses of Parliament, at Margarets, Westminster, Aug. 13. 1644*, 1644, p. 57; Masson, III, 262; Stern, I, ii, 484. Todd notes (I, 1826, 64) that his friend James Bindley was the first to find this reference. See also Milton's reference to Palmer's sermon above under date of August 6, 1644.

AUGUST 24-26. STATIONERS PETITION AGAINST MILTON'S BOOK ON DIVORCE.

Die Sabbati, Augusti 24°, 1644. . . .

Ordered, That the Petition from the Company of Stationers, be read on *Monday* Morning next. . . .

Die Lunæ, Augusti 26°, 1644.

PRAYERS.

The humble Petition of the Company of Stationers, consisting of Booksellers, Printers, and Bookbinders, was this Day read;

and ordered to be referred to the Consideration of the Committee for Printing; to hear all Parties; and to state the Business; and to prepare an Ordinance upon the whole Matter; and to bring it in with all convenient Speed: And they are, to this Purpose, to peruse the Bill formerly brought in concerning this Matter. They are diligently to inquire out the Authors, Printers, and Publishers, of the Pamphlet against the Immortality of the Soul, and concerning Divorce.

Sir *Philip Stapilton*, Sir *Tho. Widdrington*, Mr. *Stephens* and Mr. *Baynton*, are added to this Committee.

Journals of the House of Commons, III, 605-606; Masson, III, 164-165, 265 ff.

SEPTEMBER. BEGINS TO NOTICE FAILURE OF SIGHT.

Decennium, opinor, plus minus est, ex quo debilitari atq; hebescere visum sensi, eodémq; tempore lienem, visceráq; omnia gravari, flatibusq; vexari: & mane quidem, siquid pro more legere cœpissem, oculi statim penitus dolere, lectionemq; refugere, post mediocrem deinde corporis exercitationem recreari; quam aspexissem lucernam, Iris quædam visa est redimire: haud ita multò post sinistrâ in parte oculi sinistri (is enim oculus aliquot annis prius altera nubilavit) caligo oborta, quæ ad latus illud sita erant, omnia eripiebat.

Milton, *Epistolarum Familiarium Liber Unus*, 1674, p. 40; CM, XII, 66. This is from Milton's letter to Philaras, dated September 28, 1654.

[It is ten years, I think, more or less, since I felt my sight getting weak and dull, and at the same time my viscera generally out of sorts. In the morning, if I began, as usual, to read anything, I felt my eyes at once thoroughly pained, and shrinking from the act of reading, but refreshed after moderate bodily exercise. If I looked at a lit candle, a kind of iris seemed to snatch it from me. Not very long after, a darkness coming over the left part of my left eye (for that eye became clouded some years before the other) removed from my vision all objects situated on that side.]

Masson, IV, 640.

SEPTEMBER 16. DIVORCE BOOK ATTACKED BY PRYNNE.

[Prynne regrets] the late dangerous increase of many *Ana-baptisticall, Antinomian, Hereticall, Atheisticall opinions, as of the soules mortality, divorce at pleasure, &c.* lately broached, preached, printed in this famous City, which I hope our grand Councell will speedily and carefully suppresse.

William Prynne, *Twelve Considerable Serious Questions touching Chvrch Government*, 1644, p. 7; Masson, III, 299; Parker, *Milton's Contemporary Reputation*, p. 73. The date is that of the Thomason copy in the British Museum.

OCTOBER 9. BROTHER CHRISTOPHER FINED AS DELIN-QUENT.

9 Oct 44 for 2 quarters at Midsummer last a house Ludgate Hill 7.10.0.

British Museum Add. MS. 24,501, fol. 56. See the note to the entry under date of June 21, 1644.

OCTOBER 16. PUBLICATION OF WORK ATTRIBUTED TO MILTON.

Jus Populi.

Todd (I, 1826, 224) quotes from a volume of tracts in the Archiepiscopal library at Lambeth, in which, after the entry of "John Milton's Speech for unlicensd Printing" and after two more titles attributed to Milton, this title is mentioned as *"His Jus. Populi."* Todd also notes (p. 225) that someone has added on the title page of the *Jus Populi* in this collection the initials J.M. as those of the author. Todd points out, however, that Milton is an unlikely choice as author because at one point the anonymous author condemns divorce for any other cause than adultery, a sentiment which Milton is unlikely to have shared. It is customarily assigned to Henry Parker, as in the Thomason catalogue, from which the above date is taken. See also CM, XVIII, 637.

OCTOBER 31. ANSWER TO MILTON'S DIVORCE BOOK REGISTERED.   𝔘ltimo 𝔒ctobris 1644

Master Lee.   Entred . . . under the hands of Master CARILL and Master WHITAKER warden, *An Answeare to a booke intituled The doctrine & discipline of divorse &c* . . . . vjᵈ.

Eyre and Rivington, Stationers' Registers, I, 135; Stern, I, ii, 485.

NOVEMBER (?). BROTHER CHRISTOPHER FINED (?).

Hunter's manuscript collections from Sequestration of Delinquents' Books from January, 1643, to December, 1644; British Museum Add. MS. 24,501, fol. 56. The entry is fragmentary and not very legible, consisting apparently of the date, November, 1644, followed by the amount, twenty shillings. Presumably it means that as a Royalist Christopher Milton was taxed in this amount, but I do not feel sure. I have not found the originals.

NOVEMBER 7. HERBERT PALMER'S BOOK ATTACKING MILTON REGISTERED.

7th ꝶ𝖔𝖇. 1644

Thomas Underhill Entred . . . by order of the Comons house of Parliam^t *a Sermon called The glasse of Gods providence &c preached at a solemne fast before both houses of Parl. Aug: 13th 1644,* by **Herbert Palmer** . . . vj^d.

The Stationers' Registers, ed. Eyre and Rivington, I, 136; Stern, I, ii, 326, 484. See the entry above under date of August 13, 1644.

NOVEMBER (?). PALMER'S SERMON ATTACKING MILTON PUBLISHED.

The Glasse of Gods Providence towards his Faithfvll Ones. Held forth in a Sermon preached to the two Houses of Parliament, at Margarets, Westminster, Aug. 13. 1644.

By Herbert Palmer. The exact date of publication is uncertain. But since it was entered in the Stationers' Registers on November 7, it is likely to have appeared soon afterwards. The Thomason catalogue dates it according to the date of delivery of the sermon.

[Milton published his translation of Bucer] *about a week before this calumnious digression was preach'd; so that if he* [Palmer] *knew not Bucer then, as he ought to have known, he might at least have known him some months after, ere the Sermon came in print.*

Milton, *Tetrachordon*, 1645, sig. A2v; CM, IV, 66. Milton's phrase for the time elapsed since the preaching of the sermon, "*some months,*" would be entirely accurate for the interval since August 13.

NOVEMBER 7. LETTER TO CHRISTOPHER MILTON AT
WELLS AS ROYAL COMMISSIONER OF EXCISE.

Gentlemen/

Concerninge the busines att Bridgwater you may please to
receive this accompt of my service in psuance of your Comaundꝑ.
J deliūed your Letter to the Sub-governor and discoursed the
busines with him att large, And as for the busines in it self,
J find, he verrie well approoves it, and your authoritie but saies
that he was not able to afford you, power & force to make it good,
for that the force which must doe it, was att the Leager before
Taunton, and that the fforce in the Towne were all of the
Townsmen who peticion & ꝑtest against the busines in such sort
that he durst not adventure to ayd me in the ꝑsecution of your
expresse direccoñ (J meane concerninge Pitt the Clothier) al-
leaginge farther that he had advised with Parliamᵗ men about
this busines who doe expresslie affirme and mayntayne that this
busines ought not to be sett on foote but that the Contribution
must be spared, J answeared that his Maᵗⁱᵉ: intended it shoulbe
soe when this was setled, but he replied your Comisss: is positive
and absolut, without any such declaracoñ from his Ma:ᵗⁱᵉ. And
for that Cause the people are soe much affrighted att the busines,
sayinge whilst one is setlinge they shalbe ruined by thother &
by both togeather. Att our second meetinge J told him J had
fownd foraigne goodꝑ (vizt) wyne and salt brought in from
Sea. & prayd his ayd in that he answeared me J should doe what
J would but he could not nor would afford me any ayd vntill
he had received answeare & direccoñ from Mʳ Windham, wish-
inge both you and me to forbare a while, J was ꝑmised to have
a farther answeare Tuesday night on Mʳ Wyndhams retorne of
his and your Leꝑ touchinge this busines, but Mʳ Wyndham
sent noe answeare wensday, Mʳ Burton and J were once resolved to make an attempt on Pitt and on the forraigne goodꝑ,
but we concluded if we were once bafled att the first we should
be scorned. (if not beaten) att the next, soe that nothing is donn
att present but what J have written, And if you resolve of any
way to ꝑceed J wish you would make one Jorny to see the ffirst

act playd, and J will wayt on you any day you shall appoynt (god willinge) and to that end J have sent this bearer of purpose, And if you give me leave to tell you myne oppynion, J must needȝ saie the busines will neū goe on fayerlie vntill the kinge declare himself that the Contribution shall fall as this doth sett vpp. that one man may not pay both, or that you gett a Mandamus, or that the Leager be off from Taunton Gent'. all J can saie is this, I shalbe readie to putt in practise & execution any your Comaundȝ and remayne/

Crewkerne 7th Your Lovinge ffreind & servant
Novem̄ 1644/   John Hutchins:/
     [Endorsed, f. 280v.]
To the Wor:^{ll} Christopher Milton Esquier
and the rest of his Ma^{te} Com:^{rs} of Excise for
the County of Som̄s^t att Wellȝ this present

Leave this att the fflower de Luce with
Captaine West in Wellȝ./

British Museum Harleian MS. 6802, ff. 279-280v.; quoted also in Add. MS. 19,142, fol. 79v. This letter, I believe, has not previously been noticed.

NOVEMBER 14. ANONYMOUS ANSWER TO *DOCTRINE AND DISCIPLINE* LICENSED.

To preserve the strength of the Mariage-bond and the Honour of that estate, against those sad breaches and dangerous abuses of it, which common discontents (on this side Adultery) are likely to make in unstaied mindes and men given to change, by taking in or grounding themselves upon the opinion answered, and with good reason confuted in this Treatise, I have approved the printing and publishing of it.
Novemb. 14 1644. JOSEPH CARYL.

Anon., *An Answer to a Book, Intituled, The Doctrine and Discipline of Divorce*, 1644, facing title page; Parker, p. [170].

NOVEMBER 19. DIVORCE BOOK ANSWERED BY ANONY-
MOUS AUTHOR.

An Answer to a Book, Intituled, The Doctrine and Discipline
of Divorce, or, A Plea for Ladies and Gentlewomen, and all
other Maried Women against Divorce. Wherein, Both Sexes
are vindicated from all bonadge of Canon Law, and other mistakes whatsoever: And the unsound Principles of the Author
are examined and fully confuted by authority of Holy Scripture, the Laws of this Land, and sound Reason. Concil. Anglic.
Anno 670. Can. 10. Nullus conjugem propriam nisi (ut sanc-
tum Evangelium docet,) fornicationis causa relinquat. London,
Printed by G. M. for William Lee at the Turks-Head in Fleetstreet, next to the Miter Taverne. 1644.

From the title page of the first edition. Reprinted in Parker, *Milton's
Contemporary Reputation*, pp. 170 ff., in facsimile. The book is a sober,
sensible answer to Milton's arguments, attempting to prove that in-
compatibility is not sufficient ground for divorce. It contains a few sly
digs at Milton like the following (p. 16): "We believe you count no
woman to due conversation accessible, as to you, except she can speak
Hebrew, Greek, Latine, & French, and dispute against the Canon law
as well as you." The book was registered on October 31, licensed on
November 14, and published (according to the manuscript date on the
Thomason copy) on November 19. See Masson, III, 299. The name
of the author is unknown.

. . . at length a book was brought to my hands, entitl'd *An
Answer to the Doctrine and Discipline of Divorce.* . . . When as
the Doctrin of Divorce had now a whole year bin publisht the
second time, with many Arguments added, and the former ones
better'd and confirm'd, this idle pamflet comes reeling forth
against the first Edition only . . . [written by] an actual Serv-
ing-man.

Milton, *Colasterion*, 1645, pp. 3-5; CM, IV, 235, 237. In *Colasterion*, after ridiculing Prynne, Milton unmercifully satirizes the anonymous *Answer*.

Joh. Miltons book of Divorce answered.

Anthony Wood's manuscript note in his own copy of his *Athenae
Oxonienses*, 1691, Bodleian Library, call-number Wood. 431.a., I, 881.
After the note as quoted follow a few letters or numbers which I cannot
make out, probably a reference to an earlier page.

John Milton · NOVEMBER 1644

NOVEMBER 23. *AREOPAGITICA* PUBLISHED.

Areopagitica; A Speech Of M^r. John Milton For the Liberty of Vnlicenc'd Printing, To the Parlament of England. [Four lines of Greek verse, signed "Euripid. Hicetid."] This is true Liberty when free born men Having to advise the public may speak free, Which he who can, and will, deserv's high praise, Who neither can nor will, may hold his peace; What can be juster in a State then this? Euripid. Hicetid. London, Printed in the Yeare, 1644.

Title page of the Thomason copy. Facsimiles in CM, IV, facing p. 293, and in *A Seventeenth-Century News-Letter*, Volume III, No. 2 (December, 1944), p. 7. The date is from the last-named (the Fulton copy now in the Yale University Library), which bears the inscriptions "Ex Dono Authoris" and "nou. 23" on the title page. The Thomason copy is dated one day later. The translation is noted in CM, XVIII, 266, 267, 537, 605. According to A. Geffroy (*Étude sur les Pamphlets Politiques et Religieux de Milton*, 1848, p. 232) the original manuscript of this book is preserved in the Bodleian Library, but no biographer of Milton has been able to find any trace of it.

Postremò de typographia liberanda, ne veri & falsi arbitrium, quid edendum, quid premendum, penès paucos esset, eóq; ferè indoctos, & vulgaris judicii homines, librorum inspectioni præpositos, per quos nemini ferè quicquam quod supra vulgus sapiat, in lucem emittere, aut licet aut libet, ad justæ orationis modum Areopagiticam scripsi.

Milton, *Defensio Secunda*, 1654, pp. 91-92; CM, VIII, 132-134.

[Finally I wrote *Areopagitica*, according to the model of a regular speech, about the liberty of printing, so that the decision about what was true and what was false, what should be published and what suppressed, should not be entrusted to a few almost uneducated persons, men of mediocre judgment, chosen to inspect books, who allow and deign to permit almost no one to bring to light any knowledge which he possesses above that of the common people.]

His next public work, and which seem'd to bee his particular Province, who was so zealous in promoting Knowlege, was *Areopagitica*, written in manner of an Oration, to vindicate the Freedom of the Press from the Tyranny of Licensers; Who either inslav'd to the Dictates of those that put them into Office, or prejudic'd by thir own Ignorance, are wont to hinder ye comming out of any thing [new or] which is not consonant to the common receiv'd Opinions, and by that means deprive the public of the benefit of many usefull labours.

The "earliest" biography, fol. 142; Darbishire, p. 25. The words "new or," here placed in brackets, are crossed through in the manuscript.

Areopagitica, viz for ye libertie of ye Presse.

Aubrey, fol. 64; Darbishire, p. 11.

Areopagitica; A Speech of *John Milton* for the Liberty of Unlicensed Printing, to the Parliament of *England*. 4*to*.

Phillips, p. [1]; not in Darbishire.

Areopagitica: A speech for the liberty of unlicensed printing, to the Parliament of England. Lond. 1644. qu. written to vindicate the freedom of the Press from the Tyranny of Licensers, who for several Reasons deprive the publick of the benefit of many useful Authors.

Wood, I, 882; Darbishire, p. 42.

NOVEMBER 23. PRESENTS COPY OF *AREOPAGITICA* TO UNKNOWN FRIEND.

Ex Dono Authoris nou: 23.

Inscription on the title page of a copy of *Areopagitica* recently acquired by Yale University from Dr. John Fulton. See *A Seventeenth-Century News-Letter*, Volume III, Number 2 (December, 1944), p. 7, where the title page is reproduced in facsimile. The name of the recipient is unknown. Dr. Fulton kindly informs me that this volume had previously belonged to Sir David Dundas of Ochtertyne and to Charles W. G. Howard. The "Ex Dono Authoris" is written below the English translation of Euripides and the date at the left of the imprint.

NOVEMBER 23. MANUSCRIPT CORRECTIONS IN COPIES OF *AREOPAGITICA*.

A number of copies of *Areopagitica* are known in which various manuscript corrections have been made in the text. One example is the change of "warfaring" to "wayfaring" on p. 12. It has been conjectured that these changes are in Milton's hand and that their presence indicates that the volumes which possess them were presentation copies; such is the opinion of G. A. Bonnard in the *Review of English Studies*, IV (1928), 434-438. This view is opposed by Helen Darbishire, *ibid.*,

VII (1931), 72-73. Copies so annotated are in the Lausanne Library (T. 999), the Bodleian Library (Wood. B. 29 and E.H.4.F.50), the British Museum (C.55.c.22.[9], the Thomason copy), the library of Trinity College, Dublin (the presentation copy to Patrick Young), and the collection of Mr. and Mrs. Adrian van Sinderen of Brooklyn. See French, "The Autographs of John Milton," #20.

In this connection may be mentioned a copy of *Areopagitica* advertised in Catalogue 620 of Maggs Brothers (1936), item 4, of which the title page is reproduced in facsimile in the catalogue. It bears on the title page the Latin line: "Qui libellos suppresserūt, iidem suppressēre literas" [The same men who have suppressed books have suppressed literature]. The handwriting resembles Milton's. See CM, XVIII, 537.

NOVEMBER 24. PRESENTS COPY OF *AREOPAGITICA* TO GEORGE THOMASON.

Ex Dono Authoris Nouemb^r. 24:

Inscriptions on the title page of the Thomason copy of *Areopagitica* in the British Museum. The "Ex Dono Authoris" is written below the Greek verses quoted from Euripides, and the date at the left of the imprint. The handwriting somewhat resembles that in Dr. Fulton's copy, but it is impossible to tell whether or not it is the same. On p. 12 the word "warfaring" has been corrected by hand to "wayfaring." See CM, XVIII, 551; French, "The Autographs of John Milton," #19; Masson, III, 277; Stern, I, ii, 482.

DECEMBER 16. ALLOWANCE TO BROTHER CHRISTOPHER FOR CHILDREN (?).

[December 16, 1644. Paid to Mrs. Elijah (or Elizabeth) Webster for keeping Mr. Milton's children.]

British Museum Add. MS. 24,501, fols. 23, 56. For fuller comment on these records, see above under date of July 1, 1644.

DECEMBER 21. JOHN HALL TELLS SAMUEL HARTLIB HE WISHES TO KNOW MILTON.

Worthy S^r.

. . . J am much Ambitious of ye Accquaintance of Mr Milton, (who is here s^d to be ye Author of ye excellent discourse of Education y^w were pleased to impart) J beseech y^w be a means to bring vs to a Correspondency, if y^w can. . . .

S. Johns.   Y^r affectionately devoted
Dec: 21.   Sērvt in x^t
                                  J Halls

[Addressed outside:] To his honourd freind Mr Samuel Hartlibb, at his house in Dukes-place London.

From the original letter in the possession of Lord Delamere; printed in part in G. H. Turnbull, *Hartlib, Dury and Comenius*, p. 39. Although the signature is illegible to me, Professor Turnbull identifies it as John Hall's; and he assigns the letter to the year 1644, though it does not appear on my photostatic copy. Apparently Hartlib had sent Hall a copy of Milton's *Of Education*, which Hall here acknowledges. If Hartlib responded to Hall's request, Milton may thus have met in 1644 or 1645 a man who was to help him in his secretaryship years later.

DECEMBER 28. SUMMONED BEFORE HOUSE OF LORDS FOR EXAMINATION.

Die Sabbati, 28° die Decembris [1644]. . . .

The Wardens of the Stationers Company gave the House an Account, "That they have used their best Endeavours to find out the Printer and Author of the scandalous Libel; but they cannot yet make any Discovery thereof, the Letter being so common a Letter; and further complained of the frequent Printing of scandalous Books by divers, as *Hezechia Woodward* and *Jo. Milton*."

Hereupon it is ORDERED, That it be referred to Mr. Justice *Reeves* and Mr. Justice *Bacon*, to examine the said *Woodward* and *Milton*, and such others as the Master and Wardens of the Stationers Company shall give Information of, concerning the printing and publishing their Books and Pamphlets; and to examine also what they know concerning the Libel, who was the Author, Printer, and Contriver of it: And the Gentleman Usher shall attach the Parties, and bring them before the Judges; and the Stationers are to be present at their Examinations, and give Evidence against them.

Journals of the House of Lords, VII, 116; Masson, III, 291; CM, XVIII, 364. The House had been concerned for some time about the "libel," the story of which Masson gives in some detail. Its title has not been given, but it might very well be that given in the Thomason catalogue under date of December 9, 1644, the exact date of the first notice of it taken by the House. It is a single sheet entitled "Alas pore Parliament, how art thou betrai'd?" It bears the manuscript note by Thomason: "Written by some Independent against Ld. Gen. Essex and Ld. Manchester, and scattered about the streets in the night."

Woodward, who had written a book attacking bishops, appeared as ordered and was released on giving bail on December 31, but nothing more is heard of Milton in this connection. Grierson conjectures (*Milton and Wordsworth*, 1937, p. 58) that the poet had influential friends who protected him, but we have no proof.

The Assembly of Divines then sitting at Westminster, though formerly obliged by his learned Pen in the defense of Smectymnyus, and other thir controversies with the Bishops, now impatient of having the Clergies Iurisdiction, as they reckon'd it, invaded, instead of answering, or disproving what those books had asserted, caus'd him to be summon'd for them before the Lords: But that house, whether approving the Doctrin, or not favoring his Accusers, soon dismiss'd him.

The "earliest" biography, fols. 141v-142; Darbishire, p. 24. The writer made several changes in the text; they are carefully given in Miss Darbishire's notes.

Upon his publication of the said three books of Marriage and Divorce, the *Assembly of Divines* then sitting at *Westminster* took special notice of them, and thereupon, tho the Author had obliged them by his pen in his defence of *Smectymnus* and other their Controversies had with the Bishops, they impatient of having the Clergies jurisdiction (as they reckon'd it) invaded, did, instead of answering, or disproving what those books had asserted, cause him to be summoned before the House of Lords: but that House, whether approving the Doctrine, or not favouring his Accusers, did soon dismiss him.

Wood, I, 882; Darbishire, p. 41.

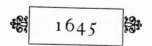

1645

PLANS TO MARRY MISS DAVIS (?).

[Milton planned to move from Aldersgate] but in the interim before he removed, there fell out a passage, which though it altered not the whole Course he was going to Steer, yet it put a stop or rather an end to a grand Affair, which was more than probably thought to be then in agitation: It was indeed a design of Marrying one of Dr. *Davis's* Daughters, a very Handsome and Witty Gentlewoman, but averse as it is said to this Motion; however, the Intelligence hereof, and the then declining State of the King's Cause, and consequently of the Circumstances of Justice *Powell's* Family, caused them to set all Engines on Work, to restore the late Married Woman. . . .

Phillips, pp. xxv–xxvi; Darbishire, p. 66. Not much is known of the Davis family.

WRITES SONNET TO A YOUNG LADY.

Lady that in the prime of earliest youth. . . .

Milton, *Poems*, 1645, p. 50; Cambridge Manuscript, p. 9; CM, I, 61. Neither the date nor the identity of the young lady addressed in this sonnet is at all certain. It has frequently been thought to have been written to the Miss Davis whom Milton is said to have contemplated marrying, and it is therefore here placed near the reference to that action. In Smart's edition of the sonnets (pp. 58 ff.) the editor suggests the young lady in question was a daughter of George and Katharine Thomason.

FATHER BECOMES ACQUAINTED WITH MOTHER-IN-LAW ANNE POWELL.

[Anne Powell testified on June 4, 1656, that] she did knowe John Milton deceād late father of the dēft . . . and knewe ye said John Milton dēcd for about twoe yeares . . . before their [his and Richard Powell's] seuerall deceases. . . .

From Anne Powell's deposition in the Ashworth-Milton case, June 4, 1656, *q.v.* Although it is hard to believe that the father of the groom and the mother of the bride should not have met until three years after their marriage, that is what this statement says. Since Mary Powell returned to her poet-husband at about this time, it is of course possible that in the entertainment held on that occasion they may first have met. The elder Milton died on March 13, 1647.

WIFE RETURNS.

Nor though hee sent severall pressing invitations could hee prevayl wth her to return, till about foure yeers after, when Oxford was surrendr'd (the nighness of her Fathers house to that Garrison having for the most part of the mean time hindred

any communication between them) shee of her own accord came,
& submitted to him; pleading that her Mother had bin the inciter of her to that frowardness.

The "earliest" biography, fol. 141v; Darbishire, pp. 22-23.

Of his Gentleness and Humanity hee likewise gave signal
proof in receiving home, and living in good accord till her death
with his first Wife, after shee had so obstinately absented from
him: During which time, as neither in any other Scene of his
life, was hee blemish'd with the least Unchastity.

The "earliest" biography, fol. 143v; Darbishire, p. 31.

[When there was talk of Milton's marrying Miss Davis]
the Intelligence hereof, and the then declining State of the
King's Cause, and consequently of the Circumstances of Justice
Powell's Family, caused them to set all Engines on Work, to
restore the late Married Woman to the Station wherein they a
little before had planted her; at last this device was pitch'd
upon. There dwelt in the Lane of St. *Martins L-Grand*, which
was hard by, a Relation of our Author's, one *Blackborough*,
whom it was known he often visited, and upon this occasion the
visits were the more narrowly observ'd, and possibly there
might be a Combination between both Parties; the Friends on
both sides concentring in the same action though on different
behalfs. One time above the rest, he making his usual visit, the
Wife was ready in another Room, and on a sudden he was surprised to see one whom he thought to have never seen more,
making Submission and begging Pardon on her Knees before
him; he might probably at first make some shew of aversion
and rejection; but partly his own generous nature, more in-
clinable to Reconciliation than to perseverance in Anger and
Revenge; and partly the strong intercession of Friends on both
sides, soon brought him to an Act of Oblivion, and a firm League
of Peace for the future; and it was at length concluded, That
she should remain at a Friend's house, till such time as he was
settled in his New house at *Barbican*, and all things for her reception in order; the place agreed on for her present abode, was
the Widow *Webber's* house in St. *Clement's* Church-yard,

whose Second Daughter had been Married to the other Brother many years before. . . .

Phillips, pp. xxvi-xxvii; Darbishire, pp. 66-67; CM, XVIII, 377. Miss Darbishire identifies the Blackborough referred to here as either Hester (Jeffrey) Blackborow or her son Abraham (p. 340).

. . . he could not prevail with her to come back, till about 4 years after when the Garrison of *Oxon* was surrendred (the nighness of her Father's house to which having for the most part of the mean time hindred any communication between them) she of her own accord returned and submitted to him, pleading that her Mother had been the chief promoter of her frowardness.

Wood, I, 881; Darbishire, p. 40.

HUMPHREY MOSELEY ARRANGES TO PUBLISH MILTON'S POEMS.

THE STATIONER TO THE READER

It is not any private respect of gain, Gentle Reader . . . *but it is the love I have to our own Language that hath made me diligent to collect, and set forth such* Peeces *both in Prose and Vers, as may renew the wonted honour and esteem of our English tongue; and it's the worth of these both English and Latin* Poems, *not the flourish of any prefixed* encomions *that can invite thee to buy them, though these are not without the highest Commendations and Applause of the learnedst* Academicks, *both domestick and forrein: And amongst those of our own Countrey, the unparallel'd attestation of that renowned Provost of* Eaton, *Sir* Henry Wootton. . . . *The Authors more peculiar excellency in these studies, was too well known to conceal his Papers, or to keep me from attempting to sollicit them from him. Let the event guide it self which way it will, I shall deserve of the age, by bringing into the Light as true a Birth, as the Muses have brought forth since our famous* Spencer *wrote; whose Poems in these English ones are as rarely imitated, as sweetly excell'd. . . . Thine to command* HUMPH. MOSELEY.

Poems, 1645, sigs. a3-a4v; CM, I, 414-415. Although this negotiation cannot be dated, it must have begun some little time before January 2,

1645/6, the date of the publication of the volume (*q.v.*). Even the writing of the preface must have been done some time before the finished volume was out. It is therefore dated here simply 1645.

"Lycidas" imitated by Andrew Marvell (?).

The last distemper of the sober Brain.

Marvell, "Fleckno, *an English Priest at* Rome," line 28, in *The Poems & Letters of Andrew Marvell*, ed. H. M. Margoliouth, 1 (Oxford, 1927), 83. Pierre Legouis (*Andre Marvell*, 1928, p. 58) considers this an imitation of line 71 of "Lycidas." As to the date of the poem, which is uncertain, Margoliouth (1, 235) says: "The incidents, but not necessarily the composition, of this satire belong to the spring of 1645 or 1646." He does not give a date for the composition, but Legouis suggests that it was written about 1645.

Sonnet to Lady Margaret Ley.

Daughter to that good Earl, once President. . . .

Milton, *Poems*, 1645, p. 51; Cambridge Manuscript, p. 9; CM, 1, 61. In the Cambridge Manuscript the poem is entitled, "To yᵉ Lady Margaret Ley." For details about the lady, see above under date of August, 1642. There is wide variation among editors and critics as to the date, but 1645 is as likely to be correct as any other. It must obviously have been written before the appearance of the 1645 edition of the poems.

Fragment of Greek verse written.

Philosophus ad regem quendam qui eum ignotum & insontem inter reos forte captum inscius damnaverat τὴν ἐπὶ θανάτῳ πορευόμενος *hæc subito misit.*

Milton, *Poems*, 1645, part ii, p. 70; CM, 1, 280-281. The date here assigned is merely a guess; there seems to be no information whatever about the time when Milton wrote these lines. Professor Hughes dates them 1645. The "os" of the last Greek word is represented in the original by an abbreviation.

[To a certain king who unknowingly condemned a philosopher, unknown and innocent but taken by chance among prisoners, the philosopher, walking to his death, suddenly sent these lines.]

NEW EDITIONS OF *THE DOCTRINE AND DISCIPLINE OF DIVORCE*.

The Doctrine & Discipline of Divorce . . . 1645.

There were two editions of this work of 1645, of which both the title pages (except for the date) and the texts are substantially the same as that of February 2, 1644. The variants are carefully recorded in CM, III, 522 ff. But whereas the editor of that volume recognizes three variant issues in 1645, Parker (*Milton's Contemporary Reputation*, pp. 271-272) gives good reasons for holding that there were rather two editions. See also above under date of February 2, 1644.

JANUARY (?). PROPOSAL TO COMMISSION MILTON IN THE ARMY (?).

I am much mistaken, if there were not about this time a design in Agitation of making him Adjutant-General in Sir *William Waller's* Army; but the new modelling of the Army soon following, prov'd an obstruction to that design; and Sir *William*, his Commission being laid down, began, as the common saying is, to turn *Cat in Pan*.

Phillips, p. xxviii; Darbishire, p. 68; Stern, I, ii, 152. This idea, if Phillips is correct about its ever having existed, must have come up before February, 1645, for the New Model ordinance was passed by the House of Commons on January 28, 1645, and by the House of Lords on February 15. Phillips assigns it to the time when Milton's wife had returned and they had moved to the Barbican. By the Self-denying Ordinance, passed April 3, 1645, Waller and others laid down their commissions. Stern ridicules the whole idea and thinks that Phillips must have been confusing his uncle with another man of the same name. Phillips, however, would hardly have been likely to make this particular mistake, whether or not he is correct in the present instance.

FEBRUARY 7. PUBLICATION OF FEATLEY'S ATTACK ON DIVORCE BOOKS.

Witnesse a Tractate of Divorce, in which the bonds of marriage are let loose to inordinate lust, and putting away wives for many other causes besides that which our Saviour only approveth, namely, in case of Adultery.

Daniel Featley, Καταβάπτισται κατάπτυστοι. *The Dippers Dipt. or, The Anabaptists Duck'd and Plvng'd over Head and Eares*, 1645, sig. B2v, "Epistle Dedicatory to Parliament," dated January 10, 1644 [i.e., 1644/5]. Thomason's copy is dated by him on the title page in manuscript February 7, 1644[/5]. Featley mentions Milton in the same breath with *The Bloudy Tenent* and *Man's Mortality*. Featley's book went through several editions. The third, also 1645, has the same passage. See Parker, *Milton's Contemporary Reputation*, p. 74.

. . . that Doctor, who in a late equivocating Treatise plausibly set afloat against the Dippers, diving the while himself with a more deep prelatical malignance against the present state, & Church-government, mentions with ignominy the Tractate of Divorce.

Milton, *Tetrachordon*, 1645, sig. A5v; CM, IV, 69; Masson, III, 311.

MARCH 4. *TETRACHORDON* PUBLISHED.

Tetrachordon: Expositions Upon The foure chief places in Scripture, which treat of Mariage, or nullities in Mariage. On Gen. 1. 27. 28. compar'd and explain'd by Gen. 2. 18. 23. 24. Deut. 24. 1. 2. Matth. 5. 31. 32. with Matth. 19. from the 3^d. v. to the 11th. 1 Cor. 7. from the 10th to the 16th. Wherin the Doctrine and Discipline of Divorce, as was lately publish'd, is confirm'd by explanation of Scripture, by testimony of ancient Fathers, of civill lawes in the Primitive Church, of famousest Reformed Divines, And lastly, by an intended Act of the Parlament and Church of England in the last yeare of Edvvard the sixth. By the former Author J. M. [Four lines of Greek verse.] Euripid. Medea. London: Printed in the yeare 1645.

From the title page of the first edition; facsimile in CM, IV, facing p. 63. The text begins on p. 63. The Thomason copy has the manuscript date on the title page, "march. 4th," and the year 1645 has been changed in manuscript to 1644, i.e., 1644/5.

Tres enim ea de re tractatus olim scripsi . . . Alterum qui Tetrachordon inscribitur, & in quo quatuor præcipua loca Scripturæ super ea doctrina quæ sunt, explicantur.

Milton, *Epistolarum Familiarium Liber Unus*, 1674, p. 43; CM, XII, 72. This is from Milton's letter to Leo Aizema, dated February 5, 1654/5.

[For I formerly wrote three tracts about this subject . . . The second, which is entitled *Tetrachordon*, and in which are explained the four principal places of Scripture which bear on that doctrine.]

Tetrachordon [of Divorce].

Aubrey, fol. 64; Darbishire, p. 11. The brackets appear thus in the manuscript.

... then *Colasterion,* and after *Tetrachordon.* ...

The "earliest" biography, fol. 141v; Darbishire, p. 23. These words follow immediately after the mention of Milton's *Doctrine and Discipline of Divorce.*

The other in prosecution of the first, was styled, *Tetrachordon.*

Phillips, p. xxv; Darbishire, p. 65.

Tetrachordon: Expositions upon the Four chief Places in Scripture, which Treat of Marriage, or Nullities in Marriage, on *Genesis* 1.27,28. Compar'd and Explain'd by *Genesis* 2.18, 23,24. *Deut.* 24.1,2. *Matt.* 5.31,32. with *Matt.* 19. from the 3d. to the 11. *verse.* 1 *Cor.* 7. from the 10th. to the 16th. Wherein the Doctrine and Discipline of Divorce, as was lately Published, is confirmed by Explanation of Scripture, by Testimony of Ancient Fathers, of Civil Laws, in the Primitive Church, of Famousest Reformed Divines: And lastly, by an intended act of the Parliament and Church of *England* in the last year of *Edward* the Sixth. 4*to.*

Phillips, pp. [li]-[lii]; not reprinted in Darbishire.

(7) *Tetrachordon: Expositions upon the four chief places in Scripture, which treat on marriage,* on Gen. 1. 27, 28, &c. Lond. 1646. qu.

Wood, 1, 881; Darbishire, p. 41. Wood's date must be a clerical error.

MARCH 4. *COLASTERION* PUBLISHED.

Colasterion: A Reply To A Nameles Ansvver Against The Doctrine and Discipline of Divorce. Wherein The trivial Author of that Answer is discover'd, the Licencer conferr'd with, and the Opinion which they traduce defended. By the former Author, J. M. Prov. 26. 5. Answer a Fool according to his folly, lest hee bee wise in his own conceit. Printed in the Year, 1645.

From the title page of the first edition; facsimile in CM, IV, facing p. 233. The text begins on p. 233. The Thomason copy bears the manuscript date "March. 4th." on the title page, with the year 1645 changed in pen to 1644. The Greek word "kolasterion" means prison or punishment.

Tres enim ea de re tractatus olim scripsi . . . Tertium, Colasterion, in quo cuidam Sciolo respondetur.

Milton, letter to Leo Aizema, February 5, 1654/5; *Epistolarum Familiarium Liber Unus*, 1674, p. 43; CM, XII, 72.

[For I formerly wrote three tracts about that matter . . . The third, *Colasterion*, in which a reply is made to a certain pretender to learning.]

Colasterion.

Aubrey, fol. 64; Darbishire, p. 11.

. . . then *Colasterion*. . . .

The "earliest" biography, fol. 141v; Darbishire, p. 23.

Lastly, he wrote in answer to a Pragmatical Clerk, who would needs give himself the Honour of Writing against so great a Man, his Colasterion or Rod of Correction for a Sawcy Impertinent.

Phillips, p. xxv; Darbishire, pp. 65-66.

Colasterion: A Reply to a nameless Answer against the Doctrine and Discipline of Divorce. Wherein the Trivial Author of that Answer is discovered, the Licenser conferr'd with, and the Opinion which they traduce defended. 4*to*.

Phillips, p. [li]; not reprinted in Darbishire.

(8) *Colasterion: A reply to a nameless answer against the doctrine and discipline of divorce*, &c. printed 1645. qu.

Wood, I, 881; Darbishire, p. 41.

SENDS COPIES OF PROSE BOOKS TO PATRICK YOUNG.

Ad doctissim[um] virum, Patri[cium] Junium Joann[es] Miltonius hæc sua, unum in f[as]culum conjecta mittit, paucis h[u]jusmodi lectori[bus] contentus.

Milton, autograph inscription on an early page in a collection of tracts now in the library of Trinity College, Dublin. The inscription is reproduced in facsimile in Sotheby, p. 121; see French, "The Autographs of John Milton," #21; CM, XVIII, 269, 548. The following tracts are included: *Of Reformation, Of Prelatical Episcopacy, The Reason of Church Government, Animadversions, An Apology for Smectymnuus, The Doctrine and Discipline of Divorce, The Judgement of Martin*

Bucer, Colasterion, Tetrachordon, and *Areopagitica.* Though the inscription is undated, it is here placed under the year 1645 because the latest books in the group appeared in that year. The bracketed portions represent letters near the margin which have been torn away, but there can be little doubt about them. I have not seen the original but have depended on the facsimile and on accounts by Sotheby and others.

Milton may have presented this volume to Young because of his erudition, since Anthony Wood calls him (*Athenae Oxonienses,* 1721, I, Fasti, 170) "the most eminent *Grecian* of his time," or because he was Keeper of the King's Library. Another reason may have been Milton's interest in Young's proposed edition of an early Greek manuscript of the Septuagint, which for several years had been eagerly awaited by learned men and which in 1645 the Assembly of Divines at Westminster urged Young to finish for publication (*ibid.*). But Young never finished the work. All Milton's writings here included, except possibly *Areopagitica,* have a strongly Biblical content.

[To the most learned man, Patrick Young, John Milton sends these works of his bound into one volume, content with a few such readers.]

APRIL 11. POET (OR HIS FATHER) WITNESSES WILL OF WILLIAM BLACKBOROW.

John Milton

[In brief summary, William Blackborow of the parish of St. Anne's, Aldersgate, citizen and leatherseller, bequeathes as follows:

(1) To his wife Hester, land and buildings in Muckingford (Essex) and in Tilbury and household stuff and plate.

(2) To his son William, the reversion of the above and other lands and buildings in Mucking and Tilbury.

(3) To his son Abraham, the reversion of the above and £140 in leather and parchment.

(4) To his daughter Hester, the reversion of the above, failing heirs to Abraham, £250 on the day of her marriage or on reaching the age of 20, and a part interest in other property in Tilbury and elsewhere.

(5) To his daughter Joan, the reversion of the above and an equal interest in the other property.

(6) To his daughter Jane, a similar arrangement to that for Joan.

(7) To various cousins and friends, including his "brother" John Jeffrey of Bely in the parish of Maldon, Essex, small amounts of money for mourning.

The will is signed by William Blackborow in the presence of John Milton, Edward Wright, and Thomas Bridges, and dated April 11, 1645.]

Prerogative Court of Canterbury, London, 82 Twisse; *Athenaeum*, 1880, I, 566; French, "The Autographs of John Milton," #103; CM, XVIII, p. 624. It is not certain whether the signer was the poet or his father, since the document in the Prerogative Court is a copy and not the original. But in view of the father's age and approaching death, it is more likely to have been his son.

MAY 8. ATTACKED BY EPHRAIM PAGITT.

They preach, print, and practise their hereticall opinions openly: for books, *vide* the bloody Tenet, witnesse a tractate of divorce in which the bonds are let loose to inordinate lust.

Ephraim Pagitt, *Heresiography: or, A description of the Heretickes and Sectaries of these latter times*, London, 1645, sig. A3v; Masson, III, 155; Parker, *Milton's Contemporary Reputation*, pp. 74-75. Since I have not been able to see a copy of the first edition, my text is taken from Parker's. The date is that entered on the Thomason copy. The book was entered in the Stationers' Registers on March 5, 1645.

JUNE 14 (?). ALLEGED AUTHOR OF *THE KING'S CABINET OPENED.*

The Kings Cabinet opened: Or, Certain Packets of Secret Letters & Papers, Written with the Kings own Hand, and taken in his Cabinet at Nasby-Field, June 14. 1645. By Victorious Sᵣ. Thomas Fairfax . . . Together, with some Annotations thereupon. Published by speciall Order of the Parliament. [ornament] London, Printed for Robert Bostock, dwelling in Pauls Church-yard, at the Signe of the Kings-head, 1645.

[Manuscript note written under the line "Together . . . thereupon":] by I: Milton

From a copy in the Sutro Library in San Francisco. Described by G. F. Sensabaugh, "A Milton Ascription," *Notes and Queries*, CXCIV (August 6, 1949), 337. Professor Sensabaugh doubts that Milton really had anything to do with this book and believes that "the only significance to be attached to this ascription" by some anonymous later writer "is that it tells something, however little, about Milton's reputation and fame." I am indebted to the kindness of the librarian of the Sutro Library in sending me a photostatic copy of the title page of this pamphlet. Although the editor of the catalogue of the Thomason Tracts dates it June 14, 1645, it is not likely that, whether Milton had any hand in it or not, it could have been written, printed, and published on the same day as the event which it recounts. But for lack of a more definite date it is entered here under that day.

JUNE 20. JOHN ROUS BUYS COPIES OF MILTON'S BOOKS FOR THE BODLEIAN.

June 20, 1645. Sold to Mr Rowse for ye Publik Liberary./. by *Tho. Robinson.* . . .

Miltons doctrine of diuorce 0-2-0

. . . Concerning ye Liberty of Printing ....0-0-[10].

Bodleian Library, Library Papers, Bills to 1763, p. 30 (?); W. D. Macray, *Annals of the Bodleian Library*, 1890, p. 101. In the photostatic copy which I have used the price of the second title is somewhat blotted, but it is almost certainly ten pence. These two books by Milton are part of a group of twenty-six titles sold to Rous on the date given. They include works by Prynne, Burton, Selden, Ross, Goodwin, Sir Thomas Browne, and others.

SEPTEMBER (?). MOVES TO HOUSE IN BARBICAN.

Not very long after the setting forth of these [divorce] Treatises, having application made to him by several Gentlemen of his acquaintance, for the Education of their Sons, as understanding haply the Progress he had infixed by his first undertakings of that nature, he laid out for a larger House, and soon found it out. . . . [Milton's wife, it was decided,] should remain at a Friend's house, till such time as he was settled in his New house at *Barbican*, and all things for her reception in order.

Phillips, pp. xxv-xxvii; Darbishire, pp. 66-67. The date is that conjectured by Masson, III, 442-443. The house, which was no. 17 Barbican, was standing until 1864 or 1865, when it was torn down to make way for the Metropolitan Railway. An illustration of it may be found in the *Illustrated London News* for July 16, 1864. Further information may be found in the *Athenaeum*, 1864, II, 123-124, 603; *Bookworm*, II (1889), 173-176; *Good Words*, XXXIV (1893), 134-135. In this last article David Masson reproduces the illustration mentioned above. A pane of glass from this house is said (in the *Bookworm* article just mentioned) to have been sent to Toledo, Ohio; but I have been unable to find any trace of it.

A small fragment of material said to be part of a brick from this house was presented by Moses C. Tyler to the Yale University Library, where it is now preserved. Since it is merely a jagged, nondescript piece, there is no way to identify it except by the accompanying records. The label on the box reads: "To Yale College. Fragment of brick from the house in Barbican, London, in which John Milton lived from 1645 to 1647 (Vide other side of this cover). Taken from [several illegible words, two of which look like "fire" and "ruins"] & presented to Alma Mater by Moses C. Tyler Class of '87." Inside the cover of the box containing the piece is this statement: "To this house Milton moved from Aldersgate St, when deserted by Mary Powell: here he received her back, together with her parents, brothers & sisters: here he [received?] pupils & wrote for them the Hist. of England: here his aged father died: from this house he removed to Holborn with garden looking upon Lincoln's Inn Fields."

SECOND EDITION OF PAGITT'S ATTACK PUBLISHED.

These I terme Divorsers, that would be quit of their wives for slight occasions; and to maintaine this opinion, one hath published a Tractate of divorce, in which the bonds of marriage are let loose to inordinate lust, putting away wives for many other causes, besides that which our Saviour onely approveth; namely in case of adulterie, who groundeth his Error upon the words of God, *Gen.* 2. 18. *I will make him a helpe meet for him.* And therefore if she be not an helper, nor meet for him, he may put her away, saith this Author.

Pagitt, *Heresiography*, second edition, 1645, p. 142, quoted from Parker, *Milton's Contemporary Reputation*, p. 75. The date is uncertain, but it must be after that of the first edition (May 8, 1645), and before that of the third, in 1647. The sentence about Milton quoted from the first edition is also retained in the second. Parker calls attention to the obvious similarity between this passage and that from Featley's *Dippers Dipt*, quoted earlier under date of February 7, 1645.

OCTOBER 6. POEMS REGISTERED FOR PUBLICATION.
6° [October 1645] . . . .

Master Mozeley. Entred . . . under the hands of Sʳ NATH: BRENT and both the wardens a booke called *Poems in English & Latyn*, by Mʳ **John Milton** . . . vjᵈ.

Eyre, *Stationers' Registers*, 1, 196. The volume did not appear until the following January.

OCTOBER 17. ALLOWANCES FOR CHRISTOPHER MILTON'S CHILDREN.

[An account book of the Committee of Sequestrations in London shows an entry under October 17, 1645, of two pounds and fourteen shillings paid to Mrs. Elijah Webster for keeping Mr. Christopher Milton's children. A similar entry from the Books of Sequestration of Delinquents differs only in showing eighteen shillings. It is followed by the amount of thirteen pounds and twelve shillings, probably the total of allowances to date.]

From Joseph Hunter's notes, British Museum Add. MS. 24,501, f. 23. He gives the first reference as being on fol. 50 and the second as fol. 56. I have not seen the originals. The readings are somewhat uncertain because of Hunter's difficult handwriting.

NOVEMBER (?). HAS PORTRAIT DRAWN AND ENGRAVED BY WILLIAM MARSHALL FOR *POEMS*.

IOANNIS MILTONI ANGLI EFFIGIES ANNO
ÆTATIS ViGess: Pri:

The portrait serves as the frontispiece to Milton's *Poems*, which appeared on January 2, 1645/6 (*q.v.*). It is reproduced in Fletcher's facsimile, 1, 153 and in other places. The label quoted above occurs in the oval surrounding the figure, which appears seated beside an open window looking out on a wooded scene. Surrounding the oval are figures representing Melpomene, Erato, Urania, and Clio. Below is the four-line Greek verse inscription given below, and at the lower right-hand corner of the page the signature: "W. M. sculp."

Despite some vague resemblances to the Onslow portrait of 1629 and somewhat more marked similarities to the Faithorne picture of 1670, this does not look much like any other known picture of Milton. Yet Milton's reference to it in his *Pro Se Defensio* (quoted below), slighting though it is, proves almost conclusively that it was made from life expressly for publication in the *Poems* of 1645/6. Probably, however, Marshall used the Onslow portrait also, since this one bears some resemblance to that, and since the statement that this is a likeness of Milton at the age of 21, though far from the truth here, is precisely true of that. There is no trace of Marshall's original drawing. It is here entered under the latter part of 1645 because that seems a reasonable time for it to have been made for inclusion in the *Poems*.

Discussion of it may be found in Masson, III, 456-459; Williamson, *Milton Tercentenary*, pp. 5, 47; and elsewhere.

[Likeness of John Milton, Englishman, made in the twenty-first year of his age.]

Narcissus nunc sum . . . quia tu effigiem mei dissimilimam, *praefixam poematibus* vidisti. Ego verò si impulsu & ambitione Librarii, me imperito Sculptori, propterea quòd in urbe alius eo belli tempore non erat, infabrè scalpendum permisi, id me neglexisse potiùs eam rem arguebat, cujus tu mihi nimium cultum objicis.

Milton, *Pro Se Defensio*, 1655, p. 84; CM, IX, 124.

[I am now (according to Milton's antagonist More) a "Narcissus" . . . because you have seen a picture, most unlike me, "prefixed to my poems." But if, through the urging and ambition of the bookseller, I allowed myself to be unskillfully engraved by an inexperienced artist because in that time of war there was no other in the city, this demonstrates rather that I neglected that very thing (vanity) which you accuse me of having too much cultivated.]

'Αμαθεῖ γεγράφθαι χειρὶ τήνδε μὲν εἰκόνα
Φαίης τάχ' ἂν, πρὸς εἶδος αὐτοφυὲς βλέπων
Τὸν δ'ἐκτυπωτὸν οὐκ ἐπιγνόντες φίλοι
Γελᾶτε φαύλου δυσμίμημα ζωγράφου.

Milton, *Poems*, 1645, frontispiece; *Poems*, 1673, part II, p. 71; CM, I, facing p. 402 (facsimile); Masson, III, 459.

The date of these Greek verses must obviously lie between the time when Marshall finished his engraving so that Milton could look at it, and the time of the appearance of the book on January 2, 1645/6. The contractions in the original are spelled out here.

[That an unskilful hand had carved this print
You'd say at once, seeing that living face;
But, finding here no jot of me, my friends,
Laugh at the botching artist's mis-attempt.]

Masson's translation, III, 459.

NOVEMBER 12. SIR CHENEY CULPEPPER INQUIRES ABOUT MILTON AS A TEACHER AND MENTIONS HIS *OF EDUCATION*.

Mʳ Hartlib

... J pray (as you shall haue oportunity) inform your selfe of the charge on wᶜʰ a schollar may be wᵗʰ Mʳ Milton; that (yf J haue occasion) J may satisfy suche wᵗʰ whome (till he be more knowne) that consideration is like to waygh, There are some good sprincklings in his (as J conceiue it to be) letter of Education, but (vnder fauor J conceiue) there is not descendinge enought into particulars, but rather a generall notion of what experience onely can perfecte. ...

9:ᵇᵉʳ 12ᵗʰ   Your affect: frind

45.   Ch: Cul.

[Addressed outside:] ffor Mʳ Hartlib at Dukes place London.

From a letter from Sir Cheney Culpepper to Samuel Hartlib now in the collection of Lord Delamere; printed in part in G. H. Turnbull, *Hartlib, Dury and Comenius*, p. 39. Though the signature is much abbreviated, Professor Turnbull ascribes it to Culpepper.

NOVEMBER 24. ROBERT BAILLIE'S ATTACK PUBLISHED.

Concerning Divorces, some of them goe farre beyond any of the *Brownists*, not to speake of Mr *Milton*, who in a large Treatise hath pleaded for a full liberty for any man to put away his wife, when ever he pleaseth, without any fault in her at all, but for any dislike or dyspathy of humour (mmmm); for I doe not know certainely whither this man professeth *Independency* (albeit all the Hereticks here, whereof ever I heard, avow themselves *Independents*); what ever therefore may be said of Mr. *Milton*, yet Mr. *Gorting* and his Company were men of renown among the *New-English Independents*, before Mistrisse *Hutchinsons* disgrace; and all of them do maintaine, that it is lawfull for every woman to desert her husband, when he is not willing to follow her in her Church-way, and to take her selfe for a widow, loosed from the bond of obedience to him, onely because he lives without that Church whereof she is become a member.

Robert Baillie, *A Dissuasive from the Errours of the Time*, 1645, p. 116; Masson, III, 467; Parker, *Milton's Contemporary Reputation*, p. 75. The date comes from Thomason's manuscript note on his copy of the second impression, where he dates this November 24 and that January 22. In a letter dated November 25, 1645, Baillie refers to "my Dissuasive from the errors of the time, which is now abroad" (*Letters and Journal*, II [1775], 168). The note "mmmm" refers to pp. 144-145 later in the book, where Baillie quotes at length from pp. 6, 15, 16, 63, and 76 of Milton's *Doctrine and Discipline of Divorce*.

Mr. *Milton* permits any man to put away his wife upon his meer pleasure, without fault and without cognizance of any Iudge.

Baillie, *ibid.*, marginal note.

Mr. Milton *permits any man to put away his wife upon his meere pleasure without any fault, and without the cognisance of any Iudge*, p. 116.

Ibid., sig. ¶¶.

WINTER. BROTHER CHRISTOPHER LIVES IN EXETER.

Christopher Milton did inhabit in this Citty within sea[ven] moneths before the surrender of the same into the hands of his Excellency Sir Thomas Fairefax [on April 13, 1646].

From a certificate dated May 16, 1646, *q.v.*

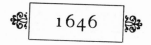

1646

BEGINS WRITING *SAMSON AGONISTES* (?).

In "The Date of *Samson Agonistes*," *Philological Quarterly*, XXVIII (1949), 145 ff., William R. Parker carefully reviews the evidence about the date of composition of Milton's tragedy and "guesses" that it was "begun in 1646 or 1647" and finished in 1652 or 1653. Allan H. Gilbert (*ibid.*, pp. 98 ff.) similarly argues for an early date. But no very tangible evidence has yet been presented.

POWELL FAMILY VISITS WITH MILTON.

But it was not only by Children that she [Milton's wife Mary] increas'd the number of the Family, for in no very long time after her coming, she had a great resort of her Kindred with her in the House, *viz.* her Father and Mother, and several of her Brothers and Sisters, which were in all pretty Numerous; who upon his Father's Sickning and Dying soon after went away.

Phillips, p. xxvii; Darbishire, p. 67. The date is very vague, but may be placed some time in 1646. It was probably, by Phillips's method of describing it, some time after the birth of the Miltons' daughter Anne on July 29, 1646, and certainly before the death of Milton's father in March, 1647; certainly also before the death of Richard Powell on or about January 1, 1647.

FATHER-IN-LAW RICHARD POWELL MOVES TO OXFORD.

Richard Powell of Forrest hill in the County of Oxon, Esq\`./ ... diserted his dwellinge and went to Oxford and lived there whiles it was a Garrison holden for the Kinge against the Parliam\`\`. and was there at the tyme of the Surrender. . . .

From Powell's petition of December 8, 1646, *q.v.* Although the time of Powell's move from Forest Hill to Oxford is uncertain, the latter city surrendered on June 24, 1646; Masson, III, 472.

DATI WRITES HIM THREE LETTERS, ALL OF WHICH ARE LOST.

... scribis, ternas te jam olim ad me dedisse, quas ego periisse scio.

From Milton's letter to Dati, April 21, 1647, *q.v.* The dates of the lost letters can be only generally set. See CM, XVIII, 528.

[You write that you have already sent me three letters, which I know have been lost.]

ATTRIBUTED SELF-PORTRAIT.

There being still extant a sketch of an head of MILTON upon board, indeed rather a drawing or painting, &, by what I can remember, no ways curious, except that it is given out to have been drawn by himself. And, upon recollection, I think I have heard his wife say so.

A letter from Roger Comberbach to William Cowper, Clerk of the Parliament, December 15, 1736, quoted by Francis Peck, *New Memoirs of the Life and Poetical Writing of John Milton*, London, 1740, p. 104.

A portrait which might answer the description was described by Edward Walford in "An Unknown Portrait of John Milton," in the

Antiquarian Magazine and Bibliographer, II (1882), 1–4; the portrait is reproduced facing p. 1. The portrait is said to bear Milton's name, "Joannis Miltoni," and his spread-eagle arms. On the back are said to be the words, "Mr. John Milton, Back Library, No. 14." The portrait is of a stocky man with flowing hair crowned with laurel. It bears no resemblance to the other accepted pictures of Milton.

It belonged in 1908 to Mrs. Morrison, was exhibited at Cambridge in that year, and is described by Dr. Williamson in his *Milton Tercentenary*, pp. 25, 35. Williamson scouts the idea that Milton painted it, but thinks it was based on that of Richardson.

The only evidence of date is Walford's statement that the age of the subject is about 38–40.

Writes Complimentary Poem to Alexander Rosse?

On Mel Heliconium written by M^r. Rosse Chaplain to his Matie.

These shapes, of old transfigur'd by the charmes

. . . .

From poisnous weedes a sweet, & Wholsome Jyuce.

J:M:

Written in manuscript on a blank leaf following the dedication in a copy of Alexander Rosse's *Mel Heliconium* now in the New York Public Library. The printed date on the title page, 1642, has been changed in pen to 1646. The entry is reproduced in facsimile in Sotheby, facing p. 112. See French, "The Autographs of John Milton," #85; CM, XVIII, 357, 516, 589. The resemblance of the writing to that of other known specimens by Milton is very tenuous, and most scholars feel uncertain about Milton's connection with the writing. It should always be remembered that there were an extensive number of men in Milton's day whose initials were J.M.

Imitated by Marvell?

Legouis believed that lines 53–56 of Marvell's "The Garden" echoed lines 147–150 of "Il Penseroso," and that they were written about this time. See his *Andre Marvell*, Paris, 1928, p. 58. The argument is not very convincing.

Writes Poem on "New Forcers of Conscience."

On the forcers of Conscience.

Thus entitled in the Trinity Manuscript, p. 48; published in his *Poems*, 1673, with the title, "On the new forcers of Conscience under the Long PARLIAMENT," p. 69; CM, I, 71. The date is highly dubious. Smart gives no date, Hanford (*Modern Philology*, XVIII, 481) dates it 1646, as does Hughes, and Stevens (*Modern Philology*, XVII, 31) puts it early in 1647.

ATTACK BY DANIEL FEATLEY REPRINTED.

The Dippers Dipt.
In this fourth edition, 1646, sig. A4, the attack on Milton noted in previous editions is repeated. The first edition appeared February 7, 1644/5.

SONNET XII.

On the Same [*i.e., Tetrachordon*]

I did but prompt the age to quit their cloggs. . . .
Poems, 1673, pp. 56-57; Trinity Manuscript, pp. 43, 46; CM, I, 62. In the manuscript the first version bears the title, "On the detraction wch follow'd upon my writing certain treatises"; the word "detraction" was later crossed out. On p. 46 it is without title. It is not included in the 1645 volume of Milton's poems.
Stevens (*Modern Philology*, XVII, 27-28) thinks that this poem was written before Sonnet XI ("A book was writ of late called *Tetrachordon*"), and that it was produced in 1644. Hanford (*ibid.*, XVIII, 481), agrees on the order, but dates it 1645-46. Hughes dates it 1646 with a question mark. Smart makes no attempt to date either sonnet.

SONNET XI.

A Book was writ of late call'd *Tetrachordon*. . . .
Poems, 1673, p. 56; Trinity Manuscript, pp. 46, 47; CM, I, 62. On theories as to date, see the notes to Sonnet XII above.

JANUARY 2. *POEMS* PUBLISHED.

Poems/of/Mr. John Milton,/Both/English and Latin,/ Compos'd at several times./ Printed by his true Copies./ The Songs were set in Musick by/Mr. Henry Lawes Gentleman of/ the Kings Chappel, and one/of His Maiesties/ Private Musick./—Baccare frontem/ Cingite, ne vati noceat mala lingua futuro,/Virgil, Eclog. 7./Printed and publish'd according to/ Order./ London,/ Printed by Ruth Raworth for Humphrey Moseley,/ and are to be sold at the signe of the Princes/ Arms in S. Pauls Church-yard. 1645.

John Milton · JANUARY 1646

From the original title page; CM, I, 1-325. This volume has several times been reproduced in facsimile, most notably in Fletcher, I, 153 ff. Facsimiles of the title page are given in CM, I, facing p. 1, and in other places; the separate title page of the Latin section, which forms the second part of the volume, is reproduced in CM, I, 153 (verso).

The Latin quotation may be translated: "Wreathe my forehead with baccar, that no evil tongue may harm [me] the future poet."

The title page occurs in two states, in one of which the "S." of the last line is omitted. Fletcher shows both states.

Thomason's copy (British Museum, E. 1126) bears the date, marked in pen on the title page: "Jan: 2ᵈ."

Curiously enough, there are no specific references to this volume distinctly by the early biographers, except the partial ones given by Wood just following the present entry. They mention the publication of his poems, but not in such language as to distinguish between the volumes of 1645 and 1673.

(11) *Poemata: quorum pleraque intra annum aetatis vigesimum conscripsit author*, &c. Lond. 1645. oct. (12) *A mask.—* printed 1645. oct. (13) *Poems*, &c.—printed the same year.

Wood, I, 882; Darbishire, p. 42.

Fletcher believes (I, 150) that the Latin poems were bound and issued separately.

JANUARY (?). MAKES MANUSCRIPT CORRECTIONS IN POEMS (?).

No proof of this assertion is available, except that the copy of the *Poems* in the New York Public Library bears a note in ink at the top of p. 57, beside the title of "Lycidas," in a hand which might be Milton's. The note reads: "Mʳ King fell. of Xᵗ." Symbols beside this note and by the phrase "a learned Friend" in the subtitle of the poem show that it was intended to be inserted at that place. See an article by Joseph B. Gilder in the New York *Times Book Review*, July 5, 1925, p. 11; French, "The Autographs of John Milton," no. 22; CM, XVIII, 550.

The assertion about corrections, which would indicate something more ambitious than this one change, comes from John Nichols, *Literary Anecdotes of the Eighteenth Century*, IX (London, 1815), 778; see also French, "The Autographs of John Milton," no. 23a, and CM, XVIII, 550. According to Nichols, John Sharp owned a copy of the *Poems* in 1761 which contained "many manuscript stanzas, for aught I know, in Milton's own handwriting, and several interlined hints and fragments." Dr. Johnson, to whom he showed it, was much pleased with it. But the wording of the statement is highly unconvincing, and no trace of the volume has been found since Nichols's reference to it.

JANUARY (?). JOHN EVELYN ACQUIRES A COPY OF
MILTON'S *POEMS*.

A copy of the *Poems* of 1645 with Evelyn's monogram in gold on
the sides and the back was sold at Sotheby's in 1894 for £63. Its later
history is not known. See *Book Prices Current*, VIII (1895), 424;
ibid., X (1897), 402-403; Luther S. Livingston, *Auction Prices of
Books*, III (New York, 1905), 227. Since there is no clue to the time
when Evelyn bought it, it is entered here.

JANUARY (?). SAMUEL PEPYS AND THE EARL OF
ANGLESEY ACQUIRE A COPY OF MILTON'S *POEMS*.

A copy of the *Poems* of 1645 containing Pepys's signature and
that of Lord Anglesey, who recorded that he paid two shillings for it,
belonged to Sir Richard Tangye; see Dr. Williamson's *Milton Tercentenary*, 1908, p. 118. The date when Pepys bought it is not given,
but since it is possible that he might have purchased it at this time, it
is entered here. Its history since 1908 is not known. Neither is it clear
from Williamson's note which of the two owners got the book first,
or which Earl of Anglesey it was. Williamson mentions Pepys's name
first.

JANUARY (?). RECEIVES REQUEST FROM JOHN ROUS,
LIBRARIAN OF THE BODLEIAN, FOR COPIES OF HIS
WRITINGS.

Ad Joannem Roüsium Oxoniensis Academiæ Bibliothecarium.

De libro poëmatum amisso quem ille sibi denuò mitti postulabat, ut cum aliis nostris in Bibliotheca publicâ reponeret, Ode
Joannis Miltonj.

Strophe I

Gemelle cultu simplici gaudens liber . . .

Quis te, parve liber, quis te fratribus
Subduxit reliquis dolo?
Cum tu missus ab urbe,
Docto jugiter obsecrante amico,
Jllustre tendebas iter
Thamesis ad incunabula. . . .

Milton's manuscript ode to Rous, bound now in the second part of
his *Poems*, 1645 (Bodleian MS. Lat. Misc., f. 15), following the
second title page. See the main entry for this poem under date of January 23, 1646/7.

John Milton · JANUARY 1646

[To John Rous, Librarian of Oxford University.

An ode of John Milton about a lost volume of my *Poems* which he (Rous) asked to be sent to him again, so that he might replace it in the public library with my others.

Double book rejoicing in a single cover . . .

Who, little book, stole you by fraud from the rest of your brothers when, at the urgent plea of my learned friend, you were sent from the city and took your glorious journey to the cradle of the Thames? . . .]

From the above excerpt from Milton's ode of January 23, 1647, and from the presentation inscription in the volume of his prose works which is now in the Bodleian, the inference seems sound that Rous asked Milton to send him a collection of his writings, both prose and verse. The prose volume could not have been sent earlier than the beginning of 1645, since it contains, among other titles, *Tetrachordon* and *Colasterion*. The poems, of course, were not available until after January 2, 1646. The date here used, some time in January, 1646, is therefore based on the assumption that shortly after learning of the issue of Milton's *Poems*, which first gave him some name in literature which was not so ephemeral as the prose pamphlets, Rous requested copies of all his writings. This date is purely hypothetical; it may have been any time before the latter part of 1646. In any case, enough time between this request and January 23, 1647, must be allowed for the request to reach Milton, for Milton to send the books, for the poems to be lost, for Rous to write another letter requesting a replacement, and for Milton to write the ode which he dated January 23, 1647.

JANUARY (?). SENDS PROSE WORKS AND POEMS TO JOHN ROUS.

Doctissimo viro, probóqz Librorum Æstimatori Joanni Roüsio, Oxoniensis Academiæ Bibliothecario, gratum hoc sibi fore testanti Joannes Miltonius opuscula hæc sua in Bibliothecam antiquissimam atqz celeberrimam adsciscenda libens tradit, tanquam in memoriæ perpetuæ Fanum, emeritamqz, uti sperat, invidiæ, calumniæqz vacationem; si Veritati Bonóqz simul Eventui satis litatum sit. Sunt autem

De reformatione Angliæ lib. 2.

De Episcopatu Prælatico lib. 1

De ratione politiæ Ecclesiasticæ lib. 2.

Animadversiones in Remonstrantis Defensionem lib. I

Apologia lib. I

Doctrina, et disciplina divortii lib. 2

Judicium Buceri de Divortio lib. I

Colasterion lib. I

Tetrachordon in aliquot præcipua scripturæ loca de Divortio instar lib. 4

Areopagitica, sive de libertate Typographiæ Oratio

De Educatione Ingenuorum epistola

Poemata Latina, et Anglicana sporsim.

Presentation inscription in the volume of Milton's collected works in the Bodleian which is now catalogued as 4°. F. 56. Th.; French, "The Autographs of Milton," # 24; Sotheby (facsimile), p. 120; CM, XVIII, 269, 548. The date of the inscription and of the sending of Milton's books to Rous is uncertain, but it must be after the receipt of Rous's request (catalogued above as January, 1646) and Milton's Latin ode of January 23, 1647.

[To the most learned man, and excellent judge of books, John Rous, Librarian of the University of Oxford, on his testifying that this would be agreeable to him, John Milton gladly forwards these small works of his, with a view to their reception into the University's most ancient and celebrated Library, as into a temple of perpetual memory, and so, as he hopes, into a merited freedom from ill-will and calumny, if satisfaction enough has been given at once to Truth and to Good Fortune. They are—'Of Reformation in England,' 2 Books; 'Of Prelatical Episcopacy,' I Book; 'Of the Reason of Church-government,' 2 Books; 'Animadversions on the Remonstrant's Defence,' I Book; 'Apology against the same,' I Book; 'The Doctrine and Discipline of Divorce,' 2 Books; 'The Judgment of Bucer on Divorce,' I Book; 'Colasterion,' I Book; 'Tetrachordon: An Exposition of some chief places of Scripture concerning Divorce,' 4 Books; 'Areopagitica, or a Speech for the Freedom of the Press;' 'An Epistle on Liberal Education;' and 'Poems, Latin and English,' separately.]

Masson, III, 647.

John Milton · JANUARY 1646

Antistrophe [1]

Quis te, parve liber, quis te fratribus
Subduxit reliquis dolo?
Cum tu missus ab urbe,
Docto jugiter obsecrante amico,
Jllustre tendebas iter
Thamesis ad incunabula
Cærulei patris,
Fontes ubi limpidi
Aonidum, Thyasúsqz sacer
Orbi notus per immensos
Temporum lapsus redeunte cælo,
Celeberqz futurus in ævum. . . .

Antistrophe [2]

Quin tu, libelle, nuntii licet malâ
Fide, vel oscitantiâ,
Semel erraveris agmine fratrum,
Seu quis te teneat specus,
Seu qua te latebra, forsan unde vili
Callo teréris institoris insulsi,
Lætare felix, en iterum tibi
Spes nōva fulget posse profundam
Fugere Lethen, vehiqz superam
In Iovis aulam remige pennâ. . . .

From Milton's Ode to Rous, January 23, 1647, *q.v.*

[Who, little book, stole you by fraud from the rest of your brothers when, at the urgent plea of my learned friend, you were sent from the city and took your glorious journey to the cradle of the Thames, the blue father, where are the limpid fountains of the Muses and the sacred dance, known to the world while the heavens have revolved through immense stretches of time, and to be famous forever? . . .

But you, little book, although by the bad faith of a messenger or by laziness you have wandered from the company of your brothers, whatever cave or whatever shady place may contain you, where perhaps you are rubbed to pieces by the dirty, tough hand of a stupid hawker, rejoice and be happy. Lo! new hope shines for you again that you can escape from Lethe and be carried on winged oar to the high court of Jove.]

Masson (III, 648, note) repeats Warton's story of how these two presentation volumes were almost lost to the Bodleian for a second time when a book-collector named Nathaniel Crynes was allowed to have his pick of certain volumes then in the library. "Fortunately Mr. Crynes did not care for the Milton volumes, and so they went back to the shelves."

January 22. Reissue of Baillie's Book Containing Attack on Milton.

Robert Baylie, *A Dissvasive*, second impression, 1645. The Thomason copy in the British Museum bears a manuscript note on the title page: "2de Impression"; and another: "Jan: 22th." With a few trifling alterations in spelling and punctuation, the section on Milton is identical with that in the first impression, noted above under date of November 24, 1645.

February 9. Writes Sonnet to Henry Lawes.

To my freind Mr Hen. Laws Feb. 9. 1645
Harry, whose tunefull & well-measur'd Song. . . .

Milton, Cambridge Manuscript, p. 43; Henry and Williams Lawes, *Choice Psalmes put into Musick For Three Voices*, 1648, sig. a2 (but the pagination is irregular); Milton, *Poems*, 1673, p. 57; CM, I, 63. The sonnet occurs three times in the manuscript with numerous changes. The heading quoted above is from the first occurrence. The second, also on the same page, begins: "To M^r: Hen: Lawρ on the publishing of his Airρ/ Harry, whose tuneful & well-measur'd Song. . . ." The third, on p. 45, is: "To M^r: H. [first written "Hen.," then the "en" deleted] Laweρ [the "e" added over a caret] on [next appeared "the publishing of," later deleted] his Aireρ/ Harry whose tunefull & well-measur'd Song." In Lawes's volume it stands: "To my Friend M^r. Henry Lawes./ Harry, whose tunefull and well measur'd song . . . J. Milton." In the *Poems* of 1673 it is "*To Mr. H. Lawes, on his Aires./* XIII./ Harry whose tuneful and well measur'd Song. . . ." Facsimiles are found in Fletcher, Facsimile, I, 43, 368, 445, 449.

February 17. Attacked in Print by John Bachiler.

I know it is objected that many dangerous Bookes come out by my Licens. . . . To this I answer.

First, The Books which meet with *harshest* censure, such as the *Bloody Tenet*, the Treatise about *Divorce*, and others that have Affinitie with these, I have been so farre from licensing, that I have not so much as *seene* or *heard* of them, till after they have been commonly sold abroad. . . .

John Bachiler

John Goodwin, *Twelve Considerable Cautions*, 1646, facing the title page, sig. Av; William Haller, *Tracts on Liberty*, 1934, I, 137-138; Parker, *Milton's Contemporary Reputation*, p. 76. The quotation is from the statement of John Bachiler, the licenser, published in Goodwin's book. The "Treatise about *Divorce*" is presumably Milton's *Doctrine and Discipline of Divorce*, which is frequently coupled with Roger Williams's book in contemporary attacks. The date is taken from the Thomason copy in the British Museum, on the title page of which the "6" of the date is erased, and the date written in: "feb. 17 1645."

FEBRUARY 26. DIVORCE VIEWS ATTACKED BY EDWARDS.

154. That 'tis lawfull for a man to put away his wife upon indisposition, unfitnesse or contrariety of minde arising from a cause in nature unchangeable; and for disproportion and deadnesse of spirit, or something distastefull and averse in the immutable bent of name; and man in regard of the freedome and eminency of his creation, is a law to himself in this matter, being head of the other sex, which was made for him, neither need he hear any judge therein above himself.

155. 'Tis lawfull for one man to have two wives at once.

Thomas Edwards, *Gangræna*, 1646, p. 34. The paragraphs quoted are two of a long list of heresies of various kinds which the author condemns. The bibliography of this book is somewhat confused. Thomason's copy, from which this text is taken, has the year 1646 crossed out in pen and 1645 substituted (i.e., 1645/6), and "feb: 26th" added. Yet Robert Baillie wrote in the late fall or winter of 1645: "some late books have done them [the ministers of London] good; especially Mr. Edwards's Gangrena"; *Letters and Journal*, II (1775), 177. A Second Part is dated May 28 by Thomason, and a Third Part December 28. A second edition of *Gangræna* also appeared in 1646, and at least three editions of a First and Second Part. All have references to Milton, but they vary considerably. Those which Thomason dated are here entered under his dates; the others are grouped together under June, 1646.

See also Masson, III, 467-468; Parker, *Milton's Contemporary Reputation*, pp. 76-77.

Of Marriages and of Parents and children Vid. Miltons *doctrine of divorce.*

Edwards, *ibid.*, marginal note.

APRIL 20 OR 25. BROTHER CHRISTOPHER TAKES COVENANT.

These are to certifie that Christopher Milton of London in the County of Middlesex Esqz. did freely & fully take the Nationall Covenant and subscribe the same.

Vpon the ffive and twentieth Day of Aprill 1646. The sayd Covenant being administered unto him according to order by me Wiłłm Barton Minister of John zecharies London.

[Endorsed] Mr Christopher Milton Took the Oath this 8th of August 1646.   Tho: Vincent.

Public Record Office SP 23/187, p. 199; Hamilton, p. 63. In another document (Composition Papers, second series, xiv, 193) which Hamilton also quotes (p. 62) the date is given as April 20, and Christopher's residence is given as Reading, Berks, rather than London.

MAY 16. AFFIDAVIT OF BROTHER CHRISTOPHER'S RESIDENCE AT EXETER.

We doe hereby certifie that diuerse credible persons now dwelling in this cittie haue witnessed before vs that Christopher Milton did inhabit in this City within sea[ven] moneths before the surrender of the same into the hands of his Excellency Sir Thomas Fairefax. Giuen at Exeter vnder our hands this sixteenth day of May 1646.   J Bury
                    Ed: Wolfe.

[Endorsed] Christopher Milton
        No: 732
        7°. Sept. 1646
        Intrat^r./
        Rep: 21: Dec. 49
        ffine—200 łi.
B. 228.
P. 13.
X. 434.
Ta. 107.

John Milton · MAY 1646

Public Record Office SP Dom 23/187, p. 201; Hamilton, pp. 63-64. Exeter had surrendered on April 10, 1646; see Masson, III, 485.

Christopher Milton . . . was a Com^r. for the Kinge, vnder the greate seale of Oxford, for sequestringe the Parliam^{ts} ffreinds of three Countyes, and afterwards went to Excester, and liued there, and was there at the tyme of the surrender. . . .

From the record of August 25, 1646, *q.v.*

MAY 28. PUBLICATION OF STORY OF EFFECT OF MILTON'S DIVORCE VIEWS ON MRS. ATTAWAY.

There are two Gentlemen of the Inns of Court, civil and well disposed men, who out of novelty went to hear the women preach, and after Mistris *Attaway* the Lace-woman had finished her exercise, these two Gentlemen had some discourse with her, and among other passages she spake to them of Master *Miltons* Doctrine of Divorce, and asked them what they thought of it, saying, it was a point to be considered of; and that she for her part would look more into it, for she had an unsanctified husband, that did not walk in the way of *Sion*, nor speak the language of *Canaan*; and how accordingly she hath practised it in runing away with another womans husband, is now sufficiently known to M^r. *Goodwin* and M^r. *Saltmarsh*, and one of the lies like all the rest in M^r. *Edwards Gangraena*.

Thomas Edwards, *The Second Part of Gangræna*, 1646, part 2, pp. 10-11; Masson, III, 189 ff.; Parker, *Milton's Contemporary Reputation*, pp. 76-77. On the bibliography of Edwards's book see the entry of February 26, 1646. Parker's text is given as being from the second edition, p. 9.

There are other references to the activities of Mrs. Attaway in the book, including a series of letters between her and William Jenney, a preacher who left his wife and children, as she did her husband, to run off to Jerusalem or Jericho. Her name appears in at least one place as Atomy. In various forms of the book these items occur on pp. 87-89, 119-121, and 220-223.

Masson dates the episode itself "in and about 1644," but because of the difficulty of being sure of either the date or the authenticity of it, mention of it is here confined to the entries from Edwards which describe it.

The date of this entry is that of the Thomason copy.

MAY-JUNE. SIR ROBERT PYE TAKES POSSESSION OF FOREST HILL.

Anne Powell the widdow of Richard Powell late of Forresthill in ye Countye of Oxford Esqr. maketh oath, y^t Laurence Farre seruant to Sr Robert Pye ye elder of Westmr: K^{nt}. did in the month of May or beginning of June 1646, in the behalfe and for ye vse of his sayd Master Sr Robert Pye ye elder, Enter and take possession of ye cheife Mansion house of Forresthill wth ye appurten^{ts}. (mortgaged to ye sayd Sr Robert Pye by ye sayd Richard Powell by his deed dated June 30th. 1640.) before any sequestraćon layd vpon that or any other part of ye sayd Richard Powells estate: W^{ch} possession the sayd Robert Pye or his assignes hath euer since continued.

Anne Powell.

Jurat coram Comissionar.
   31° December 1650
      R M

Public Record Office, SP Dom 23/109, p. 524; Hamilton, p. 90. This document is given here because it furnishes the background for the later law-suit between Pye and Milton over this property; see below under date of February 11, 1647. For further details see French, *Milton in Chancery*, chapters VI, VII, VIII, and corresponding appendixes.

And it is deposed by Ann Powell widow, That for non-payment of the said 1510^{li}. the said Sr Robert Py entred vpon the said premisses in May or June 1646 before any sequestraćon layd therevpon.

John Reading's report, January 1, 1650, Public Record Office, SP Dom 23/109, p. 517. Other references occur in other documents; see Hamilton, pp. 56, 85, 101.

JUNE (?). ATTACK BY EDWARDS REPRINTED.

The attack on Milton's divorce views printed under date of February 26, 1645/6, is found in several editions which can be dated only within the year 1646. Substantially the passage as there given is found in *Gangræna*, second edition, p. 34, in *The First and Second Part of Gangræna*, p. 29, and in the third edition of the latter title, p. 29. I have not seen the second edition of *The First and Second Part*, but probably the second edition of *Gangræna* takes its place. The placing of this entry here under the month of June is a mere approximation.

John Milton · JUNE 1646

JUNE 5. WILL OF WILLIAM BLACKBOROW, WITNESSED BY MILTON, PROVED.

A summary of the will is given above under date of April 11, 1645, the date of its being signed by Milton and others. It was proved in the Prerogative Court of Canterbury on June 5, 1646, and is catalogued as 82 Twisse. See J. and G. F. Matthews, *Abstracts of the Probate Acts of the Prerogative Court of Canterbury*, IV (London, 1906), 83; *Athenaeum*, 1880, I, 566; William McMurray, *The Records of Two City Parishes*, London, 1925, p. 213. The will was proved by Hester Blackborow, relict, and their son William, executors. Administration was granted.

JUNE 16. FATHER-IN-LAW RICHARD POWELL'S PROPERTY APPRAISED AND SOLD.

[Endorsed] A Coppy of ye Inventory, w^th: ye prices of ye goods, as they were appraysed ye 16th. of June 1646.

Jn a Trunke of Linēn as followeth:
1: pre of Sheetes: 5 Napkins: 6: y^rds. of broad
Tiffany: 3: pre of Pillow beares: 1: Hand
Towell. 1: Hollan Cubboard Cloth. 1: remnant
of new Holland   00-16-00

Jn ye Backside.
240: pieces of Tymber. 200: loades of fire-
wood. 4: Carts. 1: Wane. 2: old Coaches.
1: Mare-Colt. 3: Sowes. 1: Boare. 2: Ewes.
3: pcells of boards   156-12-2
  Jn ye Wooll-house, Hoppes at   002-00-00
  Jn ye Comon, 100: Butts at   60-00-00
        one Bull   01-10-00
M^r. Eldridge hath in his hand as much ⎫
Tymber as he was to give M^r. Powell for it ⎬   100-00-00
At Lusher's ffarme, The piece of Corne in y^e
great Field at   42-00-00
The Broad Meddow eaten vp by ye Souldiers; ⎫
One greate ground eaten vpp   ⎬   —not praysed
One Ground called Pilfrance at   ⎭   10-00-00
More 1: piece of Wheate   06-13-04

[147]

Mr. Powell hath at Forresthill, 16. yard land,⎫
wch. was vsually sett at 8^{li}. or 9^{li}. yeere;⎬   not praysed
and the Tith of all ye field ⎭

M^r. Powell hath at Wheatley, 1. House & 3.⎫
yrd. Land, Free land: & 3 yrd. Land & halfe⎬   474-00-00
vpon Lease. ⎭

      Wee have in our hands,

Wee have in money	23-00-00
32. pieces of Silver	
2. little Silver spoones	
1. broken Silver spoone	
1 Clock Bell at	02-00-00
14: q^rters of Mastline at	14-00-00
5. q^rters of Malt	05-00-00
6: Bushells of Wheate	01-02-00

     Jn ye Studdy or Boyes chamber wch. should
have followed next after ye Little chamber over
ye Pantry
1: Bed-stedd, wth. greene Curtaines & Vallons laced.
1. feather bedd. 1. feather bolster. 1. pre
of blanketts. 1. yellow Coverlid. 1: old
horseman's Coate wth. Silver buttons.
1. great chaire. 1. great Chest. 2: Court
Cupboards. One standing Press wth.
Drawers.   02-13-00

     Sold vnto M^r. Matthew. Appletree all ye goods in this Jn-
ventory appraysed, y^t. is to say ye Household goods.

Jn ye Hall	01-04-00
Jn ye Great Parlour	07-00-00
Jn ye Little Parlour	03-00-00
Jn ye Kitchin	01-04-00
Jn ye Pastry	01-10-00
Jn ye Pantry	00-10-00
Jn ye Bakehouse	03-06-00
Jn ye Brew-house	03-06-00
Jn ye Vpper dary house	01-12-00

Jn yᵉ Seller	01-15-00
Jn yᵉ Stilling Roome	01-01-00
Jn yᵉ Cheese-presse house	00-12-06
Jn yᵉ Matted chamber	04-16-00
Jn yᵉ chamber over yᵉ Hall	02-18-00
Jn yᵉ chamber over yᵉ little Parlour	03-15-00
Jn yᵉ two little chambers over yᵉ Kitchin	01-00-00
Jn ye Servants chamber	02-00-00
Jn yᵉ little chamber over yᵉ Pantry	03-03-00
Jn yᵉ Studdy or Boyes chamber	02-13-00
Jn Mʳˢ. Powells chamber	08-04-00
Jn Mʳˢ. Powells Closett	02-09-06
Jn yᵉ roome next yᵉ Closett	01-10-00
Jn yᵉ Roome over yᵉ Wash-house	07-09-00
Jn Mʳ. Powell's Studdy	01-14-00
Jn yᵉ same roome more Liñen	00-16-00
Malt; Mastline; Wheate; A Clocke & Bell	22-02-00
Jn yᵉ backside: 4. Hogges: 2. Ewes: 1. Mare & fold: 3. parcells of board: 240. pieces of Tymber: 200. load, or thereabouts, of fire-wood: 1. Wayne, 4. Carts 2. Coaches	156-12-02
Wood lying in yᵉ Common, 100. Butts	60-00-00
Jn yᵉ wooll-house Hoppes	02-00-00
A Bull	01-10-00
	310-12-02

Witnesse
John
Clontno
[?]
his Marke

Witnesse
8 his marke.
Vesing his marke

Sold these goods yᵉ 16. of June 1646. by vs whose names are vnder written for yᵉ Suͫe of Three hundred thirty and five pounds vnto yᵉ abovesaid Mʳ. Appletree, & pd. yᵉ same time to John King in pt of payment yᵉ Suͫe of Twenty Shillings; & yᵉ Rest to bee pᵈ. at yᵉ. delivery

John Webb:
Richard Vivers
John King.

Vera Copia. Ex^{ta}

27°. febr. 1650.   Tr: Pauncefote Reg^r.

J make oath this is a true Copie

         Tr. Pauncefote,

         R.M.

[On a separate piece of paper, probably originally part of the above:]

     Jn ye first Cart.

1. Arras worke chayre.	1. Tapestry Carpett.
6. Thrum chayres.	1. Wrought carpett.
6. wrought stooles.	1. Carpett greene wth. fringe.
2. Old greene carpetts.	3: Window Curtaines.

Public Record Office, SP Dom 23/110, pp. 547-548; *Calendar of the Committee for Compounding*, p. 1440; Hamilton, pp. 92-94. It should be noted that this is a true copy, not the original inventory. Probably the original is lost. In 1791, apparently, Thomas Warton had it, either permanently or on loan. In his edition of Milton's *Poems upon Several Occasions* (London, 1791, second edition, p. xxxi), he says: "I have now before me an original 'Inventorie of the goods of Mr. Richard Powell of Forresthill, in the county of Oxon, taken the 10th of June A.D. 1646.' . . . By the number, order, and furniture of the rooms, he appears to have lived as a country gentleman, in a very extensive and liberal style of house-keeping." The document printed above fits his description. Warton also adds: "I have also seen in Mr. Powell's house at Forresthill many papers, which shew the active part he took in favour of the Royalists. With some others relating to the Rangership of the Shotover forest, bearing his signature." This note is repeated in Todd, 1 (1826), 269.

The exact spellings of the names of the witnesses who made their marks without being able to write is not clear. I give the nearest transliteration which I can.

This inventory is written in a hand which is strikingly like Milton's. Since Milton was probably a better business man than Powell, was soon to hold public office under the new government, and was Powell's creditor in a considerable sum of money, it is quite possible that he should have written the inventory. See also the entirely different summary of Powell's property given below under date of November 21, 1646, which also looks as if it might be in Milton's hand.

For other references to the inventory and sale of Powell's goods, see Hamilton, pp. 82-83, 88, 111.

JUNE 24. SURRENDER OF OXFORD, AFFECTING THE POSSESSIONS OF MILTON AND THE POWELLS.

. . . 11. That all Lords, Gentlemen, Clergymen, Officers, Soldiers, and all other persons in *Oxon*, or comprised within this Capitulation, who have Estates Real or Personal, under or liable to Sequestration, according to Ordinance of Parliament, and shall desire to compound for them (except Persons by Name excepted by Ordinance of Parliament from Pardon) shall at any time within Six Months after rendring the Garrison of *Oxford*, be admitted to compound for their Estates; Which Composition shall not exceed Two Years Revenue for Estates of Inheritance; and for Estates for Lives, Years, and other Real and Personal Estates, shall not exceed the Proportion aforesaid for Inheritances according to the Value of them: And that all persons aforesaid, whose Dwelling Houses are sequestrated (except before excepted) may after the rendring of the Garrison, repair to them, and there abide, convenient time being allow'd to such as are placed there under the Sequestration, for their Removal.

And it is agreed, That all the Profits and Revenues arising out of their Estates (after the day of entring their Names as Compounders) shall remain in the hands of the Tenants or Occupiers, to be answered to the Compounders when they have perfected their Agreements for their Compositions; and that they shall have liberty and the General's Pass and Protection for their peaceable repair to, and abode at their several Houses or Friends; and to go to *London* to attend their Compositions, or elsewhere, upon their necessary occasions, with Freedom of their Persons from Oaths, Engagements, and Molestations, during the space of Six Months; and after, so long as they prosecute their Compositions, without wilful default or neglect on their part, except an Engagement by promise not to bear Arms against the Parliament, nor wilfully to do any Act prejudicial to their [i.e., the Parliament's] Affairs, so long as they remain in their Quarters. And it is further agreed, That forthwith after their Compositions made, they shall be forthwith restored to, and enjoy their Estates, and all other Immunities, as other Subjects do, together with the Rents and Profits from the time of entring their Names, discharged of Sequestrations, and from Fifth and Twentieth Parts, and other Payments and Impositions, except such as shall be general, and common to them with others.

Bulstrode Whitelocke, *Memorials of the English Affairs*, 1732, p. 211; John Rushworth, *Historical Collections*, Part IV, Vol. I (1701), pp. 282-283; Masson, III, 472-473. Since Milton and the Powells owned property near Oxford, they were both affected by this article of the terms of surrender.

JUNE 27. FATHER-IN-LAW RICHARD POWELL GRANTED PASS TO LEAVE OXFORD.

Sir Thomas Fairfax *Knight* Generall *of the Forces raised by the* Parliament.

Suffer the Bearer hereof 𝕸𝖗 𝕽𝖎𝖈𝖍𝖆𝖗𝖉 𝕻𝖔𝖜𝖊𝖑𝖑 𝖔𝖋 𝖋𝖋𝖔𝖗𝖗𝖊𝖘𝖙𝖍𝖎𝖑𝖑 𝖎𝖓 𝖙𝖍𝖊 𝕮𝖔𝖚𝖓𝖙𝖞 𝕺𝖝𝖔𝖓 who was in the City and Garrison of OXFORD, at the Surrender thereof, and is to have the full benefit of the *Articles* agreed unto upon the Surrender, quietly and without let or interruption, to passe your Guards with 𝕳𝖎𝖘 Servants, Horses, Armes, Goods, and all other necessaries, and to repaire unto *London* or elsewhere upon 𝕳𝖎𝖘 necessary occasions. And in all Places where he shall reside, or whereto he shall remove, to be protected, from any Violence to 𝕳𝖎𝖘 Person, Goods, or Estate, according to the said *Articles*, & to have full Liberty at any time with in Six Months, to goe to any convenient Port, and to Transport 𝕳𝖎𝖒-selfe, with 𝕳𝖎𝖘 Servants, Goods, and Necessaries beyond the Seas, And in all other things to enjoy the Benefit of the said *Articles*. Hereunto due obedience is to be given, by all Persons whom it may concerne, as they will answer the contrary. *Given under my Hand and Seale the* 𝟤𝟩𝖙𝖍 Day of 𝕵𝖚𝖓𝖊 1646.

𝕿. 𝖋𝖆𝖎𝖗𝖋𝖆𝖝.

To all Officers and Souldiers vnder my Command, and to all others whom it may Concerne.

[Endorsed] 𝕽𝖎𝖈𝖍𝖆𝖗𝖉 𝕻𝖔𝖜𝖊𝖑𝖑 𝕹° 1137
𝕯𝖊𝖈: 1646
𝕽𝖊𝖕: 1°: 𝕺𝖈𝖙 49 𝖋𝖋𝖎𝖓𝖊 180ˡ.

Public Record Office, SP Dom 23/194, p. 407; Hamilton, p. 75. The words printed in boldface are in manuscript; the rest is a printed form. The order of Dec. 8, 1649, dates this June 20, but the original, as above, is dated June 27. Probably Powell went very soon to Milton's house in London, where he died a few months later; see below under date of January 1, 1647.

JULY 15. FATHER-IN-LAW RICHARD POWELL'S LUMBER ASSIGNED TO THE TOWN OF BANBURY FOR REPAIRS.

Die Mercurii, 15° die Julii. . . .

A Petition of the inhabitants of *Banbury*, was read; complaining, That the One Half of the Town is burned down, and Part of the Church and Steeple pulled down; and there being some Timber and Boards at one Mr. *Powell's* house, a Malignant, near *Oxford*, they desire they may have those Materials assigned them, for the repair of their Church and Town.

It is ORDERED, That this House thinks fit to grant this Petition; and to desire the Concurrence of the House of Commons therein, and that an Ordinance may be drawn up to that Purpose.

Journal of the House of Lords, VIII, 433-434; Hunter, p. 32 (passing mention, not text); Hamilton, p. 111 (passing mention); Stern, I, ii, 388, 490; Masson, III, 482.

Die Mercurii, 15° Julii, 1646. . . .

The humble Petition of the inhabitants of *Banbury* was read, And

It is thereupon *Ordered*, That the Timber and Board cut down by one Mr. *Powell*, a Malignant, out of *Forrest* Wood near *Oxford*, and sequestered, being not above the value of Three hundred Pounds, be bestowed upon the Inhabitants of the town of *Banbury*, to be employed for the Repair of the Church and Steeple, and Rebuilding of the Vicarage House and common Gaol there; And that such of the said Timber and Boards, as shall remain of the Uses aforesaid, shall be disposed by the Members of both Houses which are of the Committee for *Oxfordshire*, to such of the well-affected Persons of the said Town, for the Rebuilding of their Houses, as to the said Members, or major Part of them, shall seem meet.

Journals of the House of Commons, IV, 617-618; Masson, III, 482.

[Anne Powell complains on December 14, 1649] That the hono^{ble} howse of Parliament vpon some misinformačon not takinge notice of the said Artickles did in July one thowsand sixe hundred fortie sixe order the said wood to severall uses which was there vpon togeither with the rest of his goods and moveables seized and carried away by the Sequestrato^{rs} to the Comittee for Oxoñ contrary to the said Artickles.

From Anne Powell's petition of December 14, 1649, *q.v.* The action is mentioned in other documents, such as the certificate of June 1, 1650, and Anne Powell's petition of October 20, 1652 (?).

The greatest pt of the psonall estate of the said Powell by Ordinance of Parliam^t of the 15th. of August 1646 was given to the Church & Towne of Banbury) the rest of his the said Powells estate is now in question before the Comissioners for Articles . . .

Will: Drap:
Tho Apletree.

From a letter of June 1, 1650, *q.v.*

JULY 29. DAUGHTER ANNE BORN.

My daughter Anne was born July the 29th on the fast at eevning about half an howre after six 1646.

British Museum, Add. MS. 32,310, in Milton's own hand in his family Bible; Darbishire, p. 336.

Anne my Daughter was born July the 29th. the day of the Monthly fast between six & seavn, or about half an hour after six the Ev'ning 1646.

British Museum, Add. MS. 4244, f. 52v (Birch's transcript of Mrs. Milton's Bible, which is no longer extant); Stern, I, ii, 490; Masson, III, 483, and IV, 335. Both of Masson's entries contain curious errors, though quite different from each other. In the transcript in Volume III he reads "morning" instead of "Ev'ning"; in Volume IV he corrects this error but introduces a new one which was not in Volume III: for "the Ev'ning" he reads "she living."

. . . the first fruits of her [Mary Powell Milton's] return to her Husband was a brave Girl, born within a year after; though, whether by ill Constitution, or want of Care, she grew more and more decrepit.

Phillips, p. xxvii; Darbishire, p. 67.

AUGUST 6. FATHER-IN-LAW RICHARD POWELL PETITIONS TO COMPOUND FOR HIS ESTATES.

To the hon^{ble}: the Comittee sitting at Goldsmiths hall for Composicons./

The humble peticon of Richard Powell of fforrest hill in the County of Oxon. Esqz./

Sheweth

That you^r peticoners estate for the most parte lying in the Kings Quarters he did adhere to his Maiestys pty against the forces raised by the Parliam^t: in this vnnaturall warr, for which his Delinquency, his estate lyeth vnder Sequestracon./ He is comprised within those articles at the surrender of Oxford./

And humbly prayes to be admitted to his Composicon according to the said Articles./

And he shall pray &c

Richard Powell:/

Rec^d: 6°: Augusti 1646

26°: Novembr 1646 Refer'd to the Sub-Comittee

Public Record Office, SP Dom 23/194, p. 400; Calendar of the Committee for Compounding, p. 1439; Hamilton, pp. 75-76. See also Brereton's reports of March 4, 1650/1, and January 7, 1652/3.

AUGUST 7. BROTHER CHRISTOPHER PETITIONS TO COMPOUND.

To the hon^{ble}. Com^{tee}. for Composicons with Delinquents sittinge att Goldsmiths Hall./

The humble peticon of X̄popher Milton of Reddinge in the County of Berks Esqr./

Sheweinge,

That he executed a Comission of Sequestracons vnder the greate seale at Oxford for three Countyes, and was at Exeter at the tyme of the Surrender thereof late made vnto the Parliam^{te}.

And humbly prayes, that he may be admitted to Compound, and to receiue the benefitt of those Artickles:

And he shall pray &c./

Christopher Milton.

7: August: 1646.

Refer'd to ye Sub Com^{ttee}.

Public Record Office, SP Dom 23/187, p. 196; Calendar of the Committee for Compounding, p. 1448; Hamilton, p. 128.

AUGUST 7 (?). BROTHER CHRISTOPHER SUBMITS SCHEDULE OF HIS POSSESSIONS FOR COMPOUNDING.

A true perticuler of all the Estate Reall and Personall of me, Xp̄ofer Milton of Reddinge in the County of Berks, a Councello͡ʳ. at Lawe./

That I am seized in fee to mee and my heires in possession, of and in a certaine Messuage or Tenemᵗᵉ. Scituate Standinge and beinge within St. Martins parish Ludgate called the signe of the Crosse Keyes, and was of the yeerely value, before theis troubles—40ˡⁱ.

Personall estate J haue none but what hath bin seized and taken from mee, and converted to the vse of the State./

This is a true perticuler of all my estate reall and personall for which J onely desire to compound to free it out of Sequestraĉon, and doe submitt vnto and vndertake to satisfye and pay such ffine as by this Comᵗᵉᵉ. for Composiĉons with Delinquents shall be imposed and sett to pay for the same in order to the freedome and dischardge of my person and estate./

Chr̄: Milton./

Public Record Office, SP Dom 23/187, p. 197; Calendar of the Committee for Compounding, p. 1448; Hamilton, pp. 128-129. Although undated, this document accompanies Christopher Milton's petition of August 7, and may therefore be regarded as bearing about the same date.

AUGUST 8. BROTHER CHRISTOPHER TAKES OATH.

Mʳ Christopher Milton Took the Oath this 8ᵗʰ of August 1646.   Tho: Vincent.

Endorsement on the verso of the certificate of Christopher Milton's having taken the covenant; see under April 20 or 25, 1646.

AUGUST 25. BROTHER CHRISTOPHER'S PETITION ACTED ON AND HIS FINE SET.

Christopher Milton of Reddinge in the County of Berks Esqʳ. Councello͡ʳ. at Lawe./

His Delinquency that he was a Com^r. for the Kinge, vnder the greate seale of Oxford, for sequestringe the Parliam^{ts} ffreinds of three Countyes, and afterwards went to Excester, and liued there, and was there at the tyme of the surrender, and is to haue the benefitt of those Articles, as by the Deputy Gouerno^{rs}. certificate of that place of the 16th of May 1646. doth appeare.

He hath taken the Naconall Couenant before Willm̄ Barton minister of John Zacharies the 20th. of April 1646, and the negative oath heere the 8^t. August 1646./

He compounds vpon a perticular deliuered in vnder his hand by which he doth submit to such ffine &c. and by which it doth appeare,

That he is seized in ffee to him and his heirs in possession of and in a certaine messuage or Tentē scituate in St. Martins parish Ludgate called the signe of the Crosse Keys, and was of the yeerely value before theis troubles—40l^{i}./

Personall estate he hath none./

Will Thomson.

25 August 1646   fyne att the 3^d is 200l^{i}.
Jero^m Alexander.

Public Record Office, SP Dom 23/187, p. 193; Calendar of the Committee for Compounding, p. 1448; Hamilton, p. 62. An almost identical version of this record is found in SP Dom 23/54, pp. 681-682. Aside from trivial differences of spelling and the like, it differs from the above in omitting the two names at the end and, what is more important, in adding an alternative fine below that of 200 pounds given here. After the line reading "ffine at a 3^d:—200l^{i}," it adds: "at a 10th—080." As the later records will show, 80 pounds was the fine actually imposed.

The Town Clerk of Reading has courteously sent me the following quotation from John Man's *The History and Antiquities of the Borough of Reading*, 1816, p. 16: "When the peace of the country was restored . . . the new government compelled the royalists to compound for their estates. . . . In the list of the compounders returned to government, are the following gentlemen of this town: . . . Christopher Milton £80.0.0."

It appears that John Milton had some hand in this affair, perhaps by speeding up action of the petition, perhaps in bringing about a lowering of Christopher's fine. Edward Phillips's account (p. vi) speaks of "his composition made by the help of his Brother's Interest, with the then prevailing Power." Newton (*Paradise Lost*, 1749, I, lv) repeats this idea: "His brother Christopher Milton . . . was a strong royalist, & after the civil war made his composition thro' his brother's interest." We might add here Phillips's note (p. vi) about Christopher's later career: "But when the war was ended . . . and his composition made . . . he betook himself again to his former Study and Profession, following Chamber-Practice every Term, yet came to no Advancement in the World in a long time, except some small Employ in the town of *Ipswich*, where (and near it) he lived all the latter time of his Life." But more detailed information will be found later in the present records.

SEPTEMBER 7. BROTHER CHRISTOPHER'S FINE FURTHER ACTED ON.

7°: Septem͡br. 1646. . . .
Christopher Milton of Redding in Com Berkes Esq͡r.
Councello͡r: at Lawe - - - - - - { 0080: Att a Tenth:
{ 0200: At a third:

Public Record Office, SP Dom 23/3 (Order Book), p. 228; Calendar of the Committee for Compounding, p. 1448; Hamilton, p. 129.

By the Com͡rs. for Compounding 7° Sept: 1646
Christopher Milton of Reading in the County of Berk Councellor at Law was fined as followeth ffor an estate in fee in possession 40͡li p Ann for w͡ch his ffine was set at a 1/3 200͡li at 1/10 80͡li He was a Com͡r to sequester estates He came in vpon the Articles of Exceter.

Exaied 15° ffebr 1656. T Bayly Reg͡r.

Public Record Office, SP Dom 23/34 (Registrar's Certificates), p. 107; Hamilton, p. 129.

SEPTEMBER 24. BROTHER CHRISTOPHER PAYS HALF OF HIS FINE.

[Endorsed:] Extract of the Bonds Entred into by the Severall psons. within named To Michaell Herringe & Richard Wareinge Late Trers att the Receipt of Goldsmiths Hall./ . . .

[Cou]nties . . . Bērks . . . .

The names of the psons seq͡red. and place where theire Estate Lyes . . . Christopher Milton of Redding in the County of Berks. Esq͡r. . . . .

The names of the Securities and place of theire aboade . . .
William Keech of ffleetstreete London. Goldbeater. . . .
The Penalties of the bonds . . . 80:00:00. . . .
The date thereof . . . 24th Sept: 1646. . . .
Some due & payable . . . 40:00:00. . . .
Time when . . . 24th Decr. 1646. . . .
27 Sept. 1655 Ex^{ta} Dan: Hancock.

Public Record Office, SP Dom 23/82, p. 653; Hamilton, p. 130. In the original record the various items are arranged in vertical columns, with many entries under each. This entry seems to indicate that Christopher filed a bond for 40 pounds with the Commissioners on September 24, 1646, and that he was therefore expected to provide similar security for the other 40 pounds on December 24. Since there is a check mark against his name (like a capital V), we may suppose that he met these demands.

[Headed:] a Breviate of Accompts kept by vs Richard Waring and Michael Herring Tresūrers att Goldsmiths Hall with Delinquents. . . .
M . . . Milton Chr°: of Reading Berks. . . .
ffines . . . 0080/00/0. . . .
ffirst payments . . . . 24: of Sept 1646 0040/00/0. . . .
second payments . . . - - - . . . .
Rests . . . 0040/00/0

Public Record Office, SP Dom 23/43, p. 60. Like the preceding selection, the material in this one in the original is arranged in a series of columns, though it is changed here to paragraph form for ease in reproducing.

Christopher Milton, of Reading, in the county of Berks, esq., and William Keeth, of Fleet Street, London, goldbeater, bound to the same treasurers, the 24th of September, 1646, in . . . £80. With condition to pay £40 the 24 of December then next, together with [such other sum and sums of money as the House of Commons shall order to be paid as a further fine for Christopher Milton's delinquency.]

Hamilton, p. 129. Hamilton gives as his reference simply "Composition Papers." I have not found the original. The passage in brackets is as given in Hamilton.

OCTOBER 10. DIVORCE WORKS MENTIONED BY JOHN WILKINS (?).

The second edition of Wilkins's *Ecclesiastes*, 1647 (*q.v.*), mentions Milton's divorce books. Presumably the reference is also found in the first edition, which is dated October 10, 1646, by Thomason. But since I have not seen it, I can not be sure. Parker, *Milton's Contemporary Reputation*, p. 77, also uses the edition of 1647 for quotation.

NOVEMBER 21. FATHER-IN-LAW RICHARD POWELL'S GOODS INVENTORIED FOR COMPOUNDING.

A particular of the reall and personall Estate of Richard Powell of fforrest Hill

He is seised of an estate in fee of the Tythes of Whatley, in the parish of Cudsden, and three yard lands and a halfe there, together with certayne Cottages, worth before these times p annū } 040-00-0

This is morgadgd to Mr Ashworth for ninetye nine yeares for a security of four hundred pownds as appeares by deed bearing date the 10th of Jann: in the 7th of King Charles./

a lease for 99 years defeated by the paym^{te} of 400^l the 30 of Jan: 1642 ap^p unpd

His personall estate, in corne and household stuffe amounts too .... } 500-00-0

Jn Timber and wood 400-00-0

Jn debts upon specialityes and otherwise owing to him .... } 200-00-0

He oweth upon a statute to John Mylton .. 300-00-0

He is indebted more before these times by specialityes and otherwise to seuerall psons as appeares by affidauit .... } 1200-00-0

He lost by reason of these warres three thousand powndes.

This is a true pticular of the reall and personall estate that he doth desire to compound for with this honb^l: Comittee, wherein he doth submitt himselfe to such fine as they shall impose according to the Articles of Oxford wherin he is comprized. Rec^d: 21°: Novemƀr: 1646.   Richard Powell

Public Record Office, SP Dom 23/194, p. 403; Calendar of the Committee for Compounding, p. 1439; Hamilton, pp. 76-77.

A true copy of the text given above is found in SP Dom 23/110, p. 543. At the end is the note: "Vera Copia Tr: Pauncefote Reg^r." Several endorsements on the back refer to other papers on the Powells included in the sequestrators' records. The only discrepancy between the two versions is the omission, in the copy, of the marginal note.

There are three or four different handwritings in this document. One is that of the body of the document, a hand vaguely reminiscent of Milton's, though there is no reason to suppose that it is his. The second is that of the marginal note, "a lease . . . unpd," which is almost illegible and may be incorrectly transcribed. The third is Powell's signature, which may possibly be the same as number two, though it looks somewhat different. It is entirely different, by the way, from his signature to the document of December 4, 1646. The fourth is that of the date.

DECEMBER 4. FATHER-IN-LAW RICHARD POWELL TAKES THE COVENANT AND OATH.

These are to certifie, that Richard Powell of fforresthill in the County of Oxford Esquire did freely & fully take the Nationall Covenant and subscribe ye same, uppon the ffourth day of December 1646. The sayd covenant being administered unto him, according to order, by me,

Wiłłm Barton

(66.) Minister of John Zecharies London.

Probat. est.

[Endorsed:] Richard Powell of fforrest hill in the County of Oxford Esqr Took the oath this 4th of Decem♭ 1646.

Tho: Vincent

Public Record Office, SP Dom 23/194, p. 401; Calendar of the Committee on Compounding, p. 1439; Hamilton, p. 77.

DECEMBER 4. FATHER-IN-LAW RICHARD POWELL MAKES OATH OF HIS TRUE DEBTS.

Richard Powell of fforrest hill in the County of Oxford, maketh oath that the seüall summes of money mencōned to be oweing by him in his particular annexed to his petition at Gouldsmyths hall are trulie and reallie oweing by him. And further deposeth that he is the worse in his Estate att Leaste three thousand pounds by reason of these warres. And that the aforeẽd debtes were by him oweing before the beginning of this Parliament and are still oweing

Ric. Powell.

Jur.' 4° die Decembr. 1646.

John Page.

Public Record Office, SP Dom 23/194, p. 406; Calendar of the Committee for Compounding, p. 1439; Hamilton, p. 77.

DECEMBER 8. FATHER-IN-LAW RICHARD POWELL'S PETITION ACTED ON AND HIS FINE SET.

Richard Powell of Forrest hill in the County of Oxon, Esqr./

His Delinquency that he diserted his dwellinge and went to Oxford and lived there whiles it was a Garrison holden for the Kinge against the Parliam^{te}. and was there at the tyme of the Surrender, and to have the benefit of those Articles as by S^r. Thomas ffairfax certificate of the 20th. of June 1646. doth appeare.

He hath taken the Naconall Couenant before Wiłłm Barton minister of John Zacharies the 4th. of December 1646. and the negative oath heere the same daye./

He compounds upon a perticuler deliuered in vnder his hand, by which he doth submitt to such ffine &c. and by which it doth appeare,

That he is seized in ffee to him and his heirs in possession, of and in the tythes of Whatley, in the parish of Cudsden, and other Lands and Tents there, of the yeerely value before theis troubles—40^{li}./

That he is owner and possessed of a personall estate in goods, and there was oweinge vnto him in good debts, in all amountinge vnto 600^{li}.; and there is 400^{li}. more in Tymber which is alledged to be questionable./

That he is endebted by Statutes and bonds—1500^{li}.

He hath lost by reason of theis warrs—3000^{li}./

He craues to be allowed 400^{li}. which by a demise and lease dated the 30th. of January 1642 of the lands and Tents aforesaid is secured to be paid vnto one Thomas Ashworth gen. and is deposed to be still oweinge./

D. Watkins.

8 December 1646.   ffine at 2 yeeres value

Jero^m Alexander   180^ll:—

Public Record Office, SP Dom 23/194, p. 387; Hamilton, p. 78. A practically verbatim copy is found in SP Dom 23/54, p. 973, from which the signatures at the end are omitted, but which adds in their place: "Resolution of ye Comm:^ttee."

DECEMBER 16. SONNET ON MRS. GEORGE THOMASON.

On ye religious memorie of Mrs Catharine Thomason my christian freind deceas'd 16 Decem. 1646.

When Faith and Love which parted from thee never. . . .

Milton, Trinity Manuscript, pp. 44, 45; *Poems*, 1673, p. 58; CM, I, 63-64; Fletcher, I, 43, 446-449. There are three drafts of this sonnet in the Manuscript, of which only the first has a title, that given above, which was later scored through. The first line of the poem as quoted above is from the version in the *Poems* of 1673, in which the poem appears as sonnet 14. The first identification of the subject of this sonnet-elegy as the wife of Milton's bookseller-friend George Thomason was made by Smart, who furnishes a good deal of information about her on pp. 78 ff. and 161 ff. of his edition of the sonnets.

DECEMBER 16 (OR 15). OBTAINS CERTIFICATE ON FATHER-IN-LAW RICHARD POWELL'S BOND OF 1627.

Cert' in Canc' Dnī regis per me Thomā Hampson Barronettū Clīcu &c Decimo Sexto Die Decembris Año xxij^do Caroli Regni.

Endorsement on Statute Staple of June 11, 1627, *q.v.*

[Certified in the Chancery of our Lord the King by me, Thomas Hampson, Baronet and Clerk, etc., on the sixteenth day of December in the 22nd year of the reign of Charles.]

Cer in Canc. Dnī Rρ per me Thomā Hampson Barronettū Clīcu &c xv^to die Decemb^r A°: xxij^do. Car Rρ &c.

Public Record Office, L.C. 4/200, f. 265; French, *Milton in Chancery*, p. 293. The reason for the discrepancy of one day between the two versions is not clear.

[Certified in the Chancery of our Lord the King by me, Thomas Hampson, Baronet and Clerk, etc., on the 15th day of December in the 22nd year of King Charles etc.]

DECEMBER 23. FATHER-IN-LAW RICHARD POWELL'S
FINE FOR COMPOUNDING SET AT 180 POUNDS.

23°: December 1646. . . .
Richard Powell of fforest-hill in the County of Oxoñ
Esqᵣ:..0180: At a Tenth.

Public Record Office, SP Dom 23/3. Powell's name is one of about
fifteen whose fines were set at this time. See also above under date of
December 8, 1646.

DECEMBER 24. BROTHER CHRISTOPHER PAYS SECOND
HALF OF FINE (?).

The documents quoted above under date of September 24, 1646,
show that Christopher Milton paid 40 pounds on September 24 and that
a similar sum remained to be paid on December 24. See the note to the
earlier entry for the reason for believing that he paid the later sum
promptly.

DECEMBER 28. ATTACK BY EDWARDS REPUBLISHED.

Thomas Edwards, *The Third Part of Gangræna*, 1646, pp. 26-27,
113-116, 188. The text is substantially the same as that given in the
Second Part, May 28, 1646. The date is that of the Thomason copy.
A reference to this volume occurs in Robert Baillie's letter to William
Spang of about this time. (In Baillie's *Letters and Journal*, 1841, II,
416, the letter is undated, but it comes between one of December 25,
1646, and another of January 26, 1647.) Baillie says: "The increase
of all heresies here is very great, as you will perceive . . . in the third
part of Mr. Edwards's Gangrena."

DECEMBER 30. WITNESSES LAST WILL AND TESTAMENT
OF FATHER-IN-LAW RICHARD POWELL.

In the name of God Amen—I Richard Powell of fforresthill
alias fforsthill in the Countie of Oxon' Esquire being sick and
weak of bodie, but of perfect minde and memorie I praise God
therefore; This thirtieth daie of December in the yeare of our
lord God, One thousand six hundred ffortie and sixe, Doe make
and declare this my will and Testament in manner and forme
following ffirst and Principallie J Comend my soule to the
handes of Almighty God my maker trusting by the meritts
Death, and passion of his sonn Jesus Christ my Redeemer to
haue life euerlasting: And my bodie J comitt to the earth from

whence it came to be decentlie interred according to the discretion of my Executor hereafter named And for my worldlie estate which God hath blessed me withall J will and dispose as followeth./ Imprimis J giue and bequeathe vnto Richard Powell my eldest sonn my house at fforresthill alias fforsthill in the Countie of Oxford with all the houshould stuffe and goods there now remaineing and Compounded for by me since at Gouldsmiths hall, togeather with the woods and Timber there remaineing and all the landes to my said house of fforresthill belonging and heretofore therewith vsed, together with the ffines and profitts of the said landes and tenements to the said Richard Powell and his heires and assignes for euer. To this intent and purpose, and it is the true meaning of this my last will, that my landes and goods shalbe first employed for the satisfieing of my debts and ffunerall expenses, and afterwardes for the raiseing of portions for his brothers and sisters soe farr as the estate will reach, allowing as much out of the estate aboue menc̄oned vnto my said sonn Richard Powell as shall equall the whole to be deuided amongst his brothers and Sisters, that is to saie the one halfe of the estate to himselfe, and the other halfe to be deuided amongst his brothers and sisters that are not alredie prouided for, Jn which deuision my will is that his sisters haue a third parte more than his brothers. My will and desire is that my said Sonn Richard doe out of my said landes and personall estate herein mentioned, satisfie his mother my dearely beloued wife Ann Powell, that bond I haue entered into for the makeing her a Joynture which my estate is not in Condition now to dischardge: And lastlie I doe by this my last will and testament make and ordaine my sonn Richard Powell my sole executor of this my last will; And I doe hereby revoke all former wills by me made whatsoeuer, And my will farther is that in Case my said sonn Richard Powell shall not accept the Executorshipp, then I doe hereby Constitute and appointe and doe earnestly desire my dearely beloued wife Ann Powell to be my sole executrix, and to take vpon her the mannageing of my estate abouementioned to the vses and purposes herein expressed: And in case she doe refuse the same then I desire my loueing freind Master John Ellstone of fforesthill to take the executorshipp vppon him and to performe this my will as is here before expressed, to whome I give twentie shillings, to buy him a Ring. And my earnest desire is that my wife and my sonn have no difference concerning this my will and estate. Item J giue and bequeathe to my sonn Richard Powell all my houses and landes at Whately in the Countie of Oxford, and all other my estate reall and personall in the kingdom of England and dominion of Wales to the vse intent and purpose aboue herein expressed: And my desire is that my daughter Milton be had a reguarde to in the satisfieing of her portion and adding thereto in Case my estate will beare it; And for this estate last bequeathed in case my sonn take not upon him the Executorshipp, then my will is my beloved wife shall be sole executrix vnto whome I giue the landes and goods last aboue mentioned to the vses and purposes herein mentioned. Jn Case she refuses then J appoint Master John Ellstone my executor to the vses and purposes aboue mentioned: Jn witnes hereof I haue hereto put my hand and Seale, the daie and yeare first aboue written. ffor the ffurther strengthening of this my last will, J doe Constitute and appoint my loueing freinds Sir John Curson, and Sir Robert Pye the elder knights to be overseers of this my last will, desireing them to be aideing and assisting to my executor to see my last will performed according to my true meaneing herein expressed, for the good and benefitt of my wife and Children, And I give them as a token of my loue twentie shillings a peece to buy them each a Ring for their paines taken to aduise and further my executor to performe this my will: Richard Powell. Subscribed Sealed and acknowledged to be his last will in the presence of James Lloyd: John Milton   Henry Delahay./

Somerset House, P. C. C., 52 Fines; Masson, III, 636-637. In the margin near the beginning is the note: "T^m [testamentum] Richardi Powell." See also David H. Stevens, "Mary Powell's Lost Dowry," *Milton Papers*, Chicago, 1927, pp. 7-13. Apparently no part of the dowry was ever paid. This will was proved on March 26, 1647, by Richard Powell's relict Anne, and again on May 10, 1662, by his son Richard.

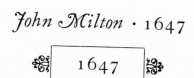

DIFFICULTIES IN RECOVERING LOAN TO POWELL AND LEGAL STEPS TOWARDS DOING SO.

[Sir Robert Pye, attempting to seize Forest Hill for a debt of Richard Powell to him,] hauing lately had and taken possession of the p^rmisses soe conueyed to him as aforesayd, is now, and lately hath binn hindered, and interrupted in the peaceable injoym^t thereof by one John Melton of London geñ who p^rtend℘ that hee hath some former Jnterest, and Estate of and in the same p^rmisses by and from the sayd Richard Powell by Mortgage Statute Recognizance Judgment, or some other Tytle Estate or Jnterest deriued from the sayd Richard Powell p^rcedent to yor. Orato^rs said Estate. And the sayd John Melton being often in a friendly manner desired by your Orato^r to discouer, and make knowne vnto him what estate Title Jnterest or Engagement hee hath or may clayme of or in the premisses or any parte thereof from the sayd Richard Powell, hath from tyme to tyme and still doth vtterly refuse to discou^r and make knowne the same vnto yor Orato^r whereby yor Orato^r cannot injoy the p^rmisses according to his Estate before menc̄oed, and sett forth contrary to Lawe, and Equity. . . .

From Sir Robert Pye's bill against Milton, February 11, 1647, *q.v.* The date is not made definite, but it must have been before February 11, probably fairly recently.

[Richard Powell owes interest to Milton,] which the said Richard Powell from tyme to tyme hath refused or neglected to pay though hee hath often bene in all freindlye manner thereto required by this Defeñdt wherefore and for that this Defeñdt hath now present occasions for his said moneys true it is, That hee this Defendt intendeth and indeauoureth by Due Course of lawe to putt the said Statute in execution, for the recouerye of his said iust true Debt and Damages . . . .

From Milton's answer to Pye's bill, February 22, 1647, *q.v.* A good deal of meeting and discussion between Powell and Milton, and between Pye and Milton, seems to be implied in these excerpts.

[Powell and William Hearne have not paid their debts to Milton;] and whereas they did not pay it to him, as is said: by our writ we have commanded you that the bodies of the aforesaid Richard Powell and William Hearne (if they were laymen) should be taken and held safely in our prison till they should have satisfied the aforesaid debt to the said John, and that all the lands and chattels of the said Richard and William in your county should be diligently extended and appraised by the oath of honest and lawful men of your said county by whom the truth of the matter might be the better known, according to the true value of the same, and that they should be seized into our hand in order that the same might be delivered over to the said John until full satisfaction should be made for the aforesaid debt according to the form of the statute published and provided at Westminster for the recovery of men's debts. And that you should make known to us in our Chancery on a certain day now past, wherever it should then be, by your sealed letters, how you executed our said order, and that you should have there our said writ. On which day as specified in our said writ you returned to us in our Chancery that the aforesaid Richard Powell was dead.

From the parliamentary order of July 16, 1647, to Sheriff William Cope of Oxfordshire, *q.v.* The writ here described has not been found. The date must have been early in 1647, probably in January, since Cope's return states that Powell is dead. The original document is in Latin.

SAMUEL HARTLIB MENTIONS MILTON IN HIS NOTES ABOUT EDUCATION.

[1] [M^r. Miltons *cancelled*] Academie. and Mr Lawrence Academie.

There should bee a Chamber or Office of Conference better then Nennidat [?].

An Office of Learned Addresse.

A Colledge for Mechanical Jnuentions. . . .

[2] S W. Wallers Colledge at Winchester. or Plantatio of Hampshire.

John Milton · 1647

A Worke-house at Winchester. . . .
Foundation of an Academy. his [removing of Mr Milton. *cancelled*] p'ses Dr Coxe. . . .

[3] Comissioners for the Act of the Councel for schooling

1	Mr Dury	6.	Needham.
2	Pell	7.	Milton.
3	Rand.	8	Collier seint.
4.	Dr Horne.		Heyling Wall.
5	Ramis. Dantine.		Eres. Tonge.

These three fragments are from the manuscripts of Samuel Hartlib in the collection of Lord Delamere; printed in part in G. H. Turnbull, *Hartlib, Dury and Comenius*, p. 40. Professor Turnbull thinks that although they are not dated, they probably belong to 1647 and concern the Office of Address. Since the handwriting is difficult to read, some of my transcriptions are not dependable, especially "Nennidat," "Ramis. Dantine," and "seint." But it is at least clear that, in attempting to formulate plans for changes in the system of education, Hartlib thought highly enough of Milton to mention him occasionally. The first two parts contain a great deal more than the few lines given above, whereas the third is complete as given.

DIVORCE WORKS MENTIONED BY JOHN WILKINS.

Of Divorce and Polygamy.
Lumbard li. 4. Aquinas in Supplem. p. 3.
The Casuists.
Wigandus de divortiis.
Beza de Polyg. & divortiis.
Edm: Bunny: *Of Divorce for adultery and marrying again.*

M. Milton { *Treatise.* *Vindication.* *Tetrachordon.*

Dove.

John Wilkins, *Ecclesiastes*, second edition, 1647, p. 87; Parker, *Milton's Contemporary Reputation*, p. 77. The first edition appeared in October, 1646; Thomason's copy is dated October 10. The whole book is chiefly a bibliography of books on various phases of religion. In an indirect way Milton is also mentioned under two other headings, through his connection with Smectymnuus. Under the title of "Concerning *Episcopacy* there are these Authors" on p. 51 are two columns of writers, the first headed *"Pro"* and the second *"Con."* One name under the first

is "B^p *Hall*," and one under the second is "*SMECTYMNWS.*" Under the section "Concerning Presbytery" on p. 52, one reference under the "*Con*" column is "The forecited Discourses that are for Episcopacy."

WRITES MARGINAL NOTES IN BEST'S *MYSTERIES DIS-COVERED* (?).

[1] To Election both Vocation and Adoption are Termes synonymal.

[2] Quod attinet ad Christi Personam . . . Filij Dei dici vix mereantur.

Paul Best, *Mysteries Discovered*, 1647, the Bodleian Library copy catalogued as Pamph. 84 (39), title page and pp. 16-18 respectively; CM, XVIII, 341-344 (text and translation), 572 (notes). The history of this note as a possible Miltonic annotation and the reasons for which it has been attributed to Milton by some readers are given in the last-named reference. The case is not strong. See also CM Fourth Supplement.

Best was considered an alarmingly heretical writer. On June 10, 1645, on information from the Assembly of Divines as to his blasphemies, the House of Commons had committed him to the Gatehouse prison, and on January 28, 1645/6, they resolved that an ordinance should be prepared to punish him with death; see *Journals of the House of Commons*, IV, 170, 420, as referred to in W. H. Hart, *Index Expurgatorius Anglicanus*, London, 1872 ff., p. 124, # 131. He was, however, released and lived until 1657.

BEFORE APRIL 21. RECEIVES LETTER FROM CARLO DATI.

Perlatis inopinatò Literis ad me tuis, mi Carole, quantâ, & quam novâ sim voluptate perfusus . . . scribis, ternas te jam olim ad me dedisse, quas ego periise scio . . . ais, ex quo Florentiâ discessi, meâ de salute solicitum, semperq; mei memorem fuisse . . . Exequias Ludovici Regis à te descriptas libenter lego, in quibus Mercurium tuum . . . agnosco.

From Milton's letter to Dati, April 21, 1647, *q.v.*

[With how great and what new pleasure I was filled, my Charles, on the unexpected arrival of your letter . . . you write that you had sent me three letters before, which I now know to have been lost . . . you say, that from the time of my departure from Florence you have been anxious about my health and always mindful of me . . . I am reading with pleasure your description of the funeral ceremony to King Louis, in which I recognize your style.]

Masson, III, 652-654.

PAGITT'S ATTACK REPUBLISHED.

[1] We have *Atheists* too many. . . . They preach, print and practise their hereticall opinions openly: for books, *vide* the bloody Tenet, witnesse a Tractate of divorce, in which the bonds are let loose to inordinate lust: a pamphlet also in which the soule is laid asleep from the houre of death unto the hour of judgement, with many others. . . .

[2] Concerning Divorces, Mr. *Milton* permits a man to put away his wife upon his meere pleasure, without any fault in her, but for any dislike, or disparity of nature. . . .

[3] *Divorcers*. These I terme Divorcers, that would be quit of their Wives for slight occasions; and to maintain this opinion, one hath published a Tractate of divorce, in which the bonds of marriage are let loose to inordinate lust, putting away wives for many other causes, besides that which our Saviour only approveth; namely in case of adulterie, who groundeth his errour upon the words of God, *Gen.* 2. 18. *I will make him a helpe meet for him.* And therefore if she be not an helper, nor meet for him, he may put her away, saith this Author. Which opinion is flat contrary to the words of our Saviour. . . .

Ephraim Pagitt, *Heresiography*, 1647 (third edition), sig. A4v, pp. 87, 150. The first selection is from the Epistle Dedicatory to the Aldermen of London, and is repeated from the first edition; the third selection first appeared in the second edition; the second, from a chapter on the Independents, appears in this edition for the first time. See Parker, *Milton's Contemporary Reputation*, pp. 74-75.

In the fourth edition, which is also dated 1647, these allusions come on pp. 86-87 and 145-146. Pagitt must have died about this time, since his will (92 Fines) was proved in the Prerogative Court of Canterbury on May 29, 1647: Matthews, *Year Books of Probate*, IV, 257.

JANUARY (?). SLIGHTING ALLUSION BY HENRY VAUGHAN (?).

The King Disguis'd.

Written about the same time that Mr. John Cleveland wrote his.

A King and no King! Is he gone from us,
And stoln alive into his Coffin thus?

. . .

Thou Royal Riddle, and in every thing
The true white Prince, our Hieroglyphic King!
Ride safely in his shade, who gives thee Light:
And can with blindness thy pursuers smite. . . .

Henry Vaughan, *Thalia Rediviva*, 1678, pp. 1-2; *The Works of Henry Vaughan* (ed. L. C. Martin), Oxford, 1914, II, 605-606. Mr. Martin notes (II, 704) that the Thomason copy of *Thalia Rediviva* bears a note on this poem, referring to the line dating this poem as about the same time as John Cleveland's: "Jan: 21 1646 London by Jo: Cleveland Poet." The copy of Cleveland's "The King's Disguise" in the Thomason collection is so dated. Miss Louise Imogen Guiney (*Quarterly Review*, CCXX [1914], 358) interpreted the last line quoted above as a reference to Milton, though of course Milton was not blind at this time. The normal interpretation of the line needs no such personal reference to Milton or anyone else.

JANUARY (?). JOHN ROUS REQUESTS REPLACEMENT COPY OF MILTON'S *POEMS* FOR BODLEIAN LIBRARY.

Ad Joannem Roüsium . . . De libro poëmatum amisso quem ille sibi denuò mitti postulabat. . . .

Nam te Roüsius sui
Optat peculi, numeroqz justo
Sibi pollicitum queritur abesse,
Rogatqz venias ille cujus inclyta
Sunt data virûm monumenta curæ:
Teqz adytis etiam sacris
Voluit reponi quibus et ipse præsidet
Æternorum operum custos fidelis,
Questorqz gazæ nobilioris,
Quam cui præfuit Jön
Clarus Erectheides
Opulenta dei per templa parentis
Fulvosqz tripodas, donaqz Delphica,
Jön Actæâ genitus Creüsâ. . . .
Jbis honestus,

John Milton · JANUARY 1647

Postquam egregiam tu quoqz sortem
Nactus abis, dextri prece sollicitatus amici.
From Milton's Ode to Rous, January 23, 1647, *q.v.*

[To John Rous . . . about a lost volume of my *Poems* which he asked to be sent to him again. . . . For Rous seeks you (the book) for his own possession, and complains that you, though promised to him, are missing from the just number; and he, to whose care are given the illustrious monuments of men, asks you to come. He has wished you to be placed again in the sacred shrines over which he himself presides, the faithful guardian of immortal works and the custodian of a nobler treasure than that over which Ion presided, the famous son of Erectheus in the rich temples of the god his parent, and the gilded tripods and Delphic gifts—Ion, born of Actaean Creusa. . . . You shall go in honor after you leave, having obtained an eminent fate, solicited by the request of a fortunate friend.]

It should be noticed that Rous twice asked for copies of Milton's work, if we can take this ode at its face value. The first request has been filed under the date of January, 1646; it was more general than this one, asking for Milton's writings in general. Somewhere along the way or after arrival in the Bodleian, the copy of the *Poems* of 1645 which Milton included evidently became lost. Thereupon Rous made his second request, of which this is the only record. Neither one is accurately datable, but it is likely that this second one came not so long before Milton answered it with his ode of January 23, 1647.

JANUARY 1. FATHER-IN-LAW RICHARD POWELL DIES.

Anne Powell the Widdowe of Richard Powell of fforesthill in y^e. County of Oxoñ Esquire maketh Oath that ye said Ric: Powell her late Husband died neere the first day of January in the yeare of our Lord one Thousand sixe Hundred fowrtie sixe, at the Howse of M^r. John Milton Scituate in Barbican London:—

Jur coñ. Com^riis/   Anne Powell.
27° Feb: 1650 R. M.

Public Record Office, SP Dom 23/110, p. 547; Hamilton, pp. 50-51. There are numerous other references to Powell's death in the many composition papers of this time. His will was proved on March 26 of this year.

[173]

JANUARY. SIR EDWARD POWELL TAKES OVER MILTON'S
FATHER-IN-LAW RICHARD POWELL'S PROPERTY AT
WHEATLEY.

[Asking to be allowed to compound for property in Wheatley
assigned to him by Richard Powell in 1641 as surety for a debt
of 300 pounds, Sir Edward Powell states] That yor pet^r for
non paym^t of the said mony entred vpon the p^{r}misses in January 1646.

From Sir Edward Powell's petition of August 28, 1650, *q.v.* For
further light on Richard Powell's hopelessly tangled financial affairs, of
which this is only one small sample, the reader may be referred to my
Milton in Chancery, 1939, chapters VI and VIII, and to David H.
Stevens's "Mary Powell's Lost Dowry," in his *Milton Papers*, 1927,
pp. 7-13.

JANUARY 19. SATIRIZED FOR DIVORCE VIEWS IN A
BROADSIDE (?).
Divorcer.

To warrant this great Law of Separation,
And make one two, requires high aggravation:
Adultry onely cuts the Marriage-knot,
Without the which Gods Law allowes it not.
Then learn to seperate from sin that's common,
And man shall have more Comfort from a woman.

Anon., *A Catalogue of the severall Sects and Opinions in England*,
1647, reproduced in William Haller, *Tracts on Liberty*, 1934, I, 131;
Parker, *Milton's Contemporary Reputation*, p. 77; Raymond, pp. 84-
85. This work is a single-sheet broadside containing numerous engrav-
ings of various sects and heresies with accompanying verses like the one
quoted above. The picture accompanying these lines shows a man beat-
ing a woman. Thomason's copy is dated in manuscript, "Jan: 19th," and
"1646" substituted for "1647" erased. Parker doubts that there is any
direct reference to Milton here, but since so many other writers alluded
to him as one of the divorce writers, it is strongly probable that this author had him in mind as one of the leading exponents of what he considered this heresy.

JANUARY 23. WRITES ODE FOR JOHN ROUS TO ACCOM-
PANY PRESENTATION COPY OF *POEMS*.

Ad Joannem Roüsium Oxoniensis Academiæ Bibliothecarium
De libro poëmatum amisso quem ille sibi denuò mitti

postulabat, ut cum aliis nostris in Bibliotheca publicâ reponeret,
Ode. Joannis Miltonj

Strophe 1

Gemelle cultu simplici gaudens liber . . .

Antistrophe [1]

Quis te, parve liber, quis te fratribus
Subduxit reliquis dolo? . . .

Antistrophe [2]

. . . en iterum tibi
Spes nōva fulget posse profundam
Fugere Lethen, vehiqz superam
Jn Jovis aulam remige pennâ;

Strophe 3.

Nam te Roüsius sui
Optat peculi . . .

Antistrophe [3]

Ergo tu visere lucos
Musarum ibis amœnos,
Diámqz Phœbi rursùs ibis in domum
Oxoniâ quam valle colit
Delo posthabita,
Bifidoqz Parnassi jugo:
Jbis honestus,
Postquam egregiam tu quoqz sortem
Nactus abis, dextri prece sollicitatus amici.
Jllic legéris inter alta nomina
Authorum, Graiæ simul et Latinæ
Antiqua gentis lumina, et verum decus. . . .

Milton's Ode to Rous, now bound in the second part of his *Poems*,
1645, which is catalogued as Bodleian MS. Lat. Misc., f. 15; reproduced
in facsimile in Sotheby, facing p. 114, and in Fletcher, I, 458-462. The
date comes from Milton's own heading in the 1673 edition of his *Poems*,
which is given below. It cannot be decided for certain, of course, whether
the ode and the book were actually sent to Rous on the same date on
which the ode was written, but presumably the two dates would be
close together.

[An Ode of John Milton to John Rous, Librarian of Oxford University, concerning a lost volume of my *Poems* which he asked to be sent to him again, so that he might replace it in the public library with my others.

Strophe 1.

Double book rejoicing in a single cover . . .

Antistrophe 1.

Who, little book, stole you by fraud from the rest of your brothers? . . .

Antistrophe 2. . .

Lo, new hope shines for you again that you can escape from Lethe and be carried on winged oar to the high court of Jove.

Strophe 3.

For Rous seeks you for his own possession. . . .

Antistrophe 3.

Therefore you shall go to see the delightful groves of the Muses, and you shall go again to the divine home of Phoebus, where he lives in the Oxford vale, preferred above Delos and the double summit of Parnassus. You shall go in honor when you leave, having obtained an eminent fate, solicited by the request of a fortunate friend. There you shall be read among the great names of authors, ancient stars and the true ornament of both Greek and Latin races. . . .

Only part of the text of the ode is reproduced here, partly because some of it is irrelevant, and partly because sections of it have been given elsewhere as records of Rous's first request for Milton's writings (January, 1646), Milton's response in sending them (January, 1646), and Rous's second request for a replacement (January, 1647).

Jan. 23. 1646.

Ad *Joannem Rousium* Oxoniensis Academiæ Bibliothecarium. Milton, *Poems*, 1673, part 2, pp. 90-94; CM, I, 316-325; Fletcher, I, 143-145. It is conceivable that the date here given means January 23, 1646, by modern dating. But the overwhelming likelihood is that it means 1646/7. First, that is the usual method of dating. Second, it is not likely that Milton could have received the request from Rous, have sent him the required texts, have received word back again from Rous of the loss of a volume, and have written this longish Latin ode—all within three weeks at the longest. Masson interprets the date as 1647 "certainly" (III, 645).

FEBRUARY 2. BROTHER CHRISTOPHER'S SON THOMAS
BAPTIZED AT ST. CLEMENT DANES CHURCH, LONDON.

Baptizinges 1646 . . . Februarij Thomas Milton sonne of
Christophor and Thomazine —— 2.

Parish Register of St. Clement Danes, London; N & Q, xi, vii
(1913), 21, 113. Perceval Lucas assembles some information about him
in the last-named reference. He married Martha, daughter of either Sir
William Fleetwood of Aldwincle or Charles Fleetwood of Northampton. Thomas Milton died in 1694 and was buried in St. Dunstan's in
the West on October 17 of that year. His will was proved by his relict
Martha on December 3, 1694. She later married William Coward,
M.D., and removed to Ipswich, where his will was proved in 1724.

FEBRUARY 11. BROUGHT TO COURT BY SIR ROBERT PYE
OVER LATE FATHER-IN-LAW'S PROPERTY IN FOREST
HILL.

To the right Honble the Comm^{rs} of the Great Seale of England.
Vndecimo die ffebruarij. 1646./
    Maydwell
Humbly complayning sheweth vnto yor Hono^{rs}, your daily
Orato^r Sr Robert Pye of Westm^r in the County of Midd'ρ knight
That whereas Richard Powell of fforsthill in the County of
Oxōn Esqr did, by his deed Jndented bearing date the thirtieth
day of June in the sixteenth yeare of the Raigne of o^r Souaigne
Lord King Charles, for and in consideracōn of the sume of One
thowsand ffour hundred poundρ payed vnto him by yor Orato^r
graunt vnto yor Orato^r All that Manno^r or Lo^{pp} of fforresthill
āls fforstill āls ffosthill, with diuers other Landρ in fforsthill
aforesayd. To haue and to hould all the sayd Landρ and p'misses
to yor Orato^r his exec^{rs} Adm^{rs} and Ass's for and dureing the
terme of one and thirty yeares, with a Prouiso therein conteyned
that if the sayd Richard Powell his ex^{rs} or adm^{rs} or any of them
should well and truly satisfie, and pay or cause to be satisfyed
and payd vnto yor Orato^r his Executo^{rs} or adm^{rs} the full sumē
of ffifteene hundred pōwndρ & ten on the first day of July Anno
1641. That then the estate, and terme of one and thirty yeares
to cease and bee voyd as in and by the sayd recited Jndenture,

ready to bee shewed to this Honble Court more att large may appeare. Which sayd sumē of ffifteene hundred & ten poundę or any parte thereof was not satisfyed att the sayd day limitted in the sayd recited Jndenture nor att any tyme since vnto yor Orato^r, whereby the sayd estate, and terme of One and Thirty yeares of and in the p^rmisses is become absolute. But now soe it is May it please yor Hono^{rs} that yor Orato^r hauing lately had and taken possession of the p^rmisses soe conueyed to him as aforesayd, is now, and lately hath binn hindered, and interrupted in the peaceable injoym^t thereof by one John Melton of London geñ who p^r"tendę that hee hath some former Jnterest, and Estate of and in the same p^rmisses by and from the sayd Richard Powell by Mortgage Statute Recognizance Judgment, or some other Tytle Estate or Jnterest deriued from the sayd Richard Powell p^rcedent to yor. Orato^{rs} said Estate. And the sayd John Melton being often in a friendly manner desired by your Orato^r to discouer, and make knowne vnto him what estate Title Jnterest or Engagement hee hath or may clayme of or in the premisses or any parte thereof from the sayd Richard Powell, hath from tyme to tyme and still doth vtterly refuse to discou^r and make knowne the same vnto yor Orato^r whereby yor Orato^r cannot injoy the p^rmisses according to his Estate before mencōed, and sett forth contrary to Lawe, and Equity. Jn Consideracōn whereof, and for-as-much as yor Orato^r hath noe remedy by the Common Lawe of this Realme to know the truthe of such engagem^{tę} if any such bee whereby hee may bee releeued for his sayd debt vnlesse the sayd John Melton shall or will upon his Corporall Oath discouer and sett forth what Statute Judgem^t Recognizance Mortgage or other Estate or Jnterest hee hath or may clayme in, out of, or vnto the p^rmisses or any parte thereof by from or vnder the sayd Richard Powell. And vpon what Consideracōn the same was obtained And whether the same bee not, or ought not to bee vacated released and determyned. To the End therefore that the sayd John Melton may vpon his oath sett forth the truth thereof, and may also make a full and pfect answer to all and singuler other the p^rmisses. May it please your hono^{rs}. to graunt vnto your sayd Orato^r his Matie most gratious writt of Subpena to bee directed vnto him the sayd John Melton commaunding him att a certeyne day, and vnder a certeine payne therein to bee limitted psonally to bee and appeare in his M^{tie} high Court of Chauncery then and there to answere the p^{r}misses And to stand to, and abide such further Order and direction therein as to yor Hono^{rs} shall seeme most agreable to equity and good Conscience. And your Orato^r shall: &c./ Kel: sen./

Jntr.

Bulstrode Whitelocke.

Public Record Office, C2 Charles I/P 10/15; French, *Milton in Chancery*, pp. 297-298; London *Times Literary Supplement*, December 21, 1935, p. 879; CM, XVIII, 615-616 (description only, no text). For a running story of the suit and further details concerning Pye and other people mentioned in the proceedings, see *Milton in Chancery*, Chapter VIII and accompanying notes. Pye's bill of complaint is reproduced in facsimile facing p. 111.

FEBRUARY 22. ANSWERS SIR ROBERT PYE'S BILL OF COMPLAINT.

The answere of John Milton gent to the Bill of Complaynt of Sr Robert Pye Knight Complaynaunte./
Jurat 22°. ffeb.
1646. Rob't. Aylett
Smythe./

The said Defeñdt saueinge to himself nowe and all tymes hereafter all advantage of exception to the vncertaintie and insufficiencie of the said Bill of Cōmplt for answere therevnto hee this Defeñdt sayth That hee this Defeñdt. Doth not knowe That Richard Powell in the said Cōmplts said Bill named did at anie tyme for anie Considerracōn at all, or otherwise by his Dede in the Bill pretended or otherwise graunt, or otherwise Convey vnto the said Complainaunte. All or anie parte of the mannor or Lordshippe of fforesthill al's. fforsthill al's. ffosthill in the said Bill mencōed or anie other lands in ffosthill aforesaid for anie terme whatsoeu^r or vppon anie pvisoe whatsoeu^r to bee voide or Determined, for non payment of anie sumē of money

[179]

whatsoeu[r], Nor Doth this Defendant Knowe that the same or anye such terme or estate as in the said Bill is mencōed, became absolute for the same, or anie such Cause as in the said Bill is pretended. Howbeit this Defendant saith That hee this Defendant Conceiveth it to bee true That the sayd Richard Powell in his life tyme was lawfullye seised in his Demesne as of ffee or of some other good and lawfull estate of inheritance or otherwise was possest of some longe terme of yeares yett to come of and in the said mannor lands and premisses in the said Bill mencōed enablinge him to make the graunt hereafter mencōed./ And that the said Richard Powell, beinge thereof soe seised or possessed as aforesaid and beinge iustly and truely indebted vnto this Defeñdt in the sumē of three hundred pounds of lawfull English money for repayment whereof with Damages, for the forbeareance thereof, Hee the said Richard Powell togeather with one William Hearne of London gouldsmith did by one statute staple bearinge date on or about the elleventh Day of Julye in the third yeare of his ma[ties]. Raigne that nowe is become bound to this Defeñdt in the sumē of five hundred pounds to bee paid at middsomēr then next, which said statute was Defeazansed to bee void vppon payment of three hundred and twelue pounds to this Defendant his heires executors or administrators on or about twelueth Day of December next after the Date of the said statute as by the said statute and Defeazance readdye to bee shewed to this hōble Court, whereto for more Certaintye therein this Defeñt referreth himselfe is Doth and may more fully, and at large appeare./ And, this Defeñdt further saith, That the said three hundred and twelue pounds or anie part thereof was not paid according to the said Defeazance the twelueth Day of December or at any tyme since to or to the vse of this Defeñdt But all the said three hundred and twelue pounds togeather with Damages for the forbearance thereof for Divers yeares last past is iustly and truely oweinge vnto this Defeñdt, which the said Richard Powell from tyme to tyme hath refused or neglected to pay though hee hath often bene in all freindlye manner thereto required by this Defeñdt wherefore and for that this Defeñdt hath now present occasions for his said moneys true it is, That hee this Defendt intendeth and indeauoureth by Due Course of lawe to putt the said Statute in execution, for the recouerye of his said iust true Debt and Damages aforesaid, as hee hopeth vnder the favour of this hōble Court is lawfull for him this Defeñdt to Doe without anie wronge at all as hee Conceiveth to the Cōmplt whose tytle to the premisses sett forth by the said Bill is of his owne shewinge subsequent to the said statute, Nor Doth this Defeñdt knowe of anie possession the Cōmpt hath or ought to haue in the premisses or anie part thereof or howe or when hee entred, or that this Defeñdt hath any wayes Disturbed interrupted or Disquieted him therein, or intends soe to Doe otherwise then in a legall waye for recouerye of his Debt and Damages aforesaid./ And saith that hee Claymeth noe other tytle estate or interrest whatsoeuer in or to the premisses, but by vertue of the said statute which hee neuer refused to Discouer or sett forth to the said Cōmplt, And this Defeñdt saith That the said statute ought not to be vacated released or Determyned for the reasons aforesaid But vppon receipt of his said Debt of three hundred pounds with Damages for the forbearance thereof yett vnsatisfyed togeather with this Defendts Costs at Lawe and Charges in this hōble Court occationed by the non payment of the said Debt in tyme hee this Defeñdt is and wilbe readdye and willinge to Deliuer vpp the same to be Cancelled./ Without that, That anie other matter or thing Clause sentence Article or allegacōn in the said Bill of Compl^t conteyned and not before herein sufficiently answ^{r}ed vnto confessed and avoided denyed or Traversed is true soe & in such sort manner and forme as in & by the said Bill of Compl^t the same are sett forth & alledged All which matters & things this Defend^t is & wilbee readie to averre iustify maintaine & prove as this hō^{ble} Co^{r}t shall award And prayeth to bee thence dismissed wth his reasonable Costs & charges in this behalfe most wrongfully sustained./   Jo: Bradshawe.

Public Record Office, C2 Charles I/P 10/15; London *Times Literary Supplement*, March 14, 1936, p. 224; French, *Milton in Chancery*, pp. 298-300; CM, XVIII, 398-400.

MARCH 13 (?). FATHER DIES.

He dyed, about 1647. . . .

Aubrey, f. 64; Darbishire, p. 10. Aubrey originally wrote: "He dyed, in that yeare, that the Army marched thorough the City," but later crossed out all but the first two words and wrote "about 1647" above them. March 13 is taken as the approximate date because he was buried on March 15 (*q.v.*). In describing the elder Milton's last days and death Mr. Brennecke (*John Milton the Elder and his Music*, New York, 1938, p. 148) unfortunately misprints the year of his death as 1637. He also wrenches a phrase out of its context and gives a somewhat misleading idea. Edward Phillips (p. xxiii; Darbishire, p. 64) tells of "the Old Gentleman living wholly retired to his Rest and Devotion, without the least trouble imaginable." Mr. Brennecke tells how the elder Milton "died, in the spring of 1637, both suddenly and peacefully, and surely 'without the least trouble imaginable.' "

. . . his Father (who died very aged about 1647) . . .

Wood, I, 883; Darbishire, p. 47.

MARCH 15. FATHER BURIED IN ST. GILES' CRIPPLEGATE.

Burrialls in March 1646. . . John Melton gentleman—15.

Parish Register of St. Giles' Cripplegate, London; Masson, III, 643. See also W. Denton, *Records of St. Giles' Cripplegate*, London, 1883, p. 160. In an account in the *Gentleman's Magazine* (LX, 1790, 837), the writer gives the date as 1656/7.

[His father was] buried in Cripple-gate-ch: from his house in the Barbican.

Aubrey, f. 64; Darbishire, p. 10.

. . . hee [John Milton the poet] happen'd to bee bury'd in Cripplegate where about thirty yeer before hee had by chance also interrd his Father.

The "earliest" biography, last sentence; Darbishire, p. 34.

[The poet] was buried in the grave of his Father (who died very aged about 1647) in the Chancel of the Church of S. *Giles* near *Cripplegate, London.*

Wood, I, 883; Darbishire, p. 47.

MARCH 15. INHERITS PART OF FATHER'S ESTATE.

. . . the moderate Patrimony his Father left him . . . His moderate Estate left him by his Father. . . . By the great fire in 1666 hee had a house in Bread street burnt: wch was all the Real Estate hee had.

The "earliest" biography; Darbishire, pp. 31, 32, 33. From this entry it seems clear that the house in Bread Street was part of the poet's inheritance.

The Estate which his Father left him was but indifferent, yet by his frugality he made it serve him and his. . . . By the great Fire which hapned in *London* in the beginning of *Sept.* 1666, he had a house in *Breadstreet* burnt, which was all the real Estate that he had then left.

Wood, I, 884; Darbishire, p. 48.

AFTER MARCH 15. TUTORING IN BARBICAN HOUSE.

And now [after the death of his father and the return home of the Powell family] the House look'd again like a House of the Muses only, tho the accession of Scholars was not great. Possibly his proceeding thus far in the Education of Youth may have been the occasion of some of his Adversaries calling him Pædagogue and Schoolmaster: Whereas it is well known he never set up for a Publick School to teach all the young Fry of a Parish, but only was willing to impart his Learning and Knowledge to Relations, and the Sons of some Gentlemen that were his intimate Friends; besides, that neither his Converse, nor his Writings, nor his manner of Teaching ever savour'd in the least any thing of Pedantry; and probably he might have some prospect of putting in Practice his Academical Institution, according to the Model laid down in his Sheet of Education. The Progress of which design was afterwards diverted by a Series of Alteration in the Affairs of State. . . .

Phillips, pp. xxvii-iii; Darbishire, pp. 67-68. The date seems to be fixed by that of the death (and burial) of Milton's father, since the wording of Phillips's reference here implies that this condition followed the death of the elder Milton. For an analysis of Milton's work as a teacher and of the pupils whom he instructed, see Masson, III, 656-660. Masson here collects information about Edward and John Phillips, Richard Heath, Mr. Packer, Cyriack Skinner, Henry Lawrence, Sir Thomas Gardiner of Essex, Richard Barry, 2nd Earl of Barrimore, and Richard Jones, later Viscount and then Earl of Ranelagh.

MARCH 26. FATHER-IN-LAW RICHARD POWELL'S WILL PROVED.

See the note to the record of Powell's will above, under date of December 30, 1646. The will was proved by his relict Anne Powell before Sir Nathaniel Brent, LL.D., in the Prerogative Court of Canterbury. See *The Year Books of Probate*, ed. J. and G. F. Matthews, London, IV (1906), 264.

APRIL (?). POEMS IMITATED BY ROBERT BARON.

[1] Hence loathed Melancholy . . . .

[2] Ring out yee Christall Spheares . . . .

[3]   . . . *Euphrosyne*

Right goddesse of free mirth come lead with the . . . .

[4] Hence, hence fond mirth, hence vaine deluding joyes . . . .

[5] The Goddesses so debonaire, and free . . . .

[6] Not trickt and frounc't up

As in the fresh flowry May. . . .

[7] Bring the Faire Primrose (that forsaken dyes) . . . .

Robert Baron, Ερστοπαιγνιον. Or, the Cyprian Academy, London, 1647. The selections given are from Book I, pp. 54, 55; Book II, pp. 3, 28, 34, 43, 45. These are by no means all the echoes of Milton in the book, but they are some of the most obvious. In the British Museum copy (C.71.cc.4) of the edition of 1648 some previous owner or reader has checked these and various others. The date used above is that of the catalogue of the Thomason tracts. The Thomason copy, however, lacks title page and date. Baron's plagiarisms of Milton have been pointed out by Warton (Milton's *Poems upon Several Occasions*, second edition, London, 1791, pp. 403-407), William Godwin (*Lives of Edward and John Phillips*, 1815, p. 287), and other later critics. Warton gives many passages. Todd (VI, 1826, 399 ff.) adds to Warton's list. See also Parker, *Milton's Contemporary Reputation*, pp. 23-24.

APRIL (?). RECEIVES LETTER FROM CARLO DATI.

[With how great and what new pleasure I was filled, my Charles, on the unexpected arrival of your letter. . . . Immediately, however, when I came upon that passage where you write that you had sent me three letters before, which I now know to have been lost. . . . As to what you say, that from the time of my departure from Florence you have been anxious about my health and always mindful of me. . . . This you must have read for yourself long ere now, if that poem reached you, as now first I hear from you it did. . . . Yet, even in the midst of these evils, since you desire to be informed about my studies. . . . I am reading with pleasure your description of the funeral ceremony to King Louis, in which I recognize your style . . . which befits the president of a club of wits. . . .]

These excerpts from Milton's reply to Dati, dated April 21, 1647 (*q.v.*), are the only indications which we have of the nature of Dati's letter. The original is lost, though a later letter of November 1, 1647, given below, survives.

APRIL 7. DIVORCE BOOKS MENTIONED BY EDWARD HYDE.

I thank you for your friend Lilburne, and desire you to send me as many of his books as you can. I learn much by them; and in earnest I find a great benefit by reading ill books. . . . And so I gain very much law by reading Mr. Prynne. . . . And Mr. Cornelius hath delivered me (but as lent by you to him to be restored) your bundle of heresies and frenzies, which sure does not comprehend a moiety of the new propagated doctrines, except Mr. Milton's opinions of wedlock (from whence a race of goodly conclusions will naturally flow) be received and confirmed as orthodox by the assembly.

State Papers Collected by Edward, Earl of Clarendon, II (1773), 363; Stern, I, ii, 485. The quotation is from a letter of April 7, 1647, from Edward Hyde (not then Earl of Clarendon) to Sir Edward Nicholas. See also *The Calendar of Clarendon Papers*, I (1872), 372.

The original letter, from which I neglected to take an adequate quotation, is in the Bodleian, MS. Clarendon 29, f. 183. It is dated "Jersey y[e]. 7th of April 1647" and endorsed "To Secretary Nicholas Apr: 7°:"

APRIL 21. WRITES LETTER TO CARLO DATI.

Carolo Dato Patricio Florentino.

10. Perlatis inopinatò Literis ad me tuis, mi Carole, quantâ, et quam novâ sim voluptate perfusus, quandoquidem non est ut pro re satis queam dicere, volo ex dolore saltem, sine quo vix ulla magna hominibus delectatio concessa est, id aliquantum intelligas. Dum enim illa tua prima percurro, in quibus elegantia

cum amicitia pulchre sane contendit, merum illud quidem gaudium esse dixerim, præsertim cum uti vincat amicitia, operam te dare videam. Statim vero cum incido in illud quod scribis, ternas te jam olim ad me dedisse, quas ego periisse scio, tum primum sincera illa infici, tristíq; desiderio conturbari, cœpta est lætitia; mox etiam gravius quiddam subit, in quo vicem meam dolere persæpe soleo, quos forte viciniæ, aut aliqua nullius usus necessitudo mecum, sive casu, sive lege conglutinavit, illos nullâ re aliâ commendabiles assidere quotidie, obtundere, etiam enecare mehercule quoties collibitum erit; quos, mores, ingenium, studia, tam belle conciliaverant, illos jam pene omnes, aut morte, aut iniquissimâ locorum distantiâ invideri mihi, & ita confestim è conspectu plerumq; abripi, ut in perpetua fere solitudine versari mihi necesse sit. Te, quod ais, ex quo Florentiâ discessi, meâ de salute solicitum, semperq; mei memorem fuisse, gratulor mihi sane, par illud utriq; & mutuum accidisse, quod ego me solum sensisse meo fortasse merito arbitrabar. Gravis admodum, ne te celem, discessus ille & mihi quoq; fuit, eosq; meo animo aculeos infixit, qui etiam nunc altius inhærent, quoties mecum cogito tot simul sodales atq; amicos tam bonos, tamq, commodos unâ in urbe longinquâ illâ quidem, sed tamen charissimâ, invitum me, & plane divulsum reliquisse. Testor illum mihi semper sacrum & solenne futurum Damonis tumulum; in cujus funere ornando cum luctu & mœrore oppressus, ad ea quæ potui solatia confugere, & respirare paulisper cupiebam, non aliud mihi quicquam jucundius occurrit, quam vestrum omnium gratissimam mihi memoriam, tuiq; nominatim in mentem revocasse. Id quod ipse jamdiu legisse debes, siquidem ad vos carmen illud pervenit, quod ex te nunc primum audio. Mittendum ego sane sedula curaveram, ut esset ingenii quantulumcunque, amoris autem adversum vos mei, vel illis paucis versiculis, emblematis ad morem inclusis, testimonium haudquaquam obscurum. Existimabam etiam fore hoc modo, ut vel te vel alium ad scribendum allicerem; mihi enim si prior scriberem, necesse erat, ut vel ad omnes, vel si quem aliis prætulissem, verebar ne in cæterorum, qui id rescissent, offensionem

incurrerem; cum permultos adhuc superesse istic sperem, qui
hoc à me officium vendicare certe potuerint. Nunc tu omnium
primus, & hâc amicissimâ Literarum provocatione, & scribendi
officio ter jam repetito debitas tibi à me jampridem respondendi
vices reliquorum expostulatione liberasti. Quanquam fateor accessisse ad illam silentii causam, turbulentissimus iste, ex quo
domum reversus sum, Britanniæ nostræ status, qui animum
meum paulo post ab studiis excolendis, ad vitam & fortunas
quoquo modo tuendas necessario convertit. Ecquem tu inter tot
Civium commissa prælia, cædes, fugas, bonorum direptiones,
recessum otio Literario tutum dari putes posse? Nos tamen etiam
inter hæc mala, quoniam de studiis meis certior fieri postulas,
sermone patrio haud pauca in lucem dedimus; quæ nisi essent
Anglice scripta, libens ad vos mitterem, quorum judiciis plurimum tribuo. Poematum quidem quæ pars Latina est, quoniam
expetis, brevi mittam; atq; id sponte jamdudum fecissem, nisi
quod, propter ea quæ in Pontificem Romanum aliquot paginis
asperius dicta sunt, suspicabar vestris auribus fore minus grata.
Nunc abs te peto, ut quam veniam, non dico Aligerio, & Petrar-
chæ vestro eadem in causa, sed meæ, ut scis, olim apud vos lo-
quendi libertati, singulari cum humanitate, dare consuevistis,
eandem impetres (nam de te mihi persuasum est) ab cæteris
amicis, quoties de vestris ritibus nostro more loquendum erit.
Exequias Ludovici Regis à te descriptas libenter lego, in quibus
Mercurium tuum, non compitalem illum & mercimoniis addictum, quem te nuper colere jocaris, sed facundum illum, Musis
acceptum, & Mercurialium virorum præsidem, agnosco. Restat
ut de ratione aliqua & modo inter nos constet, quo literæ deinceps
nostræ certo itinere utrinq; commeare possint. Quod non admodum difficile videtur, cum tot nostri Mercatores negotia apud
vos, & multa, & ampla habeant, quorum Tabellarii singulis heb-
domadis ultro citroq; cursitant; quorum & navigia haud multo
rarius hinc illinc solvunt. Hanc ego curam Jacobo Bibliopolæ,
vel ejus hero mihi familiarissimo, recte, ut spero, committam. Tu
interim, mi Carole, valebis, & Cultellino, Francino, Frescobaldo,
Malatestæ, Clementillo minori, & si quem alium nostri amantio-

rem novisti; toti deniq; Gaddianæ Academiæ, salutem meo nomine plurimum dices. Iterum vale.

Londino, Aprilis 21. 1647.

Milton, *Epistolarum Familiarium Liber Unus*, 1674, pp. 28-32; CM, XII, 44-53. The holograph manuscript of the letter in Milton's hand is in the New York Public Library. No complete facsimile has been published, but parts may be found in Sotheby, p. 122; in J. F. Marsh, *Papers connected with the Affairs of Milton and his Family* (Chetham Society Publications, Vol. XXIV, 1851), frontispiece; and in CM, XII, facing p. 50. See French, "The Autographs of John Milton," #25.

There are few differences in text between the manuscript version of this letter and that published in 1674. Aside from negligible variations in spelling and punctuation, the verbal variants as listed in CM, XII, 385-386 are as follows (with references to the lines above): 1 *Florentino*] Florentino Joannes Miltonius Londinensis S. P. D.—9 in illud quod] in quod—19 abripi] tolli—40 scribendum allicerem] scribendum in Angliam allicerem—43 incurrerem] caderem—45 primus, & hâc amicissimâ Literarum provocatione, & scribendi officio ter jam repetito debitas tibi à me jampridem respondendi] primus insperato hoc tuo per literas invitatu, ne dicam priorum illarum jacturâ debitas jam tibi a me respondendi—53 Literario tutum] literario alicubi tutum—58 jamdudum] jampridem—67 addictum, quem te nuper colere jocaris, sed] additum, sed—78 Clementillo minori] Clementillo—81 *Londino*, Aprilis 21. 1647] Londini Pascatis feriâ tertiâ MDCXLVII.

For Dati's comment on this letter, see his answer, dated November 1, 1647.

[Letter to Charles Dati, Nobleman of Florence.

With how great and what new pleasure I was filled, my Charles, on the unexpected arrival of your letter, since it is impossible for me to describe it adequately, I wish you may in some degree understand from the very pain with which it was dashed, such pain as is almost the invariable accompaniment of any great delight yielded to men. For, on running over that first portion of your letter, in which elegance contends so finely with friendship, I should have called my feeling one of unmixed joy, and the rather because I see your labour to make friendship the winner. Immediately, however, when I came upon that passage where you write that you had sent me three letters before, which I now know to have been lost, then, in the first place, that sincere gladness of mine at the receipt of this one began to be infected and troubled with a sad regret, and

presently a something heavier creeps in upon me, to which I
am accustomed in very frequent grievings over my own lot:
the sense, namely, that those whom the mere necessity of neighbourhood, or something else of a useless kind, has closely con-
joined with me, whether by accident or by the tie of law, *they*
are the persons, though in no other respect commendable, who
sit daily in my company, weary me, nay, by heaven, all but
plague me to death whenever they are jointly in the humour
for it, whereas those whom habits, disposition, studies, had so
handsomely made my friends, are now almost all denied me,
either by death or by most unjust separation of place, and are
so for the most part snatched from my sight that I have to live
well-nigh in a perpetual solitude. As to what you say, that from
the time of my departure from Florence you have been anxious
about my health and always mindful of me, I truly congratulate
myself that a feeling has been equal and mutual in both of us,
the existence of which on my side only I was perhaps claiming
to my credit. Very sad to me also, I will not conceal from you,
was that departure, and it planted stings in my heart which
now rankle there deeper, as often as I think with myself of my
reluctant parting, my separation as by a wrench, from so many
companions at once, such good friends as they were, and living
so pleasantly with each other in one city, far off indeed, but to
me most dear. I call to witness that tomb of Damon, ever to be
sacred and solemn to me, whose adornment with every tribute
of grief was my weary task, till I betook myself at length to
what comforts I could, and desired again to breathe a little—
I call that sacred grave to witness that I have had no greater
delight all this while than in recalling to my mind the most
pleasant memory of all of you, and of yourself especially. This
you must have read for yourself long ere now, if that poem
reached you, as now first I hear from you it did. I had carefully
caused it to be sent, in order that, however small a proof of
talent, it might, even in those few lines introduced into it em-
blem-wise, be no obscure proof of my love towards you. My
idea was that by this means I should lure either yourself or

some of the others to write to me; for, if I wrote first, either I
had to write to all, or I feared that, if I gave the preference to
any one, I should incur the reproach of such others as came to
know it, hoping as I do that very many are yet there alive who
might certainly have a claim to this attention from me. Now,
however, you first of all, both by this most friendly call of your
letter, and by your thrice-repeated attention of writing before,
have freed the reply for which I have been some while since
in your debt from any expostulation from the others. There was,
I confess, an additional cause for my silence in that most turbulent state of our Britain, subsequent to my return home, which
obliged me to divert my mind shortly afterwards from the
prosecution of my studies to the defence anyhow of life and
fortune. What safe retirement for literary leisure could you
suppose given one among so many battles of a civil war, slaughters, flights, seizures of goods? Yet, even in the midst of these
evils, since you desire to be informed about my studies, know
that we have published not a few things in our native tongue;
which, were they not written in English, I would willingly send
to you, my friends in Florence, to whose opinions I attach very
much value. The part of the Poems which is in Latin I will send
shortly, since you wish it; and I would have done so spontane-
ously long ago, but that, on account of the rather harsh sayings
against the Pope of Rome in some of the pages, I had a suspicion they would not be quite agreeable to your ears. Now I beg
of you that the indulgence you were wont to give, I say not to
your own Dante and Petrarch in the same case, but with singular
politeness to my own former freedom of speech, as you know,
among you, the same you, Dati, will obtain (for of yourself I
am sure) from my other friends whenever I may be speaking
of your religion in our peculiar way. I am reading with pleasure
your description of the funeral ceremony to King Louis, in which
I recognize your style—not that one of street bazaars and mercantile concerns which you say jestingly you have been lately
practising, but the right eloquent one which the Muses like, and
which befits the president of a club of wits. It remains that we

agree on some method and plan by which henceforth our letters may go between us by a sure route. This does not seem very difficult, when so many of our merchants have frequent and large transactions with you, and their messengers run backwards and forwards every week, and their vessels sail from port to port not much seldomer. The charge of this I shall commit, rightly I hope, to Bookseller James, or to his master, my very familiar acquaintance. Meanwhile farewell, my Charles; and give best salutations in my name to Coltellini, Francini, Frescobaldi, Malatesta, Chimentelli the younger, anyone else you know that remembers me with some affection, and, in fine, to the whole Gaddian Academy. Again Farewell!

London: April 21, 1647.]

Masson, III, 652-654; CM, XII, 44-53.

It may be this and Milton's other published letters to Dati which are referred to in a statement by Angelo Fabroni in his *Vitae Italorum*, XVI (Pisa, 1795), 32-33: "Extant quidem Aegidii Menagii, ad quem saepe literas mittebat (1), Alexandri Mori, Joannis Miltonii, Thomae Bartolinii, Nicolai Vistenii, Friderici Gronovii, Petri Lambecii, Nicolai Heinsii, ut de ceteris nostrisque sileam, honorificentissima de ipso testimonia. . . . [Note] (1) *Hic viginti & amplius Datii epistolas emisit in libro, quem inscripsit* Mescolanze, *ex quibus apparet fuisse inter eos quasi quamdam societatem communium studiorum.*" [There are extant most complimentary testimonies in honor of Dati by Giles Menage, to whom Dati often sent letters, by Alexander More, John Milton, Thomas Bartolini, Nicholas Visteni, Frederick Gronovi, Peter Lambech, Nicholas Heinsius, not to mention myself and others. . . . He (Menage) issued twenty and more letters of Dati in a book which he entitled *Miscellanies*, from which it appears that there was among them a sort of society of common studies.] Menage's *Mescolanze*, in the two editions which I have seen (Rotterdam, 1692, and Venice, 1736) contains many letters from and to Dati and many references to him. But I have been unable to find any to or from Milton.

APRIL 26. SATIRIZED FOR DIVORCE VIEWS.

That a man may lawfully put away his wife if she be not a meet helper.

Anon., *These Tradesmen are Preachers in and about the City of London. Or A Discovery Of The Most Dangerovs And Damnable Tenets*, 1647. This broadside is a collection of satires on the heretical teachings of the period, of which that quoted is number 20. Two others, vaguely related to Milton's later writings, actually or by later criticism, are that the soul dies with the body and that God is the author of the sinfulness of people. The tract is described in *Catalogue of Prints and Drawings in the British Museum Division I . . . Satires*, 1 (1870), 374-376, and in William Haller's *Tracts on Liberty*, 1 (1934), 131. Haller gives a facsimile, facing p. 56. This allusion is given in Parker's *Milton's Contemporary Reputation*, p. 77. The date is from Thomason's copy in the British Museum.

JULY 16. OBTAINS EXTENT ON POWELL'S OXFORDSHIRE PROPERTY.

Carolus dei grā Angl' Scotie ffranc' & hibñ' Rex fidei defensor &c vic' Oxōn sal'tm Cum Ricus Powell' de fforest hill' in Cōm tuo gen' & Will's hearne Civis & Aurifabr' london vndecimo die Junij Anno regni nrī tcīo coram Nichō hide Milite tunc Capitali Justic' nrō ad plīta coram nōb tenend' assign' recogn' se debere Johī Milton de vniūsitat' Cantebr' gen' quingent' libr' quas eidem Johī soluisse debuissent in ffesto Natiuitatis scī Johīs Baptē tunc p'x futur' Et eas ei non soluer' vt dicebatʳ Per brē ñrm tibi nup p'cepimˢ qd' corpora p'dcōr' Ricī Powell' & Willī hearne (si laici essent) capi & in prisona ñra donec eidem Johī de debito p'dcō satisfecissent saluo custodiri & omīa t'ras & catalla ipōr' Ricī & Willī in balliua tua p sacr'm pbor' & legāl homī de eadem balliua tua p quos rei vītas melius sciri potuisset iuxta verum valorem eor'dem diligent' extendi appciari & in manū ñram seīri fac' vt ea p'fat' Jōhi quousqz sibi de debito p'dcō plene satisfc'm foret libāri fac' iuxta formam statuti apud West'm p hmoī debit' recupand' inde edit' & puis Et qualit' dcm' p'ceptum ñrm fores execut' scir' [fac'] nōb in Cancellar' nrām ad c'tum diem iam pt'it' vbicunqz tunc foret p lrās tuas sigillat'. Et qd' hēres ibi dcm' brē ñrm, Ad quem diem in dcō brī ñro content' tu nōb in Cancellar' nrām p'dcām retorn' qd' pñoīat Ricūs Powell' mortuus est Tibi igitʳ p'cipimˢ qd' corpus pd'ci Willī hearne (si laicus sit) capi & in prisona nrā donec eidem Johi de debito p'dcō plene satisfecit saluo Custodiri & omīa t'rās & catalla ipīus Willī in balliua tua necnon tam omīa t'rās & ten' que fuerunt p'dcī Ricī Powell' dcō tempore recognicōis debiti p'dcī aut inqūi postea nisi alicui hered' infra etatem

existen' iure hereditario discenderunt quī omīa boni & catalla
que ferunt p'dcī Ricī tempore mortis sue in dcā balliua tua p
Sacr'm ꝓbor & legal' hoīm de eadem balliua tua p quos rei vītas
melius sciri potit iuxta verum valorem eor'dem diligent' extendi
& ap'pciari & in manū ñram seīri fac' vt ea p'fat' Johī milton
quousqz sibi de debito p'dcō plene satisfac'm fuīt libāri fac'
iuxta formam Statuti p'dcī Et qualit hoc p'ceptum ñrm fuis
execut' scir' fac' nōb in Cancellār' nrām p'dcām a die scī michīs,
ꝓ'x futur' in tres septimanas vbicunqz tunc fuīt p lrās tuas
sigillat' Et hēas ibi hoc brē T'me ipō apud West'm xvj° die
Julij Anno r'ñ vicesimo t'cio./

lenthall' P.

[*Endorsed*] Execūco ipsius brīs' patet in quadam Inquisicōne
huic brī' annēx.

Will's Cope Ar'
vic'

Public Record Office, Certificates on Statutes Staple, C 228/6;
J. M. French, "The Powell-Milton Bond," *Harvard Studies and
Notes in Philology and Literature*, xx (1938), 67; French, *Milton
in Chancery*, 293-294.

[Charles by the grace of God King of England, Scotland,
France, and Ireland, Defender of the Faith, etc. To the Sheriff
of Oxford, greeting. Whereas Richard Powell of Forest Hill
in your county, gentleman, and William Hearne, citizen and
goldsmith of London, on the 11th day of June in the third
year of our reign (*i.e.*, 1627) before Nicholas Hyde, knight,
then our Chief Justice, at a session appointed to be held before
us, acknowledged that they owed John Milton of the University of Cambridge, gentleman, five hundred pounds which they
were bound to pay to the said John at the feast of the Nativity
of St. John the Baptist then next ensuing (*i.e.*, June 24); and
whereas they did not pay it to him, as is said: by our writ we
have commanded you that the bodies of the aforesaid Richard
Powell and William Hearne (if they were laymen) should be
taken and held safely in our prison till they should have satisfied the aforesaid debt to the said John, and that all the lands

and chattels of the said Richard and William in your county should be diligently extended and appraised by the oath of honest and lawful men of your said county by whom the truth of the matter might be the better known, according to the true value of the same, and that they should be seized into our hand in order that the same might be delivered over to the said John until full satisfaction should be made for the aforesaid debt according to the form of the statute published and provided at Westminster for the recovery of men's debts. And that you should then make known to us in our Chancery on a certain day now past, wherever it should then be, by your sealed letters, how you executed our said order, and that you should have there our said writ. On which day as specified in our said writ you returned to us in our Chancery that the aforesaid Richard Powell was dead. We ordered you therefore that the body of the aforesaid William Hearne (if he were a layman) should be taken and safely held in our prison till he should have fully satisfied the said John of the aforesaid debt, and that all the lands and chattels of the said William in your county, and also all the lands and tenements which belonged to the aforesaid Richard Powell at the said time of the recognizance of the said debt or the inquisition afterwards, unless they had descended by any law of inheritance to any heir under age then living—that all these goods and chattels which were possessed by the aforesaid Richard at the time of his death in your said county should be diligently extended and appraised, by the oath of honest and lawful men of your said county by whom the truth of the matter might be the better known according to the true value of the same, and seized into our hand, that they might be delivered to the said John Milton till full satisfaction should be made to him for the said debt according to the form of the statute aforesaid. And you are to make known to us in our Chancery aforesaid within three weeks of the day of St. Michael next to come (*i.e.*, September 29), wherever it shall then be, by your sealed letters, how you have executed this order of ours. And you shall have there this writ. Witness myself at Westminster,

[194]

the sixteenth day of July in the twenty-third year of our reign (1647).

Lenthall, Speaker.

The execution of the same writ appears in a certain inquisition annexed to this writ.

William Cope, Esq., Sheriff.]
French, *Milton in Chancery*, pp. 104-105.

[Anne Powell testified in 1656] That shee doth knowe y^t the said nowe defēndt did about the latter end of ye yeare of our Lord god 1647. or ye beginninge of the yeare 1648. extend the free landꝑ of ye said Richard Powell in Whateley in ye Countie of Oxoñ aforesaid, as alsoe ye tithe Corne there belonginge to the said Richard Powell vpon the said Statute and was possessed thereof by vertue of the said Extent, and as this dēpt crediblie heard did afterwardꝑ Reextend the saide premisses but howe the said Reextent was made or for what cause as is Jntērted shee cannot certenly say. . . .

From Anne Powell's deposition in the Ashworth-Milton suit, June 4, 1656, *q.v.* The "Reextent" mentioned here is not clear, unless it refers to Milton's taking possession of the property on November 20, 1647.

AUGUST 5. AS RESULT OF MILTON'S EXTENT, POWELL'S WHEATLEY PROPERTY IS SUBJECTED TO INQUISITION.

Oxōn ss Inquisicō indentat' capt' apud Civitat' Oxōn in Cōm pd' quinto die Augusti Anno regni dñi nrī Caroli dei grā Anglī Sccie ffranc' & hibñie Regis fidei defensoris &c' vicesimo t'cio coram me Willō Cope Ar' vic' Cōm pd' virtute brīs dcī dñī Regis mihi directi & huic Inquisicōni annēx & Sacr'm Johīs hunt Ricī Phillips Willī Sadler Triumph de St Pauli Johīs Slatford Willī Cooper Willī Yannynge Johīs Wild' Jacobi Colkyer Willī Michell' Thome hore & Anthīj Slatter ꝑbōr' & legl'm hominū de ballīa mea Qui dicunt sup Sacr'm suū qd' Ricus Powell geñ in brī p'dcō noīat' die Recogniconis debī in brī p'dcō mencōnat' scilt' vndecimo die Junij Anno regni dcī dñī Regis nunc Anglī &c' t'cio in brī p'dcō mencōnat' seīt' fuit in dmcō suo vt de feodo de & in tota illa porcōn decimar' grani cum ꝑtiñ in Whateley in

pochia de Cuddesdeñ in Cōm pd' clari Annui valoris in omibz
exit' vlt^{ra} reprīs viginti sex librar' triū solidōr' & quatuor denar'
Ac de & in vno mesuagio duōbz horreis vno Cottagio & vñ virgat t're & dimid' vnius virgat' terr' contineñ triginta & septem
acras & vnam Rodam t're tres acras prati & octo acras & dimid'
vnius acre pastur' cum ptiñ iaceñ & existeñ in villa & Campis
de Whateley pd' in pōch de Cuddesden' pd' clari Annui valoris
in omībz exit' vlt^{le} repris' quindecim librar' Ac vlt'ius Jur' p'dcī
sup Sacrm' suū p'dcm' dicunt qd' p'dcūs Ricūs Powell' post pd'
diem Recognicōnis debī p'dcī in eōdm brī mencōnat' scīlt p'dcō
vndecimo die Junij Anno t'cio sūpdcō & ante diem Capcōnis
huius Jnquisicōnis seīt' fuit in d'mcō suo vt de feodo de & in
duōbz virgat' t're cum ptiñ' iaceñ & existeñ in Whateley pd'
contineñ quadragint' octo acr' & vñ rod' terr' arabili & quatuor
acr' prati cum ptin' clari Annui valoris in omībz exit' vlt^{le} repris'
tres decem librar' sex solidor' & octo denarior' Ac de & in vno
Cottagio cum ptin' in Whateley p'd' modo in tenur' siue occupacōne cuiusdam Walt'i Symons clari Annui valoris in omībz exit'
vlt^{le} repris' viginti solidor' Ac de & in vno alio Cottagio cum
ptin' in Whateley pd' modo in tenur' siue occupacōne cuiusdam'
Rīci Clarke clar' Annui valoris in omībz exit' vlt^{le} repris' viginti
solidor' Ac de & in vno mesuagio cum ptin' in Whateley pd' in
tenur' siue occupacōne cuiusdam Thome Church clari Annui
valoris in omībz exit' vlt^{le} repris' viginti solidor' Ac etiam de
& in vno alio Cottagio cum ptin' in Whateley pd' in tenur' siue
occupacōne Cuiusdam Willī Platt clari Annui valoris omībz exit'
vlt^{le} repris' tresdecim solidor' & quatuor denarior' Ac vltius Jur'
p'dcī sup Sacr'm suū p'dcm' dicunt qd' Anna Powell vid' que
fuit vxor p'dcī Ricī seit' existet de & in t'cia parte omñ & siñglor'
p'missor' p'dcōr' cum ptin' vt de lībo teñto p t'nno vite sue vt
dote sua ex dotacōne p'dcī Rīci quondam viri sui qdqz p'dcā
Anna adhuc supstes & in plena vita existit vidēlt apud Whateley
p'dcām Omnia que quidem p'missa p'dcā cum p'tin' ego p'fat'
vic dcō die Capcōnis huius Jnquisicōnis in manus dcī dnī Regis
cepi & seīri feci Deniqz Jur' p'dci' sup Sacr'm suū p'dcm dicunt
qd' p'dcus' Ricūs Powell tempore mortis sue nulla hūit bona

seu catalla nec hūit aliqua alia siue plura terr' sentēta in dcā
ballīa mea ad noticiam Jur' p'dcor' que extendi aut seiri possunt
Jn cuius rei testimonie tam ego p'fat' vic' q'm Jur' p'dcī huic
Jnquisicōni Sigilla nrā die & Anno primo sup'dcis apposuim⁸./

Will's Cope Ar'

vic'

Public Record Office, Proceedings on Statutes Staple, C 228/6;
J. M. French, "The Powell-Milton Bond," *Harvard Studies and Notes
in Philology and Literature*, xx (1938), 68; French, *Milton in Chancery*, 294-295.

[Oxford, ss. An inquisition drawn up and taken at the city
of Oxford in the aforesaid county on the fifth day of August in
the twenty-third year of the reign of our Lord Charles by the
grace of God King of England, Scotland, France, and Ireland,
Defender of the Faith, etc. (*i.e.*, 1647), before me, William
Cope, Esq., Sheriff of the said county, by virtue of a writ of our
said Lord the King directed to me and annexed to this inquisition, and the oaths of John Hunt, Richard Phillips, William
Sadler, Triumph de St. Paul, John Slatford, William Cooper,
William Yanning, John Wild, James Colkyer, William Michell, Thomas Hore, and Anthony Slatter, honest and lawful
men of my county. Who say on their oath that Richard Powell,
gentleman, named in the aforesaid writ, on the day of the recognizance of debt mentioned in the aforesaid writ, that is on the
eleventh day of June in the third year of the reign of our said
Lord the now King of England, etc. (1627), mentioned in the
aforesaid writ, was seized in his demesne as of fee of and in all
that portion of the tithes of corn with the appurtenances in
Wheatley in the parish of Cuddesdon in the said county, of the
clear annual value in all issues over and above reprises of
£26-3-4; and of and in one messuage, two barns, one cottage,
and one yard and a half of land, containing thirty-seven acres
and one rod of land, three acres of meadow and eight acres and
a half of pasture with the appurtenances lying and being in the
town and fields of Wheatley aforesaid in the parish of Cuddesdon aforesaid, of the clear annual value in all issues over and
above reprises of £15; and further the jurors aforesaid on their

oath aforesaid say that the aforesaid Richard Powell after the said day of recognizance of debt aforesaid mentioned in the same writ, that is on the said eleventh day of June in the third year aforesaid, and before the day of the taking of this inquisition, was seized in his demesne as of fee of and in two yards of land with appurtenances lying and being in the said Wheatley, containing forty-eight acres and one rod of arable land and four acres of meadow with appurtenances, of the clear annual value in all issues over and above reprises of £13-6-8; and of and in one cottage with appurtenances in Wheatley aforesaid now in the tenure or occupation of one Walter Symons, of the clear annual value in all issues over and above reprises of 20s.; and of and in one other cottage with appurtenances in Wheatley aforesaid, now in the tenure or occupation of one Richard Clarke, of the clear annual value in all issues over and above reprises of 20s.; and of and in one messuage with appurtenances in Wheatley aforesaid in the tenure or occupation of one Thomas Church, of the clear annual value in all issues over and above reprises, of 20s.; and also of and in one other cottage with appurtenances in Wheatley aforesaid in the tenure or occupation of one William Platt, of the clear annual value in all issues over and above reprises of 13s. 4d.; and further the jurors aforesaid on their oath aforesaid say that Anne Powell, widow, who was the wife of the aforesaid Richard, stands possessed of and in a third part of all and singular the premises aforesaid with the appurtenances as of freehold for the term of her life as her portion from the endowment of the aforesaid Richard her former husband, and that the said Anne now survives and exists in full life at Wheatley aforesaid. All which premises aforesaid with their appurtenances I, the aforesaid sheriff, on the said day of the taking of this inquisition, have taken and caused to be seized into the hands of our Lord the King. Finally, the aforesaid jurors on their aforesaid oath say that the aforesaid Richard Powell at the time of his death had no goods or chattels and had no other or further lands in my said county to the knowledge of the said jurors which could be extended or seized. In testimony of which matter both I, the aforesaid sheriff, and the aforesaid jurors have affixed our seals to this inquisition on the day and year first above written.

William Cope, Esq., Sheriff.]

French, *Milton in Chancery*, pp. 105-106.

. . . The 5ᵗ of August 1647, the Sheriffe of the County of Oxford, upon an Jnquisition taken upon the said Statute, did seise into the Kings hand, certaine Messuages, Lands, and Tithes in Whateley, whereof the said Rich: Powell in his life was seised in his Demesne, as of fee, a third part whereof Anne his wife of [*sic*] for life, as her dower of the cleare Yearly value of 58 ˡ. 3ˢ. 4ᵈ.

From Milton's petition of March 4, 1650/1, *q.v.*

. . . By vertue of an Extent and An Inquisicōn therevpon taken before the Sherriffe of the County of Oxoñ in the Citty of Oxoñ by the oath of lawfull men of the said County vpon the fifth day of August Jn the yeare of our Lord One Thousand six hundred ffortie and seaven itt was then and there found that the said Richard Powell att the time of the Acknowledgement of the said Statute That is to say vpon the Eleventh day of June in the said Third yeare of the late King was seized in his Demesme as of ffee of and in . . . . [Here follows almost verbatim the wording of the remainder of William Cope's return as quoted above.]

From Milton's answer to Elizabeth Ashworth's bill of complaint of February 22, 1653/4, *q.v.*

SEPTEMBER OR OCTOBER (?). MOVES FROM BARBICAN TO HIGH HOLBORN.

It was not long after the March of *Fairfax* and *Comwel* [*sic*] through the City of *London* with the whole Army, to quell the Insurrections *Brown* and *Massy*, now Malecontents also, were endeavouring to raise in the City against the Armies proceedings, ere he left his great House in *Barbican*, and betook himself to a smaller in *High Holbourn*, among those that open backward into *Lincolns-Inn* Fields, here he liv'd a private and quiet

Life, still prosecuting his Studies and curious Search into Knowledge, the grand Affair perpetually of his Life. . . .

Phillips, pp. xxviii-xxix; Darbishire, p. 68. Masson (III, 667) dates the move conjecturally in September or October, since Fairfax's march through London had occurred on August 6 and 7, 1647. Masson ventures the conjecture (III, 668) that the house "may still be extant."

He lived in several places. e.g. Holborn neer K's gate.

Aubrey, f. 68; Darbishire, p. 4. On this residence of Milton's see Cunningham, *London*, 1927, p. 338; Stow, *Survey of London* (1908), I, 77, II, 87 ff.; Walford, *Old and New London*, IV, 547-549, III, 50. Cunningham locates it between the Great and Little Turnstiles, fronting on Holborn and backing on Lincoln's Inn Fields.

SEPTEMBER 25. ANOTHER JOHN MILTON CHARGED WITH TREASON.

Die Sabbati, 25° *Septembris*, 1647, *Post Meridiem*. . . .

Resolved, &c. That . . . *John Milton* junior . . . be forthwith indicted of High Treason at the King's Bench. . . .

Journals of the House of Commons, V, 317. There is no reason to connect this document with Milton the poet, though he was "John Milton Junior" as was the poet. See my "Mute Inglorious John Miltons," *Modern Language Quarterly*, I (1940), 370. The incident out of which this indictment grew was the invasion of the House of Commons by a mob of Londoners on July 26, 1647; see Masson, III, 551. The John Milton Junior of this reference appears again in the *Journals* on October 1, when the House issued a hue and cry for him and his fellow-invaders, who by this time, however, had disappeared. It seems unwise to print here in any fulness either of the entries in the *Journals*, since they will serve merely to add strength to a mistaken identification.

A number of further references to a John Milton who is probably the same person appear later on in the *Journals* of both Commons and Lords during 1648. The references in the former are V, 452; in the latter X, 196-203, 213-215, 217-219, 307-308.

OCTOBER. ATTRIBUTED EPITAPH.

An Epitaph.
He whom Heaven did call away
Out of this Hermitage of clay . . .
When this cold numnes shall retreate
By a more y^n Chymick heat.
J. [?] M. O^{ber}.
1647./

This 54-line poem, written in an old hand in a copy of Milton's *Poems* of 1645 in the British Museum, was first discussed and attributed to Milton by Henry Morley in the London *Times* for July 16, 1868. It received wide discussion in the *Times* and other newspapers, in *Notes and Queries*, in the *Athenaeum*, and elsewhere. David H. Stevens, *Reference Guide to Milton*, # 2629, 2654, and 2656, gives a list of some of these references. An extensive collection of clippings on this subject is to be found in the British Museum under the title of "A Miltonic Controversy" (shelf-mark 11826.k.16). A brief summary of the relevant information is given in CM, XVIII, 595, where the text of the poem is given in full. The first of the two initials at the end is uncertain: it may be J or P or T or R, since it is obscured by the library stamp which occurs at that spot. Few critics have accepted it as Milton's, and the likelihood of its being genuine is very slim indeed. Even if the initials were surely J.M., and even if the handwriting were surely that of the seventeenth century, it would still be extremely foolhardy to attribute it to Milton simply because of those two facts. But it is mentioned here for the sake of completeness of the record.

OCTOBER 18-21. SIR ROBERT PYE AND MRS. ANNE POWELL ASSESSED ON PROPERTY IN FOREST HILL AND WHEATLEY.

An Assessment made vppon the Jnhabitants of the several Towneships Hamlets libertyes and Tythinges in Bullington Thame and Dorchester Hundreds . . . for six months incurred since the 25th day of March last past . . . taken at Whatley in the sayd county on Munday & Thursday the eighteenth & one & twentith dayes of October . . . 1647

fforesthill		li̇ s̄ ð
Sr Robert Pye K^t ....04-07-00 . . .		
Whetely		
Mrs Anne Powell wid. ....00-06-09. . . .		

From an assessment roll of Oxfordshire in the Public Record Office, of which I have lost the exact reference. The two sets of figures come from membranes 3 and 4. Though various Powells are named in this list, Milton's name does not occur.

NOVEMBER 1. LETTER FROM CARLO DATI.

All' Jll^{mo}. Sig: Gio: Miltoni Londra

Quando era morta in me ogni speranza, bench' uiuiss^o. il desiderio di riceuer Lettere di V. S. ueggo comparirmi una sua sopra

qñto io possa esprimere con questa penna gratissima. O quanti
motiui di smisurata allegrezza arrecò nel mio cuore quella pic-
cola carta! carta scritta da amico si virtuoso, e si caro; che dopo
si lungo tempo da si remota prouincia, mi portò nuoue della
salute di lei quanto bramata altrettanto dubbiosa, e mi accertò
che di me si manteneua memoria tanto fresca, e si amoreuole
nell' anima gentiliss^a. dl Sig^r. Gio: Miltoni. Conobbi ancora in
quale stima fosse appò di Lei la mia Patria, che frà suoi pregi
annouera d'auer nella grande Jnghilterra (come disse ql Poeta
diuisa dal nrō Mondo) chi le sue glorie magnifica, ama i suoi
Cittadini, celebra i suoi scrittori, e nel suo bello Idioma si pro-
priamente, e si politam^{te}. pscrive, e ragiona. E qsto appunto mi
mosse a rispondere Toscanam^{te}. alla lra Latiniss^a. di V. S., di
cui è dote singulariss^a. rauuiuare le lingue morte, e le straniere
far proprie, sperando che le sia p esser grato il suono di qlla che
ella si ben parla, e possiede. Per la stessa cogione piglierò ard^e.
di pregarla a uolere onorare co' suoi uersi la gloriosa memoria
del Sig^r. Franc^o. Rouai egregio Poeta Fiorentino immaturam^e.
defunto, e p qnto io credo da lei ben conosciuto. Lo stesso hanno
fatto a mia petizione i s^{ri}. Niccolò Einsio, e Isac Vossio Olandesi
miei amici, e Prōni Sing^{mi}., e letterati famosi dll' età nostra. Era
il Sig^r Francesco nobile di nascita, dotato dlla natura d'ingegno
eleuatissimo, e arricchito dall' arte, e dallo studio indefesso delle
scienze più belle. Intendeua beniss^o. la lingua Greca parlaua la
Franzese, scriueua stupendamente la Latina, e la Toscana. Cantò
Tragedie, ualse nelle Canzoni liriche, nelle quali lodò gl' Eroi, è
depresse i Vizi, e particolarm^e. in qlle sette fatte contro a i sette
Capitali. Era manieroso, cortese, amato da i Principi, di costumi
incorrotti, e religiosissimi. Mori Giouane senza auer publicato
l'ope sue. da gli amici di esso a lui si preparano Esequie sontuose,
solo in qsto mancheuoli c̄h dll' Oraz^e funerale a me è stā imposta
la Carica. Se ella si compiacerà, com' io spero di mandarmi in
tal proposito qualche frutto dl suo ameniss^o. ingegno si ob-
bligherà nō me solo, ma ttā la mia Prā e publicate che saranno
le Poesie dl Sig^r. Fran^o. e le lodi dl med^o. da me le ne saranno
inuiate le copie. Mà già che hò cominciato a parlar dlla nostra

lingua, e de' nostri Poeti piacemi participare a' V. S. una dlle mie Osseruazioni che negl' auanzi dl tempo concedutimi dalle occupaz^i. mercant^i. uò talora facendo sopra i nostri scrittori.

L'altrieri mentre io faceua reflessione sopra quel ternario dl Petrarca Trionf. d'Amor. c. 3

> Dura legge d'Amor, mà benche obliqua
> seruar conuiensi poch' ella aggiugne
> di cielo in terra uniuersale antiqua.

Veddi che già il dottiss. Casteluetro aueua notato questo luogo auer qualche simiglianza con q̄l d'Orazio l. 1. Ode 23.

> Sic uisum Veneri, cui placet impares
> formas, atq. animos, sub iuga ahenea
> sæuo mittere cum ioco.

Ottimam^{te}. imitato dal suscitatore della Poesia Pindarica, e Anacreontica Gabbriello Chiabrera, nella Canzonetta 18^a.

> Ah c̄h uien cenere
> penando un amator benche fedele;
> cosi uuol Venere
> nata nell' Ocean nume crudele.

Nei quali uersi nō solo si riconosce qualche particella presa da Orazio, si come il restante trasportato da Tibullo non senza notabil miglioramento, appò il quale L. 1. Eleg. 2 contro a i reuelatori dei segreti amorosi si legge q̄sta minaccia.

> Nam fuerit quicumq. loquax is sanguine natā
> is Venerem e rapido sentiet esse mari.

Doue parendomi che l'Aggiunto *rapido* dato al mare operi poco, o niente leggeidi *rabido* dalla qual uoce, co'l far solo capouolgere una Lettera, resulta grandissima forza al concetto di Tibullo, che uuole esprimere Venere rigorosa, e crudele in punire un tal delitto. A questa Correzzione si oppongono tutti i testi stampati, e ttī i Comentari del med^o. Poeta i quali leggono *rapido*, epiteto molto più conueniente al ueloce corso dei fiumi, che all' impeto dl mare, mà tutauia da molti poeti anche al mare applicato.

Catullo de Berecȳth. et Aty.

> Rapidum salum tulistis truculentaq. Pelagi

Virgilio in o p dir meglio con lo Scaligero Corn. Seu. in Aetna
    Sicuti cum curuo rapidum mare cernit^r. æstu.
Seneca Ercol. Eteo. uerso 552
    —et rapidū mare
Taurus puellæ uector Assiriæ scidit.
Valerio flacco Argon. L. 4
    —rapidum uentis certantibus æquor'
Claudiano.
    Jlle Tyron rapidi p tot discrim^a. ponti
Et altri ancora; mà osseruisi che tutti parlano di tempeste,
ouero cercano di esprimere la furia dl Mare tempestoso, che però
gli torna acconciam^e. il chiamarlo rapido, e Catullo nell' Argonaut. benissimo nomino rapido il Mare di Ellesponto pche p lo
flusso, e reflusso corre in q̄llo stretto continuamente. Mà a Tibullo leua ttā la bizzaria il dire
    Sentiranno i loquaci esser dal sangue
    e dal rapido mar Venere nata
piutosto che
    e dal rabbioso Mar Venere nata.
    Fauoriscono q̄sta mia opinione tutti quei Poeti i quali hanno
chiamoto il mare. ferū, sæuū, insanū, iratū, e altrimenti p espres-
sione de crudeltà; Ma doppiamente illustrano i luoghi da me
considerati. Seneca nel Ipolito u. 273
    Diua nō miti generata ponto
E Virgil. Æneid. L. 5. u. 802 che fà dire a Nettuno parlante
a Venere
    Fas omne est Cytherea meis te fidere regnis
    unde genus ducis: merui quoque sæpe, furores
    Compressi, et *rabiem* tantā cæliq. *marisq*.
Confermano la mia lezione il medesimo Virgil. il q̄le disse—
rabies Scyllæa   Valerio flacc. L. 4. u. 508 in circa
    Turbine sic rabido populos atq. æquora longè
    transabeunt, nullaq. dat^r. considere terra.
E u. 582 —   — pontū penetrauerit ulla
    cū ratis, et rabidi steterint in gurgite montes
Silio. Italico. L. 13

Agmina ut aspexit, rabidi ceu bellua ponti.
Jl medesimo errore appunto è trapassato nella Poetica d'Orazio
appō il quale Comunemente si legge parlandosi d'Orfeo
    Dictus ob hoc lenire tigres, rabidosq. Leones
doue ciascheduno di mediocre ingegno conosce quanto sia freddo,
e scontinuato concetto il dire c̄h il Canto d'Orfeo auesse virtù
di appiaceuolire i Leoni uelocissimi, e quanto meglio torni come
leggono il Cruquio, e il Lambino in alcuni manuscritti
    Dictus ob hoc lenire tigres, rabidosq. Leones
sendo proprijssimo l'appiaceuolire i rabbiosi, aggiunto conueniente a i Leoni. Onde Cornelio Gallo, o come meglio si crede
Massimiano Poeta Eleg. pª.
    Fracta diu rabidi compescitur ira Leonis.
benc̄h appō il medesimo si legga Eleg. 5
    tu cogis *rapidas* affectus discere tigres
che p le stesse ragioni del Luogo d'Orazio tornerebbe meglio
rabidas come le chiamo Virgil. Georg. 2. u. 151—
    At rabidæ tigres absunt, et sæua Leonū
    semina—
Mà troppo p auuentura mi sono auanzato, e co'l discorso, e con
l'ardire; tornando adunq. al mio primo scopo che fù di emendare
Tibullo, e illustrare il Chiabrera dico esser notissº. il nascimento
di Venere dal mare, come largamente notarono.
    Natal Conte Mitolog.
    Lilio Greg. Geraldi de Dijs Gentiū syntag. 13.
    Martino Del Rio sopra il uerso 273. dll' Ipolito di Seneca.
e Lodouico dlla Certa in Virg. Aen. L. 5. u. 802—
Non è meno certo che appō i poeti l'esser nato dal mare fù tenuto
indizio infallibl' di crudeltà. come disse A gell. L. 15. c. 21
    Ferocissimos, et immanes, et alienos ab omni humanitate
tanquā e mari genitos Neptuni filios dixerunt.
Jl medesimo Tibullo Eleg. 4. L. 3—
    Nam nec te uasti genuerunt æquora ponti.
Catullo nell' Argonaut.
    quod mare conceptū spumantibus expuit undis?

Ouid. nell' epist. di Arianna a Teseo.

    Nec pater est Aegeus, nec tu Pittheidos Aetræ
      filius: auctores saxa fretumq. tui.

Omero nel xvi°. dll' Iliade. u. 34.

    —γλαυκὴ δὲ σ' ἔτικτε θάλασσα,
    πέτραι τ' ἠλίβατοι, ὅτι τοι νόος ἐστὶν ἀπηνὴς.

cio, è

    Tu dal Ceruleo mar, dall' alte pietre
    nascesti, p̄ch sei di mente cruda.

    E il nr̄o Torquato Tasso dei sopracitati Poeti anzi emulo che imitatore canto nel xvi°. dlla sua Gerusalemme

    Ne te Sofia produsse, e non sei nato
    dell' Azio sangue nò tu, te l'Onda insana
    dl mar produsse, e il Caucaso gelato
    e le mammͤ allattar di Tigre Ircana

Ne giunga nuouo ad alcuno che Venere Dea si piaceuole e si graziosa sia chiamata dal Chiabrea nume crudele p̄che Orazio pure la dissē

    Mater sæua cupidinum

E Seneca nell' Ercole Eteo u. 543—

    Timende matri teliger sæuæ puer.

Partecipo a V. S. queste mie Considerazioni sicuro d'esser compatito, e auuertito amoreuolmͤ. dalla sua esquisita dottrina come la prego instantemͤ. supplicandola a p̄donarmi se l'affetto eccessiuo, l'essere stō si lungo tempo senza sue, e la gran lontananza mi hanno fatto eccedere i limiti prescritti alle lettere. Duolmi in estremo c̄h le turbolenze del Regno abbiano turbati i suoi studi, e stō ansiosamͤ. attendendo le sue Poesie nelle quali credo che mi si porgerà largo campo di ammirare la finezza dl suo ingegno, eccetto però in q̄lle che sono in disprezzo della mia Religione, le quali benche proferite da bocca amica possono esser ben compatite, mà non lodate; q̄sto tt̄auia nō mi sia d'impedimento a riceuer l'altre, scusando la mia zelante libertà. Frà tanto mentre io prego il Cielo che la faccia, e conserui felice, ella mi conserui dandomene segno co' suo gratissimi comandamͭͭ.

tutti li amici da me in nome di V. S. salutati affettuosam^e. la riu-
eriscono.

D V. S. Jll^ma.   Fir^e. p^o. 9bre. 1647

Ser. Deuot^mo.

Carlo Dati.

The original manuscript, or perhaps Dati's copy, is in the New
York Public Library. The letter is printed in full, with the abbreviations
expanded, in CM, XII, 296 ff. There is a partial facsimile in J. F. Marsh's
Papers Connected with the Affairs of Milton and his Family (published
by the Chetham Society, 1851), frontispiece. I am grateful to my colleague, Dr. Remigio U. Pane, for helping me to decipher the manuscript
of this letter.

A good many letters from Dati to various friends, chiefly French
and Italian, are given in Gilles Menage's *Mescolanze d'Egidio Menagio*,
Venice, 1736; but no letters to Milton are included. Angelo Fabroni's
Vitae Italorum, XVI (Pisa, 1795), 32-33, contains a brief biography
of Dati.

No verses by Milton on Rovai, if he ever wrote them in answer to
this request, have been found; nor has Milton's copy of Rovai's poems,
if Dati sent them to him, been found.

[To the most illustrious Signor John Milton, London:

When all hope of receiving letters from you was dead in
me, most keen as was my desire for such, lo! there arrives one
to delight me more than I can express with this most grateful
pen. O what feelings of boundless joy that little paper raised in
my heart—a paper written by a friend so admirable and so dear;
bringing to me, after so long a time and from so distant a land,
news of the welfare of one about whom I was as anxious as I
was uncertain, and assuring me that there remains so fresh and
so kind a remembrance of myself in the noble soul of Signor
John Milton! Already I knew what regard he had for my
country; which reckons herself fortunate in having in great England (separated, as the Poet said, from our world) one who
magnifies her glories, loves her citizens, celebrates her writers,
and can himself write and discourse with such propriety and
grace in her beautiful idiom. And precisely this it is that moves
me to reply in Italian to the exquisite Latin letter of my honoured friend, who has such a very singular faculty of reviving

dead tongues and making foreign ones his own; hoping that there may be something agreeable to him in the sound of a language which he speaks and knows so well. I will take the same opportunity of earnestly begging you to be pleased to honour with your verses the glorious memory of Signor Francesco Rovai, a distinguished Florentine poet prematurely dead, and, to the best of my belief, well known to you: this having already been done at my request by the very eminent Nicolas Heinsius and Isaac Vossius of Holland, peculiarly intimate and valued friends of mine, and famous scholars of our age. Signor Francesco was noble by birth, endowed by nature with a genius of the highest kind, which was enriched by culture and by unwearied study of the finest sciences. He understood Greek excellently, spoke French, and wrote Latin and Italian wonderfully. He composed Tragedies, and excelled also in lyrical Canzoni, in which he praised heroes and discountenanced all vice, particularly in one set of seven made against the seven capital sins. He was well-bred, courteous, a favourite with our Princes, of uncorrupted manners, and most religious. He died young, without having published his works: a splendid obituary ceremonial is being prepared for him by his friends, faulty only in the fact that the charge of the funeral oration has been imposed upon me. Should you be pleased to send me, as I hope, some fruit of your charming genius for such a purpose, you will oblige not me only, but all my country; and, when the Poems of Signor Francesco are published, with the eulogiums upon him, I will see that copies are sent you.—But, since I have begun to speak of our language and our poets, let me communicate to you one of the observations which, in the leisure-hours left me from my mercantile business, I occasionally amuse myself with making on our writers. The other day, while I was reflecting on that passage in Petrarch's *Triomf' d'Amor*, C. 3: . . .

I communicate to you these considerations of mine, sure of being excused, and kindly advised by your exquisite learning in such matters as I submit, urgently begging you to pardon me if excess of affection, the sense of being so long without you, and our great intimacy, have made me exceed the limits proper for a letter.—It is an extreme grief to me that the convulsions of the kingdom have disturbed your studies; and I anxiously await your Poems, in which I believe I shall have large room for admiring the delicacy of your genius, even if I except those which are in depreciation of my Religion, and which, as coming from a friendly mouth, may well be excused, though not praised. This will not hinder me from receiving the others, conscious as I am of my own zeal for freedom. Meanwhile I beg Heaven to make and keep you happy, and to keep me in your remembrance, giving me proofs thereof by your generous commands. All friends about me send you salutations and very affectionate respects.

Your most devoted,

Florence, 1st Nov. 1647.   Carlo Dati

Masson, III, 680-683. The translation in CM, XII, 297-313, is by Professors Mabbott and McCrea. Masson's translation is incomplete, omitting most of the central section on philology: I have left out still more, indicating the omission by a row of dots. Nothing of biographical import is found in the omitted passage, which is given in full in the original Italian.

AFTER NOVEMBER 1 (?). CONTRIBUTES TO ROVAI MEMORIAL VOLUME (?).

Carlo Dati invited Milton, in his letter of November 1, 1647 (*q.v.*), to contribute complimentary verses to a volume in honor of Francesco Rovai, saying that Heinsius and Vossius had already done so. Milton may have furnished verses, but none have been found. The *Poesie di Francesco Rovai*, ed. N. Rovai, Florence, 1652, seems to contain no Miltonic writings. Dati's letter of December 4, 1648, makes no mention of them. But a manuscript or printed volume with such poetry may yet be found.

NOVEMBER 20. TAKES POSSESSION OF WHEATLEY.

[In a statement in 1651 Milton says that the Sheriff of Oxfordshire seized Wheatley in 1647,] The wch Messuages, and Premisses, the said Sheriffe, by virtue of a Liberate, did the 20th of Novem: 1647, deliver unto the Petitioner [i.e., Milton],

To hold unto him, and his Assignees, as his ffranktenement, untill he were satisfied his said Debt of 500ˡⁱ, with damages, costs,
and Charges. As by a Copie of the Liberate, and the Execution
thereof, deposed by the said Thomas Gardner, appeares.

From Milton's petition of March 4, 1650/1, *q.v.*

By vertue of which extent Jnquisic̄on and a liberate therevpon . . . the said porc̄on of tithes with the Appurtennances
and alsoe All and singuler the lands Tenements Cottages and
premises with their Appurtennances vpon the Twentieth day of
November in the Twenty Third yeare aforesaid were delivered
to this Defᵗ by the said Sherriffe to hold to him and his assignes
as his ffreehold vntill hee should be fully satisfied of his said
Debt.

From Milton's answer to Elizabeth Ashworth, February 22, 1653/4,
q.v.

NOVEMBER 20. ALLOWS MOTHER-IN-LAW ANNE POWELL HER SHARE OF INCOME FROM WHEATLEY.

And this Defᵗ conceiveth that the said Tithes lands and premises were chardged by the said Jury with the Dower of the
said Anne vpon the said Annes makeing knowne her clayme
and Right therevnto by reason whereof her said Dower was
Allowed vnto her by this Defᵗ as hee conceiveth Rightfully
vntill vpon his composic̄on aforesaid and the Refusall of the
Com̃ittee to Admitt the said Anne to Any composic̄on And their
expresse Order to this Defᵗ to take and Receiue the whole Rents
yssues and proffitts of all the sayd Tithes lands and premises As
by the said Order Appeareth this Defᵗ then Refused Any longer
to Allow the said Dower to the said Anne and hath since Received the whole proffitts.

From Milton's answer to Elizabeth Ashworth, February 22, 1653/4,
q.v. The date used is that of Milton's obtaining the property of Wheatley,
as explained under this same date.

[Milton valued his Powell estate at eighty pounds] Out of
wᶜʰ he was allowed the thirds wᶜʰ he paid to Mʳⁱˢ Powell for her
Dower.

From the court order of June 7, 1653, *q.v.*

NOVEMBER 27 (?). SIR ROBERT PYE PREPARES REPLY
TO MILTON.

... Wherevnto the said p^t. replied the 27th of No: 1647. ...
From the order of the Court of Chancery, June 16, 1649, *q.v.* The
actual replication of Pye referred to here, as filed in the Chancery records,
is dated Hilary, 22 Charles I, and is therefore filed under January-
February, 1648. For a possible explanation of the conflict of dates, see
that entry.

DECEMBER 3. SIR ROBERT PYE ASSIGNS FOREST HILL TO
HIS SON JOHN.

[John Reading says in a report of January 1, 1650/1:] That
afterwards the said S^r. Robert Py by his Indenture dated the
3°. December 1647 In consideracōn of the naturall loue and
affection which hee bore to the petitioner [John Pye] being
one of his sonns, did graunt assigne and sett ouer, the said premisses and all his estate therein then to come and vnexpired vnto
the peticōner his executors and assignes.
Public Record Office, SP Dom 23/109, p. 518; Hamilton, p. 56.
Similar references are found in Hamilton, pp. 85 and 521.

DECEMBER 14. DIVORCE VIEWS ATTACKED BY SION
COLLEGE MINISTERS.

Errours touching Marriage and Divorce ...
That, Indisposition, unfitnesse or contrariety of minde (*beti-
wixe man and wife*) arising from a cause in nature unchangeable, hindring and ever likely to hinder the main benefits of
conjugall society, which are solace, and peace; are a great reason of Divorce, *&c*^t.
[Marginal note:] 'Doctrine and Discipline of divorce, by *I.
M.* Lond. 1644 p 6: Peruse the whole Book.
*A Testimony to the Truth of Jesus Christ, and to our Solemn League
and Covenant; as also against the Errours, Heresies and Blasphemies of
these times, and the Toleration of them: Wherein is inserted A Catalogue
of divers of the said Errours, &c. ... Subscribed by the Ministers of
Christ within the Province of London, Decemb. 14 &c. 1647.*, 1648,
p. 19. Referred to in Masson, III, 676, and quoted as above in Parker,
pp. 77-78. The long list of signers of this document, given on pp. 35-38,

is composed of men connected almost exclusively with Sion College: Calamy, Gataker, Love, Wall, and others.

Thomason's copy has the 8 of 1648 crossed out in pen and the date "Jan: 18 1647" [*i.e.*, 1647/8] added.

1648

WINTER. PROFITS FROM WHEATLEY.

. . . this Def^t that winter season [1647-48] . . . could not make any thing thereof saue onely Two powndes and Thirteene shillings rent out of the Cottages not being Able to lett the rest of the premises vntill the Lady day [March 25] following. . . .

From Milton's answer to Elizabeth Ashworth's bill, February 22, 1653/4, *q.v.*

TWO POEMS INCLUDED IN WILLIAM SANCROFT'S MANUSCRIPT ANTHOLOGY.

[1]   Ψ. *136.*

1. Lett us with a gladsom mind
   Praise the Lord; for He is kind.
   For his Mercies ay endure,
   Ever faithfull, ever sure.

. . . .

26. Lett us therfore warble forth
    His mighty Majestie, & worth.
    For &c.
    That His Mansion hath on High,
    Above the reach of Mortall Eye.
    For his Mercies ay endure,
    Ever faithfull, ever sure./.
    J. Milton. poëm. p. 13. (done at 15 years old.

[2]   *On the Morning of Christ's Nativitie.* 1629.
     This is the Month, & this the happy Morn,

John Milton · 1648

Wherein the Son of Heavens Eternal King,
Of wedded Maid, & Virgin Mother born,
Our great Redemtion from above did bring:
For so the holy *Sages* once did sing,
That He our deadly forfeit should release,
And wth His Father work us a perpetual Peace.

. . . .

27.

But See! the Virgin blest
Hath layd her Babe to Rest;
Time is o^r tedious Song should here have ending:
Heaven's youngest-teemed Starr
Hath fixt her polisht Carr,
Her sleeping Lord wth Handmaid-Lamp attending:
And all about ye Courtly Stable
Bright-harnest Angels sitt in Order serviceable./.

Jo Miltons. poëms. p. 1.

Bodleian Library, MS. Tanner 466, pp. 34-35 and 60-66; or by other pagination, ff. 20v-21; 33v-36v. The references to this manuscript, first noticed by Warton, are misleading. Warton mentioned them (Milton's *Poems*, 1791, p. v) as follows: "Perhaps almost the only instance on record, in that period of time, of their [Milton's minor poems] having received any, even a slight, mark of attention or notice, is to be found in archbishop Sancroft's papers at Oxford. In these papers is contained a very considerable collection of poetry, but chiefly religious, exactly and elegantly transcribed with his own hand, while he was a fellow of Emanuel college, and about the year 1648, from Crashaw, Cowley, Herbert, Alabaster, Wootton, and other poets then in fashion. And among these extracts is Milton's ODE ON THE NATIVITY, said by Sancroft to be selected from 'the first page of John Milton's Poems.' Also our author's version of the fifty-third Psalm, noted by the transcriber, I suppose as an example of uncommon exertion of genius, to have been done in the fifteenth year of the translator's age." Warton gives as his reference: MSS. Coll. Tann. Num. 465, ff. 34, 60.

An effort to check Warton's reference and to get photostatic copies of the pages in question caused the Keeper of Western Manuscripts in the Bodleian, Mr. R. W. Hunt, some perplexities. But with great kindness and persistence he kept after them until he found them. It will now be noticed that the manuscript is not No. 465 but 466, the location is not *folios* 34 and 60 but *pages* 34 and 60, and the psalm is not 53 but 136. And yet, except for the number of the psalm, and the slip of

[213]

writing *folio* instead of *page*, Warton was correct, since MS. 466 is part of a larger volume originally called 465.

Warton's date seems reasonable. Sancroft, later to be Archbishop of Canterbury, was appointed fellow and tutor of Emmanuel College, Cambridge, in 1642 (*DNB*), so that he would have been likely to know of and be interested in Milton's 1645 volume of poems. And the page reference given for the Psalm 136 fits the 1645 edition but not that of 1673; the Nativity poem begins on p. 1 in each edition. The text, too, is that of 1645.

Although the spelling, capitalization, and punctuation are very widely different from Milton's printed volume, as the selections given above will show, there are no verbal variants in the Psalm. In the Nativity poems there are four:

52 Peace] *Peace* (*with the word* Calme *written above*)
53 or] nor
86 dawn] Day
171 wrath] wroth

The second and third of these seem like the normal slips to be found in any copying. The first seeems to represent an amendment suggested by the copyist. The fourth curiously anticipates the edition of 1673, which has "wroth" for the 1645 version "wrath."

This collection is noticed by Parker, p. 23, but without particular comment other than that Warton's mistaken reference to the fifty-third Psalm is noted.

SAID TO BE WORKING ON HISTORY OF ENGLAND.

Milton is not only writing a Vniv. History of Engl. but also an Epitome of all Purchas Volumes. Haack.

[Marginal note:] Milton. Histi Anglic. Purchas.

From Samuel Hartlib's "Ephemerides" in the collection of Lord Delamere; printed in G. H. Turnbull, *Hartlib, Dury and Comenius*, pp. 40-41. Although no date appears on the photostat of the page from which this note is taken, Professor Turnbull says this notebook is dated 1648. See also the entry below dated: "Before March 13" 1649.

In connection with this mention of the writings of Purchas, Professor Turnbull calls attention to the following extract from a letter of Benjamin Worsley to Hartlib on June 27, 1648: "This calls to mind Purchase his workes, which I wonder extreamly, is so neglected or rather scorned by our great Bookemen, whereas there is scarse a Genius lives, that may not find some delight in them, lett him be addicted to what study he will. J have often wished, that as he himselfe digested all the discourses of manners, policy, & Religion, into one, which he calls his Pilgrimage: And as others have digested some other parts of his discourses, of the norwest passage of Chynæ & of other parts, according to

their particular fancies; That some would collect all his Naturall History, with out abbreviating or Epitomizing it, for this would spoyle,
which had J not beene prevented, I had long agoe vndertaken." No
epitome of Purchas by Milton is known, although Milton uses him frequently in his *History of Moscovia* and a few times in his Commonplace
Book. The name "Haack" at the end of the note probably refers to
Theodore Haak, translator and scholar, from whom apparently this information came to Hartlib.

SENDS TWO COPIES OF HIS *POEMS* TO DATI.

Fino l'anno passato risposi alla cortesissima, ed elegantissima
Lettera di V. S. Illmo. . . . Ho di poi riceuuto due copie dlle sue
eruditissime Poesie. . . .

From Dati's letter to Milton, December 4, 1648, *q.v.* Possibly these
poems were Milton's response to Dati's request of April 21, 1647, for a
poetic contribution, though they hardly seem appropriate.

[As far back as the end of last year I replied to your very
courteous and elegant letter. . . . Since then I have received two
copies of your most erudite Poems. . . .]

SONNET TO LAWES PRINTED.

To my Friend Mr Henry Lawes.

Henry and William Lawes, *Choice Psalms*, 1648, sig. a^v; Fletcher, 1,
368; CM, I, 63. For further details see above under date of February 9,
1645/6.

SECOND EDITION OF BARON'S IMITATIONS OF MILTON.

Robert Baron, 'Ερωτοπαίγνιον, 1648, *passim*. This is a later edition of
the work noticed above under date of April, 1647.

JANUARY OR FEBRUARY (?). SIR ROBERT PYE REPLIES TO MILTON'S ANSWER TO HIS BILL OF COMPLAINT.

Maydwell The Replicacōn of Sr Robtē Pye K^t Complaynant
                to the Answere of John Melton geñtl Defend^t./
The said Complaynñt for Replicacon saith, that hee doth & will
averr, maintaine & justifie his said Bill of Complaint & all &
everie the matters thingę & allegacōns therein Contayned to bee
just true, Certaine & sufficient in the lawe to bee Answered vnto,
And that the Answere of the said Defend^t is verie vntrue in-
certaine & insufficient in the lawe to bee Replied vnto for the

manifest faultp & impfeccōns therin contayned, And for further
Replicacōn this Repliant saith in all & everie thinge & thingp
as in his said Bill of Complaint hee hath sayed, wth out that y^t.
anie other matter thing or thingp materiall in the said Def^t Answere to bee Replied vnto, and not heerin sufficientlie Replied
vnto is true, All wch matters & thingp this Repliant is readie to
averr & prove as this honō^ble Court shall Award, and prayeth as
in his said Bill of Complaint hee hath alreadie praied.

Smith. Hill: 22° Car Rp./

Public Record Office, C2 Charles I/P 98/30; London *Times Literary Supplement*, March 14, 1936, p. 224; French, *Milton in Chancery*,
pp. 300-301. The date of this document is uncertain. The later decree
in the case, handed down on June 16, 1649 (*q.v.*), mentions it as of
November 27, 1647; the document itself, as will be seen, is dated in
Hilary term, 22 Charles I (i.e., 1647/8), which was from January 24
to February 12. Both documents contain mistakes, but that of the reply
itself here seems more likely to be right. In *Milton in Chancery* I catalogued it under the earlier date. It may be that the document was prepared on November 27, which would be virtually the last day of the
Michaelmas term, so that it may actually not have reached the court
until the following, or Hilary, term.

JANUARY 17. OCCASIONALLY ATTRIBUTED WORK,
NOVAE SOLYMAE, REGISTERED FOR PUBLICATION.

𝕿𝖍𝖊 17th 𝖔𝖋 𝕵𝖆𝖓𝖚𝖆𝖗𝖕 1647. . . .

Master Legatt. Entred . . . under the hands of Master
DOWNHAM and Master LATHAM warden a booke called
Novae Solymae . . . vj^d.

Stationers' Registers, I, 286. This book, written in Latin and translated and published in 1902 by Walter Begley with an attribution to
Milton, is not accepted as by him by any responsible scholar today. It is
mentioned here simply for completeness. See CM, XVIII, 636.

JANUARY 18. SION COLLEGE ATTACK PUBLISHED.

A Testimony to the Truth of Jesus Christ. . . .

See the entry above under date of December 14, 1647, which seems
to have been published on January 18, 1648.

MARCH 25. LEASES PROPERTY IN WHEATLEY.

... [Lady Day, 1648] Att what time this De‘t [Milton] did lease the said Tithes and, Cottages to John Robinson ... for six yeares from thence fully to be compleat & ended reserveing the yearely rent of threescore pounds and the said lands Tenements and rest of the said premisses to John Cadbury and Graland Page for ye same terme of yeares att the severall yearely rents of Twentie pounds a peice. ...

From Milton's answer to the bill of Elizabeth Ashworth, February 22, 1654, *q.v.*

... hee [John Robinson] hath rented yᵉ Messuage & Landes for a yeare & vpwards & yᵉ Tithes for seaven yeares & vpwards & that this deponᵗ. doth pay to yᵉ defᵈᵗ. yearely threescore & tenne pounds for yᵉ said Messuage Lands & tythes Contribuc̄ons & taxes being deducted, & that this deponᵗ. hath paid yᵉ defᵈᵗ. Two hundred & fowrescore pounds or thereabouts in rents for yᵉ said Tythes since hee first tooke it as hee remembreth. ...

From John Robinson's deposition, January 11, 1655/6, *q.v.* I am unable to account for the discrepancies among the figures as given here.

... yᵉ said Messuage Cottage moetye of three yard Lands & tithes were lett for six yeares last past or thereabouts for fourescore pounds a yeare. ...

From John Gadbury's deposition, January 11, 1655/6, *q.v.*

APRIL. TURNS PSALMS 80-88 INTO METER.

April. 1648. J.M. *Nine of the Psalms done into Metre, wherein all but what is in a different Character, are the very words of the Text, translated from the Original.*

Milton, *Poems*, 1673, p. 143; CM, I, 134; Fletcher, I, 86. The nine Psalms as done by Milton cover pp. 143-165 of the *Poems*.

APRIL 19 (?). PAYS MOTHER-IN-LAW ANNE POWELL FIRST INSTALLMENT OF THIRDS FROM RICHARD POWELL'S ESTATE.

See the note to the entry given below under date of November 19, 1648, which suggests that the proper date of that entry may be April 19.

APRIL 24. APPOINTED TO LEVY ASSESSMENTS (?).

Die *Lunae*, 24 *April*. 1648.

An Ordinance of the Lords and Commons assembled in Parliament, for the bringing in the Arrears of the Assessments for the Army, within the City of *London* and Liberties thereof, with the Names of the Persons in each Ward appointed for executing the same. . . .

Tower Ward.

John Bennet.
Andrew Richard.
William Bateman.
Henry Sweet.
John Milton.
Thomas Burnell.
Gilbert Keat.
John Langley.
Nathaniel Wright.
George Hanger.

Journals of the House of Lords, x, 229-230. It is not likely that this reference applies to the poet, who lived too far from the Tower to be chosen for such work. But there is nothing impossible about it, and the reference is therefore included with a question.

JULY 29. ATTACKED FOR DIVORCE VIEWS.

These following [errors of doctrine] *are so grosse, they need no further Confutation.* . . .

In the doctrine of divorce by *Iohn Milton*. That unfitnesse or contrariety of minde betwixt man and wife, from a naturall cause which hindereth solace and peace are a great reason of divorce.

T. C., *A Glasse for the Times . . . with a briefe Collection of the Errors of our Times . . . Collected by T.C. a Friend to Truth*, 1648, pp. 5-6; Todd, 1 (1826), 63; Parker, pp. 77-78. The Thomason copy bears the date July 29.

AUGUST (?). WRITES SONNET TO LORD FAIRFAX.

Fairfax, whose name in armes through Europe rings. . . .

Trinity College Manuscript, p. 47; Milton, *Letters of State*, ed.

Phillips, 1694, p. xlvi; CM, I, 64. In the manuscript it bears the heading: "On ye Lord Gen. Fairfax at yᵉ seige of Colchester." Since Colchester capitulated on August 27 (Smart) or 28 (Masson), the poem must presumably date from earlier than that day. Smart, in his edition of the sonnets, p. 84, dates it before August 17, since in the poem the Scots, who were defeated at the battle of Preston on that day, seem to be still unbeaten.

Mʳ J. Milton made two admirable Panegyricks (as to sub-limitie of Witt) one on Ol: Cromwel. & the other on Th: Lᵈ. Fairfax, both wᶜʰ his nephew Mʳ Philips hath; but he hath hung back these 2 yeares, as to imparting copies to me, for yᵉ Collect. of mine wᵗʰ you. Wherefore J desire you, in yʳ next, to intimate *yʳ desire*, of having these 2 copies of verses aforesayd. Were they made in the comendacion of yᵉ Devill, 'twere all one to me. tis the ὕψος [height] yᵗ I looke after. I have been told 'tis beyond Waller's, or any thing in that kind.

John Aubrey, letter to Anthony Wood, received May 25, 1684, Bodleian Library, MS. Wood F 39, fol. 372; Darbishire, p. 342. In the original manuscript the last two letters of the Greek word are abbreviated.

AUGUST 17. JOHN SADLER SENDS REGARDS TO MILTON THROUGH SAMUEL HARTLIB.

My Deare frind   Aug: 17: 4[8?]
   . . . Jf J write not againe to my good frind Dʳ. Coxe, J pray excuse it to him. . . . if you see Mʳ. Melton J beseeche you present my reall service to him; J spare him in not writing.
                        Yr. most affectionate
                        [Signature cut off]

From a letter, said to be by John Sadler, to Samuel Hartlib in the collection of Lord Delamere; printed in part in G. H. Turnbull, *Hartlib, Dury and Comenius*, p. 41. Although this reference is very vague, the likelihood of its being to the poet Milton is strengthened by the many other allusions to him in Hartlib's papers, by the association of his name with Dr. Cox's in Hartlib's notes of 1647 about education, and by the later slight connection of Milton with a Mrs. Sadleir (Masson, IV, 529-531). For the last figure of the date and for the signature, neither of which is visible on my photostatic copy, I have drawn on Professor Turnbull's book.

SEPTEMBER 29. RECEIVES RENTS FROM WHEATLEY.

. . . Att Michalmas One Thousand six hundred ffortie and eight (the said leases con[tinuing] from the ffiue and Twentieth of March before) Thirty and One pownds Thirteen shillings and Eight pence. . . .

From Milton's answer to Elizabeth Ashworth's bill of complaint, February 22, 1653/4, *q.v.*

OCTOBER 25. DAUGHTER MARY BORN.

My daughter Mary was born on Wednesday Octob. 25th on the fast day in the morning about 6 a clock 1648.

From Milton's family Bible, British Museum, Add. MS. 32,310, front flyleaf. The entry is apparently in Milton's own hand. The page containing this and other entries has been reproduced a number of times, including Dr. Williamson's *Milton Tercentenary*, facing p. 1. See my "The Autographs of John Milton," #71; Darbishire, p. 336; Masson, III, 689.

Mary my Daughter was born on Wednesday Octob. 25, on the Fast Day in the Morning about 6 a clock 1648.

The Milton-Powell family Bible, now lost. I quote Thomas Birch's transcript, British Museum Add. MS. 4,244, f. 52v; Masson, III, 483, 689; IV, 335; Stern, I, ii, 492. See my "The Autographs of John Milton," #86.

NOVEMBER 7. DAUGHTER MARY BAPTIZED.

[Baptisms, November 7, 1648:] Mary, daughter of John Milton, Esq., and Mary, his wife.

Parish Register, Church of St. Giles in the Fields, London; provided to me by the kindness of Rev. E. R. Moore, rector. Published in my "The Baptism of Milton's Daughter Mary," *Modern Language Notes*, LXIII (1948), 264-265.

1648. Nov. 7 bap. Mary d. of John Milton Esq and Mary his wife. Register of St Giles in the Fields. For this I am indebted to my friend M[r] Adams, who has made very large extracts from this & other London Registers.

British Museum, Add. MS. 24,491, fol. 191 (also numbered 347). Yale University has a photostatic copy of this whole set of manuscripts, called "Chorus Vatum," containing Joseph Hunter's enormous biographical and genealogical collections.

NOVEMBER 13 (?). PAYS MOTHER-IN-LAW ANNE POWELL HER THIRDS.

[Milton] did pay or cause to bee payed vnto . . . Anne Powell . . . the seuerall sūmes of money menċoned and Expressed in the sixe seuerall Acquittances or Receiptes . . . [the second of which is dated] November yᵉ 13ᵗʰ 1648. and is for the sūme of 3ˡⁱ. 6ˢ. 8ᵈ.

From Anne Powell's deposition in the Ashworth-Milton suit, June 4, 1656, *q.v.* See the note to the similar entry for November 19, 1648.

NOVEMBER 19 (?). PAYS MOTHER-IN-LAW ANNE POWELL HER THIRDS FROM RICHARD POWELL'S PROPERTY.

[Milton] did pay or cause to bee payed vnto this dēpt shee beinge the said Anne Powell . . . the seuerall sūmes of money menċoned and Expressed in the sixe seuerall Acquittances or Receiptes nowe shewed to this dēpt one whereof is dated Nouember yᵉ 19ᵗʰ 1648: and is for yᵉ sūme of fiftie shillinges . . . and that the said monyes were payed to this dēpt in satisfaction of her thirdϼ for yᵉ times then beinge of and in the said landϼ and tithes, And this dēpt acknowledgeth that she did thereupon giue the said Acquīttances or Receiptes vnto or for the said defēndt and that this dēpts name sett to the same Respectivelie was of the proper hand writeinge of herselfe this dēpt. . . .

From Anne Powell's deposition in the Ashworth-Milton suit, June 4, 1656, *q.v.* It seems likely that Mrs. Powell's dating (or that of the court scribe) is here at fault. The other five dates given are November 13, 1648, April 23, 1649, October 20, 1649, April 10, 1650, and October 12, 1650. Since the regular pattern here is one of six-months intervals, the proper date here may be April 19 rather than November 19. The eye of the copyist may easily have caught the wrong word at this point. The original receipts have not been found.

DECEMBER 4. CARLO DATI WRITES MILTON A LETTER.

Illᵐᵒ. Sig. e Pron. Ossᵒ.

Fino l'anno passato risposi alla cortesissima, ed elegantissima Lettera di V. S. Illᵐᵒ. affettuosaᵐ. ringraziandola dlla memoria che p sua grazia si compiace tenere della mia osseruanza. Scrissi, come fo adesso in Toscano, sapendo che la mia Lingua è a lei si cara, e familiare che nella sua bocca non apparisce straniera. Ho di poi riceuuto due copie dlle sue eruditissime Poesie dlle q̄li nō mi poteua arriuare donatiuo più caro, p chè quantunque piccolo racchiude in se ualore infinito p esser una Gemma dl Tesoro dl Sig: Gio: Miltoni. E come disse Teocrito;

ἦ μεγάλα χάρις
δώρῳ ξὺν ὀλίγῳ, πάντα δὲ τιμαῦτα τὰ πὸρ φίλων.

Gran pregio ha' picciol dono, e merta onore
Cio che uien da gl'amici.

Le rendo adunque q̄lle grazie che maggiori p me si possono e prego il Cielo che mi dia fortuna di poterle dimostrare la mia deuozione verso il suo merito. Non ascondere alla reneuolenta di V. S. Illma. alcune nuoue che son certo le saranno gratissime. Il Ser^{mo}. Granduca Mio Siḡ. s'e compiaciuto conferirmi La Cattedra, e Lettura dlle Lettere umane dell' Academia Fiorentina uacata p la morte dll' Eruditiss°. S^r. Giov^l. Doni gentiluomo fiorentino. Questa è carica onoreuolissima, e sempre esercitata da Gentiluomini, e litterati di q̄sta Patria, come già dal Politiano, da' due Vettori, e due Adriani lumi dlle Lettere. La p̄tā Settimana p la morte dl Ser^{mo}. Pr̄npe Lorenzo di Tosc^a, Zio dl Granduca Regnante feci l'orazione funerale, come dlla sia publicata sarà mia cura inuiarne Copia a V. S. Illma. Hò alle mani diuerse opere, quali a Dio piacendo triero [avanti] p farne q̄llo [guidi]-cheranno meglio i mie' dotti, e amoreuoli amici. Il Sr Valerio Chimentelli e stō eletto da S. Altezza p Professore delle Lettere Greche in Pisa con grande espettazionne dl suo ualore.

I SS^{ti}. Frescobaldi, Coltellini, Francini, Galilei, et altri infiniti unitam^t. Le inuiano affettuosi saluti. ed io come più d'ogn' altro obbligato, con ricordarle il desiderio de suoi comandi mi ratifico p sempre uiuere.

Di V. S. Illma.

Firente, 4 xbre. 1648.   [no signature]

[Endorsed:] All' Illmo. Sig^r e Pron Oss°. Il Sig^r. Giouanni Miltoni. [Londra.]

British Museum, Add. MS. 5016*, ff. 9-10v; Milton's *Works*, Pickering, 1851, I, cxcv-vi; CM, XII, 312 ff. The words enclosed in brackets are no longer visible in the original manuscript but are taken from earlier transcripts. Though the letter is not signed, no one has questioned its genuineness or its attribution to Dati. The readings of some words, especially "delle," "dlla," and the like, are not exactly certain; former editors have ignored many of the abbreviations.

Masson (III, 691) quotes an interesting sentence from Salvino Salvini's *Fasti Consolari dell' Accademia Fiorentina*, Florence, 1717, p. 554, to the effect that Dati intended to publish letters which he had received from distinguished literary men like Milton, Vossius, Heinsius, and others; but he seems not to have done so.

[Most Illustrious Sir and Most Honoured Master,

As far back as the end of last year I replied to your very courteous and elegant letter, thanking you affectionately for the kind remembrance you are pleased to entertain of me. I wrote, as I do now, in Italian, knowing my language to be so dear and familiar to you that in your mouth it scarcely appears like a foreign tongue. Since then I have received two copies of your most erudite Poems, and there could not have reached me a more welcome gift; for, though small, it is of infinite value, as being a gem from the treasure of Signor John Milton. And, in the words of Theocritus:—

[the Greek is here quoted again]

"Great grace may be
In a slight gift: all from a friend is precious."

I return you therefore my very best thanks, and pray Heaven to put it in my power to show my devoted appreciation of your merit. There are some pieces of news which I will not keep from you, because I am sure, from your kindness, they will be agreeable to you. The most Serene Grand Duke my master has been pleased to appoint me to the Chair and Lectureship of Humanity in the Florentine Academy, vacant by the death of the very learned Signor Giovanni Doni of Florence. This is a most honourable office, and has always been held by gentlemen and scholars of this country, as by Poliziano, the two Vettori, and the two Adriani, luminaries in the world of letters. Last week, on the death of the Most Serene Prince Lorenzo of Tuscany, uncle of the reigning Grand Duke, I made the funeral oration; when it is published, it shall be my care to send you a copy. I have on hand several works, such as, please God, may lead to a better opinion of me among my learned and kind friends. Signor Valerio Chimentelli has been appointed by his Highness to be Professor of Greek Literature in Pisa, and there are great expectations from him. Signors Frescobaldi, Coltellini, Francini, Galilei, and many others unite in sending you affectionate salutations; and I, as under more obligation to you than any of the others, remain ever yours to command.

Florence, Dec. 4, 1648.

(Addressed on the outside:) To the most illustrious sir and most honored master, the signor John Milton, London.]

Masson, III, 690-691. A somewhat altered translation is given in CM, XII, 313 ff. See also my "The Autographs of John Milton," #106. The previous letter which Dati mentions at the beginning of his letter is probably that of November 1, 1647, given above. There is no record of Milton's having received from Dati the funeral oration of which Dati here promised to send him a copy.

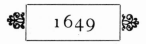

1649

AREOPAGITICA ALLUDED TO IN JOHN HALL'S *HUMBLE MOTION TO PARLIAMENT* (?).

But since this [attack on abuses in universities] would amount to a long rabble, and degenerate into some *Satyre* or *Pasquill*, rather then an *Areopagitick*, I will be content, having a publicke business in hand, to lay aside all bitternesse, though it might be advantagious to my purpose, and with due meeknesse and equanimity, draw to my last taske, and then sit downe with silent wishes and earnest expectation.

J[ohn] H[all], *An Humble Motion To The Parliament of England Concerning The Advancement of Learning: And Reformation of the Universities*, 1649, pp. 28-29; first published and described by William Haller in "Two Early Allusions to Milton's *Areopagitica*," *Huntington Library Quarterly*, XII (1949), 207-212. Professor Haller believes that the word "*Areopagitick*" probably refers to Milton's *Areopagitica*, since the *New English Dictionary* records no instance of the use of the word before Milton. The similarity of thought to Milton's in some parts of the pamphlet leads Dr. Haller to comment that Hall was "one of Milton's earliest and most attentive readers." This is one of the few early allusions to Milton's famous book. I am indebted to the courtesy of the officials of the Huntington Library for allowing me to have a photostatic copy of the title page and this section of Hall's book, of which they have a film copy of the original in the British Museum.

FEBRUARY 9 (?). *EIKON BASILIKE* IS PUBLISHED.

Εἰκὼν Βασιλική: The True Portraicture of His Sacred Majestie in his Solitudes and Sufferings . . . MDCXLVIII.

[MS. note on titlepage:] feb: 9ᵗʰ.

[MS. note on flyleaf:] The first Jmpression.

Taken from the Thomason copy in the British Museum; press-mark C.59.a.24. The date of the first appearance of the book is somewhat uncertain. Thomason, who usually got his copies near the day of issue, dated his as above. There were, however, some fifty editions during the year 1649, and one or more may have appeared somewhat earlier. The two following quotations indicate that some copies were available earlier; but being written later, they may be unreliable. The best study of this book is Edward Almack, *A Bibliography of the King's Book, or Eikon Basilike*, London, 1896.

Mr. John Wilson, barrister-at-law, author of the *Treatise of Monarchy*, 8vo., and of the *Vindication of Icôn Basilikè*, against Milton, told me, in person, that he bought the *Icôn Basilikè*, Jan. 31, 1648 [*i.e.*, 1648/9] for ten shillings, the very next day after the King was beheaded! Fra Thompson, D.D.

A note in a copy of Toland's *Amyntor*, quoted in Christopher Wordsworth, *Who Wrote Eikon Basilike?*, 1824, p. 53.

I saw, and read a part of the King's Book the very next Morning after that execrable Murther . . . it was not many days before I bought it my self.

Vindiciae Carolinae, 1692, p. 27.

MEMORANDVM

King *Charles* the *Second*, and the Duke of *York*, did both (in the last Session of Parliament, 1675. when I shewed them in the Lords House, the Written Copy of this Book, wherein are some Corrections and Alterations, written with the late King *Charles* the *First's* own Hand,) assure me that this was none of the said Kings compiling, but made by Dr. *Gauden* Bishop of *Exceter*, which I here insert for the undeceiving of others in this Point, by attesting so much under my hand;

Anglesey.

An advertisement opposite the title pages of some copies of Milton's *Eikonoklastes*, 1690; it also states that the memorandum was found by Edward Millington, written in the hand of Arthur Annesley, first Earl of Anglesey, in a book belonging to King Charles. This leaf is found in some copies (*e.g.*, that in the New York Public Library), and not in others (*e.g.*, the British Museum copy 599.c.24). Virtually the same statement was printed in Toland's *Life of John Milton*, 1698; see Darbishire, p. 145. It is said to have been found in 1686 by Millington, while he was auctioning off Anglesey's library, in the Earl's copy of *Eikon Basilike*.

A heated controversy about the authorship raged in England during the 1680's and 1690's. Pamphlets galore appeared on both sides, some asserting Gauden's authorship, and others maintaining that Charles wrote the book himself. The best guides to the available information on this subject are (1) Christopher Wordsworth's *Who Wrote Eikon Basilike*, 1824, and (2) Edward Almack's preface to his edition of *Eikon Basilike*, 1904. The most reasonable conclusion, it seems to me, is that Charles was responsible for the major part of the material used in the book, but that he is very likely to have depended on his friends and advisers for much clerical assistance. Since the story of the book carries him up to almost the day of his execution, he may very well have left the arranging of the latter part to Gauden or some other assistant.

FEBRUARY 9 (?). ALLEGEDLY INSERTS A PRAYER FROM SIDNEY'S *ARCADIA* IN KING CHARLES'S *EIKON BASILIKE*.

I was told Pamela's *Prayer, was transferr'd out of Sir* Philip Sidney's *Arcadia into* Ἐικων Βασιλικὴ *by a contrivance of* Bradshaw's *and* Milton's. *Sir I make no secret of it, and I frankly tell you my Author, who was Mr.* Henry Hill Oliver's *Printer, and the occasion, as he many years ago told me, was this, Mr.* Dugard, *who was* Milton's *intimate Friend, happen'd to be taken printing an Edition of the King's Book;* Milton *used his interest to bring him off, which he effected by the means of* Bradshaw, *but upon this Condition that* Dugard *should add* Pamela's *Prayer to the aforesaid Books he was printing, as an attonement for his fault, they designing thereby to bring a scandall upon the Book.*

John *Milton* · FEBRUARY 1649

From a letter from Thomas Gill to Charles Hatton, dated May 1, 1694, quoted in Thomas Wagstaffe (?), *A Vindication of King Charles the Martyr*, second edition, 1697, pp. 50-51, as transcribed in S. B. Liljegren, *Studies in Milton*, Lund, 1918, pp. 56-57. The pros and cons of Milton's guilt in perpetrating this astounding fraud are given at great length in the books by Wordsworth and Almack mentioned just above. The present editor finds it utterly impossible to accept the charge at all. The form in which it appears sounds like unadulterated slander.

I do remember very well that Mr. Henry Hills *the Printer told me that he heard* Bradshaw *and* Milton *laugh at their inserting a Prayer out of Sir* Philip Sidney's *Arcadia at the end of King* Charles's *his book and then* Milton *had jeer'd it in his answer, adding withall that they were men would stick at nothing that might gain their point and this I testifie.*

From a letter by Francis Bernard following the preceding letter and dated May 10, 1694; reprinted in the same reference. In slightly different form and under different date it reappears in Liljegren, p. 60. Quoted also in CM, XVIII, 379.

THAT nothing may be wanting I shall in the last place consider what is objected to the Prayer us'd by the King as his own in the time of his Captivity; but is, with very small Variation, the same that is said by PAMELA to a Heathen Deity in Sir PHILIP SYDNEY's *Arcadia*. This Discovery, as we said before, was first made by MILTON in his *Iconoclastes*. But Dr. GILL affirms, 'That his Patient HENRY HILL the Printer said it was put in by a Contrivance of MILTON, who catching his Friend Mr. Du GARD printing an Edition of *Icon Basilike*, got his Pardon by BRADSHAW's Interest, on Condition he would insert PAMELA's Prayer to bring Discredit on the Book and the Author of it.' I wonder at the Easiness of Dr. GILL and Dr. BERNARD to believe so gross a Fable, when it does not appear that Du GARD, who was Printer to the Parliament, ever printed this Book, and that the Prayer is in the second Edition publish'd by Mr. ROYSTON, whose Evidence is alledg'd to prove the Genuinness of the Book. And if the King's Friends thought it not his own, what made them print it in the first Impression of his Works in Folio, by ROYSTON in 62, when MILTON could not tamper with the Press? Or why did they let it pass in the last Impression in Folio by Mr. CHIS-WEL in the Year 86, when all the World knew that it was long before expos'd in *Iconoclastes?* After this I need not go about to shew that Dr. GILL had no Reason for the great Opinion he entertain'd of HENRY HILL, and how little he consulted his own Reputation by asserting that no Man was better vers'd in the secret History of those times; that he was intrusted with Intrigues by the great ones of that Government, who, as all the World knows, manag'd their Affairs after another rate. Nor will I insist upon his turning Papist in King JAMES's time to becom his Printer, as he was OLIVER's before, or any other Circumstance to lessen his Credit, since it appears that what he averr'd is inconsistent with Matter of Fact, Mr. ROYSTON, and not Du GARD, having publish'd the Celebrated Prayer which I add in this Place laid Parallel with the Original.

[Here follow the two prayers, from the *Arcadia* and from *Eikon Basilike*, on facing pages.]

John Toland, *Amyntor: Or, A Defence Of Milton's Life*, London, 1699, pp. 153 ff. This section is given to balance the hostile quotations preceding. Many others could be quoted, but they add little to the points here given. The whole business is a curiosity rather than a serious matter for Miltonists to consider.

FEBRUARY 13. PUBLISHES *THE TENURE OF KINGS AND MAGISTRATES*.

The Tenure of Kings and Magistrates: Proving, That it is Lawfull, and hath been held so through all Ages, for any, who have the Power, to call to account a Tyrant, or wicked King, and after due conviction, to depose, and put him to death; if the ordinary Magistrate have neglected, or deny'd to doe it. And that they, who of late, so much blame Deposing, are the Men that did it themselves. The Author, J. M. London, Printed by Matthew Simmons, at the Gilded Lyon in Aldersgate Street, 1649.

Title page of the Thomason copy in the British Museum. This copy has the "9" of "1649" crossed out and the date added in manuscript: "feb: 13 1648" [*i.e.,* 1648/9]. The "M" of the author's name is also extended to "Milton." For a later edition or editions, see below under date of February 15, 1649/50. The John Fulton copy at Yale has notes on the title page similar to those in the Thomason but omitting the day of the month.

... neque de jure regio quicquam à me scriptum est, donec Rex hostis à Senatu judicatus, bellóq; victus, causam captivus apud Judices diceret, capitísque damnatus est: Tum verò tandem, cùm Presbyteriani quidam ministri, Carolo priùs infestissimi, nunc Independentium partes suis anteferri, & in Senatu plus posse indignantes, Parlamenti sententiæ de Rege latæ, (non facto irati, sed quod ipsorum factio non fecisset) reclamitarent, & quantum in ipsis erat, tumultuarentur, ausi affirmare Protestantium doctrinam, omnésque ecclesias reformatas ab ejusmodi in reges atroci sententiâ abhorrere, ratus falsitati tam apertæ palàm eundum obviàm esse, ne tum quidem de Carolo quicquam scripsi aut suasi, sed quid in genere contra tyrannos liceret, adductis haud paucis summorum Theologorum testimoniis, ostendi; & insignem hominum meliora profitentium, sive ignorantiam sive impudentiam propè concionabundus incessi. Liber iste non nisi post mortem Regis prodiit, ad componendos potiùs hominum animos factus, quàm ad statuendum de Carolo quicquam quod non mea, sed Magistratuum intererat, & peractum jam tum erat.

Milton, *Defensio Secunda*, 1654 (Thomason copy), pp. 92 ff.; CM, VIII, 134 ff.

[... nor did I write anything on the prerogative of the crown, till the king, voted an enemy by the parliament, and vanquished in the field, was summoned before the tribunal which condemned him to lose his head. But when, at length, some presbyterian ministers, who had formerly been the most bitter enemies to Charles, became jealous of the growth of the independents, and of their ascendancy in the parliament, most tumultuously clamoured against the sentence, and did all in their power to prevent the execution, though they were not angry, so much on account of the act itself, as because it was not the act of their party; and when they dared to affirm, that the doctrine of the protestants, and of all the reformed churches, was abhorrent to such an atrocious proceeding against kings; I thought that it became me to oppose such a glaring falsehood; and accordingly, without any immediate or personal application to Charles, I shewed, in an abstract consideration of the question, what might lawfully be done against tyrants; and in support of what I advanced, produced the opinions of the most celebrated divines; while I vehemently inveighed against the egregious ignorance or effrontery of men, who professed better things, and from whom better things might have been expected. That book did not make its appearance till after the death of Charles; and was written rather to reconcile the minds of the people to the event, than to discuss the legitimacy of that particular sentence which concerned the magistrates, and which was already executed.]

Translated by Robert Fellowes, in *The Prose Works of John Milton*, ed. J. A. St. John (Bohn edition), 1 (1867), 259-260.

Whatever he wrote against Monarchie was out of no animosity to the King's person or out of any faction, or Jnterest but out of a pure zeall to the Liberty [of] Mankind wch he thought would be greater under a free state than under a Monarchall goverment. His being so conversant in Livy and the Rom: authors, and the greatnes, he saw donne by the Rom: com̄nwealth & the virtue of thir great Com̄anders ["Captaines" written above the line], induc't him to. . . .

Tenure of Kings & Magistrates.

Aubrey, fols. 65v, 64; Darbishire, pp. 13-14, 10. The title is from Aubrey's list of Milton's writings.

In Political matters hee had publish'd nothing. And it was now the time of the Kings comming upon his Tryal, when some of the Presbiterian Ministers, out of malignity to the Independent Party, who had supplanted them, more then from any principles of Loyalty, asserted clamourously in thir Sermons and Writings the Privilege of Kings from all accountableness, Or (to speak in the Language of this time) Non resistance & Passive Obedience to bee the Doctrine of all the Reformed Churches. This general Thesis, which incourag'd all manner of Tyranny, hee oppos'd by good Arguments, and the Authorities of several eminently learned Protestants in a Book titled *The*

Tenure of Kings, but without any particular application to the dispute then on foot in this Nation.

The "earliest" biography, f. 142; Darbishire, pp. 25-26.

. . . the form of Government being now chang'd into a Free State, he was hereupon oblig'd to Write a Treatise, call'd the *Tenure of Kings and Magistrates*.

Phillips, p. xxix; Darbishire, p. 68.

The Tenure of Kings and Magistrates; proving, That it is Lawful, and hath been held so through all Ages, for any who have the Power, to call to Account a Tyrant, or Wicked King; and after due Conviction to Depose and put him to Death, if the ordinary Magistrate have neglected or denied to do it; and that they who of late so much blame Deposing, are the men that did it themselves. 4*to.*

Phillips, p. [xlix], sig. [b4]; the pages on which Phillips gives Milton's bibliography are not numbered. Not in Darbishire.

. . . and then taking part with the Independents, he became a great Antimonarchist, a bitter Enemy to K. *Ch.* I. and at length arrived to that monstrous and unparallel'd height of profligate impudence, as in print to justifie the most execrable Murder of him the best of Kings, as I shall anon tell you. Afterwards being made Latin Secretary to the Parliament, we find him a Commonwealths man, a hater of all things that looked towards a single person, a great reproacher of the Universities, scholastical degrees, decency and uniformity in the Church . . . when he saw, upon the coming of K. *Charles* I. to his Tryal, the Presbyterian Ministers clamorously to assert in their Sermons and Writings the privileges of Kings from all accountableness, or (to speak in the language of that time) Non-resistance and Passive Obedience to be the Doctrine of all the reformed Churches (which he took to be only their malignity against the Independents who had supplanted them more than for any principles of Loyalty) he therefore to oppose that *Thesis* (which as he conceiv'd did encourage all manner of Tyranny) did write and publish from divers Arguments and Authorities. (13) *The tenure of Kings and Magistrates: proving that it is lawful,* &c. *to call*

to account a Tyrant or King, and after due conviction to depose
and put him to death, &c. Lond. 1649-50. qu.

  Wood, I, 881-882; Darbishire, pp. 39-43.

THROUGH ABOUT FEBRUARY. SECLUSION; LACK OF
REWARD FOR WRITINGS; HEAVY TAXES.

  Hanc intra privatos parietes meam operam nunc ecclesiæ,
nunc reipublicæ gratìs dedi; mihi vicissim vel hæc vel illa præter
incolumitatem nihil; bonam certè conscientiam, bonam apud
bonos existimationem, & honestam hanc dicendi libertatem facta
ipsa reddidere: commoda alii, alii honores gratìs ad se trahe-
bant: me nemo ambientem, nemo per amicos quicquam petentem,
curiæ foribus affixum petitorio vultu, aut minorum conventuum
vestibulis hærentem nemo me unquam vidit; domi fere me continebam, meis ipse facultatibus, tametsi hoc civili tumultu magna ex parte sæpe detentis, & censum ferè iniquiùs mihi impositum, & vitam utcunque frugi tolerabam.

  Milton, *Defensio Secunda*, 1654, pp. 93-94; CM, VIII, 136.

  [Such were the fruits of my private studies, which I gratui-
tously presented to the church and to the state; and for which
I was recompensed by nothing but impunity; though the actions
themselves procured me peace of conscience, and the approbation of the good; while I exercised that freedom of discussion
which I loved. Others, without labour or desert, got possession
of honours and emoluments; but no one ever knew me either
soliciting anything myself or through the medium of my friends,
ever beheld me in a supplicating posture at the doors of the
senate, or the levees of the great. I usually kept myself se-
cluded at home, where my own property, part of which had
been withheld during the civil commotions, and part of which
had been absorbed in the oppressive contributions which I had
to sustain, afforded me a scanty subsistence.]

  The Prose Works of John Milton, ed. J. A. St. John (Bohn edition),
I (1867), 260.

BEFORE MARCH 13. RESUMES WORK ON *HISTORY OF BRITAIN*.

His rebus confectis, cùm jam abundè otii existimarem mihi futurum, ad historiam gentis, ab ultima origine repetitam, ad hæc usque tempora, si possem, perpetuo filo deducendam me converti: quatuor jam libros absolveram, cum ecce nihil tale cogitantem me, Caroli regno in rempublicam redacto, Concilium . . . ad se vocat, meâque operâ ad res præsertim externas uti voluit.

Milton, *Defensio Secunda*, 1654, p. 94; CM, VIII, 136-138. This work can of course not be dated exactly. It must have covered a good deal of time, and the first reading for it must certainly have dated back to the entries in the Commonplace Book and even to the years of reading at Horton or earlier. But Milton's statement that his work was interrupted by his appointment as secretary makes it appropriate to place the entry here. See also the entry "Said to be working on History of England" under "1648."

[After these things (the *Tenure of Kings* and preceding writings) had been finished, and when I thought that now there would be plenty of leisure for me, I turned to the history of the nation, set forth from the earliest beginning, if I could, in an unbroken line down to these times. I had already finished four books, when behold, after the kingdom of Charles had been turned into a republic, and without my knowing anything of their intention, the Council . . . called me in and wanted to use my services especially for foreign affairs.]

After which [*The Tenure of Kings*] his thoughts were bent upon retiring again to his own private Studies, and falling upon such Subjects as his proper Genius prompted him to Write of, among which was the History of our own Nation from the Beginning till the *Norman* Conquest, wherein he had made some progress. When for this his last Treatise . . . [he was given] the Office of *Latin* Secretary.

Phillips, pp. xxix-xxx; Darbishire, pp. 68-69.

MARCH 13. INVITED TO BE SECRETARY FOR THE
FOREIGN TONGUES.

A Meridie 13°. Martij *1648* [Noon, March 13, 1648] . . . .

21.) That M⟨r⟩. Whitlocke, S⟨r⟩. Henry Vane, Lo. Lisle Earle
of Denbigh, M⟨r⟩. Martyn, M⟨r⟩. Lisle, or any two of them be appointed a Comittee to consider what Alliances this Crowne hath
formerly had with fforeigne States. . . .

22.) That it be referred to the same Comittee to speake w⟨th⟩
M⟨r⟩. Milton to know whether he will be employed as Secretary
for the fforreigne tongues, and to report to the Councell.

Public Record Office, Book of Orders of the Council of State, SP
Dom 25/62, pp. 85-86; *CSP Dom, 1649-1650*, p. 37 (a somewhat
shortened version); Masson, IV, 79 ff.; CM, XVIII, 365.

[After writing the *Tenure of Kings* and four books of the
History of Britain] ecce nihil tale cogitantem me, Caroli regno
in rempublicam redacto, Concilium Statûs, quod dicitur, tum
primùm authoritate Parlamenti constitutum, ad se vocat, meâque
operâ ad res præsertim externas uti voluit.

Milton, *Defensio Secunda*, 1654, p. 94; CM, VIII, 136-139. Although most of this passage has recently been quoted, it needs to be
included here also among the documents regarding Milton's appointment.

[. . . behold, after the kingdom of Charles had been turned
into a republic, and without my knowing anything of their intention, the Council of State, as it is called, then first appointed by
authority of Parliament, called me in and wanted to use my services especially for foreign affairs.]

Upon the change of Government which succeeded the Kings
death hee was, without any seeking of his, by the means of a
private Acquaintance, who was a member of the new Council of State, chosen Latin Secretary. In this public Station
his abilities and the acuteness of his parts, which had lyen hid in
his privacy, were soon taken notice of, and hee was pitch'd upon
to elude the Artifice of Ἐικὼν Βασιλικὴ.

The "earliest" biography, ff. 142-142v; Darbishire, p. 26.

Hee made no address or Court for that emploiment of Latin

Secretary, though his eminent fittness for it appeer by his printed Letters of that time.

The "earliest" biography, f. 143; Darbishire, p. 29.

He was Latin Secretary to the Parliament.

Aubrey, f. 63; Darbishire, p. 2. Aubrey first wrote "Oliver Cromwell," then crossed it out and wrote "the Parliament" above it. He also crossed out "Latin," but later wrote above it "stet."

(15) That when *Oliver* ascended the Throne, he became the Latin Secretary, and proved to him very serviceable when employed in business of weight and moment, and did great matters to obtain a name and wealth. . . . Soon after the King being beheaded to the great astonishment of all the World, and the Government thereupon changed, he was, without any seeking of his, by the endeavours of a private acquaintance, who was a member of the new *Council of State*, chosen Latin Secretary, as I have before told you. In this publick station his abilities and acuteness of parts, which had been in a manner kept private, were soon taken notice of, and he was pitch'd upon to elude *the artifice* (so it was then by the Faction called) of *Eikon Basilice.* . . .

Wood, I, 881-882; Darbishire, pp. 39, 43.

. . . for this his last Treatise [*The Tenure of Kings*], reviving the fame of other things he had formerly Published, being more and more taken notice of for his excellency of Stile, and depth of Judgement, he was courted into the Service of this new Commonwealth, and at last prevail'd with (for he never hunted after Preferment, nor affected the Tintamar and Hurry of Publick business) to take upon him the Office of *Latin* Secretary to the Counsel of State for all their Letters to Foreign Princes and States; for they stuck to this Noble and Generous Resolution, not to write to any, or receive Answers from them, but in a Language most proper to maintain a Correspondence among the Learned of all Nations in this part of the World; scorning to carry on their Affairs in the Wheedling Lisping Jargon of the Cringing *French*, especially having a Minister of State able to cope with the ablest any Prince or State could imploy for the Latin tongue; and so well he acquitted himself in

this station, that he gain'd from abroad both Reputation to himself, and Credit to the State that Employed him; and it was
well the business of his Office came not very fast upon him, for
he was scarce well warm in his Secretaryship before other Work
flow'd in upon him. . . .

Phillips, pp. xxix-xxx; Darbishire, p. 69. The best account of the
work of the office of Secretary for the Foreign Tongues is to be found
in Florence M. G. Evans's *The Principal Secretary of State*, Manchester, 1923, especially chapter 6. Among Milton's predecessors in
this position were Roger Ascham (for Queen Mary), Sir Thomas
Smith (1603-1609), Thomas Reade (1619-1624), and George Weckherlin. Weckherlin, who had been under-secretary of state from 1624
to 1641, had been chosen Secretary for the Foreign Tongues in 1644.
He retired in 1649 but was recalled in 1652 to assist Milton. Milton's
salary upon appointment was £288-13-6½. Weckherlin's career would
repay further study.

MARCH 15. APPOINTED SECRETARY FOR THE FOREIGN
TONGUES.

Die Iovis 15°. Martij 1648 [Thursday, March 15, 1648]. . . .
7.) That Mʳ. Iohn Milton be employed as Secretary for fforreigne tongues to this Councell. And that he have the same
Salarie wᶜʰ Mʳ. Weckherlyn formerly had for the said service.

Public Record Office, Order Book of the Council of State, SP Dom
25/62, p. 89; *CSP Dom, 1649-1650*, p. 40; Masson, IV, 82. This
action indicates that Milton must have replied favorably to the invitation
of March 13.

MARCH 15. REPUTED CIPHER AS SECRETARY.

Milton's cypher for secret communication with others used
by Republicans under Oliver, I had among the Royal Letters
in Clarendon's Collection, which I redeemed from perdition,
and presented to my late noble Lord of Oxford; and they are
still preserved in the Harleian Library.

From a manuscript note by William Oldys written in his copy of
Gerard Langbaine's *Account of the English Dramatic Poets* as transcribed in "Milton's Cipher and the Harleian Library," *Censura Literaria*, I (1805), 438, and x (1815), 330; CM, XVIII, 543. The cipher
has not been traced. It is very likely that this document was the same
as that used by Milton's predecessor Weckherlin, who in the records
of the Council of State was occasionally instructed to put foreign letters

into code. It may yet be found, or it may possibly have been destroyed. See also notes by Thomas O. Mabbott and others in *Notes and Queries*, CLXXXII (1942), 96, 181, 289.

AFTER MARCH 15. ORDERED TO ANSWER *EIKON BASILIKE* (?).

I take it on me as a work assign'd rather, then by me chos'n or affected.

Milton, *Eikonoklastes*, 1649, sigs. Bv-B2; CM, V, 64-65.

It is interesting to know that John Selden was several times invited by Cromwell to answer this work but refused. At least, such is the statement of his biographer David Wilkins. The following passage is taken from Wilkins's *Joannis Seldeni Jurisconsulti Opera Omnia*, I (1726), "Vita," p. xliv; it is quoted by Christopher Wordsworth in *Who Wrote Eikon Basilike?* (London, 1824), p. 96.

"Et cum Cromwellius plus semel Seldenum hortaretur, ac per amicos rogaret, ut calamum adversus librum regi Carolo adscriptum ΕΙΚΩΝ ΒΑΣΙΛΙΚΗ stringeret, contemptim ac pervicaci animo provinciam hanc detrectavit, quam Miltonus regiminis parliamentarii defensor strenuus in se suscepit."

[And although Cromwell more than once urged Selden, and asked him through friends, to unsheath his pen against the book *Eikon Basilike* written by King Charles, he scornfully and stubbornly refused that duty, which Milton undertook as the vigorous defender of the parliamentary regime.]

See also below under date of October 6, 1649, for one or two other passages which give the same implication that Milton wrote his book under orders from the government. The date of such a request must have been after March 15, when he was appointed Secretary.

MARCH (?). MOVES TO CHARING CROSS.

. . . during the Writing and Publishing of this Book [John Phillips's *Responsio*], he lodg'd at one *Thomson's* next door to the *Bull-head* tavern at *Charing-Cross*, opening into the *Spring-Garden*, which seems to have been only a Lodging taken, till his designed Apartment in *Scotland-Yard* was prepared for him.

Phillips, p. xxxiii; Darbishire, p. 71; Masson, IV, 104-107. Although the reference to Phillips's *Responsio* would seem to date this entry in 1652, the mention of a move later to Scotland Yard makes 1649 more likely. Masson dates it just after his accepting the secretaryship. In Cunningham's *London* (1927, p. 112) the location is fixed as next door to the present Drummond's Bank at Number 49 Charing Cross.

MARCH 16. *EIKON BASILIKE* REGISTERED FOR PUBLICATION.

16th [of March, 1648/9]

Master Simmons	Entred . . . under the hands of Master
This is crosed	CARILL and Master DAWSON war-
by my owne hand.	den a booke called ΕΙΚΩΝ ΒΑΣΙΛΙΚΗ.
Aug. 6, 1651	The pourtracture of his sacred Ma^ty in
Mathew Syṁons,	his solitude and sufferings . . . . vj^d
at a court held	
that day.	

Stationers' Registers, 1, 314. Why the entry in the Registers should be later than the date of issue (see above under date of February 9) is a puzzle, as is also the side note. The entry has been crossed out in the Registers.

MARCH 20. INDUCTED INTO NEW OFFICE.

That the Lord President and any four members of this Council shall be a Committee to administer the oath of secrecy unto such as shall be employed as secretaries to attend this Council.

From the records of the Council of State as given in Masson, IV, 83. Masson assumes, probably justly, that Milton was one of the persons affected by this order. Not having noticed it in my own transcriptions of the records of the Council, I can only give the entry as it appears in Masson.

MARCH 22. ORDERED TO TRANSLATE LETTERS TO HAMBURG.

Die Iovis 22°: Martij 1648 [Thursday, March 22, 1648]. . . . 6.) That the Letters now read to be sent to Hamburge in behalfe of the Company of Merchant Adventurers be approved. And that they be translated into Latine by M^r. Milton.

Public Record Office, Order Book of the Council of State, SP Dom 25/62, p. 104; *CSP Dom, 1649-1650*, p. 48; Masson, IV, 83-84. The Council had previously ordered on March 20 that these letters be written; Milton's first official work for his new position thus became the translation of them into Latin.

On Milton's Latin letters to foreign countries in general, see CM, XIII, in which they are reprinted, with some additions, from the first printed collection of 1676, and W. C. Abbott's edition in four volumes of *The Writings and Speeches of Oliver Cromwell* (Harvard University Press, 1937 ff.), which presents an enormous amount of new material concerning all Cromwell's foreign letters, whether written by Milton or not. The two important manuscript collections of these letters, neither of which is complete, but both of which are drawn on in the Columbia edition of Milton, are the so-called Skinner Manuscript in the Public Record Office and the Columbia Manuscript in the library of Columbia University. Some notes on the history of the latter may be found in *Autograph Prices Current*, IV (1918-1919), 124, and VI (1921-1922), 112.

This entry may refer to the letter of April 2 (see below), never delivered, but reprinted as No. 151 in the Columbia edition.

MARCH 25. RECEIVES RENTS FROM WHEATLEY.

. . . vpon the ffiue and Twentieth of March One Thousand six hundred fforty and nine Thirty One pownds ffoureteene shillings and fiue pence . . .

From Milton's answer to Elizabeth Ashworth's bill, February 22, 1654, *q.v.* This item comes from a long list of receipts which he has had from the Wheatley property.

MARCH 26. LATIN LETTER TO HAMBURG APPROVED.

A Meridie. 26. Martij 1649 [Morning, March 26, 1649].
. . . 26.) That the Letters now brought in by M^r. Milton to ye Senate of Hamburgh, be approved and that M^r. Isaac Lee Deputy of the Company of Merchant Adventurers there, shall be appointed Agent for the delivering of them.

Public Record Office, Order Book of the Council of State, SP Dom 25/62, p. 117; *CSP Dom, 1649-50*, p. 52; Masson, IV, 84. This letter is presumably that which Milton was asked on March 22 to do; it is probably the one described below under date of April 2, 1649.

MARCH 26. ORDERED TO MAKE NOTES ON *ENGLAND'S NEW CHAINS DISCOVERED*.

A Meridie. 26. Martij 1649 [Morning, March 26, 1649].
. . . 32) That M^r. Milton be appointed to make some observations upon a paper lately printed called old & new Chaines.

Public Record Office, Order Book of the Council of State, SP Dom 25/62, p. 117; *CSP Dom, 1649-1650*, p. 52; Masson, IV, 87. *England's New Chains Discovered*, a Leveller pamphlet by John Lilburne, had appeared on February 26 (Thomason); the sequel, *The Second*

Part of England's New Chains Discovered, was out on March 24 (Thomason, Masson). Other entries in the Order Book tell us that the Council appointed Holland and Pickering to examine persons about this book on March 27; the Council issued a warrant for the arrest of the publishers on the same day; Sergeant Dendy was ordered to search the posts for copies of the book also on the same day; and finally, still on March 27, Lilburne, Walwyn, Overton, and Prince were ordered arrested. On the following day they were all sent to the Tower of London. Both parts of the book are reprinted in Willam Haller's *The Leveller Tracts, 1647-1653*, New York, 1944, pp. 156-170 and 171-189. See also CM, XVIII, 540; W. H. Hart, *Index Expurgatorius Anglicanus*, London, 1872 ff., p. 160, #183. No answer by Milton has ever been found, unless he may possibly have had some connection with *A Declaration of the Commons Assembled in Parliament, Against a Scandalous Book Entituled, The Second Part of Englands new Chains discovered, &c. Die Martis, 27 Martii, 1649*. This book, of which copies are to be found in the Thomason collection and at Harvard in the Gay collection, is a single sheet folio, characterizes the *New Chains* as false and scandalous, and explains that the authors are to be proceeded against as traitors. Nothing in the sheet indicates Milton's hand. It is said to have been printed for Edward Husband on March 29, 1649. Several other answers to the book are recorded in the Thomason catalogue. See also W. C. Abbott, *A Bibliography of Oliver Cromwell*, Harvard, 1929, item 356.

MARCH 28. INSTRUCTED TO REPORT ON AFFAIRS IN IRELAND.

Die Mercurij 28° Martij 1649 [Wednesday, March 28, 1649]. . . . 1.) That M^r. Milton be appointed to make some observations vpon the Complicacõn of interest wch is now amongst the severall designers against the peace of the Comonwealth. And that it be made ready to be printed wth the papers out of Ireland wch the House hath ordered to be printed.

Public Record Office, Order Book of the Council of State, SP Dom 25/62, p. 125; *CSP Dom, 1649-1650*, p. 57; Masson, IV, 87, 98 ff. This material was published on May 16, *q.v.*

APRIL 2. STATE LETTER TO HAMBURG.

Senatus Populúsqz Anglicanus Magnifico et Amplissimo Civitatis Hamburgensis Senatui, Salutem

Magnifici, Amplissimi, et Spectabiles Viri, Amici charissimi,

Quantis bellorum incendijs ... Dat: a Palatio westmonasteriensi 2do April: anno 1649. stylo Anglia.

> [signed] Guliel' Lenthall. senatus populīq anglie orator.

[Endorsed:] The Letter to y^e. Senate of Hamburgh not delivered sent back by Lee. 2 April 1649./

Public Record Office, SP For 82/7, ff. 153-154 (the original manuscript); Hamilton, pp. 16-17; Masson, IV, 89; CM, XIII, 466 ff. Not included by Milton in his *Literæ Pseudo-Senatus*, perhaps because it was not delivered, as the endorsement shows. If it had been delivered, it would not now be among English records, but, if available at all, in Hamburg. The few manuscript alterations in the letter are noted in CM, XIII, 632-633.

As will be the practice followed in these Latin letters written by Milton for the government, the body of the text will not be given; but the salutation and a few words of the beginning, the ending, and any endorsements of interest will be printed here. Wherever original manuscripts are available, they will be mentioned.

The handwriting of this particular letter is so very similar to known specimens of Milton's hand that it is a great temptation to assert that he wrote it himself. It is safer, however, simply to call attention to the strong resemblance in writing between it and, say, Milton's petition of February 25, 1651, also in the Public Record Office.

[The English Senate and People to the splendid and exalted Senate of the City of Hamburg, Greeting: Splendid, exalted, and honorable sirs, our very dear friends: In how great conflagrations of war ... Given at the palace of Westminster on April 2, 1649, English style. William Lenthall, Speaker of the English Senate and People.]

APRIL 5. ATTACKED FOR DIVORCE VIEWS.

> While like the froward Miltonist,
> We our old Nuptiall knot untwist:
> And with the hands, late faith did joyn,
> This Bill of plain Divorce now signe.
> Here their New Kingdom must commence,
> And Sinne conspire with Conscience.

Christopher Wasse, *Electra of Sophocles*, the Hague, 1649, "The Epilogue . . . Addressed to her Highnesse the Lady Elizabeth," p. 3 (sig. E8); Todd, I (1826), 62; Parker, *Milton's Contemporary*

Reputation, p. 83. Dr. Parker makes the interesting comment that the earliest illustration of the word "Miltonist" found in the *New English Dictionary* dates from 1806. In Thomason's copy the "W" on the title page, the initial of the author, is extended in manuscript to "Wase"; and the date, April 5, is written in.

APRIL 9. ATTACKED BY JOSEPH HALL FOR DIVORCE VIEWS.

I have heard too much of, and once saw, a licentious pamphlet throwne abroad in these lawlesse times, in the defence, and incouragement of Divorces (not to be sued out, that solemnity needed not, but) to be arbitrarily given by the disliking husband, to his displeasing and unquiet wife; upon this ground principally, that marriage was instituted for the help and comfort of man; where therefore the match proves such, as that the wife doth but pull downe a side, and by her innate peevishnesse, and either sullen, or pettish and froward disposition brings rather discomfort to her husband, the end of marriage being hereby frustrate, why should it not, saith he, be in the husbands power (after some unprevailing meanes of reclamation attempted) to procure his own peace, by casting off this clogge, and to provide for his owne peace and contentment in a fitter match?

Wo is me; To what a passe is the world come that a Christian, pretending to Reformation, should dare to tender so loose a project to the publique?

Joseph Hall, *Resolutions and Decisions of Divers Practicall Cases of Conscience in continuall Use amongst men . . . By I.H. D.D. B.N.*, London, 1649, pp. 389-391. Thomason's copy is dated April 9, 1649. This allusion is found in Todd, I, 40; Masson, III, 62-63; Parker, *Milton's Contemporary Reputation*, pp. 78-79. Hall's reference to Milton was repeated in later editions of 1650 and 1654.

AFTER APRIL 13. TRANSLATES AND REVISES TRANSLATIONS OF LETTERS FROM PRINCESS SOPHIE TO PRINCES MAURICE AND RUPERT (?).

High born Prince, deare Brother, J must write unto you by all occasions, for J have still some news to tell, wch shall bee at this time that ye Prince Elector is heere, and that he is now altogether as we **are** against the knaves **or Skellums**, he will soone goe to his country; the Peace in France is made, my Brother Edward saith he has tak'n no employment yet. Prince Ratzevil is deadly sick they say that ye Marques Gonzaga hath poyson'd him; he is in Poland yet; the states have forbidd'n all their ministers to pray for any kings in the Church. but the French will not desist. J **so** am vext that you **have** not write**n**, **that I cannot express, yet I hope you have not for gotten me seeing I am**

the 13th of Aprill
1649

Yo^r^ faithfull sister
and humble servant
Sophie

There was a postscript of commendations in this lr̄e subscrib'd with the Electors name. wch was this

A Monsieur
Monsieur
l'Prince Maurice
Conte Palatin

My service to you brother Rupt, & brother Maurice, more I cannot say being newly arriv'd, & visitations doe hinder me/

Public Record Office, SP 18/1, no. 53; Stern, II, iii, 31, 257; CM, XIII, 506-507, 635-636; cf. CM, XVIII, 653. A facsimile is given in *Facsimiles of National Manuscripts from William the Conqueror to Queen Anne*, Part IV (1868), Charles II, numbers 45-46. There seems to be a good deal of likelihood that the translation of this letter was made by Milton, and that the parts printed here in Gothic were Milton's own additions or revisions made in his own hand. According to a pencil note on the original manuscript, the endorsement "A Monsieur . . . Palatin" is in Bradshaw's hand. The date of this work is uncertain. But see the entry for May 18, 1649.

Most deere Brother [Rupert]

Wee have not any newes concerning Rupert ye Devil unlesse what comes out in print, for no man receaves any letters from you. My Brother the Prince Elector is now heere, and cares now no more for those cursed People in England. for he hath don his duty to the K: which otherwise he might have avoyded by reason of ye affaires wch requir'd him at Cleave. Heare also are ye Scotch Commissioners who every day bring some new proposal to the K. full of impertinency, for they would not that the King should keep about him any honest men, for which they are in great favour with the Princess of Orange, who declares her selfe much for ye Presbyterians and says that Percy is ye honestest man ye King hath about him. But J beleive you care not much to know ye intricacies heere for wch cause J shall not trouble you farder, beside that you have other buisnes to doe then read my L^{trs}. onely J intreate you to take notice that J remaine

A Monsr.	Aprill ye 13th	y^r most affectionte sister
Monsr. le	1649	and Servant
Prince Rupert		Sophie

Public Record Office, SP 18/1, no. 54; CM, XVIII, 653. Discussed by Dr. Maurice Kelley in the London *Times Literary Supplement*, 1937, p. 715. Although there is no sign of Milton's handwriting in this letter, it is so closely related to the preceding one that it is unlikely he would have had one in his possession without the other; and if he translated one, he probably translated the other. But his connection with it cannot be directly proved.

APRIL 16. SALMASIUS PLANNING DEFENSE OF CHARLES I.

Cæterum periculosæ plenum opus aleæ aggrederis, Defensionem dico nuper occisi Britanniarum Regis; maxime cum vestri Ordines mediam viam secent. Laudo tamen animi tui generosum propositum, quo nefandum scelus aperto damnare sustines.

Letter of Claudius Sarravius to Claudius Salmasius, April 16, 1649, printed in *Marquardi Gudii et Doctorum Virorum ad eum Epistolæ* . . . *et Claudii Sarravii Senatoris Parisiensis Epistolæ* . . . *Curante Petro Burmanno. Ultrajecti,* 1697, p. 203. This book contains a great many references to Salmasius, his *Defensio Regia,* and the English situation in general. It unfortunately stops just about at the point when Milton's *Defensio* would appear, so that it does not furnish much information about that book. But during 1649 and 1650 there are many letters to Salmasius and a few to other people, urging Salmasius to publish his book (May 28, 1649, p. 205), suggesting that he can find material for it in *Eikon Basilike* (July 11, 1649, p. 210), announcing that a copy is on the way to him (February 5, 1650, p. 223), reporting on the first reading of it (February 18, 1650, p. 224), and the like. The series ends with a pained observation that Salmasius has gone off to Sweden and shaken off his friends (December 30, 1650, p. 248). The comments on Salmasius, though usually commendatory, are not always so. Prefixed to the volume is a long description of Salmasius, particularly on sigs. # #4-# #4v.

[You are undertaking another work full of dangerous risk, I mean the Defense of the recently executed King of the Britons; especially since your classes follow a middle way of life. And yet I praise the generous resolution of your mind, by which you undertake to condemn openly that dreadful crime.]

APRIL 20. INSTRUCTED TO EXAMINE CERTAIN LETTERS.

Die Veneris 20°. April: 1649 [Friday, April 20, 1649] . . . 17.) That the Letters brought in by M^r. Watkins be viewed by M^r. Frost or M^r. Milton to see if any of them conteyne any thing concerning the exportačon of any prohibited goods.

Public Record Office, Order Book of the Council of State, SP Dom, 25/62, p. 209; *CSP Dom, 1649-1650*, p. 100; Masson, IV, 87.

APRIL 20. PROPOSES TO RENEW LEASE IN BREAD STREET FROM GOLDSMITHS' COMPANY.

At this Courte John Milton was a suiter for the renewing of the lease of a tenem^t: in Breadstreete wherein as hee alleageth there was 4. yeares to come at o^r Lady day last & offers CL^li: ffine for 21. yeares in reūcoñ wch is to bee remembred at the next Courte of Assistantp.

The Court Book of the Worshipful Company of Goldsmiths, 1648-1651, f. 46. I owe this interesting new fact about Milton, together with several related ones later on, to the courtesy and kindness of Mr. G. R. Hughes, Clerk of the Company, who searched the records and provided me with photographs of this and the other entries. The only notice of the transaction which I have seen is that by Mr. Kenneth Rogers in "Bread Street," *London Topographical Record*, XVI (1932), 52-76. On p. 75 of this article Mr. Rogers says: "The Goldsmiths' Company have record of a receipt in 1651, from John Milton, £100 in part of £400, for the renewal of his lease in Bread Street (Prideaux)." Mr. Hughes's search of the books brought to light six different stages of this business, which will be found under the present date and those of October 5, November 5, and December 21, 1649; March 12, March 27, and July 5, 1650; December 20, 1651; and June 10, 1659. There may be further dealings in the same records which have not yet been found.

Since Milton's birthplace at the corner of Bread Street and Cheapside, in the house known as the White Bear (though his apartment may have gone under the name of the Spread Eagle), was in the possession of Eton College (see above under October 16, 1617), the present transaction can hardly have concerned that property. It probably had to do with the house called the Rose, which the elder Milton also owned in the same street.

APRIL 23. PAYS MOTHER-IN-LAW ANNE POWELL HER THIRDS.

[Milton] did pay or cause to bee payed vnto this dēpt shee beinge the said Anne Powell . . . the seuerall sūmmes of money menc̄oned and Expressed in the six seuerall Acquittances or Receiptes . . . [the third of which is dated] Aprill ye 23th Anno dnī 1649: and is for the sūmme of 9^li. 19^s.

From Anne Powell's deposition in the Milton-Ashworth suit, June 4, 1656, *q.v.*

MAY 11. APPEARANCE IN ENGLAND OF SALMASIUS'S DEFENSE OF CHARLES I.

Defensio regia pro Carolo I ad Serenissimum Magnæ Britanniæ regem Carolum II. Filium natu majorem, Heredem & Successorem legitimum. Sumptibus Regiis. Anno ƆIC IƆC XLIX.

Title page of the copy in the Thomason collection, on which Thomason entered the date May 11. This is, of course, not necessarily the date of publication. This is the book which led directly to Milton's writing his *Defense of the English People* (in Latin), and indirectly to his two later *Defenses*. A careful study of the numerous editions of this work of Salmasius (or Claude Saumaise) may be found in an article by F. F. Madan in *The Library*, Fourth Series, IV (1924), 137, 143-145. There were more than a dozen editions between 1649 and 1652.

[The Royal Defense of Charles I to the most serene king of Great Britain Charles II, his elder son by birth, heir, and legitimate successor. At the king's expense. 1649.]

Nam ne teruncio quidem ab illis factus ditior, neque Rex pauperior. Cum metuerit ne editio defensionis edicto Ordinum supprimeretur, persuasit sibi, si apponeret impensis Regis esse procuratam, hujus nominis reverentia defensionem Regiam defendi posse à publicationis inhibitione. Ideo & omnibus editionibus, quæ post primam à diversis Librariis curatæ sunt, hoc idem, quasi amuletum, adscriptum fuit.

Claudii Salmasii Ad Johannem Miltonum Responsio, Opus Post-humum, London, 1660, p. 21. Though Masson quotes several pages from this work, he does not include this particular section.

[For the printer was not in the least the richer by those words ("sumptibus regiis"), nor the king poorer. Since he feared that the edition of the *Defense* might be suppressed by decree of the Senate, he persuaded himself that if he put on it that it had been sponsored by the king's funds, the *Royal Defense* would thereafter be protected against prohibition of publication by reverence for this name. So in all editions which were brought out by various publishers after the first, this same ascription was added like an amulet.]

Nihil ergo Salmasius eo Christi testimonio pro Regum defen-sione lucratus est præter denarium vel Cæsari, vel sibi. . . . Quod ad Salmasium attinet, puto, si bene illum novi, nihil inde lucri fecisse præter materiam risûs, quam illi largiter sup-peditasti ex hac tua insulsitate. Ego sane ipse multum te derisi, plurisque hoc facio, quam centum Jacobæos, quos accepisse Sal-masium falso objecisti, pro mercede Defensionis Regiæ.

Ibid., p. 270. Other similar passages could be found. See also my note in *Notes and Queries*, 188 (1945), 53-54.

[Salmasius therefore, according to that testimony of Christ, was not at all enriched for his defense of kings more than a penny either to Caesar or to himself. . . . As for Salmasius, I think, if I know him well, no reward was given him except the material for laughter, which you have supplied him bounti-fully by this insipidity of yours. I myself have laughed a great deal at you, and I get more out of this than the hundred Jacobuses which you falsely object that Salmasius got as re-ward for the *Royal Defense*.]

Salmasius a Professor in Holland, who had in a large Treatise, not long before, maintain'd the parity of Church Governors against Episcopacy, put out *Defensio Caroli Regis*, and in it, amongst other absurdities, justify'd (as indeed it was unavoidable in the defense of that cause, which was styl'd

Bellum Episcopale) to the contradiction of his former Book, the pretensions of the Bishops.

The "earliest" biography, f. 142v; Darbishire, p. 26.

... and upon the heels of that [*Eikonoklastes*], out comes in Publick the great Kill-cow of *Christendom*, with his *Defensio Regis contra Populum Anglicanum*; a Man so Famous and cryed up for his *Plinian Exercitations*, and other Pieces of reputed Learning, that there could no where have been found a Champion that durst lift up the Pen against so formidable an Adversary, had not our little *English David* had the Courage. . . .

Phillips, p. xxxi; Darbishire, p. 70.

Soon after the publication of *Iconoclastes*, *Salmasius* a Professor in *Holland*, who had in a large Treatise not long before, maintained, as 'tis said, the parity of Church Governors against Episcopacy, did publish *Defensio regia, pro Carolo* I. *Rege Angliæ*, wherein he justified several matters, as *Milton* conceived, to the contradiction of his former book.

Wood, I, 882; Darbishire, p. 44.

AFTER MAY 11 (?). MILTON OWNS AND ANNOTATES COPY OF SALMASIUS'S *DEFENSE* (?).

I have heard of a copy of Salmasius's book, the margins of which are said to be decorated with barbarisms and solecisms detected by Milton.

Todd, I (1826), 125; CM, XVIII, 580. Nothing is known now of such a copy, if one ever existed. But Milton must certainly have owned a copy, and it is very likely that he marked in it.

AFTER MAY 11. KING CHARLES II THANKS SALMASIUS FOR *DEFENSIO* BUT DOES NOT GIVE HIM MONEY (?).

[In answer to Milton's charge in his *Defensio* that Salmasius had received 100 jacobuses for writing his book, and that Milton knew who came with the king's chaplain to bring the money to Salmasius,] Si cum Sacellano introiit, cur non edis ejus nomen, nec nomen Sacellani? At jam eum tibi, quis fuerit, indicabo. Guilelmus Morlæus fuit, qui litteras Regis Salmasio attulit, quibus Rex ipsi gratias agit pro navata defensionis opera. De Jacobæis somnia, quod & ipse vir Reverendus Morlæus testabitur, qui in his locis vivit, & paratus est omnibus, qui de hac re eum interrogabunt, quid in rei veritate sit, declarare. Litteræ ipsius Regis, quas tunc attulit, de hoc ipso fidem publicatæ facient.

Salmasius, *Ad Johannem Miltonum Responsio, Opus Posthumum,* London, 1660, p. 23. This statement comes in answer to Milton's charge in his first *Defensio* (CM, VII, 15): ". . . yea, bought for one hundred Jacobuses, a great sum to get from a needy King. I speak not of things unknown: I know who took those gold-pieces to your house in that beaded purse; I know who saw you reach out your greedy hands under pretence of embracing the king's chaplain who brought the gift, but in fact to hug the gift itself, and by taking this single fee almost to empty the king's treasury."

[If he came in with the chaplain, why do you not give his name, or the name of the chaplain? But I will tell you who he was. It was William Morley who brought the king's letters to Salmasius, in which the king thanked him for having performed the work of the defense. That about the Jacobuses is nonsense, as that man, the Reverend Mr. Morley, will testify, who lives in these places and is ready to declare to everyone who asks him about it what the truth of the matter is. That king's letters which he then brought, when published, will show the truth of it.]

GEORGE MORLEY . . . His learned acquaintance abroad were *Andr. Rivet, Dan. Heinsius* and *Claud. Salmasius,* whom he often visited; to the last of which, then abiding at *Leyden,* the King sent our Author *Morley* to give him thanks in his name for the Apology he had published for his martyr'd Father, but not with a Purse of Gold as *Joh. Milton* the impudent lyer reported.

Wood, II, 768-770; Masson, IV, 255. Wood also mentions the fact that Morley was the King's chaplain in ordinary. It is difficult to find the truth about this question whether or not the king paid Salmasius for writing his book. The passion with which both sides conducted their fight with each other does not make for truthfulness. It seems quite likely that the king should have given him something as reward for so effective a work, nor would such an action be dishonorable in the slightest. It is most unlikely that any official record of such a gift will ever be found, so that we shall have to be satisfied with these conflicting statements and from them arrive at our conclusions as justly as we can.

MAY 14. JOHN HALL ENGAGED TO ASSIST MILTON (?).

Die Lunæ 14°. Maij 1649 [Monday, May 14, 1649]. . . .
13.) That M^r. Hall shall be employed by this Councell to make Answere to such pamphletts as shall come out to ye preiudice of this Comonwealth, And that he shall have one hundred pound₽ p Anñ. for his labour wth an assurance given him from this Councell that they will take further Care of him That he shall signe the Test signed by others employed by this Councell, and that he shall have thirty pound now payd unto him in part of his pension of one hundred pound p Anñ.

Public Record Office, Order Book of the Council of State, SP Dom 25/62, p. 303; *CSP Dom, 1649-1650*, p. 139. Masson, IV, 88. There is no mention of his relation to Milton here. But in the London *Times Literary Supplement* for January 30, 1919, p. 56, a writer who signs himself J. G. M. suggests that Hall was engaged to help Milton. The same suggestion had been made by J. B. Williams in an article in the *Oxford and Cambridge Review*, no. 18 (1912), pp. 73-88.

MAY 16. MILTON'S REPORT ON IRISH AFFAIRS PUB-LISHED.

Observations upon the Articles of Peace with the *Irish* Rebels, on the Letter of *Ormond* to Col. *Jones*, and the Representation *of the* Presbytery *at* Belfast.

This is a section of about twenty pages added at the end of *Articles of Peace, made and concluded with the Irish Rebels, and Papists, by James Earle of Ormond*, London, 1649, pp. 45 ff.; CM, VI, 242 ff. The *Articles* begins in CM, VI, at p. 181. This report is that requested by the Council of State on March 28, 1649, *q.v.* Thomason's copy bears his date, May 16. Though Milton's name does not appear, its ascription to him has not been questioned. See also Masson, IV, 98 ff.; M. Y. Hughes, "The Historical Setting of Milton's *Observations on the Articles of Peace, PMLA*, LXIV (1949), 1049-1073.

Observations upon the Articles of Peace with the *Irish* Rebels, on the Letter of *Ormond* to Collonel *Jones*, and the Representation of the Presbytery of *Belfast. 4to.*

Phillips, pp. [xlix-l]; not in Darbishire.

MAY 18. INSTRUCTED TO TRANSLATE FRENCH LETTERS CONCERNING HOLLAND.

Die Veneris 18°: Maij 1649 [Friday, May 18, 1649]. . . .
26.) That the ffrench letters given into the House by the Dutch Ambassad^r to be translated by M^r. Milton, and the rest of the Letters now in the House be sent for & translated, and that the Councell doe meet tomorrow at seven in ye morning about it.

Public Record Office, Order Books of the Council of State, SP Dom 25/62, p. 325; *CSP Dom, 1649-1650*, p. 147; Masson, IV, 88; CM, XIII, 637. These letters seem to have related to the murder of Isaac Dorislaus at the Hague. Milton's translations have not been found, unless, as is barely possible, his translation of the French letter from Princess Sophie to Prince Maurice (see under April 13, 1649) may be connected with this assignment.

MAY 22. GILBERT MABBOTT RESIGNS AS LICENSER, PERHAPS BECAUSE OF MILTON'S IDEAS IN *AREOPAGITICA*.

M. *Mabbot* hath long desired severall Members of the house, and lately the Councell of State to Move the house that he might be discharged of Licencing Books for the future, upon the reasons following, *viz.*

I. *Because many thousand of scandalous and malignant Pamphlets have been publish'd with his Name thereunto, as if he had licenced the same (though he never saw them) on purpose (as he conceives) to prejudice him in his Reputation amongst the honest Party of this Nation.*

II. *Because that Imployment (as he conceives) is unjust and illegall, as to the Ends of its first Institution, viz. to stop the Presse for publishing any thing, that might discover the Corruption of Church and State in the time of Popery, Episcopacy, and Tyranny, the better to keep the People in ignorance, and carry on their Popish, Factious, and Tyrannical Designs, for the enslaving and destruction both of the Bodies and Souls of all the free People of this Nation.*

III. *Because Licencing is as great a Monopoly as ever was in this Nation, in that all Men's Judgements, Reasons, &c. are to be bound up in the Licencer's (as to Licencing;) for if the*

Author of any Sheete, Booke, or Treatise, writ not to please the Fancy, and come within the Compasse of the Licencer's Judgement, then hee is not to receive any Stampe of Authority for publishing thereof.

VI. [*i.e.*, IV] *Because it is lawfull (in his Judgement) to print any Booke, Sheete, &c. without Licencing, so as the Authors and Printers do subscribe their true Names thereunto, that so they may be liable to answer the Contents thereof; and if they offend therein, then to be punished by such Lawes as are or shall be for those Cases provided.*

A Committee of the Councell of State being satisfied with these and other Reasons of M. *Mabbot* concerning Licencing, the Councell of State reports to the House; upon which the House ordered this Day, that the said M. *Mabbot* should be discharged of licencing Books for the future.

A Perfect Diurnall, no. 304, May 21-28, 1649, p. 2531; Milton, *A Complete Collection of the Historical, Political, and Miscellaneous Works of John Milton* (ed. J. Toland), 1698, I, 23; *ibid.*, with an introduction by Thomas Birch, London, 1738, I, xxv-xxvi; Masson, III, 431, and IV, 87-88; Darbishire, p. 133. Not all the text as given here has been checked with the *Perfect Diurnall*; most of it is Birch's version, which there is however no reason to suspect. Though this entry does not specifically connect Mabbott's resignation with Milton, the next one does. The ultimate source of the passage is the *Journals of the House of Commons* for May 22, 1649.

Such was the effect of our Author's *Areopagitica*, that the following year *Mabol*, a Licenser, offer'd Reasons against Licensing; and, at his own request, was discharg'd that Office.

Toland, as in the preceding note; repeated in the selections from Birch, Masson, and Darbishire also given there. Birch, and after him Masson, points out the mistakes in this statement: (1) that the name is misspelled, and (2) that the resignation came, not in 1645, but in 1649. It may also be added that Mabbott continued to license books for some time. Entries of books and pamphlets under his hand may be found in the Stationers' Registers under dates of May 23, 1649, January 29, 1653, May 10, 1653, September 8, 1653, July 5, 1654, and July 3, 1655. Stern (I, ii, 483) thinks that Mabbott did not resign voluntarily.

See also the entry under May 25-June 1, 1649.

John Milton · MAY 1649

MAY 25-JUNE 1. STORY ABOUT MABBOTT'S RESIGNA-
TION REPRINTED.

Mr. Mabbott hath long desired severall members of the
House and lately the Counsell of State to move the house that
he might be discharged of licensing books . . . upon which the
House ordered this day that the said Mr. Mabbott should be
discharged of licensing books for the future.

> *The Kingdomes Faithfull and Impartiall Scout*, no. 16, May 25-
> June 1, 1649, p. 143; J. B. Williams, *History of English Journalism*,
> London, 1908, pp. 116-117; CM, XVIII, 632. Most of the passage has
> here been omitted because, except for minor variations in spelling, punc-
> tuation, and the like, it follows almost verbatim the version quoted above
> from *A Perfect Diurnall*. The only changes of the least importance are
> two. In the paragraph above introduced by the Roman numeral II, for
> "Popish, Factious, and Tyrannical," this version reads "Popish, Factious,
> Traitorous and Tyrannical." In the paragraph headed by Roman nu-
> meral VI (*i.e.*, IV), for "their true Names," this version reads "their
> names."
> Williams comments on this passage: "It will be noticed that all this
> is from the *Areopagitica*." Actually, it is no such close quotation as Wil-
> liams implies. Professor Parker's comment (*Milton's Contemporary
> Reputation*, p. 80, as a note on the passage, which he quotes) is closer
> to the truth: "Milton is not mentioned by name, but the possible allu-
> sions to *Areopagitica* justify, I think, the inclusion of the passage with a
> query."

MAY 30. *TENURE OF KINGS* QUOTED BY JOHN GOOD-
WIN.

[Denial of subjection is deposition.] But this Doctrine (with
a farther explication, and proof of it) hath been lately taught
them with Authority and Power, by another pen.*. . . [Marginal
note:] *Tenure of Kings and Magistrates, by *J.M. pag.* 29, 30.
&c. . . .

For, not to insist upon that saying of one, who (upon good
grounds I believe) is able to make it good against all gain-
sayers, *viz.* [marginal note: "Tenure of Kings and Magistrates
by *J. M. p.* 29] *That there is no Protestant Church from the
first Waldenses of* Lyons *and* Languedoc *to this day, but have
in a round made War against a Tyrant in defence of Religion
and civil liberty, and maintain'd it lawfull.* . . .

[253]

[The king's defenders are advised to read] a few pages (*viz.* 23. 24, 25, 26, 27.) in another book, lately also published by *J.M.* intituled, *The tenure of Kings and Magistrates.* . . .

[Two to three pages of quotation from "some pieces published of late" carry the marginal note:] Tenure of Kings and Magistrates by *J. M. pag.* 24. . . .

[The king] was not onely made (saith *J.M.*) obnoxious to the doom of Law [here follows a page of quotation] . . . [marginal note:] Tenure of Kings and Magistrates, *pag.* 35.36. . . . The same Authour elsewhere chargeth these Ministers with oft *citing him* [the King] *under the name of a Tyrant in the hearing of God and Angels and men, and charging him with the spilling of more innocent bloud by far, than ever Nero did*; with oft terming him *Agag*, &c.* [marginal note: "**Ibidem pag* 4.5."*] Not long after, to the same point, thus: *He who erewhile in the Pulpit was a cursed Tyrant, & enemy to God and Saints,* LADEN WITH ALL THE INNOCENT BLOUD SPILT IN THREE KINGDOMS, *and so to be fought against, is now, though nothing penitent, or altered from his principles, a lawful magistrate, a Soveraign Lord, the Lords anointed, not to be touched, though by themselves imprisoned.* [Marginal note: "**Ibid*, p. 6."*] . . .

[About half a page quoted, with the marginal note:] Tenure of Kings and Magistrates by *J.M.* p. 40.

John Goodwin Ὑβριστιδίκαι, *The Obstrvctovrs of Jvstice,* 1649, pp. 53, 71, 73, 78-80, 94, 123; Masson, IV, 95, 106 (mere mention without quotation); Parker, *Milton's Contemporary Reputation,* pp. 80-82. I have omitted a considerable amount of Goodwin's actual quotations from Milton intentionally, and I also missed, in my reading of the book, two references which Parker supplies: to pp. 47 and 53 of Goodwin. Thomason's copy of Goodwin's book is dated May 30, 1649. For some reason Christopher Wordsworth, in *Who Wrote Eikon Basilike?,* 1824, p. 105, dates it May 17.

MAY 30. INSTRUCTED TO EXAMINE THE PAPERS OF JOHN LEE.

Die Mercurij 30°: Maij 1649 [Wednesday, May 30, 1649]. . . . 16.) That Sʳ. Henry Mildmay Sʳ. Iohn Daͮers & Mʳ. Hol-

land or any two of them be appointed a Comittee to examine
the businesse of M\(^r\). Iohn Lee.

17.) That M\(^r\). Milton take the papers found w\(^{th}\) M\(^r\). Iohn Lee
& examine them to see what may be found in them.

Public Record Office, Order Book of the Council of State, SP Dom
25/62, p. 373; *CSP Dom, 1649-1650,* p. 165; Masson, IV, 88; CM,
XVIII, 365, 654. The next entry following those quoted here is to the
effect that John Lee is to be kept in custody until the outcome of the
examination is clear.

JUNE 11. MENTIONED APPROVINGLY FOR DIVORCE
VIEWS; PREPARING ANSWER TO *EIKON BASILIKE.*

An Answer is comming forth unto those *I*dolized [*sic*]
Meditations of the late King, with Marginall Notes upon them,
no doubt but they will be good because of some good Tenents
which the Author holds, whereof this is one, that a man may
put away his wife for lesser faults then fornication; I could
wish it were made into an Act, with this proviso that woemen
[*sic*] might not take pepper ith nose at it. . . .

    Iune 11   *Imprimatur T. I.*

*The Metropolitan Nuncio. Or Times Truth-teller, commending
Verity, condemning Falsity, reproving the Wilfull . . . collected from
divers particulers, with much labour, and here presented in one bundle
to the Reader, by I.H. Numb. 3. From Wednesday June 6, to Wednesday June 13, 1649,* last page. The CBEL attributes the editorship
to John Hackluyt. Miss Raymond (pp. 123-124) says that this news-
sheet, "although its reference to Milton's *Doctrine and Discipline of
Divorce* was eminently laudatory, was accounted an ill servant of the
Commonwealth and permitted to survive for only two issues." She gives
no quotation and no specific reference. Professor Parker (*Milton's Contemporary Reputation,* p. 82) tries to be more specific without having
been able to find the original, but is misled by her having said that only
two issues appeared, and so states that the allusion occurs in No. 2, May
31-June 6. Through the courtesy of Professor William Jackson of the
Houghton Library at Harvard University I have been able to get this
quotation in a pamphlet which Parker notes was uncatalogued in 1940.
The earliest reference which I have seen to this newsbook as commenting
on Milton comes in J. B. Williams's *History of English Journalism,* London, 1908, p. 113, where the author says that the journal was edited by
John Hackluyt, that the allusion to Milton comes in either No. 2 or No. 3,
that it refers to Milton's *Doctrine and Discipline of Divorce* as "having
good tenents," and that the title was later changed to *Mercurius Militaris.*

JUNE 11. ORDERED TO EXAMINE THE PAPERS OF MR.
SMALL.

Die Lunæ 11°: Iunij 1649 [Monday, June 11, 1649]. . . .
1.) That M^r. Milton & M^r. Serjeant shall view the papers of
M^r. Small and deliver out unto him such as are onely of private
concernm^t:, and the rest to bring to this Councell, And that M^r.
Small shall have his Liberty he putting in security to appeare before this Councell on Wednesday Sevennight next, and that his
plate, money and goods shall thereupon be free from being
kept under restraint or sealing up.

Public Record Office, Order Book of the Council of State, SP Dom
25/62, p. 422; *CSP Dom, 1649-1650*, p. 179; Masson, IV, 89; CM,
XVIII, 365. The name of the Sergeant mentioned here was Dendy.

JUNE 16. COURT OF CHANCERY DISMISSES SIR ROBERT
PYE'S SUIT AGAINST MILTON.

Sābb 16° Junij

P.   Ro. Pye mil. q'   } fforasmuch as this co^{r}t was this pñte
      Johēs Milton geñ   } Day informed by M^r. Wilcox being
L C   Def   } of the p^{te} c: that the p^t excted his
bill into this c^{r}t ag^t. the Def in Hill
tearme 1646. to wch the Def apped & in March following putt
in his answ^r. Wherevnto the said p^t. replied the 27th of No:
1647 but hath not since pceeded in the said cause as appeth by
Cert from the Deft^{te} Att yt was therfore prayed that the said
bill might be dismissed wth ordinary cost$_e$ wch is ordered accord-
ingly/

Public Record Office, C 33/192, f. 794; London *Times Literary
Supplement*, March 14, 1936, p. 224; French, *Milton in Chancery*,
p. 301. For previous actions in this suit see above under dates of February 11 and 22 and November 21, 1647, and January-February, 1648.

JUNE 23. ORDERED TO EXAMINE *MERCURIUS PRAG-
MATICUS*.

Die Saturni 23°: Iunij 1649 [Saturday, June 23, 1649]. . . .
9.) That Mr. Milton doe examine the papers of Pragmaticus,
and [report] what he finds in them to the Councell.

Public Record Office, Order Books of the Council of State, SP Dom

25/62, p. 464b (wrongly paged); *CSP Dom, 1649-1650*, p. 204; Masson, IV, 89; CM, XVIII, p. 654. The reference is to the royalist newspaper *Mercurius Pragmaticus*, edited by Marchamont Needham, later to be for a time Milton's colleague in editing *Mercurius Politicus*. On June 18 the Council had ordered Edward Dendy, Sergeant at Arms, to arrest Needham and to seize his papers, among which were undoubtedly the issues which Milton is here ordered to inspect. In the original entry the word "report" is omitted, probably through a clerical error.

JULY 13. *TENURE OF KINGS* MENTIONED.

. . . First, whatsoever hath been done in those particulars; as *in bringing the Army to the City, purging the House, removing the King*, the same hath been ʳproved Lawfull. . . .

[Marginal note:] ʳSee M. *John Goodwins Books, Right and might well met*; and his Answer to M. *Gearee*. Also, *Justice advanced: The Tenure of Kings. The Case of King Charles*.

John Canne (?), *The Discoverer. Being an Answer to a Book, entituled, Englands New Chain, The Second Part, Discovered*, 1649, p. 44. I believe that this allusion to Milton has not previously been noticed. The date is that of the Thomason catalogue.

JULY 16. ASSIGNED TO INSPECT OFFICE OF CLERK OF STATE PAPERS.

Die Lunæ 16°: Iulij 1649 [Monday, July 16, 1649]. . . . 16.) That Mʳ Randolph be continued in his place of Clarke of the papers of state at Whitehall. And that he shall have his pension of fourescore Pounds Annum paid unto him by twentie pound p Quarter, and that the first Quarter shall be paid as due at Midsummer last. And Mʳ Milton is to have an inspection into that Office.

Public Record Office, Order Book of the Council of State, SP Dom 25/62, p. 533; *CSP Dom 1649-1650*, p. 233; Masson, IV, 145.

A large part of the entries in this part of the Order Book look a great deal like the handwriting of Milton. It is of course quite possible that he might have acted as secretary in recording the proceedings of the Council; on the other hand, I hesitate to state that this is definitely his writing. But it closely resembles the known specimens.

JULY 20. *EIKON BASILIKE*, TRANSLATED INTO LATIN BY JOHN EARLE, APPEARS.

Εἰκὼν Βασιλική, Vel Imago Regis Caroli, In illis suis Ærumnis et Solitudine . . . Hagæ-Comitis. Typis S.B, Impensis J. Williams & F. Eglesfield Londinensium . . . 1649.

Title page of the copy in the Thomason collection in the British Museum. Dated by Thomason July 20 on both the title page and also a front flyleaf. The dedication to Charles II is signed on sig. A6v, "Jo: Earles."

A letter from Earle to Charles II concerning this book may be found in the British Museum, Egerton MS. 2547, ff. 1-4. Undated but signed "Your Maj^{ty} most humble and devoted Subject & Chaplaine John Earles," it asks Charles to accept "this Image and Pourtrait of your Glorious Father . . . in a language common to the most part of the world." Other letters in this collection concern the translation into French by one Marsyas.

AUGUST 10. STATE LETTER TO HAMBURG.

Senatus Populusque Anglicanus Amplissimo Civitatis Hamburgensis Senatui, Salutem. Quàm diù, quámque multis de causis . . . *Westmonasterio. Dat. August.* 10. 1649.

Literæ Pseudo-Senatûs Anglicani, Cromwellii, Reliquorumque Perduellium nomine ac jussu conscriptæ A Joanne Miltono. [woodcut of face with pennants and scrolls] *Impressæ Anno 1676*, pp. 1-3; CM, XIII, 4 ff. This letter also occurs in the Skinner MS. in the Public Record Office (SP 9/61) as letter number 1; and in the Columbia MS. in the Columbia University Library as number 35. The first title will hereafter be referred to simply as *Literæ*. For a full and careful description of this book and the several manuscripts in which Milton's letters written for the Council of State have been collected, see CM, XIII, 593-600. The notes to the latter volume give careful collations of all these versions, including also the original letters as actually sent when these can be found. The present letter, which is not the same at all as that given above under date of April 2, 1649, relates to complaints by the people of Hamburg against English traders, and by English people against traders from Hamburg. The original has not been found.

[*The Senate and People of* England, *to the most Noble Senate of the City of* Hamborough. For how long a series of past Years, and for what important Reasons . . . *Westminster, Aug.* 10. 1649.]

Letters of State, Written by Mr. John Milton, To most of the Sovereign Princes and Republicks of Europe. From the Year 1649. Till the Year 1659. To which is added, An Account of his Life. Together with several of his Poems; And a Catalogue of his Works, never before Printed. London: Printed in the Year, 1694, pp. 1 ff.; CM, XIII, pp. 5 ff. This translation of the letters was done by Milton's nephew Edward Phillips. The volume has been referred to previously as "Phillips" and will continue to be hereafter.

AUGUST 14. WARRANT FOR ARREST OF MARCHAMONT NEEDHAM.

14°: Augusti 1649 [August 14, 1649]. . . .

That a Warr^t. bee issued out to y^e. Keeper of Newgate for the apprehending of Marchamont Needham alias Pragmaticus lately prisoner in Newgate. and now escaped.

Public Record Office, Order Book of the Council of State, SP Dom 25/2, unpaged; Masson, IV, 146. Though not directly related to Milton, this item is given here because it carries on the story begun under date of June 23 above.

AFTER AUGUST 16. ACQUIRES AND AUTOGRAPHS A COPY OF *EIKON ALETHINE* (?).

Eikon Elethine, the Pourtraicture of Truths most sacred Majesty, 1649.

[Signed at the bottom of the title page:] Jo. Milton.

According to *Book Auction Records*, XXI (1924), 120, a copy of a book with the title given above was sold at Sotheby's on December 4, 1923, to Spencer for £16. It was bound with *The Faithfull Pourtraicture of a Loyall Subject, in vindication of Eikon Bazilike*, 1649. The volume came from the library of John Disney, containing the date 1810 and his note referring to Milton's signature. The catalogue describes it as having "Jo. Milton's Autograph on title." The date of the present entry comes from Thomason's note on his copy, marking it as having been received on August 16, 1649. Nothing is known of the history of the volume since 1923.

The Harvard University Library has a copy of this work bearing on the flyleaf the arms of the Bridgewaters, the family for whom Milton wrote *Comus*. Its title is Εἴκων Α᾽ΛΗΘΙΝΗ. *The Pourtraiture of Truths most sacred Majesty truly suffering, though not solely. Wherein the false colours are washed off, where-with the Painter-stainer had be-dawbed Truth, the late King and the Parliament, in his counterfeit Piece entituled* Εικων Βασιλικὴ. *Published to undeceive the World. . . . London printed by Thomas Paine and are to be sold by George Whittington at the blew Anchor in Cornhill. 1649.* The book is a chapter-by-chapter answer to *Eikon Basilike*, but omitting any reference to the notorious Pamela prayer. It is preceded by an epistle dedicatory to the Council of State.

AUGUST 20. ATTACKED BY CLEMENT WALKER FOR DIVORCE VIEWS.

There is lately come forth a Book of *John Meltons* (a Libertine, that thinketh his Wife a Manacle, and his very Garters to be Shackles and Fetters to him: one that (after the Independent fashion) will be tied to no obligation to God or man) wherein he undertaketh to prove, *That it is lawfull for any that have power to call to account, Depose, and put to Death wicked Kings and Tyrants (after due conviction) if the ordinary Magistrate neglect it.* I hope then it is lawful to put to death wicked *Cromwels*, Councels of State, corrupt Factions in Parliament: for I know no prerogative that usurpation can bestow upon them. He likewise asserteth, *That those, who of late, so much blame Deposing, are the men that did it themselves,* (meaning the Presbyterians.)

[Marginal note opposite the first part of this paragraph:] *Meltons* Book, *the Tenure of Kings and Magistrates, &c.*

Theodorus Verax [*i.e.*, Clement Walker], *Anarchia Anglicana or, The History of Independency. The Second Part,* 1649, pp. 199-200; Masson, IV, 156 (giving only the first part); Parker, *Milton's Contemporary Reputation,* pp. 82-83. Thomason's copy of this book is dated "August" on the title page of Part II and "August 20" on that of Part I. In some copies or editions of this book the passage comes on pp. 196-197. See below under date of October 24 for Walker's arrest for publishing this book.

SEPTEMBER 20. SALMASIUS CONTINUES WORK AGAINST ENGLAND (?).

Hagh, Sept. 30/20 1649

I heare Salmatius goes on with his worke, the preface of which I sent long since to your honors.

From a letter from Walter Strickland to the Council of State as given in *A Collection of the State Papers of John Thurloe,* I (1742), 127. The reference is so vague that it is hard to tell what work is being described. Salmasius's *Defensio,* which Milton was later to answer, was already out, as we have seen above, by May 11. The present writing may have been a further collection of material ready for future publication; or it may possibly have been something utterly different. But works on philology, in which Salmasius specialized, would not have been likely to attract the attention of the Council of State of England.

SEPTEMBER 29. RECEIVES RENTS FROM WHEATLEY.

. . . Att Michalmas One Thousand six hundred ffortie and nine Thirty One pownds Three shillings and Tenn pence. . . .

From Milton's answer to Elizabeth Ashworth, February 22, 1654, *q.v.*

SEPTEMBER 29. FATHER-IN-LAW RICHARD POWELL'S ESTATE NAMED IN PIPE ROLLS AS IN ARREARS.

Ricūs Powell' ar' deb' xxx ls' ꝑ ann'. de ffirma rcōrie de Yeſley cu' ptin' Ac ffirm' voc' Stafford Close cu' ptin' in Staunton st: Johns Ac vn' mes' & triu' Acr' terr' in Stanton p'dct' pcell' possession'. Regij Colleg' in Oxon'. cu' diūs' alī in R⁰ xiijᵗⁱᵒ spīficāt'. pcell' terr' Phi' Pittes gen'. Jn man' Rꝑ seit' ꝑ sepali ffin' in Camā Stellatt'. Hendū' A xxᵐᵒ Julij Anno xiijᵗᵒ Rꝑ Caroli quamdiu &c' Sicut Contʳ in R⁰ xiijᵗⁱᵒ in Item Oxon'. Ac lx ls'. de Annis pt'it' Sma iiijˣˣ x ls'. Ac xxx ls' ꝑ Richo' libbe ar' Vic' Anno xvjᵗᵒ vizꝑ ꝑ Anno' finit' ad ffestu' Michīs Anno xvijᵐᵒ sicut Contʳ in R⁰ xvjᵗᵒ in Adhuc Res' Oxon' Smᵃ cxx ls'. Ac Ciiijˣˣ ls'. de Ann' p̄t'it' Ac Cv ls'. de Arr' in R⁰ xvijᵐᵒ nondu' oñat'. Smᵃ CCCxlv. ls'.

Ricūs Powell' de fforesthill ar' deb' C ls'. ꝑ ann'. de ffirm' Coppic' voc' Roe Coppice Ac Coppice voc' Horsepath Coppice Elderston Coppice Wheatly Coppice. Coppice de Redding āls Riddinge Coppice de Thornehill' Coppice de Burrowehill'. Coppice voc' Quarrie & Lodge Coppice cu' ptin' in fforest' de Shotover & Stowoode cu' diūs' alī Coppice & terr' boscali voc' Wike Coppice Lodge Coppice Breckly Coppice & Steeplehill' Coppice' cu' diūs' ali' infra fforest' de Shotover in R⁰ xvᵗᵒ in Jtem Oxon' spīficāt'. Hendū' A ffesto Annūc' Anno xijmo Rꝑ Caroli. ꝑ t'imno lxᵗ' Annor. Reddō ad ffesta Michīs & Annūc equalr'. Tma Solūc' incipien' ad ffesta' scī Michīs Archi' Anno Dnī MDCxlvᵗᵒ. sicut contʳ in R⁰ xvᵗᵒ in Jtem Oxon' Ac CCC ls' de Annis p̄t'itis Smᵃ CCCC ls'.

Public Record Office, Pipe Rolls, E372/493, Oxford section ending at Michaelmas, 1649; Hunter, p. 31; Hamilton, p. 51. Although mentioned by Hunter and Hamilton, the record has not previously been printed.

[Richard Powell, esquire, owes 30 pounds a year from the farm and rectory of Iffley with appurtenances and the farm called Stafford Close with appurtenances in Stanton St. John and one messuage and three acres of land in Stanton aforesaid, part of the possessions of King's College in Oxford with divers others specified in the 13th roll, part of the land of Philip Pitts, gentleman, seized into the king's hand by a separate fine in the Star Chamber: to have and to hold from the 20th of July in the 14th year of King Charles until etc., as contained in the 13th roll in the Oxford section; also 60 pounds from previous years: total, 90 pounds; also 30 pounds for Richard Libbe, esquire, sheriff, in the 16th year, namely for the year ended at the feast of Michaelmas in the 17th year as contained in the 16th roll, up to here in the Oxford Residuum; total, 120 pounds; also 180 pounds from previous years; also 105 pounds of arrears in the 17th roll not yet charged; grand total, 345 pounds.

Richard Powell of Forest Hill, esquire, owes 100 pounds a year from the farm copse called Roe Copse and the copses called Horsepath Copse, Elderston Copse, Wheatley Copse, the Copse of Redding alias Ridding, the Copse of Thornehill, the Copse of Borrowhill, the Copse called Quarry and Lodge Copse, with appurtenances in the Forest of Shotover and Stowood with divers other copses and wooded lands called Wike Copse, Lodge Copse, Breckly Copse, and Steeplehill Copse, with divers others within the Forest of Shotover specified in the 15th roll in the Oxford section: to have and to hold from the Feast of the Annunciation in the 12th year of King Charles for a term of 60 years to be paid at the Feasts of Michaelmas and of the Annunciation in equal payments, the term of payment to begin at the Feast of St. Michael the Archangel in the year of our Lord 1646, as contained in the 15th roll in the Oxford section; also 300 pounds from previous years; grand total, 400 pounds.]

John Milton · OCTOBER 1649

OCTOBER 1. RICHARD POWELL REPORTED FOR FINE DUE.

At the Com^{ttee}. at Westm^r. . . .

j: Octob: 1649. . . . Powell Richard of fforest Hill in Com̄
Oxoñ Esqz — li̅   s   d
180-00-00.

Public Record Office, Fines Reported, SP 23/39; French, *Milton in Chancery*, p. 86. This is presumably the same fine of £180 already assessed on December 8, 1646, and probably still remaining unpaid. See above under that date.

OCTOBER 5. GOLDSMITHS' COMPANY VOTE TO ALLOW MILTON A LEASE IN BREAD STREET FOR 21 YEARS AT 400 POUNDS.

At this Courte was read the reporte of the view of Mr Miltons house in Breadstreete for wch hee is a suiter to renew his lease there beeing at o^r Lady day next 3. yeares to come in his old lease and hee inlarged his former offer to 200^{li}: whereupon two sum̄es was noīated vizt 420^{li}: & 400^{li}: and Jt was resolved by the Ballate box 11. against 5. that hee should paye 400^{li}: and have a lease for 21. yeares in reūcoñ or surrendring vp his old lease hee should have a new lease for 24. yeares from o^r Lady day next wch beeing made knowne to him hee craved time to consider thereof and give his answere at the next Courte of Assistantp wch is graunted to him accordingly and hee to have notice to appeare at the next Court./

The Court Book of the Worshipful Company of Goldsmiths, 1648-1651, f. 87. See note above under date of April 20, 1649.

OCTOBER 6. PUBLISHES *EIKONOKLASTES*.

ΕΙΚΟΝΟΚΛΆΣΤΗΣ in Answer To a Book Intitl'd Ε'ΙΚῺΝ ΒΑΣΙΛΙΚῊ, The Portrature of his Sacred Majesty in his Solitudes and Sufferings. The Author I.M. [three verses from Proverbs and three sentences from Sallust] . . . Published by Authority. London, Printed by Matthew Simmons, next dore to the gilded Lyon in Aldersgate street. 1649.

From the title page of the first edition, of which a facsimile is given in CM, v, facing p. 63. The text begins on p. 63. Thomason's copy bears the manuscript date "Octo: 6" on the title page, on which the initial "M" is extended to "Milton."

The Yale University Library copy acquired from Dr. John Fulton has a few manuscript corrections of errors on pages 42, 53, 72, 74, and 112; and on the title page after the initials of the author is written "Milton" in red crayon.

The volume is described fully in the Pforzheimer Catalogue, II, 720.

Professor William Haller suggests (CM, V, 323) that Milton made some use in this book of the *Eikon Alethine*, of which, as we have seen above (under date of "after August 16," 1649), he may have owned and autographed a copy.

Among a collection of ballads, tracts, and the like in the British Museum (Stowe MS. 305) is to be found a manuscript copy of *Eikonoklastes*, written in what appears to be a seventeenth-century hand (ff. 89b-136b); see the *Catalogue of the Stowe Manuscripts in the British Museum*, 1895, I, 357. There is nothing in the manuscript to indicate its relation to the book, but it is more likely to be a copy than an original.

I take it on me as a work assign'd rather, then by me chos'n or affected. Which was the cause both of beginning it so late, and finishing it so leasurely, in the midst of other imployments and diversions.

Milton, *Eikonoklastes*, 1649, sigs. Bv-B2; CM, V, 64-65.

Neque verò his substitit homo ad violationem jurium omnium factus; Modò enim à Matrimoniorum dissociatione ad Regnorum divortium transiit. Cum igitur de Regis capite inter conjuratos ageretur, & ad tam immane facinus plerique expavescerent, scripsit ad eos Tartareus furcifer, nutantesque in malam partem impulit; id præcipuè urgens, de ipsorum capite agi, nempe aut ipsis aut Regi pereundum. Cesset igitur inquisitio quis tandem sacram Regis cervicem securi nefanda præciderit, habemus carnificem, qui facinus suasit, fecit; Feci verò, ait ipse, scelus fatetur, ad se recipit, tuetur, laudat; Hoc agit impurissimo libello cui titulum fecit *Iconoclastes*, quo sanctis Caroli Regis Manibus teterrimus carnifex insultat. . . .

Pierre du Moulin, *Regii Sanguinis Clamor*, Hague, Vlacq, 1652, p. 9.

[Nor even here was there rest for one made for the violation of all rights; for he passed from the dissolution of Marriages to the divorce of Kingdoms. When, accordingly, the death of the King was in agitation among the conspirators, and most were shrinking from so huge a crime, the fiendish gallows-bird wrote for them, and shoved the waverers to the evil side, urging this in special, that their own lives were concerned, for either they or the King must perish. No need, then, for farther inquiry *who* severed the sacred neck of the King with the accursed axe: here we have the hangman who advised the deed and did it. He himself says 'I did it;' he confesses the guilt, takes it to himself, hugs it, boasts of it. This he does in his blackguardly book which he entitled *Eikonoklastes*, in which the hideous hangman insults the holy memory of King Charles.]

Masson, IV, 456.

Prodiit haud multò post attributus Regi liber, contra Parlamentum individiosissimè sane scriptus: huic respondere jussus, Iconi Iconoclasten opposui; non *regiis manibus insultans*, ut insimulor, sed reginam veritatem regi Carolo anteponendam arbitratus. . . .

Milton, *Defensio Secunda*, 1654, p. 94; CM, VIII, 138. The words in italics are quoted from Moulin's attack given above. Milton here explicitly calls the book assigned work, though no order to that effect has been found in the records.

[Not long afterwards (i.e., after Milton's appointment as Secretary) there appeared the book attributed to the king, written surely most bitterly against the Parliament. Being ordered to reply to it, I opposed *Eikonoklastes* to the *Eikon*; not, as I am accused, insulting the spirit of the king, but thinking that Queen Truth should be preferred to King Charles.]

In this public Station [as Secretary] his abilities and the acuteness of his parts, which had lyen hid in his privacy, were soon taken notice of, and hee was pitch'd upon to elude the Artifice of Ἐικὼν Βασιλικὴ. This hee had no sooner perform'd, answerably to the expectation from his Witt & Pen, in Ἐικονοκλάστης, but another Adventure expected him.

The "earliest" biography, ff. 142-142v; Darbishire, p. 26.

2 Ειχονοκλαστης printed at . . . .
Iconoclastes

Aubrey, ff. 68v, 64; Darbishire, pp. 9, 11.

In the first place there came out a Book said to have been written by the King, and finished a little before his Death,

Entituled, 'Εικων Βασιλικη, that is, *The Royal Image*; a Book highly cryed up for it's smooth Style, and pathetical Composure; wherefore to obviate the impression it was like to make among the *Many*, he was obliged to Write an Answer, which he Entituled Εικονοκλαστης, or *Image-Breaker*. . . .

ΕΙΚΟΝΟΚΛΑΣΤΗΣ In Answer to a Book, Entituled, ΕΙΚΩΝ ΒΑΣΙΛΙΚΗ, The Portraiture of his Sacred Majesty in his Solitudes and Sufferings.

Phillips, pp. xxxi and [xlix]; Darbishire, p. 69-70. The second item, which is from Phillips's bibliography, is not reprinted in Darbishire.

In this publick station [as Latin Secretary] his abilities and acuteness of parts, which had been in a manner kept private, were soon taken notice of, and he was pitch'd upon to elude *the artifice* (so it was then by the Faction called) of *Eikon Basilice*. Whereupon he soon after published (14) *Iconoclastes in answer to a book entit.* Eikon Basilice, the portrature of his sacred Majesty in his solitudes and sufferings. *Lond.* 1649-50. qu. *ib.* 1690, oct. which being published to the horror of all sober men, nay even to the Presbyterians themselves, yet by the then dominant party it was esteemed an excellent piece, and perform'd answerably to the expectation of his Wit and Pen.

Wood, I, 882; Darbshire, p. 43.

AFTER OCTOBER 6. JAMES HALES ACQUIRES PAMPHLETS BY MILTON.

Ja. Hales.

A volume of Milton's writings containing this signature is now in the Bodleian Library (Wood B 29). As described in *The Life and Times of Anthony Wood*, ed. A. Clark (1891), I, 319n, it contains the following titles:

1. *The Doctrine and Discipline of Divorce*, 1645.
2. *The Judgment of Martin Bucer*, 1644.
3. *Tetrachordon*, 1645.
4. *Colasterion*, 1645.
5. *Areopagitica*, 1644.
6. *Of Education*, 1644.
7. *The Tenure of Kings and Magistrates*, 1649.
8. *Eikonoklastes*, 1649.

Whether each title was acquired separately on its first appearance or whether Hales got them at other times cannot be decided. The volume is therefore arbitrarily entered here as a unit following the date of appearance of the latest title, *Eikonoklastes*.

OCTOBER 6–JANUARY 8, 1650 (?). WRITES *HISTORY OF MOSCOVIA*.

The study of Geography is both profitable and delightfull; but the Writers thereof, though some of them exact enough in setting down Longitudes and Latitudes, yet in those other relations of Manners, Religion, Government and such like, accounted Geographical, have for the most part miss'd their proportions. Some too brief and deficient satisfy not; others too voluminous and impertinent cloy and weary out the Reader; while they tell long Stories of absurd Superstitions, Ceremonies, quaint Habits, and other petty Circumstances little to the purpose. Whereby that which is usefull, and onely worth observation, in such a wood of words, is either overslip't, or soon forgotten: which perhaps brought into the mind of some men, more learned and judicious, who had not the leisure or purpose to write an entire Geography, yet at least to assay something in the description of one or two Countreys, which might be as a Pattern or Example, to render others more cautious hereafter, who intended the whole work. And this perhaps induc'd Paulus Jovius *to describe onely* Muscovy *and* Britain. *Some such thoughts, many years since, led me at a vacant time to attempt the like argument; and I began with* Muscovy, *as being the most northern Region of* Europe *reputed civil; and the more northern Parts thereof first discovered by* English *Voiages. Wherein I saw I had by much the advantage of* Jovius. *What was scatter'd in many Volumes, and observ'd at several times by Eye-witnesses, with no cursory pains I laid together, to save the Reader a far longer travaile of wandring through so many desert Authours; who yet with some delight drew me after them, from the eastern Bounds of* Russia, *to the Walls of* Cathay, *in several late Journeys made thither overland by* Russians, *who describe the Countreys in their way far otherwise than our common Geographers. From proceeding further other occasions diverted me. This Essay, such as it is, was thought by some, who knew of it, not amiss to be published; that so many things remarkable, dispers'd before, now brought under one view, might not hazard to be otherwise lost, nor the labour lost of collecting them.*

J.M.

ADVERTISEMENT.

This Book was writ by the Authour's own hand, before he lost his sight. And sometime before his death dispos'd of it to be printed. But it being small, the Bookseller hop'd to have procured some other suitable Piece of the same Authour's to have joyn'd with it, or else it had been publish'd 'ere now.

Milton, *A Brief History of Moscovia*, 1682, sigs. A3-A4v; CM, X, 327-329. The date is so uncertain that Hanford (*Milton Handbook*, fourth edition, p. 129) assigns it simply to the Commonwealth or early Protectorate or "possibly even as early as the Horton period." If we may believe the printer's advertisement, it was at least written before early in 1652, when Milton lost his sight. Whenever Milton wrote his preface, he referred to the composition as having taken place "many years since," a very vague phrase. It is here assigned to late in 1649 on the basis of George B. Parks's "The Occasion of Milton's *Moscovia*," *Studies in Philology*, XL (1943), 399 ff. Professor Parks thinks that it was written between October 6, 1649, and January 8, 1650, when relations with Russia were strained. He suggests that it may have been written as a precis of information needed in the foreign office.

OCTOBER 20. PAYS MOTHER-IN-LAW ANNE POWELL HER THIRDS.

[Milton] did pay or cause to bee payed vnto . . . Anne Powell . . . the seuerall summes of money menčoned and Expressed in the six seuerall Acquittances or Receiptes . . . [the fourth of which is dated] the 20ᵗʰ of October 1649: and is for the summe of tenne poundę. . . .

From Anne Powell's deposition in the Ashworth-Milton suit, June 4, 1656, *q.v.*

OCTOBER 24. ORDERED TO SEIZE PAPERS OF CLEMENT WALKER.

Die Mercurij 24°: Octobʳ: 1649 [Wednesday, Oct. 24, 1649]. . . .

8.) That a warrant be issued to Mr Milton & Mr Sergeant Dendy to veiw the bookes & papers of Mr Clement Walker that are seized at Kensington & such others as he hath here in Westminster or elswhere & to report what they finde therein to the Councell.

Public Record Office, Order Books of the Council of State, SP Dom 25/63, p. 175; *CSP Dom, 1649-1650*, p. 550; CM, XVIII, 365.

These are to will & authorize You & either of you to make yor repaire to Kensington to the House of Clement Walker, or to any other place or lodgings there or in any other place to him belonging, where you shall veiw and search all his bookes and papers, and shall secure them when you have soe searched them, and shall returne to the Councell a Report of what you finde in ye said bookes or papers that may be preiuditiall to the Comonwealth. of wch You are not to fayle and for wch this shall be yor. sufficient Warrant. Given at the Councell of State at Whitehall this 24th of Octob^r. 1649/

  Signed in ye Name & by order of the Councell
  of State appointed by Authority of Parlam^t.
  [signed] Jo: Bradshawe p^r.sid^t.

To John Milton Esqz Secretary
 for forreigne Languages
  And
To Edward Dendy Esq: Sergeant
 at Armes attending this Councell:
 [Endorsed on the back:] Warr^tt: for the Apprehension
   of Clement Walker 24th
    8^br. 1649/

Public Record Office, Warrant Books of the Council of State, SP Dom 18/6, no. 77. A copy of this warrant, of the same date but addressed to Dendy alone, is found in the Order Books, SP Dom 25/63, p. 181.

Masson states (IV, 147) that Walker had been arrested on this very day for his *Anarchia Anglicana or The History of Independency, the Second Part*, which has been noticed above under date of August 20 for its attack on Milton.

NOVEMBER 5. ACCEPTS OFFER OF GOLDSMITHS' COMPANY ABOUT LEASE IN BREAD STREET AND ARRANGES PAYMENTS.

At this Courte Mr Milton came and declared his consent to accept of the graunte of the lease made to him at A Courte of Assistantp the 12th of October last and this Courte acquainted him wth the new Covenaunt of the alienacōn ffine of x^li: for the poore according to the late order in that behalfe wherevnto hee willingly submitted and craved some respite of time for payement of his ffine wch beeing taken into consideracōn Jt is ordered that hee shall paye his ffine of 400^li: As followeth vīzt./

li

At Christmas next in parte .... 100.
At Midsomer *1650* more .... 100.
At Christmas .... *1650* more 100
At Midsomer .... 16 5 1. in full 100./

And if hee shall pay it sooner then the Wardens for the time beeing to rebate him after the rate of vi^li p Centū for what hee shall pay in before the dayes of payement.

The Court Book of the Worshipful Company of Goldsmiths, f. 96. See note above under date of April 20, 1649. Either a record has been lost here, or the clerk who made this entry made a mistake, for the decision of the Court of the Company had previously been taken on October 5, not October 12.

NOVEMBER 14. MARCHAMONT NEEDHAM SET FREE.

That a warrant be issued to the Keeper of Newgate for the discharge of Mr Needham, the said Mr Needham first takeing the test.

Public Record Office, Order Books of the Council of State, SP Dom 25/63, p. 257; *CSP Dom, 1649-1650*, p. 554; Masson, IV, 149. The warrant itself is to be found in the same volume.

BEFORE NOVEMBER 16. ANNE POWELL PETITIONS FOR RELIEF.

To the right hono^ble the Commissione^rs for breach of Artickles.

The humble Peticōn of Ann Powell Widdowe Relict of Richard Powell of fforrest Hill in the Countie of Oxon, Esqʳ.

Humblie sheweth

That yoʳ Peticōners Late husband was comprised within the Artickles of Oxford and ought to have received the benefitt thereof as appeares by his Excellencies Certificate herevnto annexed. That yoʳ said Peticōners husband by the said Artickles was to have the benefitt of his reall and psonall estate for sixe Moneth's after the rendition of the said Cittie, and to enioye the same for the future soe as he made his addresses to the Comittee at Gouldsmiths Hall to compound for the same with in that tyme. That yoʳ Peticōnerˢ said husband accordingly in August one thousand six hundred fortie sixe, peticōned the said honoᵇˡᵉ Comittee and in his Perticular incerted for Tymber and wood fower hundred pounds, but before he could pfect the same dyed.

That the honoᵇˡᵉ howse of Parliament vpon some misinformacon not taking notice of the said Artickles Did in July one thowsand six hundred fortie sixe order the said wood to severall vses which was there vpon togeither with the rest of his goods and moveables seized and carried away by the Sequestrators to the Comittee for Oxoñ contrary to the said Artickles That yoʳ Peticōner as Executrix to her said husband is now sued in severall Courts of Justice at Westminster for manie Debts due to diuerse persons and is noe waie able eyther to satisfie the same or provide a scanty subsistance for herselfe and nine Children.

She therefore humblie prayes that she maie reape that favour which the said Artickles doe affoard her by restoring to her the said Tymber and wood and other her goods soe taken away or the value thereof.

And yoʳ Peticōner shall praie &c.

[Signed] Anne Powell./

Vera Copia Exᵗᵃ. Tracy Pauncefote Regʳ.

[In margin:] A certificate was made upon this to yᵉ Comʳˢ. for releife vpon Articles. 14°. Dec: 1649.

[Endorsed:] Coppie of Mʳˢ Powell her Peticon.

Public Record Office, Composition Papers, SP Dom 23/194, p. 393;
Todd, 1 (1826), 73-74 (undated and lacking the marginal note and
the endorsement); Hamilton, pp. 78, 80; Masson, IV, 145-146 (extracts only). Hamilton makes a curious mistake about this document. On
p. 78 he gives the first few lines of it, under date of November 16, 1649,
and with a reference to p. 387 of the Composition Papers. On p. 80 he
gives the whole text under date of December 14, 1649, with reference
to p. 393 of the Papers. The original paper bears no date, perhaps because it is a true copy and not the actual one which Anne Powell handed
in. Its date must be either on or before (probably before) November 16,
since on that day (*q.v.*) the Commissioners considered it and turned it
over to the Commissioners for Compounding with the request that they
report on it within a month. It is possible that I may have missed finding
the real original among the Composition Papers.

NOVEMBER 16. ANNE POWELL'S PETITION CONSIDERED BY THE COMMISSIONERS FOR RELIEF.

Painted Chamber, Westm^r

By the Comissioners appointed for releife vpon Artickles &c
  Veidis [Friday] 16to die Novembris 1649
     Present.
Lord President of the Councell of State.
Sr Henrie Holcroft   Colonell Rowe
Sr Nath. Brent   Colonell Taylor
Colonell Cooke   Colonell Whaley
Sr Willm Rowe   Mr. Sadler.
   Mr John Hurst of Councell for the Comon-wealth
Vpon readinge the Peticon of Ann Powell Widowe Relict of
Richard Powell of fforrest Hill in the Countie of Oxford Esqr
It is ordered That a coppie of her said Peticon attested vnder
the Registers hande of this Court bee delved vnto the Comis-
sion^{rs} for Compoundinge with delinquents sittinge at Gould-
smiths' Hall whoe are desired to make Certificate vnto this
Court within one moneth from the date of this order, At what
tyme the said Richard Powe^{ll} peticoned to make his Composicon and wheyther the wood menconed in her Peticon were
expressed in his Perticular delivered in vnto them with what
else they shall thinke fitt to incert touchinge the matter of Com-

plaint sett downe in the said Peticōn. Wherevpon the Court will proceed further as they shall thinke fitt.

        Signed

           By Cōmand of the Com^{rs}.

                Tracy Pauncefote Reg^{r}.

[Endorsed:] Veidis [Friday], 16to Novemb. 1649 Mr^{s} Powell Coppie order to the Com^{rs} of Gouldsmiths' Hall.

Public Record Office, Composition Papers, SP Dom 23/194, p. 397; *CCC*, pp. 1439-1440; Hamilton, p. 79.

NOVEMBER 19. ASSIGNED LODGINGS OF SIR JOHN HIP-PISLEY IN SCOTLAND YARD, WHITEHALL.

Die Lunæ 19°: Novemb^{r}: [Monday, November 19] 1649.
. . .

4.) That M^{r}. Milton shall have the lodgings that were in the hands of S^{r}. John Hippesly in Whitehall for his accommodation as being Secretary to this Councell for forreigne Languages.

Public Record Office, Order Books of the Council of State, SP Dom 25/63, p. 274; *CSP Dom, 1649-1650*, p. 398; Masson IV, 150. For views and maps of Whitehall see Edward Walford and Walter Thornbury, *Old and New London*, III, 337, and Peter Cunningham, *London* (1927), p. 289. Cunningham speaks of Milton's residence as being in Great Scotland Yard. Masson (IV, 153) says of the Hippisley apartments that they "were, at all events, at the Scotland Yard end of the palace; for his nephew Phillips, on whose authority we saw him remove, in or about April 1649, from High Holborn to Thomson's at Spring Gardens, Charing Cross, to be near the Council, adds that he remained at Thomson's only 'till his designed apartment in Scotland Yard was prepared for him.' " But see the next following item. Masson describes this apartment briefly in "Local Memories of Milton," *Good Words*, XXXIV (1893), 137-138.

. . . *Joannis Philippi Angli Defensio pro Populo Anglicano contra*, &c. during the Writing and Publishing of this Book, he lodg'd at one *Thomson's* next door to the *Bull-head* Tavern at *Charing-Cross*, opening into the *Spring-Garden*, which seems to have been only a Lodging taken, till his designed Apartment in *Scotland-Yard* was prepared for him; for hither he soon removed from the foresaid place; and here his third Child, a

Son was born, which through the ill usage, or bad Constitution of an ill chosen Nurse, died an Infant.

Phillips, p. xxxiii; Darbishire, p. 71. However accurate some of Phillips's facts here may be, his chronology must be wide of the truth. We know from other sources that (1) Milton moved into apartments in or near Scotland Yard on November 19, 1649; (2) he moved into Petty France, which Phillips puts later than the Scotland Yard house, in December, 1651; (3) his son John was born (Phillips says in Scotland Yard) on March 16, 1651; (4) John Phillips's *Responsio ad Apologiam anonymi* (which Edward Phillips calls *Defensio pro Populo Anglicano*) did not appear until December, 1652. It therefore seems safe to accept Edward Phillips's statement of the residences and his order of giving them, but not his dating of the Scotland Yard residence and the John Phillips book as at the same time.

. . . the Son, named *John*, was born as above-mention'd, at his Apartment in *Scotland Yard*.

Phillips, p. xli; Darbishire, p. 77.

NOVEMBER 21. ORDERED TO PRESENT LADY KILLI-GREW'S LETTERS TO THE COUNCIL.

Die Mercurij 21°: Novemb[r]: [Wednesday, November 21] 1649. . . . 1°.) That the Letters concerning Lady Killegrew that are in the Custody of Mr Milton be brought to Councell, that upon consideracõn thereof some resolution may be taken about the passe desired.

Public Record Office, Order Books of the Council of State, SP Dom 25/63, p. 288; *CSP Dom, 1649-1650*, p. 401; Masson, IV, 150; CM, XVIII, 366. The desired pass was granted three days later.

NOVEMBER 29. COUNCIL OF STATE ORDERS SAL-MASIUS'S *DEFENSIO* CONFISCATED.

Die Iovis 29°: Novemb[r]: [Tuesday, November 29] 1649. . . . 5.) That a Letter be written unto the Com[rs]: of the Customes to desire them to give Order, That a very strict search may be made of such Ships as come from the Netherlands for certain scandalous bookes which are there printed against the Governm[t]. of this Comõnwealth entituled Defensio Regia, And which are designed to be sent over hither, & to desire them that if any of them upon search shall be found, that they may be sent up to the Councell of State wthout suffering any of them to be otherwise disposed of upon any pretence whatsoever.

Public Record Office, Order Books of the Council of State, SP Dom 25/63, p. 325; *CSP Dom, 1649-1650*, p. 411; Masson, IV, 150-151. It was as a reply to this book that Milton's first *Defense of the English People* was written. See also the earlier reference to this book under date of May 11, 1649.

DECEMBER 8. SALMASIUS'S BOOK IN DANGER OF SUPPRESSION IN HOLLAND; MILTON (?) MENTIONED.

Strickland, as Ambassador from England formed into a Republick, upon his third instance, hath prevailed with the States to suppress Salmasius's book written for the King, first prohibited to be printed at Leyden, afterwards finished at Amsterdam, terming it, in his memorial, a Pasquil against the Republick of England. And it is not yet determined, whether it shall be burnt, or no; which he would have. There is another lately passed the press without that danger; a confutation of our Blessed Martyr King's book, in English. I have not yet seen it. . . .

Breda, Dec. 8, 1649.

Letter of Richard Watson to William Edgman, printed in the *Calendar of the Clarendon Papers Preserved in the Bodleian Library*, ed. W. D. Macray, II (1869), 500; quoted in Wordsworth, *Who Wrote Eikon Basilike?*, 1824, p. 105. I have not seen the original. The book referred to near the end may be Milton's *Eikonoklastes* or perhaps *Eikon Alethine*.

DECEMBER 16. COMMITTEE FOR COMPOUNDING REPORTS ON ANNE POWELL'S PETITION.

Die Veneris: [Friday] 14°: Decembz: 1649.

| M^r. John Ashe. | M^r. Say. | M^r. Blagrave. |
| M^r. Trenchard. | M^r. Harby. | Coll: Birche. |

This Com^{ttee}: haueing this day receiued from the Com^{rs}: appointed for releife vpon Articles, a Copie of a Petition of Anne Powell widdow, the Relict of Richard Powell, of fforrest Hill in the County of Oxon Esqr. together with a desire from the said Com^{rs}: that this Com^{ttee}: would Certifie at what tyme the said Richard Powell petitioned to make his Composic̄on, & whether the wood menc̄oned in her Petic̄on were expressed in the pticuler of the said Richard Powell deliūed in vnto this Com^ttee: with what else this Com^ttee: shall thinke fitt to insert touching the matter of Complaint sett downe in the said petic̄on; Jt is Ordered that Certificate be accordingly made vnto the said Com^rs: That ye said Richard Powell did petic̄on this Comittee to Compound upon the Articles of Oxford the 6th. of August 1646. And that he menc̄oned in his pticuler vpon which his ffine was sett Tymber & wood to the value of 400 ł. for which he was ffined according to the said Articles of Oxoñ; And that as yet noe part of the said ffine hath bin payd, nor any Lres granted by this Com^ttee. to suspend the sequestrac̄on of that estate, or any pte thereof./

[Marginal note:] M^rs: Powell.

Public Record Office, Order Book of the Committee for Compounding, SP Dom 23/6, p. 248; *Calendar of the Committee for Compounding*, p. 1439; Hamilton, p. 81. This order is a reply to the action of November 16 above. See also the marginal note dated December 14 on Anne Powell's petition above, dated "before November 16," 1649, summarizing the present action.

DECEMBER 16. ACTS AS LICENSER FOR ACCOUNT OF TRIAL OF CHARLES I.

[December 16, 1649]

John Grismond. Entred ... under the hand of Master MILTON, secretary to the Councell of State, a booke called *Historie entiere et veritable du Proces de Charles Stuart Roy d'Anglitere* &c. . . . vj^d

Stationers' Registers, I, 333; London *Times*, January 30, 1928, p. 15e. Masson (IV, 325-326) gives a list of books licensed by Milton but does not mention this particular title. The *Times* article says that a manuscript journal of the High Court of Justice is in the Public Record Office. Such a journal is indexed there as SP Dom 16/517, but there are no evidences of comment by a licenser in it. It may also be pointed out that Gilbert Mabbott, whose resignation as licenser has been noticed above (May 22, 1649), had previously licensed the same or a similar book ("A perfect narrative of the whole proceedings of the High Co^rt of Justice in the tryall of the king") on January 22, 1649—a book which Thomason dated as having been received by him on January 20. The present book appeared on March 3, 1650, *q.v.*

DECEMBER 21. CHRISTOPHER MILTON'S FINE RE-PORTED UNPAID (?).

Christopher Milton . . . Rep: 21 : Dec. 49 ffine — 200 łi.

Endorsement on the affidavit of his residence in Exeter given above under date of May 16, 1646. This note probably refers to the same action as that of December 24 below, but probably with a mistake in one or the other of the dates. Of the two I should guess that the 24th is more likely to be accurate, but this is simply a guess.

DECEMBER 21. PAYS 100 POUNDS TOWARD LEASE OF BREAD STREET HOUSE.

At this Courte Mr Warden Courthop made knowne that hee had receaved of Mr Milton in parte of his ffine of 400^{li}. for renewing the lease of the great Messuage in Breadstreet./C^{li}./

The Court Book of the Worshipful Company of Goldsmiths, f. 110. See note above under date of April 20, 1649.

DECEMBER 21-28. SALMASIUS'S *DEFENSIO* ORDERED CONFISCATED IN HOLLAND.

The States of *Holland* sent for the *Fiscall* into their Assembly, and gave him charge in their presence, to seize upon all the books intitled *Defensio Regia pro Carolo primo ad serenissimum Magnæ Britanniæ Regem Carolum secundum* that were in the *Hague,* and have given the same charge to all the Townes in *Holland,* and this is the greatest and most reproachfull thing which in that Country can be done to any booke the State disallowes.

Severall Proceedings in Parliament, Number 13, December 21-28, 1649, p. 161. Compare the order of November 29 above for seizing copies of this book as they entered England. I have not searched for the original Dutch order, but there is considerable likelihood that the present report is true.

DECEMBER 24. BROTHER CHRISTOPHER'S FINE STILL UNPAID (?).

At the Com^{ttee}. at Westm^r. . . . .

24: Dec 1649. . . . Milton Christopher of Redding in Com̄ Berkꝑ

— łi   s   d.

200 —   —

Public Record Office, Fines Reported, SP 23/39; French, *Milton in Chancery*, p. 86. This action seems to be a repetition of that of August 25, 1646, when Christopher's fine was set. At that time two figures were mentioned: eighty pounds and four hundred pounds. The eighty pounds he paid in two installments later that year, namely on September 24 and December 24. Apparently the two hundred remained unpaid, and is here recorded for that reason.

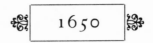

SAMUEL HARTLIB ALLUDES TO MILTON'S *AREOPAGITICA*.

There are no Licensers appointed by the last Act so that everybody may enter in his booke without License. puided the Printers or Authors name bee entered that they may bee forth coming if required. M^r. Milton.

[Marginal note:] Licensing of Bookes.

From Samuel Hartlib's diary or "Ephemerides" for 1650 in the collection of Lord Delamere; printed in G. H. Turnbull, *Hartlib, Dury and Comenius*, p. 41. Professor Turnbull thinks that this item "was no doubt communicated by Milton to Hartlib, and refers, I take it, to Bradshaw's Press Act of 1649." Masson (IV, 116-118) discusses this act, which became law on September 20, 1649. On the same page of Hartlib's manuscript there is a note that "Needham the Pragmaticus or Mercurius Britannicus got 50. lb. and is annually entertained by the State For Hue and Crie writing after the way hee was disgraced in so much that hee could not obtain a Prospovs place." This seems to be a reference to the action of the Council of State on May 24, 1650, in ordering £50 given to Needham, soon to begin editing *Mercurius Politicus*; see Masson, IV, 226.

RECEIVES INCOME OF SIXTY POUNDS FROM WESTMINSTER ABBEY (?).

His widow . . . is said to have reported . . . that, in the general depredation upon the Church, he had grasped an estate of about sixty pounds a year belonging to Westminster Abbey, which, like other sharers of the plunder of rebellion, he was afterwards obliged to return.

John Milton · 1650

Samuel Johnson, *Prefaces, Biographical and Critical, To The Works of the English Poets. By Samuel Johnson. Volume the Second,* London, 1779, p. 136. Johnson's statement is probably grounded on that of Thomas Birch in his biographical preface to *A Complete Collection of the Historical, Political, and Miscellaneous Works of John Milton,* I (1738), lxii. Birch tells of visiting Milton's granddaughter, Mrs. Foster, who informed him "that an Estate of about 60*l. per Ann.* at *Westminster,* was taken away from him at the Restoration, it belonging to the Dean and Chapter there." But Johnson's interpretation seems to owe something to his political grudge against Milton. This entry is filed under 1650 for want of a more specific date.

FINANCIAL DIFFICULTIES.

It is reported (and from the foregoing Character it seems probable) that Mr. Milton *had lent most of his Personal Estate upon the Publick Faith; which when he somewhat earnestly and warmly pressed to have restored [observing how all in Offices had not only feathered their own Nests, but had enricht many of their Relations and Creatures, before the Publick Debts were discharged] after a long and chargeable Attendance, met with very sharp Rebukes; upon which at last despairing of any Success in this Affair, he was forced to return from them poor and friendless, having spent all his Money, and wearied all his Friends. And he had not probably mended his worldly condition in those days, but by performing such Service for them, as afterwards he did, for which scarce anything would appear too great.*

Milton, *Mr John Miltons Character of the Long Parliament and Assembly of Divines,* 1681, sigs. A2-A2v, "To the Reader"; CM, XVIII, 247. The brackets are in the original text. This statement is very vague as to date, and must apply (in so far as it may be true) to a period of several years, probably chiefly to those during which he was submitting petitions for redress. The last sentence probably alludes to his work as Secretary, for which he received a salary.

ATTRIBUTED INSCRIPTION ON TOMB OF WILLIAM STAPLE.

Quod cum cœlicolis habitus, pars altera nostri,
  Non dolet, hic tantûm, me superesse dolet.
    Hoc posuit mœstissima uxor, Sara.

First printed and attributed to Milton by Thomas H. Gill in *Notes and Queries*, I (1852), 361; CM, XVIII, 594. There is no reason to accept the attribution to Milton, though it should be included here because it has been thought at one time to be his. According to Matthews's probate records, William Staple, gentleman, of the city of London, died April 4, 1648. His will, 149 Pembroke, was proved on September 16, 1650, by his relict Sarah. It is of course impossible to date the inscription on his monument (which was in the church of St. Giles Cripplegate, where Milton was later to be buried), but it seems best to place it here in the year in which the will was proved. No other connection of Milton with William Staple is known.

[Because he is gathered into the heavenly family, our other half does not grieve, but it grieves me to be left here. His most afflicted wife Sarah placed this here.]

TRACT ASCRIBED TO MILTON.

School-Lawes, or Qui Mihi in English Verse, by J.M., 1650.

A book by this title was ascribed to Milton in *Book Prices Current*, XV (1901), 511. Together with several other items, it was sold at Sotheby's on May 6-9, 1901, to Quaritch for £41. The catalogue calls it a unique poetical tract; there are no copies in the British Museum or in the Harvard College Library. The note about it in CM, XVIII, 600, points out justly that "the absence of a reference to a separate work like this from the list of Phillips, is the strongest presumptive evidence against it, and we may dismiss the attribution as chimerical."

SUPPOSED PORTRAITS (?).

Ioannes Milton aetat. 42. Ex musaeo J. Richardson. G. Vertue sculpsit, 1751.

Three portraits, which have at some time been attributed to Milton, date from about 1650. None of them can be considered to possess any reasonable degree of authenticity. I have not seen the originals of any.

1. One bearing the legend quoted above is described by Dr. Williamson in his *Milton Tercentenary*, pp. 18 and 83. Williamson describes it as "An oval, the frame of which terminates at the base in a foliated scroll in which is inserted a panel, and at the top a serpent, an apple, and lightning." The plate measures 8¾ by 6 inches. Williamson says further of it: "It does not in the least resemble the authentic portraits, and was engraved by Vertue from a drawing which belonged to Richardson and was removed from his collection, he having died six years before. The person certainly has flowing hair and wears a gown and bands, but in no other respects resembles the poet."

2. Williamson mentions another (p. 22), which was shown by the

Reverend R. C. Jenkins at South Kensington in 1866. Like the preceding one, it is said to have been dated 1650 and inscribed "Age 42." It was "a portrait of a man in dark dress with a square cut white collar and tassels and with long hair. . . . It was on canvas, 27 inches by 23 inches, and although it certainly bears some slight resemblance to the Faithorne engraving, yet the resemblance is not sufficient for us to claim it as an authentic portrait."

3. The London *Times* of April 9, 1909, p. 3e, described a newly discovered portrait of Milton signed "W. Hassel fec." It was painted on an oak panel measuring 6 by 7⅝ inches, showing a man in the prime of life. The writer suggests the date 1650 for it. It was collected in the forties by a Mr. Kennedy, taken to New Orleans in 1850, sold in 1865 to Mr. A. S. Mansfield of Boston, and exhibited in 1909 in the Fogg Art Museum of Harvard University.

The history of these portraits since 1908 and 1909 has not been traced. Professor Arthur Pope, Director of the Fogg Museum, writes me that no record of either the loan or the exhibition of the Hassel portrait can be found in the files of the Museum.

RESIDENCE IN DUKE STREET (?).

Cunningham (*London*, 1927, p. 203) says that Milton had apartments at 10 Duke Street, in which he wrote his *Defensio*, opposite the room in which Cromwell received foreign ambassadors. In view of Milton's having recently been assigned to quarters in Whitehall, this assertion is difficult to accept. There may possibly be some confusion with the fact that somewhat later Milton lived in York Street, which is only a few steps from Duke Street. The *Defensio*, which appeared early in 1651, must have been written in 1650.

SUBMITS TO CROMWELL DESCRIPTION OF MODEL REPUBLIC (?).

[Sir Thomas Phillipps is said to have presented to the Royal Society of Literature extracts of some manuscript letters of Milton to Cromwell describing a model republic.]

An anonymous article in the *Gentleman's Magazine*, New Series, VI (1836), 462. No further trace of these letters has been found. There may possibly be some confusion on the part of the writer with the Columbia Manuscript, described elsewhere. It contains copies of Milton's letters of state and of several essays on political matters. It formerly belonged to Phillipps.

STATE LETTER TO ALGIERS (?).

Most illustrious Señor whome god preserve, we receiv'd a letter from you . . . Dated at the Palace of Westm:, & signed

with the seale of the councell of State appointed by authority
of the Parliament.

Columbia MS., No. 50; CM, XIII, 495-496. Neither the date nor
Milton's authorship is certain, but it is included here because of the
likelihood that it may have been composed by Milton, and the date seems
as likely as any. In fact, the letter may be related to a record of the
Council of State dated September 20, 1650 (*CSP Dom, 1650*, p. 349).
The Admiralty Committee voted on that day to recommend to the
Council that the Council should write to the Governor of Tetuan, dis-
cussing two points. The first had to do with some Chinese, who had
refused to take a ship of his to Algiers or Tunis; the Council was to ask
him to send them his original contract with the Chinese so that they
might verify the facts. The second was concerned with his having
detained a Mr. Peach and three other Englishmen. This latter point had
come into the records several times previously; e.g., August 23, 1650
(p. 302). The present letter may also have some connection, though it
is not clear what, with the lost letter to the Governor of Tetuan which
Milton was ordered to write on January 29, 1650.

SECOND EDITION OF *EIKONOKLASTES* PUBLISHED.

'ΕΙΚΟΝΟΚΛΆΣΤΗΣ in Answer to a Book Intitl'd 'ΕΙΚΩΝ ΒΑΣΙ-
ΛΙΚΉ, The Portrature of his sacred Majesty in his Solitudes and
Sufferings. The Author J. M. [Quotations from Proverbs and
Sallust.] . . . Publish'd now the second time, and much enlarg'd.
London, Printed by T.N. and are to be sold by Tho. Brewster
and G. Moule at the three Bibles in Pauls Church-Yard near
the West-end, 1650.

From the original title page.

PRESENTS COPY OF *EIKONOKLASTES* TO THE EARL OF
CARBERY.

For my very good friend Mr. William Thomas at Laherne,
to be presented to the Right Honourable the Earle of Car-
bury. . . .

The above is supposed to be the handwriting of Mr. Milton.

Francis Blackburne, *Memoirs of Thomas Hollis*, 1780, I, 62; *A
Catalogue of the Library of the late Richard Heber*, 1835, part 6, no.
2354; Masson, IV, 246; Lowndes, *Bibliographer's Manual*, III (1900),
1566; Bernard Halliday's Catalogue 111 (1929), item 99; French,
"The Autographs of John Milton," no. 29; CM, XVIII, 270, 549. The
first quotation is said to have been written by Milton on the outside of

the brown paper leaf or flyleaf, and the second in a late seventeenth-century hand under it.

A William Thomas (1613-1689) was vicar of Laugharne, ejected in 1644, and restored in 1660; he later became Dean of Worcester, Bishop of St. David's, and Bishop of Worcester (*D.N.B.*). This is unlikely to be Milton's friend. Another, Member of Parliament from Caernarvon during the Long Parliament, who made several speeches against bishops during 1641 and 1642, sounds more likely.

Richard Vaughan, second Earl of Carbery (1600?-1686), was fined as a delinquent in 1644 and 1645, but pardoned in 1647 and afterwards remained neutral. As the husband of Alice Egerton, the lady of Milton's *Comus*, he must have been the object of some interest for Milton.

According to Blackburne, the present book was found by Richard Baron in 1755 and given by him to Thomas Hollis in 1756. Baron reprinted it in 1756.

The catalogue of Hollis's library (1817) included a copy of *Eikonoklastes*, 1650, with manuscript notes by Richard Baron and "a specimen of the Hand Writing of Mr. Milton." This is probably the copy under discussion here.

The present location of this book is not known.

PRESENTS COPY OF *EIKONOKLASTES* TO JOHN DURY.

G. Dury. 1650. Ex dono Authoris.

This inscription is written on the title page of the copy of *Eikonoklastes*, 1650, in the Grenville collection in the British Museum, shelf-mark G 11718. See Masson, IV, 246; French, "The Autographs of John Milton," no. 28; CM, XVIII, 551. The inscription, which is certainly not in the hand of Milton, is probably by Dury.

NEPHEW JOHN PHILLIPS PRESENTS COPY OF *EIKONO-KLASTES* TO JOHN BARKER (?).

Ex dono Dni John Phillips nepot Author. . . . Jo Barker.

Inscriptions on the title page of a copy of the second edition of *Eikonoklastes* now in the Sterling Library of Yale University. It is not certain that the two elements—the "ex dono" and the signature—belong together, but it seems likely that they do. The "ex dono" is in the left-hand margin just under the "Eikonoklastes," and the "Jo Barker" on the same level in the right-hand margin. Though the first part has been scored through, it is still legible. The author's initials, "J. M.," have been extended in manuscript to "J. Milton."

EIKONOKLASTES (?) POPULAR AMONG FRENCH PROT-
ESTANTS.

To return to the Objections against the French Protestants;
My Noble Antagonist saith that they had *Miltons* Book against
our precious King and Holy Martyr in great veneration. That
they will deny. But it is no extraordinary thing that wicked
Books which say with a witty malice all that can be said for a
bad cause, with a fluent and florid stile, are esteemed even by
them that condemn them. Upon those terms *Miltons* wicked
Book was entertained by Friends and Foes, that were Lovers
of Human Learning, both in *England* and *France.*

Peter du Moulin, *A Replie to a Person of Honour,* 1675, p. 40;
White Kennet, *A Register and Chronicle,* 1728, I, 23. The wording of
this allusion seems to fit *Eikonoklastes* better than the *Defensio,* but
du Moulin may perhaps be referring to that Latin work. On the other
hand, the fact that *Lewis* du Moulin translated *Eikonoklastes* into Latin
may be pertinent. At any rate, the passage is evidence that some book of
Milton's achieved high popularity among French Protestants.

CHAPTER 1 OF *EIKONOKLASTES* TRANSLATED INTO
LATIN BY LEWIS DU MOULIN.

Εικονοκλαστης Caput primum de Parliamento a Rege post-
remum indicto. A Ludovico Molinæo ad specimen Latine ex-
hibitum, unde de toto opere itidem transferendo conjectura fiat.
Londini 1650, 4to. penes me. Kennet.

Anthony Wood, *Fasti Oxonienses,* ed. Bliss, IV (1820), part 2,
p. 126; Masson, v, 216. I have not seen the book itself, but take this
title from Bliss's Wood.

[Eikonoklastes: the first chapter, concerning the Parliament
last called by the King. Exhibited in Latin by Lewis du Moulin, as a sample from which conjecture may be made in like
manner about the whole work. London, 1650, in quarto. In my
possession. Kennet.]

It is not clear from this cryptic statement whether the item referred
to is a published book or a manuscript. I have not seen it myself, nor had
Masson. The "penes me" makes it sound like a manuscript, whereas
the "Londini, 1650, 4to" sounds like the description of a printed book.

John Milton · january 1650

Imitated by Writer on Engagement (?).

[The minister who wrote animadversions against *A Plea for Non-Subscribers*, 1650] went much upon the principles of Knox, Buchanan, Lex, Rex, and Grotius, *de jure belli et pacis*; trod much in Milton's steps. . . .

The Life of Adam Martindale written by Himself, ed. Richard Parkinson, Chetham Society, 1845, p. 99. The reference is not clear, but the general situation may be quickly outlined. John Dury had published on December 4, 1649, Considerations concerning the Present Engagement, whether it may lawfully be entered into (Thomason, 1, 779); The Humble Proposals of sundry Learned Divines had followed on December 19 (1, 779); Dury had replied with Just Re-proposals to Humble Proposals on January 15 (1, 783); A Plea for Non-Scribers. Or, the Grounds and Reasons of many Ministers in Cheshire, Lancashire and the Parts adjoyning, for their Refusal of the Late Engagement came out on June 11, 1650 (1, 800); and John Dury responded on August 3, 1650 (1, 808), with Objections against the Taking of the Engagement answered. Or some Scruples of Conscience which a godly Minister in Lancashire did entertain against the Taking of the Engagement. It seems likely that the last-named title is the "animadversions" which Martindale had in mind. Incidentally, it may be worth noting that The Grand Case of Conscience concerning the Engagement Stated and Resolved, sometimes attributed to Milton, appeared on January 9, 1650.

Praised for Splendid Writing.

. . . in truth it is very hard to write good *English*; and few have attained its height, in this last frie of Books, but Mr. *Milton*.

Charles Hotham, *An Introduction to the Tevtonick Philosophie . . . Englished by D. F.*, 1650, "To the Author," sig. A3v; Todd, 1 (1826), 231; Parker, *Milton's Contemporary Reputation*, p. 84. Parker (p. 59) quotes the same passage from British Museum Sloane MS. 1325, f. 13, but without saying whether the manuscript is a copy of Hotham's book or a miscellany.

January 4. Letter of State to Senate of Hamburg.

Senatui Hamburgensi. Perspecta nobis æquanimitas . . . Valete. *Dat. Jan. 4. 1649.*

Milton, *Literæ*, 1676, p. 3; Skinner MS., No. 2; CM, XIII, 10. The date in the Skinner MS. is "Westmonasterio, Ian: 4ᵗᵒ: 1649./" The "1649" means, of course, 1649/50.

[*To the Senate of* Hamborough. Your conspicuous Favour
... Farewel. *Jan.* 4. 1649.]
Phillips, p. 6; Masson, IV, 160; CM, XIII, 11.

JANUARY 4. LETTER OF STATE TO HAMBURG APPROVED.

Die Veneris [Wednesday] the 4° of Januarij 1649. . . .

2.) That the Latin Letter prepared by Mr Milton and now
read att the Councell to bee sent to ye Senate att Hamburg bee
faire written signed and sent.

Public Record Office, Order Book of the Council of State, SP Dom
25/63, p. 467; *CSP Dom, 1649-1650*, p. 468.

JANUARY 8. ORDERED TO ARRANGE FOR PRINTING WARING'S BOOK ON IRELAND.

Die Martis [Tuesday] the 8th of Ianuarij 1649. . . .

9.) That one hundred pounds bee paid, to Mr Thomas Waring, for his paines and Charges in Compiling of a booke, con-
teyning seaverall examinations of the Bloody Massacre in Ireland, and y^t warrant doe issue out, vnto the Exigence Money
for the payment of itt;

10.) That Mr Milton doe conferr with some printers or Stationers, concerning the speedy printing of this Booke, and give
an accompt of what hee hath done therein to the Councell.

Public Record Office, Order Book of the Council of State, SP Dom
25/63, p. 486; *CSP Dom, 1649-1650*, p. 474; Masson, IV, 151; CM,
XVIII, 366. The book referred to here is almost surely Thomas Waring's
A Brief Narration of the Rebellion in Ireland, dated March 19, 1650,
in the Thomason Catalogue. It was printed by B. Alsop and T. Dunster.

JANUARY 8. ORDERED TO ANSWER SALMASIUS.

Die Martis [Tuesday] the 8th of Ianuarij 1649. . . .

11) That Mr Milton doe prepare something in answer to the
Booke of Saltmatius, and when hee hath done itt bring itt to
the Councell.

Public Record Office, Order Book of the Council of State, SP Dom
25/63, p. 486; *CSP Dom, 1649-1650*, p. 474; Masson, IV, 151.

Quod quidem munus ut susciperem, tametsi summi in republica nostrâ viri suâ authoritate perfecerunt, mihíque hoc

negotium datum esse voluerunt, ut quæ illi, Deo ductore, magnâ cum gloria gessere, ea. quod certè proximum est, contra invidiam & obtrectationem, quas in res ferrum & apparatus belli nihil potest, alio genere armorum defenderem, quorum ego quidem judicium magno mihi ornamento esse existimo, me scilicet eorum suffragiis eum esse præ cæteris, qui hanc patriæ meæ fortissimis liberatoribus haud pœnitendam operam navarem.

Milton, *Defensio*, 1651 (Madan's No. 1), sig. B2; CM, VII, 6-8.

[The greatest men in our state induced me by their authority to undertake this task and wished the work assigned to me in order that the achievement which they had accomplished with great glory under God's guidance, I might, as the next highest deed, defend by another kind of arms against envy and calumny, forces against which the steel and the equipment of war are powerless. Their judgment I consider indeed a great compliment to me, that by their decision I am the one before all others to perform this not-to-be-regretted work for the bravest liberators of my country.]

. . . me potiùs quàm alium quemvis, neque tanti nominis adversario, neque tantis rebus dicendis visum imparem, ab ipsis patriæ liberatoribus has partes accepisse communi omnium consensu ultrò delatas, ut causam & populi Anglicani, & ipsius adeò Libertatis, siquis unquam alius, publicè defenderem.

Milton, *Defensio Secunda*, 1654, pp. 2-3; CM, VIII, 4.

[(I am thankful that) I, who was neither deemed unequal to so renowned an adversary, nor to so great a subject, was particularly selected by the deliverers of our country, and by the general suffrage of the public, openly to vindicate the rights of the English nation, and consequently of liberty itself.]

The Prose Works of John Milton, ed. J. A. St. John, London, 1867, I, 216.

. . . datum mihi publicè esset illud in defensionem regiam negotium. . . .

Milton, *Defensio Secunda*, 1654, p. 47; CM, VIII, 66-68.

[I was publicly solicited to write a reply to the Defence of the royal cause. . . .]

Milton, *Prose Works*, ed. St. John, I, 238.

Prodiit deinde Salmasius; cui quis responderet, adeò non diu, quod ait Morus, dispiciebant, ut me in concilio tum etiam præsentem statim omnes ultro nominarent.

Milton, *Defensio Secunda*, 1654, p. 95; CM, VIII, 138.

[Salmasius then appeared, to whom they were not, as More says, long in looking about for an opponent, but immediately appointed me, who happened at the time to be present in the council.]

Milton, *Prose Works*, ed. St. John, I, 261.

Of civil libertie I have written heretofore by the appointment, and not without the approbation of civil power. . . .

Milton, *A Treatise of Civil Power*, 1659, sig. A5v; CM, VI, 2.

Dispiciebant igitur belluæ, quæ Ignorantiæ litarunt, Grammaticastrum aliquem famelicum qui venalem calamum parridii [*sic*] patrocinio vellet commodare. Unus inventus est, post eruditionem extra fines suos relegatam, qui Latinè scribere auderet, magnus scilicet heros quem *Salmasio* opponerent, *Ioannes Miltonus,* Quis & unde dubium, homone an vermis heri è sterquilinio editus. Quid facerent? . . . Quemadmodum ergo armis omnibus destituti premente defensionis necessitate etiam cœnum & oletum jaciunt; hi homines quibus *furor arma ministrat* in summa virorum doctorum inopia *Miltonum* arripuerunt, & illud ignobile lutum in *Salmasium* jaculati sunt.

Moulin, *Regii Sanguinis Clamor*, Hague, Vlacq, 1652, pp. 7-8. Although this passage is part of the systematic political vilification of Milton which pervades the book, it is at least based on the fact of Milton's appointment to the task.

[The beasts then, worshippers of Ignorance, looked about for some hunger-starved little man of Grammar who might be willing to lend his venal pen to the defence of Parricide. One *was* found, after they had expelled learning from their territories, who *could* undertake to write Latin—the great hero, forsooth, that they would oppose to Salmasius—JOHN MILTON. Who and whence he was no matter, whether a human being or a worm that had come yesterday from the dunghill. What should they do? . . . As therefore men destitute of all arms and with the need of defense pressing on them throw mud and filth, these men, to whom fury gives arms in this great dearth of learned men, snatched up Milton and hurled that ignoble scum of the earth against Salmasius.]

Masson, IV, 456, through "What should they do?" The last sentence, not given by Masson, has been added by the editor.

Quærebant, ut apparet, infandi parricidij auctores aliquem inter suos, huic causæ tam malæ bene tractandæ idoneum, nec inveniebant: sed tandem tandem prorepsit è gurgustio suo tenebrio quidam, & ludi trivialis magister Londinensis; qui sese obtulit de tali reperiundo, qualis ipse inventus est laborantibus, & spondere ausus est, hanc provinciam, si sibi demandaretur, non ignaviter, nec instrenue esse exequuturum: Omnibus se abundare, quæ desiderari possent, ad id opus exasciandum: Frontem ferream, cor plumbeum, animum improbum, malam linguam, stylum atrocem; Maledicendo neminem sibi posse esse parem; calumniatorem, Sycophantam, impostorem nuspiam existere, à quo vinceretur, & quem non vinceret. Convitiorum domi plenas se arcas possidere; quæ, si tot nummis refertæ essent, posse Picos anteire divitiis, qui montes aureos colunt. Nec se quidem hoc promittere, ut de pessima causa bonam concinnaret, quis enim id potest? sed omni tamen ope enixurum, ut fucum faceret credulis, & plurimum mentiendo minus cautis imponeret. Aut parricidium nulla ratione defendi posse, aut se ita defensurum esse; ut appareret iisdem artibus, quibus esset commissum, etiam fuisse defensum. Et sane plus, quam promisit, præstitit, immo plus etiam, quam ab ipso poterat exigi; ita ut expectationem eorum, qui hoc illi pensum imposuerunt, longe superarit.

Salmasius, *Ad Johannem Miltonum Responsio, Opus Posthumum*, London, 1660, pp. 1-2. If actually written by Salmasius as alleged, this book must have been done before his death, which occurred in 1653. Its publication was edited by his son.

[The infamous authors of the parricide, as appears, sought for some one among their adherents fit to handle well this bad cause, and found none; but at length there crept forth from his hovel a certain obscure scamp of a low London schoolmaster,

who offered himself to those labouring to find such an one as he
turned out to be, and ventured to promise that he would execute
the task, if it were assigned to him, neither idly nor weakly. He
had, he said, all the possible requisites in abundance for hatchet-
ing out such a work,—a forehead of iron, a heart of lead, a
mischievous spirit, an evil tongue, an atrocious style; his match
in railing could not be found; no calumniator anywhere in existence, no sycophant, no impostor, by whom he could be beaten,
or that he could not beat. He had in his possesion at home such
chests full of scurrilities that, if they were but crammed with as
many coins, he would surpass in wealth the griffins that inhabit
the golden mountains. Not that he promised to turn a very bad
cause into a good one, for who can do that? But that he would
strive by every means to get up a delusion for the credulous, and
impose it upon the less cautious by plenty of lying. Either the
parricide admitted of no sort of defence whatever, or he would
defend it so that it should come out defended by the same arts
by which it had been committed. And truly he has performed
more than he promised, more even than could be required of
him.]

Masson, VI, 206. For further allusions to Milton's appointment to this
work, see below under February 15, 1651, the day of the appearance of
Milton's first *Defensio*.

JANUARY 8. IN ILL HEALTH AND IN DANGER OF BLIND-NESS.

... cùm datum mihi publicè esset illud in defensionem regiam
negotium, eodémque tempore & adversâ simul valetudine, &
oculo jam penè altero amisso conflictarer. ...

Milton, *Defensio Secunda*, 1654, p. 47; CM, VIII, 66-68.

[... when that assignment against the *Royal Defense* was
publicly given me, and when at the same time I was afflicted not
only with ill health, but almost with the loss of my other eye.
...]

Though ill health of this sort cannot be assigned to a specific day, it
is recorded under this date because this was the day when Milton was
ordered to reply to Salmasius's *Royal Defense*.

JANUARY 9. PUBLICATION OF *THE GRAND CASE OF CONSCIENCE*, ATTRIBUTED OCCASIONALLY TO MILTON.

The Grand Case of Conscience Concerning the Engagement Stated & Resolved. Or, A strict Survey of the Solemn League & Covenant In Reference to the Present Engagement. [quotation from Seneca] . . . London, Printed by John Macock for Francis Tyton . . . 1650.

[Entry on the title page of Thomason's copy:] Jan. 9th 1649.

Title page of the Thomason copy in the British Museum, shelf-number E 589(10).

Mr. *John Milton* is also thought to be the Author of (15) *The grand case of Conscience concerning the Engagement stated and resolv'd*, &c. *Lond.* 1950 [*i.e.*, 1650]. qu. 3. sh.

Anthony Wood, *Fasti Oxonienses*, 1721, I, 265; Darbishire, p. 43. A manuscript note to the same effect is in Wood's own copy of the *Fasti*, Bodleian Library Wood 431.a, I, 882.

In 1650, there was publish'd at *London* in 4*to*, pagg. 22. a piece, intitled, *The Grand Case of Conscience concerning the Ingagement stated and resolved. Or, A strict Survey of the Solemn League and Covenant in reference to the present Engagement.* Mr. *Wood* tells us [footnote: "*Col.* 265."], that *Milton* was thought to be the Author of it; but the style and manner of writing do not the least favour that supposition.

A Complete Collection of the . . . Works of John Milton, I (London, 1738), prefatory account by Thomas Birch, xxviii. It is very unlikely that the *Grand Case* is by Milton: see T. O. Mabbott and J. Milton French, " 'The Grand Case of Conscience,' Wrongly Attributed to Milton," *Notes and Queries*, CLXXXV (1943), 302-303. Though the book is dignified and decent, and though it mentions divorce, it entirely lacks the vigor of Milton's usual writing. It is included here only for completeness.

JANUARY 14. WRITINGS TO BE DISTRIBUTED.

Die Lunæ [Monday] the 14° Ian¹: 1649. . . .

20) That Mʳ Heveningham & Mʳ Scot doe send downe to Mʳ Robinson such a number of publique Acts of Parlamᵗ: and

of Mr Miltons bookes as they shall iudge necessary to be spread in those parts.

Public Record Office, Order Book of the Council of State, SP Dom 25/63, p. 519; *CSP Dom, 1649-1650*, p. 481; Masson, IV, 151. Masson conjectures that Luke Robinson, a member of the Council, had gone abroad, and that these books were to be distributed by him as propaganda for the English government.

JANUARY 22-29. ATTACKED FOR DIVORCE VIEWS AND *EIKONOKLASTES*.

But however businesse goes with them in *Ireland* and other places they, with an impudent face, take upon them no such things, but seeme outwardly that all is their own; though inwardly their very grease melts with rage: yet, forsooth, it is the States policy to smother their sorrowes by a bustle and pretence of setling Lawes and Courts for administration of Justice, in divers Cases: as of *Wills, Administrations, Legacies, Mariages* and *Divorces*; sure when such a Court is erected these *Regicides* will choose Mr. *Mylton* (who houlds forth the Doctrine of *Divorce*, and, like a State Champion, sham'd himselfe with handling his penne to oppose those Divine *Meditations* of our late King of happy Memory) to bee Judge and then bee sure the *Junctoes* Wills must bee obeyed.

Mercurius Pragmaticus, part 2, No. 39, January 22-29, 1649/50, sig. Qq3; Masson, IV, 157; Raymond, pp. 136, 317; Parker, *Milton's Contemporary Reputation*, p. 84.

JANUARY 25. ORDERED TO TRANSLATE A LETTER FROM TETUAN.

Die Veneris [Friday] 25°: Ianuarij 1649/50. . . .

11) That the Letter of the Governo^r. of Tituan be referred to the consideration of the Comittee of the Admiralty, who are to take care that the business be put into a way of proceeding according to Law.

12) That M^r: Milton doe take care to have the above sayd Letter translated.

Public Record Office, Order Book of the Council of State, SP Dom 25/63, p. 562; *CSP Dom, 1649-1650*, p. 493; Masson, IV, 152. See also the entry below under January 29. Tituan, or Tetuan, is in Morocco, near Gibraltar.

JANUARY 29. ORDERED TO PREPARE A LETTER TO TETUAN.

Die Martis [Tuesday] 29°: Ianuarij 1649. . . .

15) That M^r. Milton doe prepare a Letter to be sent unto the Governo^r. of Tituan in Answer to his Letter to the Councell.

Public Record Office, Order Book of the Council of State, SP Dom 25/63, p. 569; *CSP Dom, 1649-1650*, p. 496; Masson, IV, 152; CM, XIII, 507, 636. The letter here referred to has not been found. But see the note to the letter to the Governor of Algiers dated simply 1650.

JANUARY 30. ONE OF ALLEGED FOUNDERS OF CALVES-HEAD CLUB.

But of all the Indignities offer'd to the *Manes* of this injur'd Prince [Charles I], nothing in my Opinion comes up to the Inhumanity and Prophaness of the **Calves Head** Clubb.

. . . my good Nature made me look upon it as a Fiction upon the Party, till happening in the late Reign, to be in the Company of a certain active Whigg, who in all other Respects, was a Man of probity enough; he assured me, that to his Knowledge 'twas true, that he knew most of the Members of that Clubb. . . .

He farther told me, that *Milton*, and some other Creatures of the Commonwealth, had instituted this Clubb, as he was inform'd, in Opposition to Bp. *Juxon*, Dr. *Sanderson*, Dr. *Hammond*, and other Divines of the Church of *England*, who meet privately every 30*th* of *January*; and, tho' it was under the Time of the Usurpation, had compil'd a private Form of Service for the Day, not much different from what we now find in the Liturgy.

That after the Restauration, the Eyes of the Government being upon the whole Party, they were obliged to meet with a great deal of Precaution; but now, says he, (and this was the Second Year of King *William's* Reign) they meet almost in a Publick Manner, and apprehend nothing.

By another Gentleman, who, about Eight Years ago, went out of meer Curiosity to see their Clubb, and has since furnish'd me with the following Papers, I was inform'd, that it was kept in no fix'd House, but that they remov'd as they saw convenient; that the Place they met in when he was with 'em, was in a blind Ally, about *Morefields*; that the Company wholly consisted of *Independants* and *Anabaptists* (I am glad for the Honour of the *Presbyterians* to set down this Remark) that the Famous *Jerry White*, formerly Chaplain to *Oliver Cromwell*, who no doubt on't came to sanctify with his Pious Exhortations, the Ribbaldry of the Day, said Grace; that after the Table-Cloth was removed, the Anniversary *Anthem*, as they impiously call'd it, was sung, and a Calves-Skull fill'd with Wine or other Liquor, and then a Brimmer went about to the Pious Memory of those worthy Patriots that had kill'd the Tyrant, and deliver'd their Country from his Arbitrary Sway; and lastly, a Collection made for the Mercenary Scribler, to which every Man contributed according to his Zeal for the Cause, or the Ability of his Purse.

Edward Ward, *The Secret History of the Calves-Head Club*, London, 1703, pp. 8-10; William Godwin, *Lives of Edward and John Phillips*, p. 279; CM, XVIII, 613. Although the story sounds apocryphal, it is quite possible that Milton and other adherents of the Commonwealth may have met regularly on January 30 to celebrate the final victory of their cause, that such a meeting may under some circumstances have acquired the grotesque features ridiculed in this account, and that it may have persisted in some form long after Milton's death. Selections from the *Secret History* are reprinted in the *Harleian Miscellany*, VI (1810), 599, and XII (1811), 218-220. The story was revived in an article in *Notes and Queries*, I, iii (1851), 390, with part of the above quotation given, but attacked by J.F.M. [John Fitchett Marsh?], *ibid.*, p. 484. It is rejected as spurious by Robert J. Allen in *The Clubs of Augustan London*, Cambridge, Massachusetts, 1933, p. 60. Edward Walford, in *Old and New London*, IV, 229-230, describes the Club, mentioning that among other details in the ceremony was an oath and protestation taken on a copy of Milton's *Defensio* and a collection taken for Milton's benefit.

FEBRUARY 2. ORDERED TO RECEIVE LETTERS AND
RECORDS OF STATE.

Die Saturni [Saturday] 2°: Februarij 1649. . . .

18) That Orders be sent to M^r: Baker M^r: Challenor M^r:
Weckherlyn M^r: Willingham or any others who have in their
Hands any publiqz papers belonging to the Comonwealth to
deliver them to M^r: Milton to be layd up in the paper Office
for publiqz service and that M^r: Baker be appoynted to order
those papers that [they] may be ready for use.

Public Record Office, Order Book of the Council of State, SP Dom
25/63, p. 600; *CSP Dom, 1649-1650*, p. 503; Masson, IV, 152; CM,
XVIII, 366. The letter to Willingham will be noticed below under date
of February 4; those to Baker, Challenor, and Weckherlin, presumably
identical, have not been found. Although this order is not limited to letters
of state from abroad, it seems likely that Milton's collection of such
letters arose from this order; his *Original Letters* (published 1743)
is therefore placed with the present entry.

And though it cannot render them [the letters from abroad
which Milton collected] more authentic, to say that they had
been long treasured up by the famous *Milton*, it may yet imply
the use he conceived they might be of, and might one day intend to make of them, to illustrate either some particular or
general history of his times. From him, they came into the possession of *Thomas Ellwood*. . . .

That history aforesaid of *Thomas Ellwood's Life*, written
by himself to the year 1683, was published in octavo 1714, a
year after his death, with a supplement concerning his writings
and the remainder of his life by *J. W.* who was *Joseph Wyeth*,
citizen and merchant of London, and for several years intimate
with him, into whose hands, among the other papers of the said
Ellwood, these letters fell; and through the hands of *J. Wyeth's* widow they came into the possession of the present editor
[John Nickolls].

*Original Letters and Papers of State, Addressed to Oliver Cromwell;
Concerning the Affairs of Great Britain. From the Year MDCXLIX
to MDCLVIII. Found among the Political Collections of Mr. John
Milton. Now first Published from the Originals. By John Nickolls, Jun.
Member of the Society of Antiquaries, London. . . . MDCCXLIII.*

The quotations are from p. iv. See also Todd, I (1826), 179-180; CM, XVIII, 555. The original manuscript collection is now in the possession of the Society of Antiquaries in London; see W. C. Abbott, *A Bibliography of Oliver Cromwell*, Cambridge, Massachusetts, 1929, item 1362. Masson (VI, 815; cf. CM, XVIII, 555) suggests that Milton may have planned a biography of Cromwell, but if my suggestion in the previous note is sound, we need neither his guess nor Nickolls's in the text to account for Milton's possession of these documents: he was simply acting as he had been directed by the Council to do. The mere fact that when he left the government he took the papers with him rather than leaving them in Whitehall means little, since many public officials did the same thing.

FEBRUARY 4. WILLINGHAM AND OTHERS ORDERED TO TURN OVER LETTERS AND OTHER PUBLIC RECORDS TO MILTON.

S^r./

Wee are informed that there are severall Letters and other papers of publique concernemeñt that are in your hands which wee have thought fitt should be brought into the paper Off[ice] at Whitehall both for the safe keeping of them and [that] they might be ready for publique use upon all occasions wee therefore desire you to deliver all the said papers to Mr Milton whom wee have appointed to receive the same and see them safely and Orderly disposed in the said paper Office./

Whitehall 4°   Signed in the Name and by Order of
February 1649/50   the [Councell] of State appointed by
                         Authority of Parliament
                         [Signed] J°: Bradshawe P^r.sid^t.

[First endorsement:] 4th. Febr: 1649 Mr Willingham to del' his Papers to M^r. Milton./

[Second endorsement, in another hand:] For Mr Willingham. these are/

[Third endorsement, in a later (?) hand:] 1649/50 Feb: 4 Domestic.

Public Record Office, SP Dom 45/20, pp. 230-231, No. 109; Todd, I (1826), 119; Hamilton, p. 47; Masson, IV, 157. In addition to the endorsements this letter bears the official seal. Several spots in the letter either have been torn away or are unreadable. These spots are marked in the above transcript by brackets around the words, which are supplied from a copy of the same letter, which is No. 110 in the same series, on pp. 232-233. Aside from being in a different hand and differing in minor points of spelling and punctuation, the copy has no significant variations from the original except that it is not sealed. This letter, it may be noted, supplements the order of February 2 to Milton to receive such letters and records.

FEBRUARY 4. LETTERS OF STATE TO PHILIP IV OF SPAIN.

[1] *Serenissimo ac potentissimo Principi* PHILIPPO QUARTO Hispaniarum Regi. *Parlamentum Reipub. Angliæ,* SALUTEM. *ANtonium Ascamum* Virum probum . . . *Dat. Feb. 4. 1649.*

Milton, *Literæ,* 1676, p. 5; Skinner MS., No. 3; Columbia MS., No. 37; CM, XIII, 14.

[*To the Most Serene and Potent Prince* Philip *the Fourth, King of* Spain. *The Parliament of the Commonwealth of* England, *Greeting.* We send to your Majesty *Anthony Ascham* . . . *Feb. 4. 1649.*]

Phillips, p. 10; Masson, IV, 160; CM, XIII, 15.

[2] *Serenissimo ac Potentissimo Principi* PHILIPPO QUARTO Hispaniarum Regi. *Parlamentum Reipub. Angliæ,* SALUTEM. Quis rerum nostrarum status sit . . . *Westmonasterio dat. Feb. 4. 1649.*

Milton, *Literæ,* 1676, p. 6; Skinner MS., No. 4; Columbia MS., No. 45; CM, XIII, 14.

[*To the Most Serene and Potent Prince,* Philip *the Fourth, King of* Spain. *The Parliament of the Commonwealth of* England, *Greeting.* WHAT is the condition of our Affairs . . . *Westminster, Feb. 4. 1649.*]

Phillips, p. 11; Masson, IV, 161; CM, XIII, 15.

FEBRUARY 4. LETTER OF STATE TO JOHN IV OF PORTUGAL.

Serenissimo Principi JOANNI QUARTO Lusitaniæ Regi. *Parlamentum Reipub. Angliæ,* SALUTEM. MUlta nos & infidæ pacis . . . *Westmonasterio dat. Feb. 4. 1649.*

Milton, *Literæ,* 1676, p. 7; Skinner MS., No. 5; Columbia MS., No. 46; CM, XIII, 18.

[*To the Most Serene Prince,* John *the Fourth, King of* Portugal. *The Parliament of the Commonwealth of* England, *Greeting.* AFTER we had suffer'd many ... *Westminster, Feb.* 4. 1649.]

Phillips, p. 13; Masson, IV, 161; CM, XIII, 19.

FEBRUARY 15. SECOND EDITION OF *THE TENURE OF KINGS* PUBLISHED.

The Tenure of Kings and Magistrates: Proving, That it is Lawfull, and hath been held so through all Ages, for any, who have the Power, to call to account a Tyrant, or wicked King, and after due conviction, to depose, and put him to death; if the ordinary Magistrate have neglected, or deny'd to doe it. And that they, who of late so much blame Deposing, are the Men that did it themselves. Published now the second time with some additions, and many Testimonies also added out of the best & learnedest among Protestant Divines asserting the position of this book. The Author, J. M. London, Printed by Matthew Simmons, next doore to the Gil- [*sic*] Lyon in Aldersgate Street, 1650.

From the title page of the Thomason copy in the British Museum, on which the "M" is extended in manuscript to "Milton," the "1650" is crossed out, and the date "feb. 15. 1649" [*i.e.,* 1649/50] is written; CM, V, 313-314, in which, however, this title page is not reproduced.

FEBRUARY 16. RECEIVES INTEREST PAYMENT FROM ROBERT WARCUPP.

The 16ᵗʰ. Day of ffebruary. 1649.

Receiued then more of Robert Warcupp Esqz one of the ffeoffees in trust of Rodolph Warcupp, late of English Esqz Deceased by the handꝑ of John Coster the summe of fiue poundꝑ of lawfull english mony in pt of payment of fifty poundꝑ principall Debt & the interest Due by bond by the sayd Rodolph Warcupp & otherꝑ vnto me John Milton esqz, J say receiued by mee ....

[Signed]   John Milton
[Marginal note:] v.ˡⁱ

[298]

The original document is now in the library of the Historical Society of Pennsylvania, by whose kind permission it is here produced. Described in *Catalogue of the Collection of Autographs formed by Ferdinand Julius Dreer*, Philadelphia, 1890, 1, 438. The signature only is reproduced in facsimile in Sotheby, facing p. 124; the text is given on p. 125. See also French, "The Autographs of John Milton," No. 107. The marginal note means "five pounds." The signature of Milton on this document agrees perfectly with other specimens of this period.

FEBRUARY 18. REAPPOINTED SECRETARY.

Die Lunæ [Monday] 18° Februarij 1649/50. . . .

That Mr Milton secretary for forreigne languages Serjeant Dendy serjeant at Armes Mr Frost the younger Assistant to Mr Frost the secretary and all the Clerkes formerly employed under Mr Frost as also the Messengers and all other Officers employed by the Councell last yeare and not dismmissed shall be againe entertained into the same employments and shall receive the same salary which was appointed them the yeare past.

Public Record Office, Order Book of the Council of State, SP Dom 25/64, p. 3; *CSP Dom, 1650*, p. 2; Masson, IV, 223. The writing looks a good deal like Milton's, but it may not be.

FEBRUARY 18. COUNCIL OF STATE ORDERS SALMASIUS'S *DEFENSIO* CONFISCATED.

To the Com^{rs}: of the Customes
Gentlemen/

Wee are informed that there are severall Copies of a booke printed at Leyden—written by Salmatius but wthout his Name to it & Jntituled defensio Regia full of virulency and bitternesse against this Comonwealth that are sent now from Holland to severall bookesellers here in London. Wee desire you to give speciall order to all yor: subordinate officers for the discovery & seizure of those bookes that they may be disposed of according to Lawe and that also the importers thereof may be also proceeded against in like manner.

WhiteHall
18° Feb^r: 1649.

Public Record Office, Order Book of the Council of State, SP Dom 25/95, p. 3; *CSP Dom, 1650*, p. 2.

FEBRUARY 23. TAKES ENGAGEMENT OR OATH OF OFFICE.

Die Saturni [Saturday] 23° Februarij 1649/50. . . .

Memorandum That Mr John Milton Secretarie for the forreigne languages Mr Edward Dendie Serjeant at Armes and Mr Gualter Frost the younger assistant to the Secretary did this day take the Engagement following. I beeing nominated by this Councell to be . . . . . [*sic*] for the yeare to come doe promise in the sight of God, That through his grace I will be faithfull in the performance of the trust committed unto mee And not reveale or disclose any thing in whole or in part directly or indirectly That shall be debated or resolved upon in the Councell, And Ordered to bee kept secrett by the said Councell without the Command direction or allowance of the Parliament or Councell.

Public Record Office, Order Book of the Council of State, SP Dom 25/64, p. 30; *CSP Dom, 1650*, p. 10; Masson, IV, 224; CM, XVIII, 366, 625. The handwriting of this entry looks like Milton's.

FEBRUARY 24. LETTER OF STATE TO JOHN IV OF PORTUGAL.

Serenissimo Principi JOANNI QUARTO Lusitaniæ Regi. *Parlamentum Reipub. Angliæ*, SALUTEM. QUotidiani ferè, & perquàm graves afferuntur ad nos nuntii. . . .

Milton, *Literæ*, 1676, p. 9; Skinner MS., No. 6; Columbia MS., No. 47; CM, XIII, 22. There is no date or place at the end as there usually is, but only (in the printed book) a row of asterisks. But the date can be supplied from the copy in the Skinner MS., which ends: "Westmonasterio. Feb: 24to. 1649."

[*To the Most Serene Prince*, John *the Fourth, King of* Portugal. *The Parliament of the Commonwealth of* England, *Greeting*. Almost daily and most grievous complaints are brought before us. . . .]

Phillips, p. 16; Masson, IV, 232; CM, XIII, 23.

MARCH (?). PROCURES PRINTER WILLIAM DUGARD'S
RELEASE FROM PRISON (?).

The Testimony of Dr. *Hooker*, and which I my self, together with Dr. *Goodall*, took from his own Mouth; and which
I have now by me, attested and subscribed with his own Hand.

Edward Hooker testifieth, that he was Corrector to Mr.
Dugard's Press, when Mr. Simons brought the Copy of *Icon
Basilike* to advise with him how to get it Printed, that Mr.
Dugard (having bought Mr. *Young's* Press) undertook it, and
it was accordingly Printed off at Mr. *Dugard's* Press, with
the Correction of the said *Hooker*. . . .

The said Mr. *Hooker* farther testifieth, that Mr. *Dugard*
having thus Printed the Book, and it coming to be known, he was
thrown into Prison, and turn'd out of *Merchant-Taylors* School
. . . and that the said Mr. *Dugard* acquainted him in the said
Letters, *That his Wife made application to President* Bradshaw
*for his Release, who told her, that he might come out if he
would take Advice of a Friend of his, and then he need not lie
in Prison; and accordingly Mr.* Milton *was sent to him, who
offer'd him his Liberty, if he would do what he would have him;
who refused his Proposals.* . . .

And Mr. *Hooker* does believe, that Mr. *Dugard's* Wife
printed *Pamela's* Prayer, taken out of Sir *Philip Sidney's
Arcadia*, with the Alterations made in it, as one of the Condi-
tions of her Husband's Release out of Prison. Witness my hand,
Nov. 20. 1669.

Ita Testor, Edw. Hooker, *Peruser of the Royal Original.*

Thomas Wagstaffe, *A Vindication of K. Charles the Martyr*, 1711,
p. 107, as reprinted in Christopher Wordsworth's *Who Wrote* ΕΙΚΩΝ
ΒΑΣΙΛΙΚΗ, London, 1824, pp. 139-140; summarized in Masson, IV,
251-252; CM, XVIII, 381. Although this story, like most of the others
having to do with the supposedly inside story of *Eikon Basilike*, sounds
pretty wild, Masson is inclined to believe that there may at least be some
truth behind it, to the extent that Dugard was a sufficiently intelligent
and respectable man to be worth attempting to convert to the Republican
cause. If so, it is possible that Milton may have been sent to try to per-
suade him to forswear further connection with Royalist books and to
print Republican ones. It is certain at least that the Council of State

issued a warrant for Dugard's arrest on February 1, 1650, and an order for the restoration of his printing press, on recognizance, on April 2, 1650; see *CSP Dom, 1649-1650*, p. 568, and *CSP Dom, 1650*, p. 76. Although Dugard seems in the version of the story above to have refused Milton's offer, and although I can find no record of his having changed his mind, the second order seems to indicate that he did. Without doubt he later printed many pro-Commonwealth books, including Milton's first *Defensio*.

MARCH 3. PUBLICATION OF ACCOUNT OF TRIAL OF CHARLES I PREVIOUSLY LICENSED BY MILTON.

Histoire entiere & veritable dv Procez de Charles Stvart, Roy d'Angleterre. .... Le tout fidelement receuïlly de pieces Authentiques & traduit de l'Anglois. A Londres, Imprimé par J. G. l'An. 1650.

Title page of the Thomason copy in the British Museum (shelf-mark E 1353). On the title page the printed "1650" is crossed out and the date "March. 3 1649" written in. Milton had licensed this book for publication on December 16, 1649. An article on this book may be found in the London *Times* for December 9, 1930, p. 15d. The writer notes that a virtual reissue of the book appeared in 1688 under the title of *L'Irrevocabilité du Test et des pénâles, prouvée par la mort tragique de Charles Stuart*. On what grounds Mr. Fortescue dated it January 20, 1649, in his catalogue of the Thomason tracts (1, 716) I do not know, except that the trial of Charles I began on that date. In *Trial of King Charles the First* (Edinburgh and London, no date) Mr. J. G. Muddiman describes at length a manuscript journal of the trial not previously printed and now in the Public Record Office. He states that the *Histoire* licensed by Milton is a "translation of the trial portion of the above 'Journal of the proceedings of the High Court of Justice.'" He dates the appearance of the *Histoire* March 3, 1650.

MARCH 12. PAYS INTEREST (FIFTY POUNDS) TO GOLD-SMITHS' COMPANY ON BREAD STREET HOUSE.

At this Courte vpon Mr Miltons request Jt is ordered that 50^{li}. parte of C^{li}. due to this Companye at Midsomer next (wch hee hath now ready) shalbee by Mr Wardens receaved vpon rebate to that time after the rate of 7^{li}. p Centū & is in parte of payem^t of 400^{li} for renewing his lease of the great Messuage in Breadstreete lately graunted to him:/

The Court Book of the Worshipful Company of Goldsmiths, 1648-1651, ff. 123v-124.

MARCH 25. RECEIVES RENTS FROM WHEATLEY.

. . . vpon the fiue and Twentieth of March One Thousand six hundred and ffifty Thirty One pownds and Tenn shillings. . . .

From Milton's answer to Elizabeth Ashworth's bill, February 22, 1654, *q.v.*

MARCH 27. IS ALLOWED REBATE ON PAYMENT OF 50 POUNDS TO GOLDSMITHS' COMPANY FOR BREAD STREET HOUSE.

At this Courte Mr Warden Smithes made knowne that hee had receaved of Mr Milton the sume of L^{li}: out of wch there is to bee returned vpon rebate after the rate of vij^{li}: p Centū accompting from yesterday when hee receaved the same to Midsomer daye next at wch time hee is to paye L^{li}. more wch is for the C^{li}. then due in pte of his ffine of 400^{li}: for renewing his lease of the great Messuage in Breadstreet for wch Mr Warden Smithes gave a receipt./

The Court Book of the Worshipful Company of Goldsmiths, 1648-1651, f. 127. See note above under date of April 20, 1649.

MARCH 28. LETTER OF STATE TO ARCHDUKE LEOPOLD OF AUSTRIA.

Serenissimo Principi LEOPOLDO AUSTRIÆ *Archiduci Provinciarum in Belgio sub Philippo Rege Præsidi.* UT primùm ad nos non sine gravissimâ querelâ perlatum est . . . *Westmonasterio Martii* 28. 1650.

Milton, *Literæ,* 1676, p. 12; Skinner MS., No. 7; Columbia MS., No. 53; CM, XIII, 28.

[*To the Most Serene Prince* Leopold, *Archduke of* Austria, *Governor of the* Spanish Low Countries, *under King* Philip. SO soon as word was brought us, not without a most grevious complaint . . . *Westminster, March* 28. 1650.

Phillips, p. 23; Masson, IV, 232; CM, XIII, 29.

MARCH 30. ORDERED TO PREPARE CREDENTIALS FOR RICHARD BRADSHAW.

Die Saturni [Saturday] 30° Martij 1650. . . .

1) That the Instructions now read to bee given to Mr Richard Bradshaw with the amendments proposed bee faire written and delivered unto him.

2) That it bee recommended to the Lords Commissioners of the great Seale to give order for the preparing of a Commission for Mr Richard Bradshaw who is to bee employed Resident from this Commonwealth to the Senate of Hamburgh according to the order of Parliament.

3) That a Credentiall letter bee likewise prepared for him by Mr Milton.

Public Record Office, Order Book of the Council of State, SP Dom 25/64, p. 137; *CSP Dom, 1650*, p. 67; Masson, IV, 224. The "credential letter" here referred to is presumably that dated April 2, *q.v.*

APRIL 1. LETTER OF CREDENTIALS FOR BRADSHAW AP-PROVED.

This letter, it appears, was "read and approved, April 1, 1650." It is among the printed *Literæ Senatûs*, &c. of Milton, and there dated April 2.

Todd, 1 (1826), 121; Masson, IV, 224. I did not find this record myself, and Todd does not give the source of his information, though the implication is that it comes from the Order Book. Masson repeats the statement.

APRIL 2. ORDERED TO ATTEND THE COMMISSIONERS OF THE GREAT SEAL.

2°: Apr 1650. . . .

Memorand. M^r. Milton to have warning to meet ye Lo^s: Com^{rs}. Whitlocke & Lisle at ye Parlam^t. doore at ten of ye Clocke to morrow morning.

Public Record Office, "Foule Book of Orders of the Councell of State," SP 25/5 (no paging); Masson, IV, 224-225; CM, XVIII, 366.

APRIL 2. LETTER OF STATE TO HAMBURG.

Hamburgensibus. DE controversiis mercatorum . . . *Westmonasterio. Dat. 2. April.* 1650.

Milton, *Literæ*, 1676, p. 16; Skinner MS., No. 8; Columbia MS., No. 54; CM, XIII, 36. This is the letter of credentials for Richard Bradshaw authorized above on March 30.

John Milton · APRIL 1650

[*To the Hamburghers.* MORE then once we have Written concerning the controversies of the Merchants . . . *Westminster, April* 2. 1650.

Phillips, p. 29; Masson, IV, 233; CM, XIII, 37.

APRIL 10. PAYS MOTHER-IN-LAW ANNE POWELL HER THIRDS.

[Milton] did pay or cause to bee payed vnto . . . Anne Powell . . . the seuerall sũmes of money menc̃oned and Expressed in the sixe seuerall Acquittances or Receiptes . . . [the fifth of which is dated] Aprill yᵉ 10ᵗʰ 1650: & is for the sũme of xˡⁱ.

From Anne Powell's deposition in the Ashworth-Milton case, June 4, 1656, *q.v.*

APRIL 11. PETER SMITH PRAISES MILTON.

April. 11. 1650.

Sⁱʳ./.

. . . I have kept Clapmarius to helpe me to pervse Milton, wch if yᵘ please to send at yᵉ next opportunity, I will give yᵘ some account how well he hath discharged his vndertakings. . . . What yᵘ intend for Mʳ. Hoskins will be seasonable vpon his returne from the Welsh circuit after Easter wherein I should com̃end Milton to be inserted for rarity, & worth, but yᵗ I feare to present a censure of what he accounts yᵉ best piece of yᵉ Nation & can further acqvaint yᵘ, yᵗ yᵉ complements, presents & reverence shewed to the present face of things, seemes more *qvàm ut penitùs sentire crederetur* [than would be believed could be felt deeply]. Yet have you a fair marke in yᵉ greatest of his designes to fixe him the education of his sonnes, wherein yᵘ are somewhat indebted by Sʳ. Henry Wottons promise of spirituall architecture: & I assure yᵘ a present of that nature from yᵘ will best sort wᵗʰ his nature & ends wherein you may com̃and at your pleasure.

Your Nephewe to serve you
Peter Smith.

[Marginal notes opposite the earlier and later portions of this quotation:] Milton. [and] Education.

From a letter in the collection of Lord Delamere; printed in G. H. Turnbull, *Hartlib, Dury and Comenius*, p. 41. Professor Turnbull thinks that the uncle to whom the letter was addressed was John Beale, and that Milton's book alluded to here is *Eikonoklastes*.

APRIL 18. FATHER-IN-LAW RICHARD POWELL'S ESTATE ORDERED RESEQUESTERED FOR FAILURE TO PAY FINE.

... Ordered the 18th. Day of Aprill 1650 to be resequestred for none paym^t of their severall fines imposed on them by Authority of Parliam^t. ... Richard Powell.

From the certificate of William Draper and Thomas Appletree, June 1, 1650, *q.v.*

APRIL 27. LETTER OF STATE TO JOHN IV OF PORTUGAL.

Serenissimo Principi JOANNI QUARTO Lusitaniæ Regi. QUod Oratorem nostrum & honorificè acceperit *Majestas Vestra* ... *Westmonasterio. Dat.* 27. *Aprilis.* 1650.

Milton, *Literæ*, 1676, p. 14; Skinner MS., No. 9; Columbia MS., No. 55; CM, XIII, 32.

[*To the Most Serene Prince,* John *the Fourth, King of* Portugal. UNderstanding that *Your Majesty* had both Honourably receiv'd our Agent ... *Westminster,* 27. *April.* 1650.

Phillips, p. 26; Masson, IV, 233; CM, XIII, 33.

APRIL 27 (?). LETTER OF STATE TO PHILIP IV OF SPAIN.

PHILIPPO HISPANIARUM REGI. Cum non ita pridem post recuperatam libertatem ... West°.

Not in Milton's *Literæ*, 1676; Skinner MS., No. 113; Columbia MS., No. 28; Hamilton, p. 10; CM, XIII, 434. Though the letter bears no date, it is probably to be dated April 27, 1650, since it probably accompanied the letter of that date to John IV of Portugal. On April 28 Edward Popham, about whom both letters were written, notified the Admiralty Committee that he had received "a copy of the credential letter sent to the king of Portugal" (*CSP Dom, 1650,* p. 134). The previous day that Committee had informed the Navy Commissioners that "The Council of State have instructed Col. Popham" about sailing for Spain (*ibid.,* p. 129). Masson dates the present letter April 27, 1650.

[To Philip, King of Spain. As, not so long after the recovery of English liberty ... Westminster.]

Not in Phillips; Masson, IV, 233; CM, XIII, 435.

APRIL 30. WRITES ORDER IN ORDER BOOK OF COUNCIL
OF STATE (?).

30°: Apr: 1650: . . .

That Mr Chambers in ye gatehouse be releasd upon his own
engagement, & twenty nobles givn him for his relief.

This order, like most of the similar ones quoted through this section
of the book, is found in two versions in the Public Record Office. One
set of Order Books of the Council of State seems to have been a first
draft, or is at least in a less finished condition than the others. Our extracts have almost always been from the better ones, though most of
the records can be quoted from both. The present entry is found in SP
Dom 25/64, p. 284; and in SP Dom 25/6 (unpaged). In the former it
is written in a hand which is decidedly not Milton's, though, as has been
mentioned from time to time, many of the others resemble his handwriting. In the latter, this entry, unlike all those in its vicinity, *does* look
like Milton's writing. A much more careful study of the writing of
these books than has as yet been made might possibly reveal more of
Milton's actual writing than any one now suspects. The attribution to
Milton was first made by Masson (IV, 225). See CM, XIII, 506, 636.
It should be added that the first line of the entry, giving the date, is
in a different hand from that of the rest, and is surely not Miltonic.

MAY 6. ORDERED TO BRING WALSALL PAPERS TO COM-
MISSIONERS.

Die Lunæ [Monday] 6° Maij 1650. . . .

(2) That Mr Milton doe attend the Lords Com^rs of the
great Seale with the papers given in by Doctor Walsall concerning the goods of felo's de se to whom it is referred to take
such course therein for the advantage of the Commonwealth as
they shall thinke fit.

Public Record Office, Order Book of the Council of State, SP Dom
25/64, p. 307; *CSP Dom, 1650*, p. 142; Masson, IV, 225; CM, XVIII,
367.

MAY 15. ORDERED TO SEARCH SUSPECTED TRUNKS.

Die Mercurij [Wednesday] 15°: Maij 1650. . . .

16) That the person brought to Towne by Cornet Ioyce be
searched by M^r. Sergeant. That the Trunks be brought to the
Sergeants Custody and be thoroughly searched by M^r. Milton
who is to report to the Councell tomorrow in the afternoone

what he findes in those Trunks. And Sr William Masham, S^r. Henry Mildmay & Mr Challenor or any two of them doe examine the said person and report to the Councell.

Public Record Office, Order Book of the Council of State, SP Dom 25/64, p. 350; *CSP Dom, 1650,* p. 163; Masson, IV, 226; CM, XVIII, 367.

MAY 24. RUMORS ABOUT AN ANSWER TO SALMASIUS BY SELDEN.

Les Anglois ne veulent répondre qu'avec l'épée à M. Saumaise et à tous ceux qui écriront contre eux pour avoir fait mourir leur roi, et ont fait cesser l'édition du livre de J. Seldenus qui étoit sur la presse, contenant la réponse à M. Saumaise. ... De Paris, ce 24 de mai, à neuf heures du soir, 1650.

From a letter of Gui Patin to Dr. Charles Spon, Paris, May 24, 1650, printed in *Lettres de Gui Patin,* II (1846), 17-18; Stern, II, iii, 258-259.

[The English do not want to reply except with the sword to Salmasius and to all those who will write against them for having put their king to death, and they have suppressed the edition of J. Selden's book which was being printed, containing the reply to Salmasius. . . . From Paris, May 24, 1650, at 9 P.M.]

Et cum Cromwellius plus semel Seldenum hortaretur, ac per amicos rogaret, ut calamum adversus librum regi Carolo adscriptum ΕΙΚΩΝ ΒΑΣΙΛΙΚΗ stringeret, contemptim ac pervicaci animo provinciam hanc detrectavit, quam Miltonus regiminis parliamentarii defensor strenuus in se suscepit.

Joannis Seldeni Jurisconsulti Opera Omnia, London, 1725, I, xliv ("Vita Joannis Seldeni," by the editor, David Wilkins); Christopher Wordsworth, *Who Wrote Eikon Basilike?,* 1824, p. 96. Though concerned here with *Eikon Basilike* rather than Salmasius's *Defensio,* and though Selden is here represented as scornful of the republic rather than in support of it, the two anecdotes may have grown from a common source or base. Nothing very definite about the whole matter seems to be available. John Aikin repeats the same story in *The Lives of John Selden, Esq. and Archbishop Usher,* London, 1812, pp. 145-146.

[And though Cromwell more than once urged Selden, and asked him through friends, to take up his pen against the book

Eikon Basilike ascribed to King Charles, he contemptuously and stubbornly refused this office, which Milton, the strenuous defender of the Parliamentary government, took upon himself.]

[When English leaders looked for someone to answer Salmasius:] *Seldenus* odiosum pensum ab humeris suis rejiciebat.

Moulin, *Regii Sanguinis Clamor*, The Hague, Vlacq, 1652, p. 8. It should be noticed that this story is almost entirely at odds with the letter of Patin. In that letter Selden had been prohibited from answering; in this, as in Wilkins's life, he spurned the idea.

[Selden threw the odious task from his shoulders.]
Masson, IV, 456.

MAY 24. COUNCIL OF STATE ENGAGES MARCHAMONT NEEDHAM.

Die Veneris [Friday] 24° Maij 1650. . . .

(20) That one hundred pounds per annum bee paid by Mr Frost quarterlie unto Mr Marchamont Needham as a pention whereby hee may bee enabled to subsist whilst hee endeavours the service of the Commonwealth and this to bee done for yeare by way of probation.

(21) That fiftie pounds bee paid unto Mr Needham by Mr Frost as a guift unto him from this Councell for his service alreadie done to the Commonwealth.

Public Record Office, Order Book of the Council of State, SP Dom 25/64, p. 385; *CSP Dom, 1650*, p. 174; Masson, IV, 226. This entry is included because of the later cooperation between Milton and Needham. Needham's chief duty was probably to be the editing of *Mercurius Politicus* as an instrument of propaganda for the government.

MAY 31. LETTER OF STATE TO HAMBURG.

Hamburgensibus. *Amplissimi, Magnifici, & spectabiles Viri, Amici charissimi,* STudia vestra quibus venientem ad vos Residentem nostrum . . . *Westmonasterio. Dat.* 31. *May.* 1650.

Milton, *Literæ*, 1676, p. 17; Skinner MS., No. 10; Columbia MS., No. 134; CM, XIII, 38.

[*To the Hamburghers. Most Noble, Magnificent, and Illustrious, our dearest Friends.* THAT your sedulities in the Reception of our Agent were so cordial and so egregious . . . *Westminster, May* 31. 1650.

Phillips, p. 31; Masson, IV, 234; CM, XIII, 39.

JUNE 1. CERTIFICATE THAT FATHER-IN-LAW RICHARD POWELL'S PERSONAL ESTATE WAS GIVEN TO TOWN OF BANBURY.

Right honoᵇˡᵉ:

In obedience to the severall Orders & lettʳˢ. of the Dates ensueing, concerneing the psons whose names are incerted, Ordered the 18ᵗʰ. Day of Aprill 1650 to be resequestred for none paymᵗ of their severall fines imposed on them by Authority of Parliamᵗ. vidz . . . Richard Powell (whose supposed reall estate is possessed by Sʳ Rob: Pie seigʳ who had by the iudgmᵗ of the late Committe of this County a lawful title therein, the greatest pt of the psonall estate of the said Powell by Ordinance of Parliamᵗ of the 15ᵗʰ. of August 1646 was given to the Church & Towne of Banbury) the rest of his the said Powells estate is nowe in question before the Comissioners for Articles whether the right thereof bee in the State or noe. . . .

Yoʳ. constant & ingaged Servants

Dedington this first   [Signed] Wiłł: Drap:
Day of June 1650   Tho Apletree

    [Marginal note:] 6 Junij: 1650 Recᵈ

    [Another marginal note:] Powell estate to be secured till yᵉ ptyᵉˢ make good their titles there.

    [Endorsed] These

To the right honoᵇˡᵉ: the Comissioners for compounding with Delinquents sitting att Westminster

present

Public Record Office, SP Dom 23/251, No. 100; *Calendar of the Committee for Compounding*, p. 1439; Hamilton, pp. 81-82.

JUNE 8. PROSPECTUS FOR *MERCURIUS POLITICUS*, LATER TO BE LICENSED BY MILTON.

    Mercurius Politicus

    Comprizing the Sūm of all Jntelligence wᵗʰ. the Affaires and

John *Milton* · JUNE 1650

Designes now on foot, in the three Naçons, of England, Jreland and Scotland

Jn defence of the Comõnwealth, and for Jnformaçon of the People.

The designe of this Pamphlett being to vndeceive the People, it must bee written in a Jocular way, or else it will never bee cryed vp: ffor those truths wch. the Multitude regard not in a serious dresse, being represented in pleasing popular Aires, make Musick to y^e. Comõn sence, and charme the Phantsie; wch. ever swayes the Scepter in Vulgar Judgem^te; much more then Reason.

J entitle it Politicus, because the present Goūnm^t is verā πολιτεία as it is opposed to the despotick forme. Jt shalbee my care to sayle in a middle way, between the Scylla and Charybdis of Scurrility and prophanes. Whitson week wilbee no fitt season to sett it flying; but J pitch vpon the next after. J desire supplyes of the best Jntelligence of State; and that Tuesday may bee the weekly day, because most convenient for dispersing it through the Nation.

J desire likewise that some Order may bee passed to authorize it./

[Endorsed:] Mercurius Politicus & its desygne 8° Junij 1650

Public Record Office, SP Dom 46/95, p. 409. Since this paper is unsigned, the authorship is uncertain. One is tempted, of course, to hazard a guess that it came from Milton, even though the handwriting is not at all like his. This temptation is increased by the statement in J. B. Williams's *History of English Journalism*, London, 1908, p. 134: "The conception of [*Mercurius Politicus*] must be attributed to John Milton, who was its editor probably from the end of the year 1650 (when the style of it suddenly alters) until the beginning of March, 1652." And there is no doubt that Milton had a good deal to do with this publication, to which he acted, curiously enough, as licenser for a considerable period in 1651. On the other hand, the old-fashioned notion that he actually wrote a considerable part of the material in the journal has been proved to be almost entirely without foundation; see J. M. French, "Milton, Needham, and *Mercurius Politicus*," *Studies in Philology*, XXXIII (1936), 236-252, and Elmer A. Beller, "Milton and *Mercurius Politicus*," *Huntington Library Quarterly*, V (1942), 479. These articles demonstrate that almost all of the so-called Miltonic material either comes from previous writings published by Marchamont

[311]

Needham or is included in later publications of his, so that the inference is virtually sure that Needham did the editorial work. This assumption is strengthened by the statement of James Heath in *A Chronicle of the Late Intestine War*, 2nd edition, 1676, p. 267: "Now appeared in Print, as the weekly Champion of the new Commonwealth, and to bespatter the King with the basest of scurrilous raillery, one *Marchamount Needham*, under the name of *Politicus*; a *Jack of all sides.* . . ." It will be remembered that on May 24 the Council of State had engaged Needham for an unspecified task, which I think we can safely interpret as the present venture. Or, as the *Cambridge Bibliography of English Literature* suggests, John Hall may have supervised the work; he had been engaged by the Council of State on May 14, 1649, to help Milton. The *CBEL* also suggests that Milton may have supervised it.

Two further items may be added. Masson expressed his belief in 1893 ("Local Memories of Milton," *Good Words*, XXXIV, 138) that Milton must have written the leading article of September 4-11, 1651, on the victory at Worcester; "it must have been wholly his." Samuel R. Gardiner felt sure in 1894 (*The History of the Commonwealth*, I, 413) that he must have written the "Ishbosheth" piece in the issue of April 3, 1651. But neither of these writers was aware of the facts about Needham given in the preceding paragraph, which seem to render their conclusions unsound.

The *Calendars of State Papers Domestic* for the 1650's show regular warrants for payments of salary to Needham, usually at the rate of £100 a year.

JUNE 12. ORDER OF RELIEF VOTED TO MOTHER-IN-LAW ANNE POWELL.

Painted Chamber Westm^r.

By the Comissione^{rs} appointed for reliefe vpon Articles of Warr/

Mercurij [Wednesday] 12mo Die Junij 1650

Vpon Longe and Deliberate Debate in the cause Dependinge before this Court betweene Ann Powell widowe, and Relict and Administratrix of Richard Powell of fforrest Hill in the Countie of Oxoñ, Esqui^r, p^{lt}; and the Late Standinge Comittee of the said Countie Defendants, and vpon consideration had of the matter of Complaint of the said Mrs Powell togeither with the Articles made vpon the surrender of the Garrison of Oxford wherein her said husband was included It appearinge vnto this Court that the goods and howsehould stuffe for which the said

M^{ris} Powell praied satisfaccon were sould and disposed of by some psons actingne vnder the authoritie of the said Com^{tee} after confirmacon of and contrarie vnto the true intent and meaninge of the said Articles, by which her said husband ought to bee restored to his reall and personall estate vnder or lyable to sequestracon havinge entred his Peticon to compound within the tyme Lymitted by the said Artickles. It appearinge alsoe by an Inventorie produced in Court that the said goods (although of farr greater value) were soe sould for three hundred thirtie five pounds vnto one Mathew Appletree of London whoe togeither with the Sequestrato^{rs} subscribed to the said Inventorie, and sale and that there is remayninge in his the said Mathew Appletrees hands as Purchaser of the said goods the some of ninetie one pounds eleauen shillings tenn pence The Court vpon the whole matter doe adiudge and declare That as to such goods and Chattles as are yet remayninge in spetie in or about the howse Late of the said Richard Powell, or otherwise vnsould or vndisposed of by the said Late Comittee or theire Agents the same shall be forthwith deliverd by the said Comittee or now Commissione^{rs} for Sequestracons in the said Countie vnto the said M^{ris} Powell./ And the said Late Comittee are to bee answerable to her for the rest of the said goods which were by theire order or appointment sold and Disposed of contrarie vnto the said Articles to the end the said M^{ris} Powell maie bee the better inabled to paie the fine imposed vpon her said husbands estate/

Signed by Comand of the Com^{rs}

Tr: Pauncefote Reg^r

[Endorsed:] Mrs Powells Order from the Committee for reliefe vpon Articles.

[Endorsed in another hand:] Anne. Powell. Articles.

Public Record Office, Composition Papers, SP Dom 23/110, p. 527; *Calendar of the Committee for Compounding,* p. 1440; Hamilton, pp. 82-83; Masson, IV, 237. A copy of this order is found on p. 549 of the same bundle. It bears the notation: "27th. febr. 1650 J make oath that this is a true copie of the ord^r made by the Court for Articles &c Tr Pauncefote." As pointed out in *Englische Studien,* LV (1921),

40-45, there is another copy in the British Museum, Add. MS. 34,326, f. 44. It is signed in the margin: "Vera Copia Tr: Pauncefote," and endorsed: "Order of yᵉ Comᵉʳˢ. for reliefe June, 12ᵗʰ, 1650: concerning the Wīdd Anne Powell." Attached to this last copy is Anne Powell's undated petition to the Council of State.

JUNE 14. ALLOWED MONEY FOR FURNISHING AN APARTMENT IN WHITEHALL.

Die Veneris [Friday] 14° Iunij 1650. . . .

(11) That Mʳ Milton shall have a warrant to the Trustees and Contractors for the sale of the Kings goods for the furnishing of his lodgeing in Whitehall with some hangings.

Public Record Office, Order Book of the Council of State, SP Dom 25/64, p. 447; *CSP Dom, 1650*, p. 549; Masson, IV, 227. The writing of the entry looks like Milton's. For the warrant itself see below under date of June 18.

JUNE 18. WARRANT FOR FURNISHING HIS APART-MENTS ISSUED.

These are to will and require you forthwith upon sight hereof to deliver unto Mʳ John Milton or to whom hee shall appoint such hangings as shall bee sufficient for the furnishing of his Lodgings in Whitehall. Given at Whitehall 18° Iunij 1650/

To the Trustees and Contractors for the sale of the late Kings goods.

Public Record Office, Order Book of the Council of State, SP Dom 25/64, p. 460; Masson, IV, 227.

JUNE 22. ORDERED TO PROCURE DATA ON THE RISING IN KENT AND ESSEX.

Die Saturni [Saturday] 22 Iunij 1650. . . .

(4) That Mʳ Milton doe goe to the Committee of the Armie and desire them to send to this Councell the booke of Examinations taken about the riseings in Kent and Essex.

Public Record Office, Order Book of the Council of State, SP Dom 25/64, p. 473; *CSP Dom, 1650*, p. 213; Masson, IV, 227; CM, XVIII, 367. The reference may be to the Royalist uprising in Kent and Essex in 1648.

JUNE 25. ORDERED TO SUMMARIZE THE INFORMATION
ABOUT THE RISING IN ESSEX.

Die Martis [Tuesday] 25° Iunij 1650. . . .

(6) That Mr Milton doe peruse the Examinations taken by
the Committee of the Armie concerning the insurrections in
Essex and that hee doe take heads of the same to the end the
Councell may judge what is fit to bee taken into Consideration.

Public Record Office, Order Book of the Council of State, SP Dom
25/64, p. 478; *CSP Dom, 1650*, p. 214; Masson, IV, 227; CM, XVIII,
267, 541. The original entry is in a hand resembling Milton's. This
order refers back to that of June 22. Any "heads" which Milton may
have made in response to this order have not been found.

JUNE 25. POEMS OF ROBERT BARON, WITH NUMEROUS
IMITATIONS OF MILTON, PUBLISHED.

Not that I doe desire to shrowd my bones
The labour of an Age in piled stones,
Or that my worthlesse Ashes should be hid
Under a skie-invading *Pyramid*. . . .

———

What needs my *Shakespear* for his honour'd Bones,
The labour of an age in piled Stones,
Or that his hallow'd reliques should be hid
Under a Star-ypointing *Pyramid*?

The first quatrain is from Robert Baron's *Pocula Castalia*, 1650, sig.
A2v; the second is from Milton's *Poems*, 1645, part i, p. 27. The
wording of the two is so close that Baron's may justly be called a
plagiarism from Milton's. Thomason's copy of Baron in the British
Museum is dated June 25. This parallel happens not to be among those
mentioned by Warton and Todd, but they make no effort to be
complete. For other borrowings by Baron, see above under dates of
April (?), 1647, and 1648.

JUNE 25. ORDERED TO SEARCH WILLIAM PRYNNE'S
HOUSE.

These are to will & require you forthwith to make yor. repaire to the studdy & Chamber of William Prynne Esquire in
Lincolns Jnne or elsewhere, which you are dilligently to search
for all writeings, letters or other papers or Record℘ belonging

to the Com̃onwealth. And alsoe for all writeings, Letters or papers by him written, or in his Custody of dangerous nature against the Com̃onwealth. all which you are to seize and seale up, and bring or cause to be safely brought to this Councell, that thereupon further Order may be given concerning them. of which you are not to fayle, and for which this shall be yor. sufficient Warrant. Given at the Councell of State at Whitehall this 25th day of June 1650

Signed in ye Name & by Order of the Councell of State appointed by Authority of Parlam^t:
[Signed:] Jo: Bradshawe. P^r. sid^t.

To John Milton Esqr:
Secr̃ to the Councell for
forreigne languages

Printed by the kind permission of Miss Dorothy Margaret Stuart from the original document in her possession. In *The New Statesman and Nation*, I (New Series, 1931), 15-16, Miss Stuart describes this document as having "reposed for upwards of two centuries in the archives of an ancient Jacobite family, and has never before been published." The handwriting, she says, is "the same ornate, clerkly hand in which all the records of the year 1650 are kept, and with the autograph signature of John Bradshawe." In Ellis's catalogue no. 344 (1939) it was offered for sale for £575. In that catalogue it was described as measuring 12 3/4 by 8 1/4 inches and as being written on "official paper of the Council of State, with Arms of the Commonwealth."

Although Miss Stuart found "no trace of any report made to the Council by their Secretary," the Ellis catalogue entry points out that Prynne was arrested five days later. The version given below from the Public Record Office is said to be a record of the issuance rather than the original, and the fact that the name of the agent is not filled in, as it is in the original, probably indicates that it was not known at the time of writing who was to take the action. The *Calendar of State Papers* catalogues it as having been issued to Sergeant Dendy.

The next succeeding entry in the records is a warrant, also unaddressed but this time without much doubt intended for Dendy, ordering him to "apprehend and . . . secure" William Prynne "in Dunster Castle for his seditious writings and practices against the Commonwealth where you shall not suffer him to have conference with any but in your presence and hearing nor to send or receive any letters but such as you shall peruse. And you are alsoe to search his house & studdy for all writeings letters papers or records that are ag^t this Commonwealth or any way belonging to it which you are to seise and send up securelie to the Councell, And what belongs onelie to himselfe you are to deliver back to him." (SP 25/64, p. 481.) This warrant also is dated June 25, 1650.

A copy of the Ellis catalogue entry may be found in the Manuscript Room of the New York Public Library in a folder of miscellaneous manuscript material relating to Milton.

These are to will and require you forthwith to make your repaire to the studdie and Chamber of William Prynn Esqz in Lincolnes Inne or elsewhere which you are dilligentlie to search for all writeings letters or other papers or records belonging to this Commonwealth And also for all writeings letters or other papers by him written or in his Custodie of dangerous nature against the Commonwealth all which you are to seize and Seale up and bring or cause to be safelie brought to this Councell that thereupon further Order may bee given concerning them. Given at Whitehall 25° Junij *1650.*

To: [blank]

Public Record Office, SP Dom 25/64, p. 480. See also *CSP, 1650,* p. 550.

JUNE 26. ORDERED TO TRANSLATE PARLIAMENTARY DECLARATION ABOUT THE SCOTCH.

Die Mercurij [Wednesday] 26° Iunij 1650. . . .

(12) That the Declaration of the Parlament bee translated into Latine by Mr Milton into Dutch by Mr Haak and into French by Monsieur Augier.

Public Record Office, Order Book of the Council of State, SP Dom 25/64, p. 483; *CSP Dom, 1650,* p. 216; Masson, IV, 228; CM, XVIII, 543. Though Todd (I, 1826, 122) associates this order with the war against the Dutch, the other commentators refer it to the war with the Scotch. Thus Masson (IV, 192, 228), Stern (II, iii, 267), and L. H. Henry (London *Times Literary Supplement,* August 17, 1933, p. 549) all so interpret it. If they are right, Milton's translation must have been a Latin version of *A Declaration of the Parlament of England, upon the Marching of the Armie into Scotland,* which Thomason annotated: "Not published till the 4th July." I have not seen a copy. Mr. Henry points out that by an order of July 2 the translation was transferred from Milton to Thomas May.

JUNE 28. LETTER OF STATE TO PHILIP IV OF SPAIN.

PHILIPPO QUARTO Hispaniarum Regi. *ANtonium Ascamum* à nobis ad Majestatem Vestram nuper missum Oratorem . . . *Westmonasterio. Dat.* 28. *Junii.* 1650.

Milton, *Literæ*, 1676, p. 17; Skinner MS., No. 11; Columbia MS., No. 138; CM, XIII, 40.

[*To* Philip *the Fourth, King of* Spain. TO our infinite sorrow we are given to understand, That *Antony Ascham,* by us lately sent our Agent to your Majesty . . . *Westminster, June* 28. 1650.]

Phillips, p. 32; Masson, IV, 234; CM, XIII, 41.

JUNE 29. SUPPOSED TRANSLATOR OF THOMAS MAY'S HISTORY OF PARLIAMENT.

A Breviary of the History of the Parliament of England. Written in Latine by T. M. and for the general good translated into English . . . 1650.

Thomason's copy is dated June 29, 1650. In an unconvincing article in *Notes and Queries* (CLXI, 1931, 129-130) Hugh C. H. Candy offers the hypothesis that the English version is by Milton. There seems to be no indication of such authorship in the text or elsewhere, and there seems to be no reason why we should accept it as having anything to do with Milton. Both Halkett and Laing (1926) and Lowndes ascribe it without question to May. The original Latin version, *Historiae Parliamenti Angliae Breviarum,* was dated by Thomason March 29, 1650. See CM, XVIII, 637.

JULY 2. RELIEVED OF TRANSLATING PARLIAMENTARY DECLARATION, NOW ASSIGNED TO THOMAS MAY.

Die Martis [Tuesday] 2° Iulij 1652 [*sic*]. . . .

(7) That the Declaration of the Parlament of England upon the marching of their Army into Scotland bee sent unto Mr Thomas May to bee by him translated into Latine to the end that it may bee sent abroad into fforeigne parts.

Public Record Office, Order Book of the Council of State, SP Dom 25/64, p. 500; *CSP Dom, 1650,* p. 228; a note by Mr. N. H. Henry in the London *Times Literary Supplement,* August 17, 1933, p. 549. This order presumably revokes the previous assignment of this work to Milton on June 26 (*q.v.*). Mr. Henry first pointed out the relevance of

[318]

this entry. The date 1652 in the heading is an obvious slip of the pen, since it is found among the orders of 1650. Like so many other orders of this period, this entry is in a hand resembling Milton's.

JULY 5. COMPLETES SECOND PAYMENT ON NEW LEASE OF THE ROSE IN BREAD STREET.

[On July 5, 1650, Milton paid the balance of the sum due for his] ffine of 400ᵘ. for renewing the lease of the great messuage in Bread Street.

From the Minute-Book of the Company of Goldsmiths under this date, furnished me by the kindness of the present clerk of the company, Mr. G. R. Hughes. For previous entries relevant to this transaction see above under dates of April 20, October 5, November 5, and December 12, 1649, and March 12 and 27, 1650. Although the wording of the present entry seems to imply that Milton had now completed all the payments required on the new lease, it more probably means that he had paid all the money due at this time. If so, he had now paid £200, or just half the stipulated amount. We have record of a further payment of £100 on December 20, 1651 (*q.v.*); perhaps another installment was paid in December, 1650, or thereabouts.

AUGUST 10. ATTRIBUTED AUTHOR OF HOSTILE INSCRIPTION ON CHARLES I.

1650 . . . Aug. 10. The Kings picture in the Old Exchange defaced and broken down by the usurpers, and this inscription set behind the head thereof, *Exit Tyrannus Regum ultimus, anno Libertatis Angliæ restitutæ primo, Anno* 1648. *Jan.* 30.

Calendrium Carolinum: or, A New Almanack, 1664, p. 29 (British Museum, shelf-number P.P.2465.a.[1]); CM, XVIII, 351, 586. Though Milton's name is not mentioned in this quotation, it is in a later one given below. It is impossible to verify the accuracy of the attribution. The Latin may be translated: "Exit the tyrant, the last of kings, in the first year of the restored liberty of England, the year 1648/9, January 30."

KING CHARLES being dead, and some foolish Citizens going a whoring after his picture, or image, formerly set-up in the old *Exchange*; the Parliament made bold to take it down, and to engrave in it's place these words:

Exit Tyrannus, Regum ultimus, Anno Libertatis Angliæ restitutæ primo, Anno Dom. 1648. *Jan.* 30.

William Lilly, *Several Observations on the Life and Death of King Charles I*, 1651, reprinted in *Select Tracts Relating to the Civil Wars in England*, ed. Francis Maseres, 1815, part i, p. 181; CM, XVIII, 586.

[On May 24, 1652, Wilhelmus Worm Olai went to the merchants' resort, "quod sua lingua Old Excens vocant," where there was a series of statues of kings;] ultimus tamen Carolus, postquam octiduum sine capite inter cæteros stetisset, totus demum loco suo exemptus est, hisce aureis characteribus superscriptis:—

> Exiit Tyrannus
> Regum Ultimus
> Anno ———
> Anno libertatis Angliæ
> Restitutæ ———

Cujus auctorem Miltonium credunt, qui cum eo die occæcatus mihi diceretur hoc epigramma meruit —

> Monstrum immane ingens Milton cui lumen ademptum
> Post hac non Regi scommata plura dabit.

Wilhelmus Worm Olai F[ilius?], "Iter Anglicum anno MDCLII die ii. Maii inceptum, die xxx. Augusti absolutum, etc." MS. Hist. 4to. 39 in the University Library, Copenhagen, described by W. D. Macray in the *Forty-Fifth Report of the Deputy Keeper of the Public Records*, as reported in *Book-Lore*, II (1885), 100-101; Fletcher, *Contributions*, pp. 64, 66-67.

[But the last one, Charles, after he had stood among the others for eight days without his head, was at last completely banished from his place, with these words written above in golden characters: "The tyrant has gone, the last of the kings, in the year ———, in the ——— year of the restored liberty of England." Of this they believe Milton the author, who, because it was told me that day that he had become blind, deserved this epigram: "That monster Milton, enormous, huge, whose sight has been snatched away, will hereafter give no more gibes to the King."

The first line of the epigram, adapted from Virgil's *Aeneid*, III, 658, was frequently used against Milton. It is found in *Regii Sanguinis Clamor* and in other writings.

AUGUST 10. WRITES NOTE ABOUT RACOVIAN CATE-CHISM.

. . . a Note under the Hand of Mr. *John Milton*, of the 10th of *August* 1650.

Journals of the House of Commons, VII, 114; Masson, IV, 438; CM, XVIII, 524, 528, 545. The entry in the *Journals* records the report on April 2, 1652, of information about the Racovian Catechism, including an examination of Milton about it and the note mentioned in the text. The note has not been found, and next to nothing is known about the contents or even about who the recipient was. It may have been addressed to the Council of State, to the printer, or to someone else; it may have been in commendation or condemnation. The Thomason Catalogue records the receipt in March, 1651, of *Catechesis Ecclesiarum in regno Poloniæ & ducatu Lithuaniæ. Cui accedit Fausti Socini Senensis vita*, and on July 8, 1652, of *The Racovian Catechisme* [of the orthodox churches in Poland and Lithuania]; also on April 2, 1652, of a single sheet containing the votes of Parliament pronouncing this book to be blasphemous and ordering all copies to be burnt (1, 832, 867, 877). See also below under April 2, 1652.

AUGUST 14. ORDERED TO INVENTORY THE RECORDS OF THE ASSEMBLY OF THE SYNOD.

14°: Aug: 1650 . . .

That M^r. Thomas Goodwyn M^r. Bifield, M^r. Bond M^r. Nye, M^r. Durye, M^r. Frost & M^r. Milton, or anie 3. of them of wch. M^r. Frost or M^r. Milton to bee one be appointed to view & to inventorie all y^e. records writings [from them unto me as they shall think fair] and papers whatsoever belonging to the assemblie of the Synod [as there shall bee occasion] to y^e. end they may bee not embezelld and may be forth comeing for the use of the Comonwealth.

Public Record Office, Order Books of the Council of State, SP Dom 25/8, p. 79; *CSP Dom, 1650*, p. 286; Masson, IV, 228; CM, XVIII, 655. The two passages in square brackets were originally written as they stand here and were later crossed out. In the margin is the note: "y^e. Synod Records."

ABOUT AUGUST 15. PETITIONS TO COMPOUND FOR WHEATLEY.

[Milton says in his petition of February 25, 1650/1] That he being to compound by the late Act for certaine land at

Whately in Oxfordshire belonging to Mr Richard Powell late
of Foresthill in the same County, by reason of an extent which
he hath upon the said lands by a Statute, did put in his Petition
about the middle of August last, wch was referrd accordingly.

Public Record Office, SP Dom 23/101, pp. 925-928; Hamilton, p.
51; Masson, IV, 240; French, *Milton in Chancery*, p. 86. If Milton
actually filed this petition, it is now lost, though other later ones survive.
Or possibly Milton had in mind the petition of August 23 (below),
which may conceivably have been a joint document though signed only
by Mrs. Powell.

AUGUST 16. ANTAGONIST SALMASIUS ARRIVES IN STOCKHOLM.

. . . Salmasius hesterno die huc advenit, ut audio. . . .

From a letter of Nicholas Heinsius to Isaac Vossius, dated August 17,
1650, "stilo Juliano," which is Old or English Style. This reference,
like several later ones, is taken from the original letter now in the Uni-
versiteits-Bibliotheek, Amsterdam; it is catalogued as III, E, 9, 15. For
directing me to these letters I take pleasure in acknowledging here my
debt to the kindness of Mr. J. W. Lever, who published extracts from
them in the *Review of English Studies*, XXIII (1947), 97 ff.; and to
Mr. H. de la Fontaine Verwey, Librarian in Chief, who supplied me
with microfilm copies of them. Although Burmann published a great
many letters of Heinsius, Vossius, and their friends in his *Sylloges Epistolarum*, most of this group are not included in his collection. The present
letter, I believe, is unpublished.

[Salmasius arrived here yesterday, as I hear.]

AUGUST 22. (See entries for August 23 below.)

AUGUST 23. MOTHER-IN-LAW ANNE POWELL PETI-TIONS TO COMPOUND, MENTIONING MILTON'S HOLD-INGS.

To the hono^ble: Commission^rs: for Composicons./

The humble peticon of Ann. Powell. Late: wife. of Richard
Powell of fforresthill in ye County of Oxoñ Esqr.
Sheweth:
That yor. pet^rs. husband being a Delinquent was comprised in
ye Articles at the surrender of Oxford: vpon which sd Articles
he having his ffine sett. died, before the payement thereof; that

contrary to the sd Articles a greate part of yor. pet^{rs}. husbands Personall estate was disposed of by the Committee of Oxford And since by ye Comittee of Articles. ordred to be restored vnto yor: pet^r. wch. sd Order as yet hath taken noe effect.

That by the late Act concerning Statutes Mortgages & extents, those persons whoe are in possession of any Delinquents. Estates by virtue thereof are to pay the Delinquents Composicon for the same.

That yor. pet^{rs}. sd huband was seised of an Estate in fee of the tiethes of Whately: and three yard lands and a halfe there with seuerall Cottages being of the yeerely value of 40^{li}; which sd Estate is nowe in the possession, of M^r. John Milton being by him extended for a debt of 300^{li}. due about. 18. yeares since, and is otherwise charged, by deed of the. 10th of January: 7°. Caroli with a Terme of 99. yeares for the payem^t. of 400^{li}. with interest, to one M^r. Ashworth, And is also liable to yor. pet^{rs}. thirds, and diuers debts vpon Bond amounting to 1200^{li}.

Yo^r. Pet^r. humbly prayes, in case yor honors will haue any fine for this Estate; that the sd charges may be considred as also the losse susteyned by the sd Comittee's wrongfull selling of her husbands psonall estate the same being the greatest pte of the Estate for wch. the sd fine was imposed.

And yor: pet^r. shall pray.

23. Aug: 1650.   Anne Powell.
Refer'd to Mr Brereton.

     Jo: Leech.
Jnt^r.

Public Record Office, SP Dom 23/110, p. 542; *Calendar of the Committee for Compounding*, p. 1440; Hamilton, pp. 83-84; Masson, IV, 240. "Jnt^r" means "entered." See the note to "About August 15" above.

AUGUST 23 (?). MOTHER-IN-LAW ANNE POWELL'S PETITION REFERRED TO BRERETON FOR REPORT.

22°: Aug 1650 . . .

Vppon the Peticon of Anne Powell late wife of Richard Powell of fforrest Hill in the County of Oxon Esqr. shewing that the Pet^{rs} said husband having a ffyne sett vppon him for his

Delinquencye dyed before paym^t. thereof made & having divers great Jncumbrances charged vppon his Estate & the Com^{ttee}: of Oxford disposing of his psonall Estate the pet^r. desires dedu-cõns & abatem^{ts}. accordingly Jt is ordered that this Case be referred vnto M^r. Brereton who is to make report thereof vnto this Com^{ttee}.

Public Record Office, SP Dom 23/11, p. 92; Hamilton, p. 84; *Notes and Queries*, II, viii (1859), 142-143. Although the date at the top is August 22, the fact that the petition itself is dated August 23 seems to indicate that the date is wrong. See also the following item.

M^{rs}: Powell pet & pert referred the 23th: of August 1650.

From the dorso of Powell's "particular" of November 21, 1646. The abbreviations "pet & pert" stand for petition and particular.

AUGUST 23 (OR LATER). REPORT PRESENTED ON MOTHER-IN-LAW ANNE POWELL'S PETITION.

. . . A petiĉon of the said Ann Powell p^{r}sented the 23º of August 1650 and Order therevpon filed H.92, and a report drawne vp by Mr Brereton vpon that Order. . . .

From the certificate of January 7, 1653, *q.v.*

AUGUST 23 (?). MILTON'S PETITION TO COMPOUND APPROVED.

22º: Aug 1650 . . .

Vppon the Petiĉon of John Milton desiring to compound for Extent vppon the Estate of the last above said Richard Powell Jt is ordered that he be admitted to Composiĉon accordingly And that it be referred vt sũp^a.

Public Record Office, SP Dom 23/11, p. 92; Hamilton, p. 92. Just above this item is the record of the referring of Anne Powell's petition to Brereton for report. If I am correct in dating that action August 23 rather than, as the manuscipt indicates, August 22, the present entry should also be August 23. The difference of a day is, however, of no importance.

AUGUST 23. FATHER-IN-LAW RICHARD POWELL'S ESTATE OWES JOHN PYE £1,238.

John Pye maketh oath y^t ouer and aboue all receipts and summes of money payd eyther to his father Sr Robert Pye the elder or to him or there assignes eyther out of ye rents and profitts of Forsthill or otherwise to his best knowledge & remembrance and according to his computaċon there was due to him the 23ᵗʰ. of August 1650. from yᵉ Executors, heyres or assignes of Richard Powell of Forsthill Esqz. deceased, vpon a Mortgage of yᵉ sᵈ Mannʳ. of Forsthill made by yᵉ sᵈ Richard Powell to yᵉ abovemenċond Sʳ Robᵗ. Pye yᵉ elder June yᵉ 30ᵗʰ. 1640. & by yᵉ sᵈ Sʳ Robᵗ. Pye assigned ouer to yᵉ deponent, the full and entire summe of One thousand, twoe hundred, thirtye & Eight pounds or thereabouts.

Jo Pye./

From John Pye's sworn statement of January 1, 1651, *q.v.*

AUGUST 23. JOHN PYE PETITIONS TO COMPOUND FOR POWELL PROPERTY.

To the Right Honoᵇˡᵉ: Cõmissiõʳˢ: for Compoundinge wᵗʰ: Delinquents

The humble Petiċon of John Pye Esqʳ.

Sheweth

That whereas one Edmund Brome Esqʳ. by deede dated October 2° 19° Jac. did demise vnto Richard Powell Esqʳ. yᵉ Mannor of fforrest hill in yᵉ County of Oxoñ for yᵉ Terme of 20 yeares & by an other deede dated 21° Julij 21° Ja: did demise vnto yᵉ said Richard yᵉ same prmises for 31 yeares to coñmence after yᵉ end of 20 yeares, vnder yᵉ yearly rent of 5ᵗ: and whereas yᵉ sd Richard Powell by his jndenture dated 30° Junij 16° Car: 1640, for yᵉ some of 1400ˡˡ pᵈ: to him by Sʳ: Robert Pye Kᵗ: did assigne all his jnterest in yᵉ prmisses to yᵉ said Sʳ: Robert Pye vppon Condiċon of redemċon vppon paymᵗ: of yᵉ some of 1510ˡˡ vpon yᵉ first of July 1641 wᶜʰ: some was not paid, soe yᵗ yᵉ said Estate became forfeited to yᵉ said Sʳ: Robert Pye, and he entered vpon yᵉ prmisses in 1646. and afterwards by jndenture dated Dec: 3ᵈ 23° Car: yᵉ said Sʳ: Robert assigned his Estate and terme vnto your petiċoner. so as he is wholy jnterested therein; and whereas yᵉ said Richard Powell, being wᵗʰⁱⁿ: yᵉ Articles of Oxford, entred his Composiċon at Goldsmiths Hall, and yᵉ fine was jmposed according to yᵉ said articles, being so adjudged by yᵉ Coñmioʳˢ: for Articles, but is since dead; Now

for as much as yᵉ said Richard Powell dyed before yᵉ Com-
posicõn was perfected;

Yoʳ: Peticoner humbly prayeth yᵗ he may either haue his
title allowed and made good vnto him according to his jnterest
therein; (he haueing yᵉ whole estate yᵗ yᵉ said Richard Powell
had therein) forfeited to him before yᵉ said Richard Powells
Delinquencie; & he entred vpon it before any squestracõn)—
or yᵗ he may haue his Debt and Damages ratified vnto him;
according to the Act of Parliamᵗ. of yᵉ first of August last.

And he shall euer pray &c

Jo. Pye/

[Endorsed:]
23. Aug. 1650.
Refer'd to Mʳ Reading.
Intratᵘˢ. Jo. Leech

Public Record Office, SP Dom 23/109, p. 521; Hamilton, p. 85;
Calendar of the Committee for Compounding, p. 1440; French, *Milton
in Chancery*, p. 86.

AUGUST 23. JOHN PYE'S PETITION REFERRED TO JOHN READING.

Die Veneris 23°. Augusti 1650 . . .

Vppon the Peticõn of John Pye Esqʳ. it is referrᵈ vnto Mʳ.
Reading to consider therevppon./

Public Record Office, SP Dom 23/11, p. 87. This entry undoubtedly
refers to Pye's petition of the same date.

According to yoʳ Order of the 23ᵗʰ. of August 1650 vpon the
peticõn of John Py Esqz desireing allowance of a Mortgage of
certaine lands of Richard Powell Esqz a delinquent deceased I
finde. . . .

From John Reading's report of January 1, 1650/1, *q.v.*

AUGUST 24. JOHN PYE'S STATEMENT OF INCOME FROM FOREST HILL.

A true and iust particular of all yᵉ rents payable yearelye to
Mʳ John Pye or his Assignes out of yᵉ Mannour of Forresthill
in the Countye of Oxoñ; taken yᵉ 24ᵗʰ daye of August. 1650./

John Milton · AUGUST 1650

	£	s	d

Edmund Mason for yᵉ cheife Mansion house
Orchards, garden, wᵗʰ yᵉ desmesnes & tyths 160.00.00/
George Ball [erased] for Abbotts wood 031.00.00/
Henry Tomlins for a Mill & 3 parcells of groūd .. 023.00.00/
George Ball for two yard land 020.00.00/
Richard Willmot for a pasture ground 07.00.00/
John Boys for a brickill 07.00.00/
George Ball for yᵉ Groues and Muche's land 001.13.04
The towne rents 043.07.04

Summe totall 293.00.08
Annuall Reprizas
Payd to ye Curate of yᵉ towne 020.00.00
To the State 0.02.06
To the Mannʳ of Yewelme 0.02.06
The yearelye rents of Forrest Hill vltra Ordinary
reprizas are .... 272.15.08.
To be diducted out of ye sayd £272. 15s. 8d.
All yearelye charges to yᵉ high-wayes, poore, heyward
and all taxes and assessements, wᶜʰ came yᵉ
last yeare to about fourtye pounds ....
Jo Pye./
[Dorso:] Mʳ Johns Pyes pticuler and Piticon.
Public Record Office, SP Dom 23/109, p. 523; Hamilton, p. 86.

AUGUST 28. ELIZABETH ASHWORTH PETITIONS TO COMPOUND FOR INTEREST IN WHEATLEY.

To the honnᵇˡᵉ: the Comissioners for compositions
The humble petition of Elisabeth Ashworth/ administratrix
to Edward Ashworth her late husband.
Sheweth:
That yʳ petitioners Husband in his life time lent vnto Richard
Powell of forest Hill in the County of oxford the soṁme of
fower hundred pounds for security wheroff the sayd powell
made a lease of ninety nine yeeres of the Tythes of Whateley

[327]

& three yard land there bearing date the 10th: of January, 7°: Caro^{ll} that in regard of the trubles y^r petitioner whose right now the sayd debte is hath not reseaued the interest of the money: That she vnderstand the sayd powell being a delinquent & died not satisfing his composition

That y^r petitioner taking notise of the late acte of the 1st. of August 1650: concerning compositions for Creditors etc desires to be admitted to a composition wherein she humbly submitts her selfe and desires she may not in the meane times be disturbed in what she doth enioy.

And she shall pray.

28 Aug. 1650   Elisabeth Ashworth.

Referred to Mr Reading, A S.

[Endorsed:] Ashworth Elizabeth
        28 Aug: 1650.

Public Record Office, SP Dom 23/64, p. 185; Hamilton, pp. 87-88; *Calendar of the Committee on Compounding*, p. 1443.

AUGUST 28. SIR EDWARD POWELL PETITIONS TO COMPOUND FOR HIS INTEREST IN FOREST HILL AND WHEATLEY.

To the Comission^{rs} for compounding for Delinquents
        estates.

The Peticon of Sr: Edward Powell kn^t & bart.

Sheweth

That about the 18° Decemb 1641 Richard Powell of fforest Hill in Com. Oxon Esqz deceased did assigne vnto him All that Tenem^t & one hundred acres of Land meadow & pasture in Whately in the County of Oxon aforesd held by Lease from the Colledge of all Soules to have & hold the same for the terme of one & twenty yeares from thence next ensueing Vpon condicon that if the said Richard Powell should repay the some of 300^{li} wth interest at the end of six monthes then the said Assignem^t to be void as apps by the same.

That yor pet^r. for non paym^t of the said mony entred vpon the prmisses in January 1646.

That the said Richard Powell at the tyme of his Death being a Delinquent had not pfected his Composicōn for the said Lands & Tenem^t

Yo^r pet^r desires that he may compound for the same according to the late Act in that behalf made.

28 Aug 1650   Edw: Powell./

Referred to Mr Brereton

AS

Public Record Office, SP Dom 23/110, p. 587; Hamilton, pp. 86-87; *Calendar of the Committee for Compounding*, p. 1443. Some additional details about financial transactions between Richard Powell and Sir Edward, some of which appear elsewhere in the present book, are given by David H. Stevens in "Mary Powell's Lost Dowry," in his *Milton Papers*, Chicago, 1927, pp. 7-13.

SEPTEMBER 19. IS ALLEGED TO HAVE BEGUN EDITING *MERCURIUS POLITICUS.*

[*Mercurius Politicus,*] the conception of which must be attributed to John Milton, who was its editor probably from the end of the year 1650 (when the style of it suddenly alters) until the beginning of March, 1652.

J. B. Williams, *History of English Journalism*, London, 1908, p. 134. This idea, which has intrigued a number of students of Milton, seems to be without foundation. Though it is true that Milton probably was closely associated with the people controlling the magazine and that he licensed it for a considerable period (see below under March 17, 1651), the supposition that he wrote the editorials, or leading articles, has been shown to be without serious ground, since many of them are reprints of Marchamont Needham's *The Case of the Commonwealth of England Stated*, and many of the remainder were later collected and published in Needham's *The Excellency of a Free State* (1656). This matter is examined in detail in my "Milton, Needham, and *Mercurius Politicus,*" *Studies in Philology*, XXXIII (1936), 236-252. The sudden alteration of style, to which Mr. Williams refers, takes place with No. 16, September 19-26, 1650. See also the entry above under date of June 8, 1650.

SEPTEMBER 29. MILTON RECEIVES RENTS FROM WHEATLEY.

. . . Att Michalmas One Thousand six hundred and ffifty Thirty Two pownds Two shillings. . . .

From Milton's answer to Elizabeth Ashworth's bill of complaint, February 22, 1653/4, *q.v.*

OCTOBER 12. PAYS MOTHER-IN-LAW ANNE POWELL HER THIRDS.

[Milton] did pay or cause to bee payed vnto . . . Anne Powell . . . the seuerall summes of money menconed and Expressed in the sixe seuerall Acquittances or Receiptes . . . [the sixth of which is dated] October the 12th 1650: And is for the summe of tenne poundꝑ.

From Anne Powell's deposition in the Ashworth-Milton case, June 4, 1656, *q.v.*

NOVEMBER 7. LETTER OF STATE TO LORD ANTHONY LEWIS, GOVERNOR OF ANDALUSIA.

Excellentissimo Domino ANTONIO JOANNI LUDOVĪCO de la Cerda Medinæ Celi Duci, Andalitiæ Præsidi. *Consilium Status Parlamenti Angliæ authoritate constitutum,* SALUTEM. ACcipimus ab Ornatissimis Viris. . . . *Westmonasterio. Dat. 7. Novemb.* 1650. Signat. Consilii sigillo: Jo. BRADSHAWE PRESES.

Milton, *Literæ,* 1676, p. 19; Skinner MS., No. 12; Columbia MS., No. 93; CM, XIII, 42.

[*To the most Excellent Lord,* Anthony John Lewis dela Cerda, *Duke of* Medina Celi, *Governor of* Andalusia. *The Council of State constituted by Authority of Parliament: Greeting.* WE have receiv'd Advice from those most Accomplish'd Persons. . . . *Westminster, Nov.* 7. 1650. Seal'd with the Seal of the Council, *J. Bradshaw,* President.

Phillips, p. 34; Masson, IV, 235; CM, XIII, 43.

AFTER NOVEMBER 24. TRANSLATES TWO LETTERS FROM SPAIN (?).

[1] THE KING OF SPAINES LETTER.

The King.

Don Francisco Fernandes Marmoleso my governor & cap^t. . . . From Madrid 24 Novem. 1650. I the King. Don Fernando Ruiz de Contreras.

Columbia MS., No. 90; CM, XIII, 491. The only proof that this letter was translated by Milton is that it is found in this manuscript of letters chiefly from his pen; we cannot be sure. The original has not been found, but there is every probability that it was in Latin.

[2] IDEM.

Don Francisco Fernandes de Marmoleso my governor and Cap.ᵗ . . . . From Madrid. 24. Nov. 1650. I the King. Don Fernando Ruiz de Contrera.

This dispatch the most Honourable governor cap.ᵗ of warre & governor of the armes in Cartagena & the Kingdome of Murcia received. In Cartagena. Munday 28. Nov. 1650. at 6. in the morning.

Columbia MS., No. 91; CM, XIII, 492.

NOVEMBER 27. MATTHEW APPLETREE ORDERED TO REPAY DEBT TO MOTHER-IN-LAW ANNE POWELL.

Painted Chambᵣ: Westmᵣ:/

Die Mercurij [Wednesday] 27° Novembris 1650

By yᵉ Comissionᵣˢ appointed for releife vpon Articles granted in tyme of warr.

Vpon motion on yᵉ behalfe of Ann Powell Widdowe Relict of Richard Powell of fforrest Hill in the County of Oxoñ Esqz praying that yᵉ determynate Ordᵣ: of this Court dated yᵉ 12ᵗʰ: of June last might be Confirmed And vpon Consideracõn had of yᵉ said Ordᵣ: togither wʰ: yᵉ grounds and reasons wherevpon yᵉ same was made The Court doe now Order (and require That yᵉ said Mathew Appletree mencõned therein do pay vnto yᵉ said Mᵣⁱˢ Powell yᵉ some of Nyntey-one pounds Eleauen shillings and tenn pence vpon or before Wednesday yᵉ 4ᵗʰ: day of Decembᵣ: next Cominge so much appearing to yᵉ Court to bee due from yᵉ said Mathew Appletree for goods and houshold stuffe of yᵉ said Richard Powell sold and deliūed vnto him by Richard Appletree, John Webb, and John King then sequestrators of yᵉ County of Oxoñ the said Matthew Appletree having subscribed to yᵉ Jnventory and sale of yᵉ said goods, and hauing paid xxˢ: to yᵉ said sequestratorˢ: in earnest of yᵉ whole paymᵗ: wᶜʰ. xxˢ: yᵉ Court do now also Order shall be paid by yᵉ said

Sequestrators vnto M^ris: Powell vpon demand, And in case ye said Mathew Appletree shall refuse or delay to make paym^t: of ye said Nynety one pounds Eleeven shillings tenn pence vnto ye said M^ris: Powell w^thin ye time lymited as aforesaid, The Court doe furth^r: Order and require, That ye said some bee brought into Court vpon Wednesday ye 4th: of Decemb^r: next Cominge by ye said Mathew Appletree, and in default thereof ye Court doe now declare, That they will proceed against ye said Mathew Appletree according to ye power and authority Comitted to them by ye Parliam^t:/

   Vera Copia Ex^ta.   Tr. Pauncefoot Regist^r:
    Tr: Pauncefote
    27°. febr. 1650
I make oath this is a true Copie.
    Tr. Pauncefote,
     R M

Public Record Office, SP Dom 23/110, p. 551; Hamilton, pp. 88-89. The note at the end makes it clear that this is a copy of the original paper, not the original, which has not been found. See also Brereton's report of March 4, 1650/1.

AFTER NOVEMBER 28. TRANSLATES ANOTHER SPANISH LETTER (?).

TO ADMIRALL ROB. BLAKE

Admirall Rob. Blake, by the hands of my servants that reside in the city of Cartagena I have received the letter which you wrote me of the 12th of this month. . . . From Madrid. 28. Nov. 1650. I the King Don Fernando Ruiz de Contrera. By the King.

Columbia MS., No. 92; CM, XIII, 494. See the note to the letters entered above under date of "after November 24."

DECEMBER 3. SIR ROBERT PYE FILES AFFIDAVIT OF FATHER-IN-LAW RICHARD POWELL'S DEBT TO HIM.

Sr Robert Pye the elder of Westm^r. K^nt. maketh oath that before the 30th. of June 1640, he redeemed a lease y^t was forfeyted by Richard Powell of Forresthill Esqr. to one Mr George

Furseman by payeing One thousand pounds to the sayd Furseman for the sayd Richard Powell; and alsoe he lent the sayd Richard Powell before the time abouemenćoned, three hundred pounds more in money, both wch suṁes together with One hundred pounds for Consideraćon, amounted to the entire summe of One thousand and fowre hundred pounds, for the securitye whereof the sayd Richard Powell did convey by his owne desyre vnto the deponent, lands in Forresthill afores^d. menćond in a deede dated 30mo Junij 1640, in such sort as in the sayd deed is expressed; wch debt is still vnpayd and no Act done eyther by this deponent or any other to his knowledge to release or inualid the sayd deede.

Robert Pye

Jur. coram Com^{rijs}
   3 Dec. 1650.
    J B

Public Record Office, SP Dom 23/109, p. 527; Hamilton, p. 89.

DECEMBER 4. JOSEPH JANE'S ANSWER TO MILTON'S *EIKONOKLASTES* ALMOST FINISHED (?).

To Mr. Smith   4/14 December.

. . . Mr. Lane hath here composed an Answer to Milton's scandalous Book which is written against the late King's most incomparable Book.

From a letter from Sir Edward Nicholas to Mr. Smith as printed in *The Nicholas Papers*, ed. G. F. Warner, I (Publications of the Camden Society, New Series, Vol. XL, 1886), 207. The Mr. "Lane" of the letter must almost surely be Joseph Jane, whose *Eikon Aklastos* appeared some time in 1651, *q.v.* The editor identifies Mr. "Smith" as Lord Hatton. The date of the letter is given in both English and continental form, as frequently happened in letters of the period. English time was ten days behind continental time.

DECEMBER 13. AFFIDAVIT ON DEED FROM FATHER-IN-LAW RICHARD POWELL TO SIR ROBERT PYE.

Richard Sherwyn of the Cittye of Westm^r in the County of Mīdds Gent maketh oath that hee was present at the Sealeing and delivery of a deede indented dated the Thirtieth day of

June in the Sixenth yeare of the reigne of the late king Charles made betweene Richard Powell late of fforresthill in the County of Oxon Esqz of the one part and Sr Robert of ffarringdon Magna in the county of Berks knt of the other part importing the granting and conveyeing vnto the said Sr Robert Pye by the said Richard Powell the Manno^r or Lo^p of fforesthill aforesaid for the Terme of Thirty one yeares With a Provisoe of the said Deede to bee voide vpon Payment of the Some of ffiftene Hundred pounds at the time specified in the said Deede Which Deede was sealed on or neere about the date thereof.

    jur. 13 Dec. 1650   Ri. Sherwyn.
    W. Molins.

    [Endorsed] M^r Py./ 25° Martij. 1651. Fine: 658. 15. 03. rec^d. 24° Jan. 1650. Fine reduced vpon the Castinge vp the allowance of the Debt:–554^l–18^s–April the 9th 1651 S.M.
    6 July 1652 confirmed at 554:18.
    Public Record Office, SP Dom 23/109, p. 529; Hamilton, p. 89. Pye's last name is omitted when he is first mentioned.

ABOUT DECEMBER 17. LETTER OF STATE TO AGENT FROM PORTUGAL.

    INTERNUNTIO PORTUGALLICO. *Illustris Domine*, LIteras tuas hujus mensis quinto decimo *Hamptonâ*. . . .
    Milton, *Literæ*, 1676, p. 21; Skinner MS., No. 118; Columbia MS., No. 60; CM, XIII, 46. Although the letter bears no date or other subscription, it must have been written about December 17, since on that day the Council of State ordered that the proposed answer to the Agent's letter should be reported to Parliament. On December 18 the House ordered a safeconduct for him to be prepared by the Council. See *CSP Dom, 1650*, pp. 472-473.

    [*To the* Portugal *Agent. Most Illustrious Lord*, WE receiv'd your Letters dated from *Hampton* the 15th of this Month. . . .]
    Phillips, p. 37; Masson, IV, 235; CM, XIII, 47. Masson dates the letter between December 17 and 19 from the *Journals of the House of Commons*, and names the Agent as Guimaraes.

DECEMBER 23. AUTHORIZED TO PRINT HIS *DEFENSIO* IN ANSWER TO SALMASIUS.

    Monday. y^e. 23th. of Decemb. 1650. . . .

That M^r. Milton doe print the treatise wch. he hath written in answer to a late booke written by Salmatius against the proceedings of this Com͞onwealth.

Public Record Office, Order Book of the Council of State, SP Dom 25/15, p. 39; *CSP Dom, 1650*, p. 479; Masson, IV, 230. There is a marginal entry: "M^r. Milton." The word "treatise" is written in above the word "answer" crossed out. The reference is to the *Defensio pro Populo Anglicano*, which was registered on December 31 and published on February 24, 1651.

DECEMBER 31. *DEFENSIO* ENTERED IN STATIONERS' REGISTERS.

Ult. die [last day] **Decembris 1650**

Wm. Dugard.   Entred . . . by order of the Councell of State, two bookes (vidlt) [that is] *The advancement of merchandize, or, certain ppositions for the improvement of the trade of this comonwealth,* &c. By **Tho. Violet** of Lon: goldsmith and **Johannis Miltoni** *Angli p populo Anglicano defentio contra Claudij Salmatij Defentiones regium,* both in Latin & English . . . xij^d

Stationers' Registers, ed. Eyre and Spottiswood, I, 357; Masson, IV, 251. Before the word "merchandize" is the word "trade," crossed out and with the note "Deleted in Register."

DECEMBER 31. MOTHER-IN-LAW ANNE POWELL DEPOSES ABOUT SIR ROBERT PYE'S TAKING OF FOREST HILL.

Anne Powell the widdow of Richard Powell late of Forresthill in ye Countye of Oxford Esqr. maketh oath, y^t Laurence Farre seruant to Sr Robert Pye ye elder, of Westm^r: K^{nt}. did in the month of May or beginning of June 1646, in the behalfe and for ye vse of his sayd Master Sr Robert Pye ye elder, Enter and take possession of ye cheife Mansion house of Forresthill wth ye appurten^{ts}. (mortgaged to ye sayd Sr Robert Pye by ye sayd Richard Powell by his deed dated June 30th. 1640.) before any sequestrac͞on layd vpon that or any other part of y^e

sayd Richard Powells estate: W^ch possession the sayd Sr Robert
Pye or his assignes hath euer since continued.

Anne Powell.

Jurat coram Comissionar
31° December 1650
R M

Public Record Office, SP Dom 23/109, p. 524; Hamilton, p. 90.

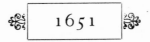

1651

EIKONOKLASTES ATTACKED BY JOSEPH JANE IN *EIKON
AKLASTOS.*

Εικων Ακλαστος The Image Vnbroaken. A Perspective of the
Impudence, Falsehood, Vanitie, and Prophannes, Published in
a Libell entitled Εικονοκλαστης against Εικων Βασιλικη Or the
Pourtraicture of his Sacred Majestie in his solitudes and Sufferings. Printed Anno Dom. 1651.

This book, of which the title means "the image unbroken," is a
chapter-by-chapter answer to *Eikonoklastes.* It was reissued in 1660
under the title *Salmasius his Dissection, q.v.* For an earlier allusion to
this book in progress see above under date of December 4, 1650.

The authorship of the book has caused some difficulty. As the title
above shows, it appeared anonymously. Wood wrote in *Athenæ
Oxonienses* (ed. Philip Bliss, III [1817], col. 592, *s.v.* "Jeanes, Henry")
of "*an Answer to John Milton's Book entit. Iconoclastes,* &c. printed
1651. qu. and said to be written by one Jeans, which I have not yet
seen." A note to this passage reads: "[By mistake, as I presume, for
Jane; and he likewise the mistaken author. See my note prefixed to that
book. BAKER.]" The editor of the Pickering edition of Milton's works
(1851, I, clxx) attributes it to Jeanes or Janes. Masson (IV, 349) treats
it anonymously. Stern (II, iii, 48, 261) says the author may be Jane or
Earle. A copy in the Yale University Library (shelf-number Ij M642.
T651) bears a note on the title page: "By John Bramhall D D Bishop
of Derry." The *DNB* and Parker (*Milton's Contemporary Reputation,* p. 88) attribute it to Joseph Jane, as does Donald Wing's *Short-
Title Catalogue, 1641-1700.*

Jane was a brother-in-law of Sir Edward Nicholas, Secretary of State,
to whom he wrote many letters of intelligence during the period of

about 1649-1660. See *The Nicholas Papers*, in the publications of the Camden Society, New Series, Volumes XL, L, LVIII, *passim; Academy*, XVII (1880), 225-226; *Gentleman's Magazine*, New Series, VI (1836), 451-468.

FEATLEY'S ATTACK REPUBLISHED.

Witnesse a Tractate of Divorce, In which the bonds of marriage are let loose to inordinate lust, and putting away wives for many other causes, besides that which our Saviour only approveth, namely, in case of Adultery.

Daniel Featley, *The Dippers Dipt*, sixth edition, 1651, sig. A4.

REISSUE OF WILKINS'S BOOK MENTIONING DIVORCE WRITINGS.

Of Divorce & Polygamy . . . M. Milton 〉 *Treatise.*
Vindication.
Tetrachordon.

John Wilkins, *Ecclesiastes*, third edition, London, 1651, p. 119; Parker, *Milton's Contemporary Reputation*, p. 77. For the first edition see above under date of October 10, 1646; the second was in 1647.

BUST EXECUTED BY SIMON OR PIERCE (?); ALSO DERIVED PUNCHEON AND SEAL.

A clay or plaster bust of Milton, now in Christ's College, Cambridge, is thought to have been made at about this time. Most students of Milton have considered it done from life; Marsh calls it "unquestionably" so. Although Masson dates it about 1654, Blackburne, Hollis, and Todd think it was done either upon the appearance of the *Defensio* or soon after. The sculptor may have been either an unidentified Pierce or Abraham Simon. It was owned at various times by George Vertue, Sir Joshua Reynolds (?), Thomas Hollis, and John Disney. It was frequently engraved, etched, or otherwise reproduced, notably by Vertue, Cipriani, and Richardson. Photographic reproductions may be found in Sotheby's *Ramblings*, the *Milton Tercentenary*, and elsewhere. A number of sculptured reproductions have also been made. For information about this bust, see Warton (1791), p. 531; Todd, I (1826), 237; Francis Blackburne, *Memoir of Thomas Hollis*, 1780, I, 86, 383; II, 620; Marsh, no. 12; *Milton Tercentenary*, pp. 14, 29, 38; Masson, VI, 757.

Probably derived from this bust were a steel puncheon and a seal. The puncheon belonged to Thomas Hollis and later to Albert Way. It is now lost. See Warton (1791), p. 531; Marsh as above; Todd, I (1826), 238; *Milton Tercentenary*, pp. 15, 79. The seal, in profile from the bust, is said to have been done by Thomas Simon, brother of Abraham. According to Blackburne (*Memoir of Thomas Hollis*, 1780, I, 81, 490; II, 573, 583, 620) the seal descended from Milton through his daughter, to her husband Foster, to John Payne, and to Hollis. Either this seal or another also belonged to Albert Way. Like the puncheon, it has also disappeared; but a wax impression of it is now in the National Portrait Gallery. Another seal, probably made from an impression of it by W. W. Rylands, is in the British Museum. See Warton, Todd, and Marsh as above, and *Milton Tercentenary*, pp. 15, 78, 79.

SICK AND ALMOST BLIND.

[In answer to the question why he delayed so long in answering Salmasius,] de aliis sanè nescio, de me audacter possum dicere, non mihi verba aut argumenta, quibus causam tuerer tam bonam, diu quærenda aut investiganda fuisse, si otium & valetudinem (quæ quidem scribendi laborem ferre possit) nactus essem. Quâ cum adhuc etiam tenui admodum utar, carptim hæc cogor, & intercisis penè singulis horis vix attingere, quæ continenti stylo atque studio persequi debuissem.

Milton, *Defensio*, 1651 (Madan's No. 1), sigs. B2v-B3; CM, VII, 10. The date might be anywhere from early in 1650 to about January, 1651. But the prefatory matter, from which this is taken, is likely to have been written near the end; it is therefore entered under the year 1651.

[. . . about others I know nothing, but about myself I can boldly say that I had no need of long search for words or arguments with which to defend so good a cause, if I had been in possession of leisure or of health sufficient for the labour of writing. Even now what health I have is so poor and precarious that I am forced to take up piecemeal, and with a break almost every hour, this piece of composition, which otherwise it would have been my duty to prosecute continuously and with unintermitted attention.]

Masson, IV, 254; CM, VII, 11.

. . . aliquot ante mensibus quam visus omnis aboleretur, quæ immotus ipse cernerem, visa sunt omnia nunc dextrorsum, nunc sinistrorsum natare; frontem totam atq; tempora inveterati quidam vapores videntur insedisse; qui somnolentâ quadam gravitate oculos, á cibo præsertim usq; ad vesperam, plerunq;

urgent atq; deprimunt. . . . Sed neq; illud omiserim, dum adhuc visûs aliquantum supererat, ut primum in lecto decubuissem, meque in alterutrum latus reclinassem, consuevisse copiosum lumen clausis oculis emicare; deinde, imminuto indies visu, colores perinde obscuriores cum impetu & fragore quodam intimo exilere. . . .

Milton, *Epistolarum Familiarium Liber Unus*, 1674, pp. 40-41; CM, XII, 68. The quotation is from Milton's letter to Leonard Philaras dated September 28, 1654. Since his sight had disappeared entirely by March, 1652 (*q.v.*), we may date this condition late in 1651.

[I observed, some months before my sight was wholly gone, that objects I looked at without myself moving seemed all to swim, now to the right, now to the left. Inveterate mists now seem to have settled in my forehead and temples, which weigh me down and depress me with a kind of sleepy heaviness, especially from meal-time to evening. . . . But I should not forget to mention that, while yet a little sight remained, when first I lay down in bed, and turned myself to either side, there used to shine out a copious glittering light from my shut eyes; then that, as my sight grew less from day to day, colours proportionately duller would burst from them, as with a kind of force and audible shot from within. . . .

Masson, IV, 640-641; CM, XII, 69.

VISITED BY IMPORTANT PEOPLE.

Milton . . . was on the first appearance of his book, visited or invited by all the Ambassadors at *London*, not excepting those of Crown'd Heads, and particularly esteem'd by *Adrian Paw* the Ambassador of the flourishing Republic of *Holland*.

Toland, p. 33; Darbishire, p. 160. On Adrian de Pauw see CM, VIII, 190-191, and XVIII, 530. This entry of course covers several years of time.

. . . for eight years before [the Restoration] he was visited by all Foreners of Note, by several Persons of Quality, and by the Ingenious of every Persuasion or Party.

Toland, p. 38; Darbishire, p. 175.

PRAISED IN DUTCH JOURNAL.

Wy sullen Vranckrijk nu voor een wijle tijts verlaten/ en gaen over zee nae Engelant: Alwaer tegens Claudius Salmasius sijn Verdedizinge des Conings Carolus de 1/ aen Carolus de 2 toe-gewijt/ een seer bondige en dappere Latijnsse Verantwoordinge voor 't Parlement uytgekomen is/ zijnde in de selbe Tale diergelijcke in dese tijden niet te vinden/ die van Politijcke saecken spreeckt: De Autheur is geweest eenen Johan Milton/ Engelsman/ eene der Secretarissen van den Raet van Staten binnen Londen/ tot wiens Tractaet (als zijnde nu in Nederlantse/ Engelsse en Fransse Tale overgeset) wy den curieusen Leser heen wijsen.

Hollandsche Mercurius, 1651, p. 16; H. Scherpbier, *Milton in Holland*, 1933, pp. 21-22; Parker, p. 85 (with translation). The exact date is not given.

[We shall now leave France for a while, and cross the sea to England, where a very compact and bold Latin Apology for the Parliament has appeared against Claudius Salmasius's Defence of King Charles I, dedicated to Charles II. No such book is to be found in the same language in these times, treating of political affairs. The author is one John Milton, Englishman, a secretary of the Council of State in London, to whose treatise we refer the interested reader, and which is translated into Dutch, English, and French.]

The translation of Milton's *Defensio* into Dutch here mentioned will be noticed shortly, but the English translation is not known. There are, however, one or two other intimations that one is being made.

ATTACKED BY JOHN ROWLAND IN *APOLOGIA*.

Pro Rege et Populo Anglicano Apologia, contra Johannis Polypragmatici, (alias Miltoni Angli) Defensionem. . . . Antverpiæ, Apud Hieronymum Verdussen, M.DC.LI.

Title page of a chapter-by-chapter retort to Milton's *Defensio*, filled with abusive epithets such as "scelestissimus" [most criminal], "insaniens Cacodæmon" [filthy lunatic], and the like. By many readers it was attributed to Bishop John Bramhall; two copies in the British Museum bear his name in manuscript as the author, and even Edward Phillips mentions him as a possible author. Actually the author was without much doubt John Rowland. It has not been translated into English.

See Masson, IV, 347-348, 536; Parker, p. 88. It was attributed to Rowland by Bramhall himself in a letter of May 9, 1654 (*q.v.*): "That silly book which he [Milton] ascribed to me, was written by one John Rowland"; and it was acknowledged by John Rowland in his *Polemica Sive Supplementum*, 1653. Two editions appeared in 1652.

[An Apology for the King and the English People against Jack-of-all-Trades, alias Milton, Englishman's Defence . . . Antwerp, published by Jerome Verdussen, 1651.]

. . . though *Salmasius* was departed, he left some stings behind, new Enemies started up, Barkers, though no great Biters; who the first Assertor of *Salmasius* his Cause was, is not certainly known, but variously conjectur'd at, some supposing it to be one *Janus* a Lawyer of *Grays-Inn*, some Dr. *Bramhal*, made by King *Charles* the Second after his Restauration Archbishop of *Armagh* in *Ireland.* . . .

Phillips, p. xxxii; Darbishire, p. 70.

On this Book our Author did not think it worth his while to animadvert, but delegated that easy task to his younger Nephew *John Philips*, now alive, who soon wrote a sufficient Answer to Bishop *Bramhal*; for so this new Antagonist was suppos'd to be cal'd.

From John Toland; Darbishire, pp. 158-159.

DEFENSIO TRANSLATED INTO DUTCH.

Joannis Miltons Engelsmans Verdedigingh des gemeene Volcks van Engelandt, Tegens Claudius sonder Naem, alias Salmasius Konincklijcke Verdedigingh. Wt het Latijn overgeset, Na de Copy gedruckt tot Londen, by Du Gardianis. 1651.

This is No. 11 in Madan's list as given under Milton's *Defensio*, February 24. The name of the translator is not given. Parker (p. 39) says that the translation was made "for the benefit of unlearned but interested Hollanders."

[John Milton Englishman's Defence of the People of England against Claudius Anonymous alias Salmasius's Royal Defence. Translated from Latin from the Copy printed at London by DuGard. 1651.]

ROWLAND'S *APOLOGY* TRANSLATED INTO DUTCH.

Verdediging voor den Koning, Ende het Volck van Enge-
land, Tegens Johannis Moey-al (alias Milton . . .) t'Hant-
werpen, By Hieronymus Verdussen, 1651.

Title page of a Dutch translation of Rowland's *Pro Rege et Populo
Anglicano*, 1651. The translator's name is not given. The book is in
duodecimo, with 251 pages of text.

[Defence of the King and the People of England against
Jack-of-all-Trades, alias Milton. . . . Antwerp, Jerome Verdussen, 1651.]

JANUARY 1. JOHN PYE MAKES OATH OF FATHER-IN-LAW RICHARD POWELL'S DEBT CONCERNING FOREST HILL.

John Pye maketh oath y^t ouer and aboue all receipts and
summes of money payd eyther to his father Sr Robert Pye the
elder or to him or there assignes eyther out of ye rents and
profitts of Forsthill or otherwise to his best knowledge & remembrance and according to his computacõn there was due to
him the 23th. of August 1650. from ye Executors, heyres or
assignes of Richard Powell of Forsthill Esqz deceased, vpon
a Mortgage of ye s^d Mann^r of Forsthill made by ye s^d Richard
Powell to ye abouemencõned Sr Robt. Pye ye elder June ye 30th.
1640. & by ye said Sr Robt. Pye assigned ouer to ye deponent,
the full and entire summe of One thousand, twoe hundred, thirtye & eight pounds or thereabouts.

Jo Pye.

Hee also deposeth, That where there is reserued by the Lease,
That the Lessee is to finde the Curate: Hee deposeth that there
is vsually paid, 20^l. to the curate of forresthall, and that there
is 5s. issueing for quit Rents of the premisses.

Jo Pye.

Jur corā Com^{rijs} 1. January 1650[/1]
Public Record Office, SP Dom 23/109, p. 525; Hamilton, pp. 90-91.

John Milton · January 1651

January 1. John reading reports on Pye-Powell finances.

According to yor Order of the 23th of August 1650 vpon the peticon of John Py Esqz desireing allowance of a Mortgage of certaine lands of Richard Powell Esqz a delinquent deceased I finde.

That Edmond Browne Esqz by Indenture dated 21° July 1623 bargained and sold to Richard Powell Esqz. The Mannor of fforresthill with the appurtennances in the County of Oxon; with the Rectory impropriate, and other lands there, from the tearme of 31. yeares, to commence from the expiracon of a former Lease thereof for 20. yeares, which did expire, the first of Nouember 1641. ffor and vnder the yearly rent of 5^{li}.

That the said Richard Powell by his Indenture beareing date the 30°. June 1640. In consideracon of 1400^{li}. therein alleaged to bee paid, did graunt bargaine sell assigne and sett ouer to S^r. Robert Py kn^t. the said Mannor of forresthill and other the premisses, for the whole tearme therein then to come, and vnexpired. Vnder this prouiso to bee voyd vpon payment of the somme of 1510^{li} the first of Iuly 1641. As by the said deed now produced vnder the hand and seale of the said Richard Powell: The sealeing and deliuery whereof is proued by Richard Sherwyn gent.

And it is deposed by Ann Powell widow, That for non-payment of the said 1510^{li}. the said S^r. Robert Py entred vpon the said premisses in May or June 1646 before any sequestracon layd therevpon.

That afterwards the said S^r. Robert Py by his Indenture dated the 3°. december. 1647. In consideracon of the naturall loue and affection which hee bore to the petitioner being one of his sonns, did graunt assigne and sett ouer, the said premisses and all his estate therein then to come and vnexpired vnto the peticoner his executors and assignes

And I finde by an affidauit of the said Sr Robert Py here taken, That before the 30° of June 1640 hee redeemed a lease forfeited by Richard Powell Esqz to George ffursman by pay-

[343]

inge 1000ʰ. to the said ffursman for the said Richard Powell, And that hee lent the said Richard Powell before the tyme aboue mentioned 300ʰ more in mony, both which sommes togeather with 100ʰ. for considerac̄on amounted to 1400ʰ. for security whereof th. said Richard Powell did Convey by his owne desire vnto the deponent the premisses by the deed before mentioned, which debt is still vnpaid, and noe act donn by him or any other to his knowledge to release, or invallid the said deed

It appeareth by a perticuler vnder the peticōners hand, that the Lands which hee holds by vertue of the said Mortgage are of the yearly vallew of 272ʰ: 15ˢ. 8ᵈ. ouer and aboue 20ʰ. therein alleaged to bee issueing out of it to the Curate and 5ˢ for cheefe Rent, both which are deposed by the petitioner.

And it is also deposed by the peticōner, That the debt intrest and charges oweing to the peticoner vpon the said mortgage, ouer and aboue all the money which hee hath receaued, doth amount vnto the somme of 1238ʰ twelve hundred thirty eight pounds.

And that hee doth not know any thinge to release or invalid the said mortgage in Law or equity.

I doe not finde that the said Richard Powell the delinquent is comprised in any exception from Composicon.

All which &c   1 Jan 1650   Jo Readinge

Public Record Office, SP Dom 23/109, pp. 517-519; Hamilton, pp. 55-57.

JANUARY 16. REVISED LIST OF OCCUPANTS OF WHITEHALL TO BE PREPARED.

Thursday yᵉ. 16ᵗʰ. of Ianuary. 1650/51. . . .

That it be referred to the Comᵗᵗᵉᵉ. for Whitehall to Consider (upon the lyst given in to this Councel of such persons as doe now inhabit wᵗʰ.in Whitehall) who are fitt to be discharged from abideing within the House any longer, And they are likewise to certifie by a lyst who they are that are to remaine.

Public Record Office, Order Book of the Council of State, SP Dom 25/16, p. 43; *CSP Dom, 1651*, p. 15; Masson, IV, 230-231. This entry is included here because it foreshadows later actions concerning Milton's quarters in Whitehall; see below under dates of April 10, May 9, and June 11, 1651.

JANUARY 16-23. *DEFENSIO* BEING PRINTED.

From *Leyden* we had this accute representation of Affaires in *Holland,* of this 17. instant, *stilo novo*. SIr, our Citie affords little (though the seat of the Muses) worthy your knowledge, onely we wonder not a little you suffer our *Salmasius* to crow and cry *Victoria* so long without bidding him battaile: Are your Wits or your Cause barren, or why is the Pen and Presse so long bringing forth?

[Editorial note at the end of this section:] Let the penner of this Epistle take notice, That a very victorious Reply to *Salmasius* is now in motion at the Presse.

Mercurius Politicus, No. 33, January 16-23, 1651, pp. 545-546; Masson, IV, 239; Parker, p. 84. Though Milton's name is not mentioned, there can be little doubt that the reference is to his *Defensio*, inasmuch as *Mercurius Politicus* was almost a government organ, Milton had a fairly close connection with it, his *Defensio* was an assigned task, and it was to appear in about a month.

JANUARY 20. LETTER OF STATE TO SPAIN POSSIBLY BY MILTON (?).

Serenissime & Potentissime Rex.

Per Excellentem Virum Dom^m Alphonsum à Cardenas Vestrum . . . Datum Westmonasterij vicesimo primo die Januarij Anno Salutis MDCL. Guilel. Lenthall prolocutor Parlamenti Reipub. Angliæ.

From the archives at Simancos, Spain; CM, XIII, 642-643. Not in Milton's *Literæ*, 1676, or in Masson, or in either the Skinner or Columbia manuscripts. That Milton had anything to do with this letter is only a guess.

[Most serene and powerful King: By the excellent man Lord Alphonsus à Cardenas your. . . . Given at Westminster the twenty-first day of January in the year of our salvation 1650 (i.e., 1650/1). William Lenthall, Speaker of the Parliament of the Commonwealth of England.]

JANUARY 22 (?). LETTER OF STATE TO PHILIP OF SPAIN.

PHILIPPO QUARTO Hispaniarum Regi. QUàm gravitèr quàmque acerbè tulerit *Majestas Vestra*, nefariam illam *Antonii Aschami* oratoris nostri cædem. . . .

Milton, *Literae*, 1676, p. 10; Skinner MS., No. 114; Columbia MS., No. 38; CM, XIII, 24. The dating of this letter is uncertain. Masson (IV, 234) dates it shortly after the letter of June 28, 1650, which is on the same subject. No forms of the letter which have been found bear any date or signature. Following Masson, the Columbia *Milton* dates it about July 1, 1650. But some of the records of the House of Commons seem to justify the date given here of January 22, 1651. From the *Journals of the House of Commons*, VI, 520-528, we can put together the following story. On January 7, 1650/1, letters to the King of Spain and to the Spanish ambassador were ordered read and then ordered reconsidered. On January 15 a letter to the King was read and recommitted; an answer to the ambassador was read and accepted. On January 16 a letter to the King was read and accepted as amended. On January 21 both were ordered sent to the ambassador, but only after being amended. On January 22 a committee was appointed to deliver both as amended. On January 24 the committee reported their safe delivery. It therefore seems reasonable to date both the present letter and that to the ambassador Cardenas January 22.

[*To* Philip *the Fourth, King of* Spain. HOW heinously, and with what Detestation your Majesty resented the Villanous Murder of our Agent, *Anthony Ascham*. . . .]

Phillips, p. 19; Masson, IV, 234; CM, XIII, 25.

JANUARY 22 (?). LETTER OF STATE TO SPANISH AMBASSADOR CARDENAS.

Legato Hispanico. *Excellentissime Domine*, COncilium Status, quam primùm per gravissima Reipub. negotia licuit. . . .

Milton, *Literæ*, 1676, p. 11; Skinner MS., No. 121; Columbia MS., No. 106; CM, XIII, 26. For the date, see the notes to the letter to the King of Spain entered under the same date. The Columbia *Milton* dates this letter, after Masson, January, 1651.

[*To the Spanish Embassador. Most Eccellent Lord*, THE Council of State, so soon as their weighty Affairs would permit 'em. . . .]

Phillips, p. 21; Masson, IV, 235; CM, XIII, 27.

JANUARY 24. SIR ROBERT PYE PAYS FINE ON POWELL PROPERTY.

Mr Py./ 25° Martij. 1651.
Fine: 658. 15. 03. rec^d. 24° Jan. 1650.

From the endorsement of Richard Sherwyn's affidavit about Powell's debt to Pye, December 13, 1650, *q.v.*

JANUARY 30. *DEFENSIO* ALMOST READY TO APPEAR.

La réponse au Livre scandaleux & diffamatoire du Sr de Saumaise alencontre de cet Estat laquelle est si fort désirée depuis long temps de plusieurs honnestes personnes, & généralement attendüe d'un chacun, est enfin prête de voir le jour, estant maintenant sous la presse & fort avancée.

Nouvelles Ordinaires de Londres, No. 30, January 23/February 2-January 30/February 9, 1650/1, p. 120. The colophon reads: "A *LONDRES*, Par *Guillaume Du-Gard*, l'an 1651/0. Par Authorité. Et se vendent par *Nicolas Bourne*, à la porte *Meridionale* de la vieille Bourse." The text above, like those used below under dates of February 27, 1651, November 25, 1652, and February 14, 1656, is from the copy in the Bibliothèque Nationale, Paris, which kindly provided me with photostats of the numbers of containing references to Milton. Dr. W. C. Abbott (*A Bibliography of Oliver Cromwell*, Cambridge, Massachusetts, 1929, item 474, p. 60) refers to it as "By John Milton [?] in 1650-52." I have not been able to learn the grounds of this attribution. Apparently no copy of this periodical is to be found in the United States; none is mentioned, at least, in the *Union List of Serials*. These passages are quoted by Charles Bastide in a little known study, "Les gazettes françaises de Londres au XVIIe siècle," *Revue de Synthèse Historique*, Paris, 1911; an offprint is in the New York Public Library. See also French, "The Date of Milton's First *Defense*," *The Library*, 5th Series, III (London, 1948), 56-58; Stevens, No. 2371.

[The reply to the scandalous and defamatory book of M. de Saumaise against this state, which has long been so much desired by many good people and generally awaited by everyone, is at last ready to see the light, being now in the press and far advanced toward publication.]

FEBRUARY 2. LETTER FROM SIR HENRY WOTTON REPRINTED.

To Master—.

Wotton's letter to Milton, originally dated April 13, 1638 (*q.v.*), was included in a reprint of this year entitled *Reliquiæ Wottonianæ. Or, A Collection Of Lives, Letters, Poems; With Characters Of Sundry Personages* and dated by Thomason, February 2. The letter, headed simply "To Master—," and bearing no date, occurs on p. 432. It is noticed in Parker, p. 85. A bookseller's catalogue of 1941 offered for sale a copy of this book bearing the arms of John Egerton, second Earl of Bridgewater, who as a young man took the part of the elder brother in the presentation of Milton's *Comus* in 1634 at Ludlow Castle.

FEBRUARY 6. LETTER OF STATE TO SENATE OF DANZIG.

ILLUSTRI & MAGNIFICO Civitatis Gedanensis Senatui. *Magnifici atque Amplissimi Domini Amici Charissimi.* FRequentes ad nos literæ mercatorum nostrorum. . . . *Westmonasterio. Dat. 6 Feb*: 1650.

Milton, *Literæ*, 1676, p. 20; Skinner MS., No. 13; Columbia MS., No. 94; CM, XIII, 44. For original letter see CM 4th Supplement.

[*To the Illustrious and Magnificent Senate of the City of* Dantzick. *Magnificent and Most Noble Lords, our dearest Friends*, MAny Letters are brought us from our Merchants. . . . *Westminster, Febr.* 6. 1650.]

Phillips, p. 35; Masson, IV, 236; CM, XIII, 45.

FEBRUARY 6. *DEFENSIO* EAGERLY AWAITED IN HOLLAND.

[A letter from the Hague by a gentleman of Leyden says:] I am thankfully glad of the promise *Politicus* gives us of *Salmasius* Answer, which we greedily expect, and *Salmasius* himself seems to desire it; *Goliah*-like, despiting all his adversaries as so many *Plgmies* [*sic*]. . . . *Hague* 16 Febr *stilo loci*, 1651.

Mercurius Politicus, No. 37, February 13-20, 1651, p. 604; Masson, IV, 329; Parker, p. 85. February 16 according to "new style," which is probably what the phrase "*stilo loci*" [according to the style of this place] means, would be ten days earlier in English reckoning, or February 6. The phrase "*Salmasius* Answer" must mean an answer to Salmasius. The reference to *Politicus* is presumably to the note given above under date of January 16-23, in which the editor of *Mercurius*

Politicus assures his Leyden correspondent that "a very victorious Reply to *Salmasius* is now in motion at the Presse."

FEBRUARY 10. ORDERED TO ATTEND MEETING WITH GUIMARAES, AMBASSADOR FROM PORTUGAL.

Monday yᵉ. 10ᵗʰ. of Feb. 1650/51. . . .

That Mʳ Milton the Secr for forreigne Languages be appointed to attend the Comittee at their meetings [with Guimaraes on Wednesday, February 12.]

Public Record Office, Order Books of the Council of State, SP Dom 25/17, p. 59; Masson, IV, 231; CM, XVIII, 367, 655. Other items in the arrangements for this meeting of Guimaraes with a committee of the Council of State were (1) that the committee should receive from him papers for the Council and transmit to him papers from the Council; (2) that they should discuss the details of a projected treaty with Portugal; (3) that the place of meeting should be the Great Chamber at the end of the Council Chamber and the time 3:00 P.M.; (4) that Charles Vane, English Agent to Portugal, should be there to assist; and (5) that Joseph Frost, son of Gualter, should act as a kind of secretary to the committee.

FEBRUARY 12. ATTENDS MEETING WITH PORTUGUESE AMBASSADOR (?).

Since Milton was ordered on February 10 (*q.v.*) to attend this meeting, there is every reason to suppose that he did so. It was scheduled to be held at 3:00 P.M. in the Great Chamber at the end of the Council Chamber.

FEBRUARY 19. REAPPOINTED SECRETARY.

Wednesday 19° Februʳʸ 1650/1. . . .

14) That Mʳ Iohn Milton be Secretary for the forreigne Languages for the tyme of the Councell.

Public Record Office, Order Book of the Council of State, SP Dom 25/65, p. 11; *CSP Dom, 1651*, p. 53; Masson, IV, 313. A similar entry occurs in SP Dom 25/18, p. 5.

FEBRUARY 20. REPLY TO SALMASIUS REPORTED ON WAY TO HOLLAND.

[A letter from] *Leyden* March 2. *new stile.* . . . Now we hear in our *Academy*, and I was told it at the *Hague* also, that your *Ambassadors* will bring with them, the Answer to *Sal-*

masius; I perceive by him, though he dreads no Antagonist, that he could wish it to write again; for, it was never calculated for this change as is since faln out.

Mercurius Politicus, No. 39 (February 27-March 6, 1651), p. 638; Masson, IV, 329; French, "Milton, Salmasius, and *Mercurius Politicus*," p. 247; Parker, p. 86. March 2, new style, would be February 20, English style.

FEBRUARY 21. OATH OF OFFICE FOR MILTON AND OTHERS PRESCRIBED BY PARLIAMENT.

Die Veneris [Friday], 21° *Februarii*, 1650. . . .

Mr. *Say* reports from the Council of State, the Form of Two Oaths . . . the other to be administred to such as the Council shall employ under them. . . .

'I *A. B.* do promise, in the Sight of God, That I will be true and faithful in the Trust committed to me, in my Employment under the Council of State: And that I will not reveal or disclose any thing, in Whole or in Part, directly or indirectly, that shall be debated or resolved upon in the Council, and ordered to be kept secret by the said Council, without the Command, Directions, or Allowance, of the Parliament or Council.'

Resolved, That the Parliament doth approve of the said Oaths to be administred to the Secretary of the Council of State, and to such other Officers belonging to the said Council of State, as the said Council shall think fit.

Resolved, That the said Council, or any Three of them, shall be, and are hereby, impowered and authorized to administer the said Oath to the said Persons accordingly.

Journals of the House of Commons, VI, 537. Presumably Milton took this oath within a short time, but we have no specific record of his doing so.

FEBRUARY 24. *DEFENSIO PRO POPULO ANGLICANO* PUBLISHED.

La réponse faite au Livre injurieux du S.r de Saumaise par le S.r Jean Milton l'un des secrétaires du Conseil d'Estat, sortit au jour lundi dernier, au grand contentement et approbation d'un chacun.

Nouvelles Ordinaires de Londres, #34, March 2/February 20-March 9/February 27, 1651, p. 136; quoted by Charles Bastide in "Les Gazettes Françaises de Londres au XVIIᵉ Siècle," an extract from *Revue de Synthèse Historique*, 1911, p. 3. This statement, if true, gives the most specific information about the appearance of the *Defensio* which we have ever had. The date of February 24 is reached in this way: February 27, the later of the two English dates of the period covered by issue 34 of the journal, is said by the journal itself to be Thursday; the preceding Monday, when the article says the book was published, was therefore the 24th. Until proved to be wrong, this date should therefore be accepted as correct.

[The reply made to the injurious book of M. de Saumaise by Mr. John Milton, one of the secretaries of the Council of State, came out on Monday last, to the great pleasure and approval of everybody.]

Joannis MiltonI Angli Pro Populo Anglicano Defensio Contra Claudii Anonymi, aliàs Salmasii, Defensionem Regiam. [Device] Londini, Typis Du-Gardianis. Anno Domini 1651.

Title page of British Museum copy catalogued as 599.c.26, which is Madan's number 1. The best discussion of the various editions of this book is F. F. Madan's "Milton, Salmasius, and Dugard," *The Library*, Fourth Series, IV (1923-24), 119-145. Those appearing between 1651 and 1695, as Madan gives them, are as follows:

1. DuGard, 1651, 4o, pp. [20], 205, [1].
2. DuGard, 1651, folio, pp. [4], 263, [1].
3. Gouda (?), 1651, 4o, pp. [10], 104, [6]; with index.
4. Utrecht (?), 1650, 12o, pp. [20], 244.
5. Unknown printer, 1651, 12o, pp. [20], 244.
6. Elzevir, 1651, 12o, pp. 260, [12]; with index.
7. Elzevir, 1651, 12o, pp. 283, [5].
8. Printer unknown, 1651, 16o, pp. 285.
9. Jansson, 1651, 12o, pp. [42], 330.
10. DuGard (?), 1651, 12o, pp. [34], 389, [21]; with index.
11. Antwerp (?), 1651, 12o, pp. 26, 319, [3]; in Dutch.
12. Gouda (?), 1652, 12o, pp. 192.
13. Utrecht, 1652, 12o, pp. 276, [12]; with index.
14. London, 1658, 12o, pp. [16], 171, [5]; with errata.
15. Translated by Washington, 1692, 8o, pp. [8], xxii, [2], 246, [2].
16. Translated by Washington, 1695, 8o, identical with #15 except for title page.

Madan noted some variations among copies of these editions and distinguished three variant issues of #1 and two of #4. Professor Maurice Kelley noted some further variations in copies in the Princeton Library in "A Note on Milton's *Pro Populo Anglicano Defensio*," *The Library*, XVII (1937), 466-467. Clarissa O. Lewis points out ("A Further Note on Milton's *Pro Populo Anglicano Defensio*," *The Library*, Fourth Series, XXIII [Transactions of the Bibliographical Society, Second Series, XXIII, 1943], 45-47) that the forty-odd copies in the University of Illinois Library show far more variations than those noted by Madan or by Kelley.

The *Defensio* is reprinted in CM, VII, 1-559, and the Index, on the ground that it may have been made by Milton, in CM, XVIII, 463, with notes at 632.

[John Milton, who wrote a book about divorce and *Eikonoklastes*, blatantly defends and takes on himself the crime of killing King Charles I] famosis in Magnum *Salmasium* paginis, quibus parricidium quod Orbis unquam vidit immanissimum & sceleratissimum, pietatis & justitiæ coloribus infucat.

Moulin, *Regii Sanguinis Clamor*, The Hague, 1652, p. 9.

[(Milton does this) in the famous pages to the great Salmasius, in which he paints with the colors of piety and justice the most monstrous and wicked parricide which the world has ever seen.]

Masson, who gives some selections from the book, does not include this particular passage, though at IV, 456, he gives a few preceding sentences. The *Regii Sanguinis Clamor* is in effect a retort to Milton's *Defensio*.

Postremò, in re tam arduâ & expectationis plenâ, neque civium meorum de me sive spem, sive Judicium illud fefellisse, neque exterorum quamplurimis cum doctis viris, tum rerum peritis non satisfecisse; adversarium verò, quamvis audacissimum, ita profligasse, ut animo simul & existimatione fracta cederet; triennioque toto, quo postea vixit, multa licet minatus ac fremens, nullam tamen amplius molestiam nobis exhiberet, nisi quod vilissimorum quorundam hominum obscuram operam subsidio sibi corrogaret, & laudatores nescio quos ineptos atq; immodicos, ad inopinatam ac recentem infamiam, siquo modo posset, sarciendam subornaret. . . .

Milton, *Defensio Secunda*, Hague, Vlacq, 1654, pp. 2-3; CM, VIII, 4. In my own copy the "a" of "multa" and the "li" of "licet" failed to print.

[(I thank God) last that in a task so hard and so full of ex-

pectation I did not fail to satisfy either the hope or the judgment of my fellow-citizens about me, or that of many foreigners, both scholars and men of affairs; that I routed my adversary, though he was most daring, so completely that he gave
up with his spirit and his fame broken; and that for the whole
three years which he lived thereafter, however much he threat-
ened and raged, he yet did no further harm to us except to secure for his assistance the obscure labors of certain most vile
men, and to suborn I know not what stupid and unrestrained
flatterers to repair as best he could his unexpected recent in-
famy.]

I have prosperously, God so favoring me, defended the pub-
lick cause of this commonwealth to foreiners.
Milton, *Considerations touching . . . Hirelings*, 1659, sigs. A7-A7v;
CM, VI, 44.

Him [Salmasius] Mr Milton, by the order of his Masters
answerd in *Defensio pro populo Anglicano*; both in more correct Latin, to the shame of the others Grammership, and by
much better reasoning. For Salmasius beeing a Forrainer, &
grossly ignorant of our Laws & Constitution (which in all Nations are the respective distinguishing Principles of Government) either brought no arguments from thence, or such onely
(and by him not seldom mistaken, or misapply'd) as were partially suggested to him by those whose cause hee had under-
taken; and which, having during the many yeers of our divisions
been often ventilated, receiv'd an easy solution. Nor had hee
given proof of deeper learning in that which is properly call'd
Politics, while hee made use of trite Instances, as that of the
Government of Bees, & such like to prove the preeminency of
Monarchy: and all along so confounded it with Tyranny (as
also hee did the Episcopal with Papal Government) that hee
might better have pass'd for a Defender of the grand Signor,
and the Council of Trent, then of a lawful King and a Reformed
Church. For this and reneging his former Principles hee was
by Mr Milton facetiously expos'd: Nor did hee ever reply,
though hee liv'd three yeers after.
The "earliest" biography, f. 142v; Darbishire, pp. 26-27.

[Salmasius's *Defensio Regia* provoked Milton's] Answer, Entituled, *Defensio Populi Anglicani, contra Claudium Anonymum,* &c.

Phillips, p. xxxi; Darbishire, p. 70.

Opera Latina, *Viz.*
Defensio pro populo Anglicano. *The same lately Translated into English.*

Phillips, p. [liii]; not in Darbishire.

Defensio populi anglicani.
Aubrey, f. 64; Darbishire, p. 11.

[In reply to Salmasius's *Defensio Regia*] he wrot and published (15) *Pro populo Anglicano defensio contra Claudii Anonymi alias Salmasii defensionem regiam.* Lond. 1651. fol. said to be written in more correct Latin than that of *Salmasius.* While *Milton* was writing the said book, his sight began to fail him, and before it was fully compleated, one of his eyes did absolutely perish.

Wood, I, 882; Darbishire, p. 44.

FEBRUARY 24. MANUSCRIPT COPIES OF THE *DEFENSIO.*

E. Geffroy stated in his *Étude sur les Pamphlets . . . de Milton,* Paris, 1848, p. 253, that the original manuscript of the *Defensio* was extant in the possession of Sir Francis Egerton. No verification of this statement has ever appeared. It is therefore likely, as Masson suggested (IV, 430), that Geffroy was confusing the manuscript with manuscript notes in a copy of the *Defensio* belonging to the Earl of Bridgewater (a member of the Egerton family), which will be noticed below.

However, an early manuscript copy is found in the Bodleian Library, shelf-mark MS. Rawl. Misc. [or D] 230. It is in duodecimo, written so as to imitate the printed letters of the book. In addition to the text of the book on pp. 1-245 and an index on ff. 124-129v, the volume contains quotations from Salmasius and some original poems about Salmasius and related subjects.

Another manuscript is in the Royal Library in Copenhagen (Old Royal, 8vo, 3579). Although it bears a note in an old hand, "This MSS. was written by Milton's own hand," it is not likely that such should be the case. It is described in the *46th Report of the Deputy Keeper of Public Records,* Appendix II, p. 71.

On these manuscripts see my "Autographs of John Milton," #32a, and CM, XVIII, 597.

FEBRUARY 24. PRESENTS COPIES OF *DEFENSIO* TO
FRIENDS.

Gualter Frost Ex dono Authoris.

Inscribed on the title page of a copy of the *Defensio* now in the
library of the University of Texas; reproduced through the courtesy
of Miss Fannie Ratchford, Librarian. See *Book Auction Records*, XIV
(1917), 479; my "The Autographs of John Milton," #34; CM,
XVIII, 552. Frost, like Milton, was employed by the Council of State.

[Gualter Frost, gift of the author.]

IOH. MAVRITIJ ex dono authoris.

Inscribed on the title page of a copy of the *Defensio* now in the British
Museum, shelf-mark 599.c.26; "The Autographs of John Milton,"
#40a; F. F. Madan in *The Library*, Fourth Series, IV (1923-24), 119-
145. Maurice, or Mauritius, has not been identified. See also CM, XVIII,
552.

[John Maurice, gift of the author.]

Liber Bibliothecæ Bodleyanæ ex dono Authoris. A°.D. 1651.

Inscribed on the flyleaf opposite the title page on Bodleian copy E.
H. 2. 20. Art. This is the folio edition, "Editio emendatior," No. 2 in
Madan's list above. The writing, which does not look like Milton's, is
said by Madan to be in the hand of John Rous, librarian of the Bodleian. See the *Bodleian Quarterly Record*, IV (1923), 56; my "The
Autographs of John Milton," #38; CM, XVIII, 552. Since this edition
was slightly later than the first, the gift must have been made later; but,
the date being unknown, the entry is placed here.

[A book of the Bodleian Library, gift of the author, A.D.
1651.]

Ch: Vane ex proprio dono Johannis Miltoni Authoris.

Inscribed on the flyleaf of a copy in the Harvard University Library,
14496.13.4.11F. The sprawling writing may be Vane's. The volume
belonged in 1908 to Sir R. Tangye. See *Milton Tercentenary*, 1908,
p. 118; my "The Autographs of John Milton," #37; CM, XVIII, 552.

[Charles Vane, the special gift of the author, John Milton.]

[1] Ex donatione Aūtoris Londini. Mense Aūgūst A°. 1651.

[2] Hocce Exemplar pretiosus *Autographo* ipsius Joannis
Miltoni.

Inscriptions in a copy in the Morgan Library in New York. The first
is on the title page, the second on a flyleaf. The first looks very much
like Milton's writing, the other like later writing. Inside the front cover
is a longer note, in Latin, suggesting that the second is in the hand of
the recipient of the book. The name of this owner, however, does not

[355]

appear anywhere. See *Book Prices Current*, XXIV (1910), 598; *Book Auction Records*, VII (1910), 431; Seymour de Ricci, *The Book Collector's Guide*, 1921, p. 410; my "The Autographs of John Milton," #40; CM, XVIII, 552.

[(1) Gift of the author, London, in the month of August, 1651.

(2) This is a valuable example of the autograph of John Milton himself.]

One further alleged presentation copy, the details of which are not known, may be mentioned here. It was sold by Libbie in 1889 for $15.50. See Luther S. Livingston, *Auction Prices of Books*, New York, III (1905), 229; my "The Autographs of John Milton," #39; CM, XVIII, 552.

Several other people are known to have possessed copies of the *Defensio*, though not necessarily presentation copies. (1) Emeric Bigot had one, which is described in the catalogue of his library (*Bibliotheca Bigotiana . . . Avctio die I. Mensis Julii, 1706*, part II, item 3813, page 100) as "Miltoni defensio pro populo Anglicano, adversùs Salmasium. *Lond.* 1651." Another copy is described in the same catalogue (part III, p. 41, second numbering, item 7702) as "Miltoni Defensio pro Populo Anglicano contra Defensionem Regiam, *in* 12. *Lond.* 1651." (2) Another copy belonged to the Earl of Bridgewater, who had acted the part of the elder brother in *Comus*, and who wrote on the title page: "Liber igni, Author furcâ, dignissimi" [The book is most deserving of being burned, the author of the gallows]. See Todd, I (1826), 127; *Gentleman's Magazine*, C (1830), ii, 506; Masson, IV, 531. This book, which belonged in 1826 to the Marquis of Stafford and in 1850 to Lord Francis Egerton, has now been lost sight of. (3) Herman Conring had one described in his catalogue [*Catalogvs Bibliothecæ Conringianæ*, 1694, pp. 198-199, item 150] as "Miltoni defensio pro populo Anglicano contra Salmasium. Londini *1651*." (4) One containing the signature "O Cromwell" on the title page, which may have been given to Cromwell by Milton, appeared several times in sales, was bought by Mr. A. T. White, and is now in the possession of his daughter, Mrs. Adrian Van Sinderen of Brooklyn. See my "The Autographs of John Milton," #33; CM, XVIII, 552. (5) Samuel Hartlib's copy is now in the Harvard University Library. Though not so inscribed, it may possibly have been a presentation copy. See my "The Autographs of John Milton," #36; CM, XVIII, 552. See also below under February 17, 1652. (6) A copy with the arms of Count Hoym on the side was sold in 1903 but has not been traced since; see *Book Prices Current*, XVII (1903), 344. (7) A copy belonging to Louis Henry, Comte de Loménie, and bearing his arms, was listed in his catalogue (*Illustrissimi & Excellentissimi Ludovici Henrici Comitis Castri-Brienij . . . Bibliothecæ . . . Catalogus . . . to be sold . . . 1724*, p. 5, item 63) and was sold again in 1911 (*Book Auction Records*, VIII [1911], 290). (8) A copy with two signatures and six autograph lines by Scaliger has been sold several times recently; see Luther S. Livingston, *Auction Prices of Books*, III, 229; *American Book Prices Current*, 1902, p. 352, and XV (1909), 545.

A copy of the *Defensio* alleged to contain manuscript corrections in Milton's hand is recorded; see my "The Autographs of John Milton," # 32b and 35; CM, XVIII, 552. It was sold at Sotheby's in 1890. There is no strong reason for accepting the Miltonic origin of the corrections. In the presentation copy in the Morgan Library noted above there is one minor correction.

FEBRUARY 25. PETITIONS TO COMPOUND FOR WHEAT-LEY.

To the Honourable the Commissioners for sequestration at Haberdashers Hall, The Petition of John Milton,
sheweth

That he being to compound by the late Act for certaine Land at Whateley in Oxfordshire belonging to Mr Richard Powell late of Foresthill in the same County, by reason of an extent which he hath upon the said lands by a Statute, did put in his Petition about the middle of August last, wch was referrd accordingly; but having had important business ever since by Order of the Councell of State, he hath had no time to proceed in the perfeting of his composition; and in the mean time finds that Order hath bin giv'n out from hence to forbidd his tenants to pay him rent. He therfore now desires he may have all convenient dispatch, and that the Order of sequestring may be recalld, and that the composition may be moderated as much as may bee, in regard that M^s. Powell the widow of the said Mr Richard Powell hath her cause depending before the Commissioners in the painted Chamber for breach of articles, who have adjudg'd her satisfaction to be made for the great damage don her by seizing and selling the personall Estate divers days after the Articles were seald. But by reason of the expiring of that Court she hath receivd as yet no satisfaction, and beside she hath her thirds out of that land, (wch was not considerd when her Husband followd his Composition, and lastly the taxes, freequartering, and finding of armes were not then considered, wch have bin since very great, and are likely to be greater.

And your Petitioner shall be ready to pay what shall be thought reasonable at any day that shall be appointed.

25. ffeb: 1650[/1].   John Milton.

M^r. Brereton is desired by ye Com^{rs} to pfect his report in Mr Miltons case by Tuesday next.   H. S.   E. W.

[Note in the left-hand margin:] J doe [substituted for "am ready toe"] swear that this debt for wch I am to compound according to my petition is a true & real debt, as will appear upon record

Jur. [sworn] 25. ffeb: 1650[/1].   John Milton.

Public Record Office, Composition Papers, SP Dom 23/101, pp. 925-928; *Calendar of the Committee on Compounding*, pp. 1439 ff.; Hamilton, pp. 51-52; Masson, IV, 243; CM, XVIII, 394. The signatures and the marginal note are unquestionably in Milton's own hand; the body of the document is probably, as Masson suggests, in the writing of his lawyer. We learn from the endorsements that Milton signed the paper, delivered it to the Committee, swore to it, and obtained action on it, all on the same day. On p. 928 is the note: "Milton John   Referred 25°. Feb: Delivered to me." This note was probably written by Peter Brereton, to whom one of the endorsements above is directed. In his report of March 4, 1651, Brereton refers to "your Order the 25th of ffeb: 1650, upon the Petition of John Milton."

Milton's signature to this document is often reproduced in facsimile; see my "The Autographs of John Milton," #108; Sotheby, facing p. 112; Todd 1 (1826), facing 84. Todd reproduces the marginal note as well as the signatures. In 1935 this document was on display on one of the prominent pedestals in the museum of the Public Record Office.

FEBRUARY 25 (?). SCHEDULE OR "PARTICULAR" OF INCOME FROM WHEATLEY.

A Particular of the Lands late Richard Powells of fforest Hill in the County of Oxford now under Extent, And for wch John Milton Esquire desireth to compound./.

The said Rich: Powell was seised in his De-
measne as of fee of the tythe Corne of Whatley and $\left.\begin{array}{r}\text{l\={i}}\\ \text{60 p ann\={u}}\end{array}\right.$
certaine Cottages then of the cleare Yearlye value
of ....

The said Richard was seised alsoe in his De- ⎱ lī
measne as of fee of three Yards ½ of Land arable ⎰20. p Annū
and pasture of the cleare yearely value of ....

Out of wch He craveth to be allowed for the ⎱ lī   ss   d
thirds, wch he paieth to Mrs Anne Powell the ⎰ 26. 13. 04
Relict of the said Richard Powell for her Dower

And alsoe craveth that his just Debt of three ⎱ lī
hundred pounds as he hath deposed, may be al- ⎰ 300.
lowed upon his Composition./. ....

John Milton

Public Record Office, Composition Papers, SP Dom 23/101, p. 929;
Hamilton, p. 91; my "The Autographs of John Milton," #110; CM,
XVIII, 395. Todd reproduces the signature in 1 (1826), facing p. 84.
Though undated, this document seems to be intended to accompany the
petition of February 25, 1651, which it follows directly in the original
records.

FEBRUARY 27. MOTHER-IN-LAW ANNE POWELL MAKES
AFFIDAVIT OF HUSBAND'S DEATH.

Anne Powell the Widdowe of Richard Powell of fforesthill
in y^e. County of Oxoñ Esquire maketh Oath that y^e. said Rich:
Powell her late Husband died neere the first day of January in
the yeare of our Lord one Thousand sixe Hundred fowrtie sixe,
at the Howse of M^r. John Milton Scituate in Barbican London:—
    Jur. [sworn] cōr. [before]   Anne Powell.
Com^{riis} [commissioners] 27° Feb: 1650
              R M.

Public Record Office, SP Dom 23/110, p. 547; Hamilton, pp. 50-
51; Todd, 1 (1826), 88. The year 1646 means 1646/7. This document is given under that date also. This sworn statement was undoubtedly made in connection with Mrs. Powell's petition to compound, since
it is mentioned in Brereton's report on her petition dated March 4, 1651,
given below.

FEBRUARY 27. MOTHER-IN-LAW ANNE POWELL SUB-
MITS TRUE COPIES OF INVENTORY OF JUNE 16, 1646,
AND COURT ORDER OF NOVEMBER 27, 1650.

[1] A Coppy of ye Inventory, wth: ye prices of ye goods, as they
were appraysed ye 16th. of June 1646. . . .

Vera Copia. Ex^{ta}

27° febr. 1650.   Tr: Pauncefote Regr.

[2] Die Mercurij 27° Novembris 1650. . . .

Vera Copia Ex^{ta}.   Tr. Pauncefoot Registr:

Tr: Pauncefote

27°. febr. 1650.

Endorsements on Anne Powell's inventory of June 16, 1646, and the
court order to Matthew Appletree of November 27, 1650, *q.v.* Like
her affidavit of her husband's death, made on this same day, these
records were mentioned in Brereton's report on her petition dated
March 4, 1651.

FEBRUARY 27. APPEARANCE OF *DEFENSIO* NOTED IN
JOURNAL.

La résponse faite au Livre injurieux du Sr de Saumaise par
le Sr Jean Milton l'un des secrétaires du Conseil d'estat, sortit
au jour lundi dernier, au grand contentement et approbation
d'un chacun.

This quotation has already appeared under date of February 24
to fix the date of appearance of the *Defensio*. The date of February 27
for the present entry is fixed by the fact that it is the latter of the two
dates given for the issue of the journal, which is dated as covering the
week February 20-27 (English style).

[The reply made to the injurious book of M. de Saumaise
by Mr. John Milton, one of the secretaries of the Council of
State, came out on Monday last, to the great content and approval of everybody.]

FEBRUARY 28. HAS RECEIVED £108 IN INTEREST ON
POWELL DEBT.

. . . J have received att seüall tymes in part of satisfacĉon of
my said iust and principall debt with daṁages for the same

and my costs of suite the some of one hundred and fowerscore
pounds or thereabouts. . . .

From Milton's affidavit of this date, *q.v.*

FEBRUARY 28. AFFIDAVIT CONCERNING RICHARD
POWELL'S DEBT.

Whereas Richard Powell of fforresthill in the Countie of
Oxford geñt and William Hearne late Cittizen and Goldsmith
of London deceased, By their writing or recognizance of the nature of a statute staple beareing date the eleaventh day of June
wch was in the third yeare of the raigne of the late King Charles
of England &c made and provided for the recoũy of debts And
taken acknowledged & sealed before S^r: Nicholas Hide K^t: then
Lord cheife Justice of the Court then called the Kings Bench
att Westm^r did acknowledge themselves to owe vnto John
Milton then of the Vniversity of Cambridge geñl sonne of John
Milton Cittizen and Scrivener of London the some of fiue hundred pounds of lawfull money of England, Which said statute
or recognizance is by a writing beareing even date therewith
defeazanced for the payment of the some of three hundred and
twelue pounds of like money vnto the said John Milton the
sonne his Executors, Adm^rs or Assignes on the twelueth day of
December then next ensuing, As by the said statute or recognizance and defeazance therevpon wherevnto relacõn being had
more att large may appeare Now J John Milton the sonne
(being one and the same partie before mencõned for Cognizee
in the said statute or recognizance) doe make oath that (since
the extending of the said statute) J have received att seũall
tymes in part of satisfaccõn of my said iust and principall debt
with damãages for the same and my costs of suite the some of
one hundred and fowerscore pounds or thereabouts, And that
there is yett remayneing due and oweing vnto mee of my said
principall money interest and costs of suite the some of three
hundred pounds or thereabouts, And J doe further make oath,
That neither J the said John Milton or any other for mee or by
my direccõn privity or consent haue or hath released or other-

wise discharged the said statute or recognizance Neither doe J
know or conceiue any reason or cause either in law or equity
why J should not receiue the said remainder of my said debt,
damages and costs of suite./

Jur̄

John Milton/ { Jur. cor. Com^ris [sworn before
the commissioners] 28° Feb 1650
E. Winslow

[Endorsed:] Milton John Esqz
4° Martij 1650
fine 130^li.

Public Record Office, Composition Papers, SP Dom 23/101, p. 931;
Todd, 1 (1826), 86; Hamilton, p. 95; CM, XVIII, 396. Masson (IV,
244) mentions it without giving the text. Presumably the signature
alone is in Milton's hand. The endorsement, added on March 4, indicates the action taken by the commissioners; other more detailed accounts will be found below under that date. A few miscellaneous notes
and figures of no particular significance are also found on the dorso; one
of them, "Milton 1298," is probably a filing number added at a later
time.

ABOUT THE END OF FEBRUARY (?). REWARDED FOR WRITING *DEFENSIO* (?).

Sed fortasse, mi homo, mi formosule homuncio, contraria
tibi tua vota sunt. Nam, si hoc fieret, periculum esset, ne non
tantum tibi jam restaret in bonis, quantum accepisti ob proditum
Regem tuum, & ad parricidii causam tutandam. Quatuor millia
librarum te inde jam in reditu habere ferunt, qui mentiri nes-
ciunt.

Salmasius, *Ad Johannem Miltonum Responsio, Opus Posthumum,*
1660, p. 16. Although not published until 1660, this book was written
before 1653, the date of Salmasius's death, and the ideas in it were in
considerable circulation among the members of his circle.

[But perhaps, my man, my pretty little man, your vows are
contrary to you. For if this should be the case, there would be a
danger that not so much goods would remain to you as you have
received for betraying the king and for defending the cause of
parricide. Those who do not know how to lie say that you have
already received in return four thousand pounds.]

[362]

Hanc intra privatos parietes meam operam nunc Ecclesiæ, nunc Reipublicæ gratis dedi; mihi vicissim vel hæc vel illa præter incolumitatem nihil.

Milton, *Defensio Secunda*, Hague, Vlacq, p. 69; CM, VIII, 137.

[This work of mine, done within my own walls, I gave without return, at one time to the church, at another to the commonwealth; neither the former nor the latter gave me in return anything but safety.]

Milton was rewarded with a thousand Pounds for this performance [*Defensio*].

John Toland, *The Life of John Milton*, 1698, p. 32; Darbishire, p. 158.

Salmasius in his *Responsio*, p. 16. says the Parliament allowed him 4000 Livres Annually for Writing for them. . . . 1000 *l.* 'tis said was besides given him for Writing his *Defence of the People of England*.

Richardson, p. xcviii; Darbishire, p. 279. It might be added that Masson (IV, 321-322) vigorously denies that Milton received any special fee for writing the book other than his regular salary as Secretary. Richardson's fantastic figure may be checked from entries of Milton's salary elsewhere in the present book.

END OF FEBRUARY (?). DURER PROTESTS AGAINST THE *DEFENSIO* (?).

. . . il declare que l'asprete qui est au liure de Monsr. Milton lui a tellement depleu qu'il a tesmoigne le mescontentement qu'il en auoit a l'autheur mesme aussi tost que le liure fust imprime.

From Dury's letter of May 30, 1655, given below.

[Durer declares that the sharpness in Mr. Milton's book so displeased him that he made known his disapproval to the author himself as soon as the book was printed.]

FAME OF *DEFENSIO*.

Nor was the heroic cause unsuccessfully defended to all Christendom against the tongue of a famous and thought invincible adversarie; nor the constancie and fortitude that so nobly vindicated our liberty, our victory at once against two the most prevailing usurpers over mankinde, superstition and tyrannie unprais'd or uncelebrated in a written monument, likely to outlive detraction, as it hath hitherto convinc'd or silenc'd not a few of our detractors, especially in parts abroad.

Milton, *The Ready and Easy Way*, 1659, p. 6; CM, VI, 116. This vague, undated reference is put here at the time of the appearance of the *Defensio* for lack of a better place. Other more definite allusions will be noted under their appropriate dates. The following reference is similarly undatable.

. . . adversarium verò, quamvis audacissimum, ita profligasse, ut animo simul & existimatione fracta cederet. . . .

Milton, *Defensio Secunda*, 1654, The Hague, Vlacq, pp. 2-3; CM, VIII, 4.

[. . . I truly so routed my opponent, most bold though he was, that he yielded with both his spirit and his fame shattered.]

Qua [in Sweden] statim à pluribus perlecta, Regina quidem, quæ & ipsa cumprimis perlegerat . . . tanta animorum facta subito mutatio est, ut qui nudiustertius summa gratia floruerat, nunc penè obsolesceret; nec ita multo post discedens num bona venia hoc uno in dubio permultis relinqueret, honoratiorne advenerit, an contemptior abierit.

Milton, *Defensio Secunda*, 1654, The Hague, Vlacq, pp. 8-9; CM, VIII, 16. The London edition, used as the text for CM, has "cum" for "num" and "unum" for "uno."

[Here it was read at once by several, by the Queen for example, who herself read it most carefully. . . . Such a change in opinion was suddenly wrought that he who had formerly flourished in the highest favor was now almost forgotten; and going away soon after by permission, he left with this one question in the minds of many people: whether he had come with greater honor or left in deeper disgrace.]

. . . our little *English David* had the Courage to undertake this great *French Goliah*, to whom he gave such a hit in the Forehead, that he presently staggered, and soon after fell; for immediately upon the coming out of the Answer, Entituled, *Defensio Populi Anglicani, contra Claudium Anonymum*, &c.

he that till then had been Chief Minister and Superintendant in the Court of the Learned *Christina* Queen of *Sweden*, dwindled in esteem to that degree, that he at last vouchsafed to speak to the meanest Servant. In short, he was dismiss'd with so cold and slighting an Adieu, that after a faint dying Reply, he was glad to have recourse to Death, the remedy of Evils, and ender of Controversies.

Phillips, p. xxxi; Darbishire, p. 70.

INDEX

Abbott, Wilbur C., vi
——, *Bibliography of Oliver Cromwell*, 296, 347
——, *Letters and Speeches of Oliver Cromwell*, see Cromwell
Abra River, see Humber
Academy, 47, 337
Actaean, 172, 173
Acts (Bible), 46
Adam, 24
Adams, Mr., 220
Adams, Philip, 86
Address, Office of, 169
Admiralty Committee, 282, 306
Adriani, Messrs., 222, 223
Aegeus, 206
Aegle, 17, 21
Aegon, 17, 20
Aelian, *Tactica*, 6
Aethra, 206
Agag, 254
Agatha, Council of, 93
Agathias, 94
Aikin, John, *Lives of John Selden, Esq. and Archbishop Usher*, 308
Aizema, Leo, 98, 123, 125
Alabaster, William, 213
"Alas, poor Parliament, how art thou betrayed!", 116
Alaunus (Alan) River, 18, 23
Alciati, Andrea, *Parerga*, 94
Aldersgate Street, 9, 10, 32, 34, 40, 43, 44, 45, 56, 82, 102, 117, 126, 129, 228, 263, 298
Aldgate, 104
Aldwinkle, co. Northants, 177
Alexander, Jerome, 163
Alexandria, 28, 29
Alfrey (Alphry), Mr., 10
Alfrey, Richard, 10
Alfrey, Thomas, 10
Algiers, 281, 282, 293
All Souls' College, Oxford, 45, 47, 328
Allen, Robert J., *Clubs of Augustan London*, 294
Almack, Edward, *Bibliography of the King's Book, or Eikon Basilike*, 225-227
Almoni, Peloni, *Compendious Discourse*, 33, 37-39
Alphesiboeus, 17, 20

Alphry, see Alfrey
Alpine, 17, 22
Alsop, B., printer, 286
Ambrose, St., 93, 94
American Book Prices Current, 357
Ames (Amesius), William, 5, 7
Amsterdam, 275
Amyntas, 17, 20
Anabaptists, 294
Anacreon, 203
Andalusia, 330; see also Lewis
Andreini, Giovanni Battista, *Adamo*, 51
Andrewes, Lancelot, *Summary view of the Government both of the Old and New Testament*, 28, 29
Anglesey, Arthur Annesley, first Earl of, 226
Anglesey, Earl of (another), 138
Answer to . . . Doctrine and Discipline of Divorce, 108, 111, 112, 124, 125
Anthemius, 73, 77
Antioch, 28, 29
Antiquarian Magazine and Bibliographer, 135
Antiquaries, Society of, 295, 296
Antwerp, 340-342, 351
Apocalypse, see Revelation
Apollo (Phoebus), 175, 176
Apollonius Rhodius, *Argonautica*, 6, 8
Appletree, Matthew, 148, 149, 313, 331, 332, 360
Appletree, Richard, 331
Appletree, Thomas, 154, 306, 310
Aquinas, St. Thomas, 169
Aratus, 8, 95
——, *Phaenomena* and *Diosemeia*, 6
Arber, Edward, see Stationers' Registers
Arcetri, 71, 74
Archimedes, 73, 77
Archivist, 36
Aretius, *Problems*, 94
Ariadne, 206
Ariosto, Lodovico, 23, 73, 77
——, *Orlando Furioso*, 78
Aristotle, 48
Armagh, Bishop of, see Ussher, James
Armorica, 18, 23
Armstrong, J. Tarbotton, 1, 2
Arnisaeus, 94
Arthur, King, 18, 23

Arviragus (Arvirach), 18, 23
Ascham, Anthony, 297, 318, 346
Ascham, Roger, 236
Ashburnham, Earl of, Catalogue . . . Of Books . . . of, 98, 99
Ashe, John, 275
Ashworth, Mr., 160, 163, 323
Ashworth, Edward, 327, 328
Ashworth, Mrs. Elizabeth, 2, 25, 46, 58, 82, 93, 103, 118, 195, 199, 210, 212, 217, 220, 221, 239, 246, 261, 268, 303, 305, 327, 328, 330
Ashworth, Thomas, 163
Asia, 28
Assembly of Divines, 117, 126, 170
Assembly of the Synod, 321
Assyrian, 204
Athenaeum, 1, 84, 127, 128, 147, 201
Athens, 27
Atomy, Mrs., see Attaway
Attaway (Atomy), Mrs., 145
Attis, 203
Aubrey, John, 219
———, *Brief Lives*, see MS. Aubrey 8 (Bodleian)
———, *Wiltshire, Topographical Collections*, ed. Jackson, 70
Augier, Mr., 317
Austin (Augustine), St., 93
Austria, 303
Autograph Prices Current, 239
Aylett, Robert, 179
Ayres, Henry, 81

B., J., commissioner, 333
B., S., printer, 258
Bachiler, John, 142, 143
Bacon, Nathaniel (?), 116
Baillie, Robert, 164
———, *Dissuasive from the Errors of the Time*, 132, 133, 142
———, *Letters and Journal*, 30, 31, 133, 143, 164
Baker, Mr., 295, 336
Baker, Sir Richard, 52
Ball, George, 327
Balsamon, 94
Banbury, 153, 154, 310
Bancroft, Richard, Archbishop of Canterbury, 37
Banquet of Jests, 11, 12
Barberini, Cardinal Francesco, 71, 74, 75

Barbican, 119, 122, 128, 129, 173, 182, 199, 200, 359
Barker, A., "Milton's Schoolmaster," 32
Barker, John, 283
Barker, R., printer, 65
Barnard, John, 30
Baron, Richard, 283
Baron, Robert, *Erotopaignion, or the Cyprian Academy*, 184, 215
———, *Pocula Castalia*, 315
Baroni, Leonora, singer, 71, 75
Barrimore, Richard Barry, second Earl of, 9, 10, 183
Barry, Richard, see Barrimore
Bartolini, Thomas, 191
Barton, William, 144, 157, 161, 162
Basil, St., 93
Basilius, 94
Bastide, Charles, "Les gazettes françaises de Londres au XVIIe siècle," 347, 351
Bateman, Richard, 45
Bateman, William, 218
Baucis, 17, 21
Baxter, Wynne E., 39, 52
Baylie, Robert, see Baillie
Bayly, T., 158
Baynton, Mr., 107
Beale, John, 306
Beamont, Mr., 29
Beaumont, Stephen, 32
Begley, Walter, *Novae Solymae*, 216
Belfast, 250
Belgium, 303
Belinus, 18, 23
Belisarius, 48
Beller, Elmer A., "Milton and *Mercurius Politicus*," 311
Belloc, Hilaire, *Milton*, 5
Bellum Episcopale, see Bishops' War
Bely, Maldon, Essex, 127
Bembo, Pietro, 27
Bennet, John, 218
Berecynthia, 203
Bernard, Francis, 227
Bernard, Richard, 30
Best, Paul, *Mysteries Discovered*, 170
Bèze (Beza), Théodore de, 94, 169
Bible, bookshop, 37, 40
Bible, Milton's, see Milton
Bibliographical Society Transactions, 352

Bibliotheca Bigotiana, 356
Bibliothèque Nationale, vi, 347
Bidenbachius, Felix, 94
Bigot, Emeric, 356
Bindley, James, 106
Birch, Colonel John, 275
Birch, Thomas, 65, 66, 220, 252
———, *Complete Collection of . . .*
Milton, see Milton
Bishops' War, 248
Blackborough, see Blackborow
Blackborow, Mr., 119
Blackborow, Abraham, 120, 126
Blackborow, Hester, 120, 126, 147
Blackborow, Jane, 126
Blackborow, Joan, 126
Blackborow, William, 126, 127, 147
Blackborow, William, younger, 126, 147
Blackburne, Francis, *Memoirs of Thomas Hollis*, 282, 283, 337, 338
Blackwater Bay (Essex), see Chelmer River
Blagrave, Daniel (?), 275
Blake, Robert, Admiral, 332
Blakiston, Noel, vi
Bliss, Philip, 284; see also Wood, Anthony, *Athenae Oxonienses*
Blue Anchor, bookshop, 259
Boccaccio, Giovanni, 73, 77
Bodleian Library, 113, 115, 138-140, 142, 174-176, 355
Bodleian Quarterly Record, 355
Boiardo, Matteo Maria, *Orlando Innamorato*, 86, 87
Bond, Dennis (?), 321
Bonnard, G. A., 114, 115
Book Auction Records, 259, 355, 356
Book-Lore, 320
Book Prices Current, 85, 138, 280, 356
Bookworm, 128
Borrowhill Copse, 261, 262
Bostock, Robert, printer, 127
Boston, Massachusetts, 281
Botsford, Mr., 29
Bottsford (Botsford), William, 29, 32
Bourne, Mr., 12
Bourne, Nicholas, bookseller, 347
Bourse, see Exchange
Bower, Thomas, 13, 14
Boys, John, 327
Brackley, Viscount, see Bridgewater

Bradshaw, John, 226, 227, 243, 269, 278, 296, 301, 316, 330
Bradshaw, Richard, 303, 304
Brainford, see Brentford
Bramhall, John, Archbishop of Armagh, 336, 340, 341
———, *Serpent Salve*, 83
———, *Works*, 83
Bray, Dr., 12
Bread Street, 183, 245, 246, 263, 270, 277, 302, 303, 319
Breckly Copse, 261, 262
Breda, 275
Brennecke, Ernest, 43, 86
———, *John Milton the Elder and his Music*, 12, 182
Brennus, 18, 23
Brent, Sir Nathaniel, 129, 184, 272
Brentford (Brainford), 84
Brereton, Peter, 155, 323, 324, 328, 329, 332, 358-360
Brerewood, Edward, *Patriarchical Government of the Ancient Church*, 28, 29
Brewster, Thomas, bookseller, 282
Bridges, Thomas, 127
Bridgewater, Earl of, 354
Bridgewater, John Egerton, Viscount Brackley, second Earl of, 79, 348, 356
Bridgewater family, 259
Bridgewater, co. Somerset, 110
Bridgewater House, 79
British, 18, 23
British Museum, 97, 98, 115, 225, 338
Britons, 18, 23
Brome (Browne), Edmund, 325, 343
Brooke, Robert Greville, second Lord, *Discourse Opening . . . Episcopacy*, 45, 46
Brooklyn, 115, 356
Brooks, Anthony, 86
Brooks Wharf, 92
Brown(e), Edmond, see Brome
Brown, John, 92
Brownbakers' Hall, 29, 32
Browne, Sir Richard, 199
Browne, Sir Thomas, 128
Brownists, 132
Bucer, Martin, 28, 91, 92, 94, 100, 105, 106, 109

————, *De Regno Christi*, 88, 91
Buchanan, George, 285
————, *Baptistes*, 85
Bull-Head Tavern, 237, 273
Bullington, co. Oxon., 201
Bunny, Edmund, *Of Divorce for Adultery*, 169
Burman, Peter, 244
————, *Sylloges Epistolarum*, 322
Burnell, Thomas, 218
Burton, Mr., 110
Burton, Robert, 128
Bury, J., 144
Butter, Nathaniel, printer, 12, 30-32, 42, 44
Byfield, Adoniram (?), 321

C., T., *Glass for the Times*, 218
Cadbury, John, see Gadbury
Caernarvon, 283
Caesar, Julius, 247
Calaber, Quintus, 6, 8
Calamy, Edmund, 212
Calendar of Clarendon Papers, 185
Calendar of the Committee for Compounding, 150, 155-158, 161, 162, 273, 276, 310, 313, 323, 326, 328, 329, 358
Calendars of State Papers, 234, 236, 238-240, 245, 250, 251, 255-257, 269, 270, 273-275, 282, 286, 292, 293, 295, 299, 300, 302, 304, 306-309, 312, 314-318, 321, 334, 335, 344, 349
Calendrium Carolinum, 319
Callimachus, 49
Calves' Head Club, 293, 294
Calvin, John, 94
Cambridge, 135
Cambridge Bibliography of English Literature, 255, 312
Cambridge Manuscript, Milton's, see MS. Milton's Minor Poems
Cambridge, Massachusetts, 294, 296
Cambridge University, 192, 193, 361
Camden Society Publications, 4, 333, 337
Canaan, 145
Candy, Hugh C. H., 83, 318
Canne, John, *Discoverer*, 257
Canterbury, 1
Capito, 94

Carberry, Richard Vaughan, Earl of, 282, 283
Cardenas, Lord Alphonsus à, 345
Carill, see Caryl
Carswell, Mr., 92
Cartagena, 331, 332
Carter, John, see Caster
Caryl, Joseph, 108, 111, 238
Cassibelaunus, 18, 22
Castelvetro, Lodovico, 203
Caster, Harbert, 13
Caster (Carter), John, 13
Caster, Sylvester, 13
Castri-Brienii, Ludovici Henrici, Comitis . . . *Catalogus*, 356
Casuists, 169
Catalogue of Prints and Drawings in the British Museum, 44, 192
Catalogue of the Milton Collection of . . . Wynne E. Baxter, 39
Catalogue of the severall Sects and Opinions in England, 174
Catalogue of the Stowe Manuscripts in the British Museum, 264
Catalogus Bibliothecae Conringianae, 356
Catalogus . . . Collegii . . . Trinitatis . . . Dublin, 36
Catechesis Ecclesiarum in regno Poloniae & ducatu Lithuaniae, 321
Cathay, vi, 267
Cato, 8
————, *De Re Rustica*, 6
Catsfield, co. Sussex, 10
Catullus, 203
————, "Argonauts," 205
Caucasus, 206
Celsus, Cornelius, 6
Censura Literaria, 236
Chalcedon, 28
Chaldee, 7
Challenor, Mr., 295, 308
Chambers, Mr., 307
Chamier, 93
Charing Cross, 237, 273
Charlemagne, 48
Charles I, King of England, 64, 68, 69, 80, 81, 84, 85, 93, 118, 119, 127, 134-136, 145, 155, 157, 162, 163, 171, 172, 177, 179, 192, 193, 195, 197-199, 225, 229-231, 233-235, 244-249, 254, 255, 257, 258, 264,

265, 275, 276, 277, 284, 293, 294, 302, 308, 319, 320, 340, 341, 352, 353

————, *Eikon Basilike*, 225-228, 234, 235, 237, 238, 244, 255, 258, 259, 263, 265, 266, 282, 301, 308, 309, 333, 336; see also (1) Salmasius's *Defensio*, (2) Milton's *Defensio*

Charles II, King of England, 225, 243, 244, 246, 248, 249, 258, 340, 341

Charybdis, 311

Chasles, Monsieur, 57

Chatterton, Thomas, 1

Cheapside, 246

Chelmer River (Idumanian River or Blackwater Bay, Essex), 17, 21

Cheshire, 285

Chetham Society Publications, 188, 207, 285

Chiabrera, Gabriel, 205, 206

————, *Canzonetta*, 203

Child, William, 13, 14

Chimentelli, Valerio, 222, 224

Chimentelli, the younger, 187, 188, 191

China, 214

Chinese, 282

Chiswell, Richard (?), printer, 228

Chloris, 17, 21

Chorus Vatum, see MS. Add. 24, 487-24, 492

Christ, Jesus, 68, 69, 88-90, 122, 129, 164, 170, 171, 211-213, 216

Christina, Queen of Sweden, 364, 365

Christ's College, Cambridge, 1, 25, 337

Church, Thomas, 196, 198

Church of England, 34, 83, 123, 124

Churchman, Theophilus, see Heylyn, Peter

Cipriani, Giovanni Battista, portrait painter, 337

Clapmarius, Mr., 305

Clarendon, Edward Hyde, Earl of, 236

————, *State Papers Collected by*, 185

Clark, A., ed., *Life and Times of Anthony Wood*, 266

Clarke, Mr., 29

Clarke, Deborah (Milton), daughter, 64, 65, 338

Clarke, Elizabeth, see Foster

Clarke, Richard, 196, 198

Cleave, 243

Clement, theologian, 45, 46

Clementillo, see Chimentelli

Cleveland, John, "The King's Disguise," 171, 172

Clio, muse, 130

Clontno, John, 149

Colchester, 219

Colkyer, James, 195, 197

Collier, Mr., 169

Colne River, 18, 22

Coltellini (Cultellino), Agostino, 187, 191, 222, 224

Columbia Manuscript, see MS. Columbia

Columbia University, vi

Columella, 6

————, *De Re Rustica*, 8

Comberbach, Roger, 134

Comenius, Johann Amos, 82; see also Turnbull, G. H., *Hartlib, Dury and Comenius*

Commissioners for Breach of Articles, 357

Commissioners for Relief upon Articles of War, 271, 272, 312, 314, 323, 325, 331

Commissioners of Great Seal, 177, 304

Commissioners of Navy, 306

Committee for Compounding with Delinquents, 155, 156, 158, 159, 310, 325, 326, 328

Committee of Army, 315

Commons, House of, 32, 85, 86, 122, 170, 251-253, 334

Comptes Rendus hebdomadaires des sceances de l'academie des sciences, 57, 60, 61, 67, 74, 78

Conring, Herman, 356

Constantine, 94

Conti, Natale, *Mythology*, 205

Contrera, Don Fernando Ruiz de, 330-332

Cooke, Colonel, 272

Cooper, William, 86, 195, 197

Cope, Sir Anthony, 2, 13, 25, 36, 46

Cope, Lady Elizabeth, 2, 13, 25, 36, 46

Cope, Sir John, 2, 13

Cope, William, 168, 193, 195, 197, 199

Corasius, 94

I Corinthians, 88, 94, 123, 124

Corker, Mr., 29

Corker, Robert, 32

Cornelius, Mr., 185

Cornhill, 259
Coster, John, 298
Council of State, 234-236, 238-240, 245, 250, 252, 253, 256, 257, 259, 260, 269, 274-276, 278, 282, 286, 292, 293, 295, 296, 299, 300, 301, 304, 306-308, 309, 312, 314-317, 321, 334, 335, 349-351, 355, 357, 360
Court Book of the Worshipful Company of Goldsmiths, see MS. Court Book
Court of Chancery, 179, 181, 192-194, 211, 256
Court of King's Bench, 200, 361
Courthope, Mr., 277
Coward, William, M. D., 177
Cowley, Abraham, 213
Cowper, William, 134
Coxe, Dr., 219
Coxe, Benjamin (?), 169
Cragg, Mr., 29
Cragg, John, 32
Cranford, Mr., 101
Cranmer, Thomas, Archbishop of Canterbury, 52, 83
Crashaw, Richard, 213
Crates, 55
Creusa, 172, 173
Crewkerne, 111
Cromwell, Oliver, 199, 219, 226, 228, 235-237, 281, 294-296, 308, 356
————, *Writings and Speeches*, ed. W. C. Abbott, 238-240
Cross Keys, Ludgate, 156, 157
Cruquius, 205
Crynes, Nathaniel, 142
Cuddesdon (Cudsden), 160, 162, 196, 197
Cullimore, W., v
Culpepper, Sir Cheney, 132
Cunningham, Peter, *London*, 200, 237, 273, 281
Curson, Sir John, 166
Cytherea, see Venus

D., G., printer, 37
DNB, see *Dictionary of National Biography*
Dalmatius, 94
Damon (i.e., Charles Diodati), 16, 186, 189
Dante, 73, 77, 187, 190
Dantine, Ramis (?), 169

Danvers, Sir John, 254
Danzig, 348
Darbishire, Helen, 114, 115
————, ed., *The Early Lives of Milton*, 2 et seq.
Dardanian, see Trojan
Dati, Carlo, 5, 6, 24, 27, 134, 170, 171, 184, 185, 188-190, 201-209, 215, 221-223
David (i. e., Milton), 248, 364
Davis, Dr., 118
Davis, Miss, 117-119
Davity, Pierre, 7
Dawson, Mr., 29, 238; see also Lawson
Declaration of the Commons . . . Against . . . the Second Part of England's New Chains Discovered, 240
Declaration of the Parliament of England upon the Marching of the Army into Scotland, 317, 318
Dedington, 310
Del Rio, Martin, 205
Delahay, Henry, 166
Delamere, Lord, v, 82, 104, 116, 132, 169, 219, 278, 306
Delilah, 84
della Casa, Giovanni, 95
della Certa, Lodovico, 205
Delos, 175, 176
Delphic, 172, 173
Denbigh, Basil Fielding, second Earl of, 234
Dendy, Edward, Sergeant-at-Arms, 240, 256, 257, 269, 299, 300, 307, 316
Denton, W., *Records of St. Giles' Cripplegate*, 182
Deputy Keeper of Public Records, Reports of, 354
Dering, Sir Edward, 31, 39
Derry, 336
Deuteronomy, 88, 123, 124
Devil, 43, 54, 219
Devizes, 70
Dictionary of National Biography, 53, 214, 283, 336
Digby, Sir Kenelm, 32
Diodati, Charles, 16-24; see also Damon
Diodati, John, *Pious Annotations upon the Holy Bible*, 83
Dion Chrysostom, 95
Dionysius Afer, 8
————, *De Situ Orbis*, 6
Disney, John, 259, 337

Dixon, James, 5
Doni, Giovanni, 222, 223
Dorchester, co. Oxon, 201
Dorian, Donald C., vi
Dorislaus, Isaac, 251
Dove, John (?), 169
Downer, John, 14
Downer, Rose, 13, 14
Downes, Mr., 31, 37
Downham, John (?), 105, 216
Draper, William, 154, 306, 310
*Dreer, Ferdinand Julius, Catalogue of
the Collection of Autographs*, 299
Drummond's Bank, 237
Dryope, 17, 21
Dublin, 83
Duck, Arthur, 13, 14
Dugard, Mrs., 301
Dugard, William, printer, 226-228, 301,
302, 335, 341, 347, 351
Duke, Grand, of Florence (?), 222,
223
Duke Street, 281
Duke's Place, London, 116, 132
Du Moulin, see Moulin
Dundas, Sir David, 114
Dunster, T., printer, 286
Dunster Castle, 316
Durer, Mr., 363
Dury, John, 82, 104, 105, 169, 283,
321; see also Turnbull, G. H., *Hart-
lib, Dury and Comenius*
———, *Considerations concerning the
Present Engagement*, 285
———, *Just Re-proposals to Humble
Proposals*, 285
———, *Objections against the Taking
of the Engagement answered*, 285
Dutch, 317, 342
Dutch ambassador, 251

ELH, 3
Earle, John, 258, 336
"Earliest" biography of Milton, see
MS. Wood D4
Edgman, William, 275
Edinburgh, 302
Edmunds, Richard, 81
Edward VI, King of England, 105,
106, 123, 124
Edward, Prince, 243
Edwards, Thomas, *Gangraena*, 143,
144, 145, 146, 164

Egerton, Alice, 283
Egerton, Sir Francis, 354, 356
Egerton, John, see Bridgewater
Eglesfield, F., printer, 258
Eikon Alethine, 259, 264, 275
Elderston Copse, 261, 262
Eldridge, Mr., 147
Eliberis, Council of, 93
Elizabeth, Lady, 241
Ellis, Messrs., booksellers, 316, 317
Ellstone, John, 166
Ellwood, Thomas, 295
———, *Life of Himself*, 295
Ely, Benjamin, 43
Ely Cathedral, 95
Elzevir, printer, 351
Emmanuel College, Cambridge, 213,
214
Encyclopaedia Britannica, 93
Englische Studien, 313
Ephesus, 28
Epiphanius, 93
Erasmus, Desiderius, 88, 92, 94
Erato, muse, 130
Erectheus, 172, 173
*Essays and Studies by Members of the
English Association*, 11
Essex, Robert Devereux, third Earl of,
85, 86, 116
Essex county, 9, 10, 183, 314, 315
Eton College, 246
Etudes Anglaises, 30, 44
Euphrosyne, 184
Euripides, 48, 95, 114, 115
———, *Hicetidae*, 113
———, *Medea*, 123
Eusebius, St., 93
Evans, Florence M. G., *Principal Sec-
retary of State*, 236
Evans, Mathew, see Ewens
Evelyn, John, 138
Ewelme (Yewelme), 327
Ewens, Alexander, 14
Ewens (Evans), Matthew, 13, 14
Ewens, Matthew, Jr., 14
Exchange (Bourse), 347
Exeter, co. Devon, 12, 133, 144, 145,
155, 157, 158, 277, 278
Eyre, see Stationers' Registers

Fabroni, Angelo, *Vitae Italorum*, 191,
207
Facsimiles of National Manuscripts, 243

Fagius, Paulus, 88, 94

Fairfax, Thomas, Baron Fairfax, 133, 144, 151, 152, 162, 199, 200, 218, 219

Faithful Portraiture of a Loyal Subject, in vindication of Eikon Basilike, 259

Faithorne, William, painter, 131, 281

Farnaby, Thomas, *Systema Grammaticum,* 29

Farre, Laurence, 146, 335

Farrerus, 94

Farringdon-Magna, co. Berks, 334

Featley, Daniel, *Dippers Dipt,* 122, 123, 129, 136, 337

Fellowes, Robert, 230

Fevardentius, 39

Field, John, printer, 85

Flaccus, Valerius, *Argonautica,* 204

Fleet Street, London, 8, 112, 159

Fleetwood, Charles, 53, 54, 177

Fleetwood, Sir William, 177

Fletcher, Harris, *Contributions to a Milton Bibliography,* 320

————, editor, *John Milton's Complete Poetical Works,* see Milton, John, *Complete Poetical Works*

Florence, 70-72, 75, 76, 184-186, 188-190, 202, 203, 207-209, 222-224

Florentine Academy, 222, 223

Flower de Luce, Wells, 111

Floyd, Dr., 81

Fogg Art Museum, Harvard University, 281

Forest Hill (Forsthill, Fosthill), co. Oxon, 14, 15, 46, 61-64, 66-70, 80, 84, 86, 134, 146, 148, 150, 152, 155, 160-162, 164-167, 173, 177, 179, 192, 193, 201, 211, 261-263, 271, 272, 275, 312, 322, 323, 325-328, 331-335, 342, 343, 357-359, 361

Forsthill, see Forest Hill

Fortescue, G. K., ed. Thomason Catalogue, see Thomason, George

Foster, Elizabeth (Clarke), granddaughter, 65, 279

Foster, Joseph, ed., *Register of Admissions to Gray's Inn,* 10

Foster, Thomas, grandson-in-law, 338

Fosthill, see Forest Hill

Fountain, Mr., lawyer, 13

Fox, William, 104

France, 7, 71, 74, 77, 192, 193, 195, 197, 243, 284, 340

Francini, Antonio, 5, 6, 187, 191, 222, 224

French, 7, 57, 78, 112, 202, 207, 208, 235, 258, 317

French, J. Milton, "The Autographs of John Milton," 1 *et seq.*

————, "Baptism of Milton's Daughter Mary," 220

————, "Chips from Milton's Workshop," 3

————, "Date of Milton's First *Defense,*" 347

————, *Milton in Chancery,* 14 *et seq.*

————, "Milton, Needham, and *Mercurius Politicus,*" 311, 329, 350

————, "Mute Inglorious John Miltons," 200

————, "Powell-Milton Bond," 193, 197

Frescobaldi, Pietro, 187, 191, 222, 224

Frontinus, *Stratagemata,* 6

Frost, Gualter, 245, 299, 309, 321, 355

Frost, Gualter, the younger, 299, 300

Frost, Joseph, 349

Fuller, Thomas, *The Holy State,* 52, 53

Fulton, Dr. John, v, 98, 113-115, 228, 264

Furseman, George, 15, 332, 333, 343, 344; see also Horseman

G., E., printer, 39, 55, 59

G., J., 302

Gadbury (Cadbury), John, 217

Gaddian Academy, 188, 191

Galilei, Vincenzo, 222, 224

Galileo, astronomer, 60, 61, 67, 70-78

Gallus, Cornelius, *Elegy,* 205

Gardiner, Samuel R., *History of the Commonwealth,* 312

Gardiner, Sir Thomas, 9, 10, 183

Gardner, Thomas, 210

Garret, William, 84

Garrod, H. W., "Milton's Lines on Shakespeare," 11

Gataker, Thomas, 212

Gatehouse prison, 170, 307

Gauden, John, Bishop of Exeter, 226

Gay collection, Harvard, 40, 240

Geffroy, A., *Etude sur les Pamphlets Politiques et Religieux de Milton,* 113, 354

Gellius, Aulus, 205
Geminus, 6
General Theological Seminary (New York), 44
Genesis, 123, 124, 129, 171
Gentleman's Magazine, 1, 182, 281, 337, 356
Gerard, 94
Gherard, Francis, 86, 87
Gibraltar, 293
Gilbert, Allan H., 133
Gilded Lion, bookshop, 228, 263, 298
Gilder, Joseph B., 137
Gill, Dr., 29, 32
Gill, Thomas, 227, 228
Gill, Thomas H., 280
Gillette, E. H., "Newly Discovered Prose Writings of John Milton," 44, 84, 85
Giraldi, Lilio G., *De Deis Gentium*, 205
God, 49, 55, 57, 87, 94, 164, 165, 170, 192, 193, 195, 197, 222, 224, 254, 260, 287, 352, 353
Godfrey of Bouillon, 48
Godwin, William, *Lives of Edward and John Phillips*, 184, 194
Golden Lyon, vessel, 87
Goldsmiths' Alley, London, 87
Goldsmiths' Company, vi, 245, 246, 263, 270, 302, 303
Goldsmiths' Hall, 155, 158, 159, 161, 165, 271-273, 325
Goliath (i. e., Salmasius), 348, 364
Gonzaga, Marquis, 243
Good Words, 9, 128, 273, 312
Goodall, Charles (?), 301
Goodwin, John, 128, 145
———, *Answer to Geree*, 257
———, *Obstructors of Justice*, 253, 254
———, *Right and Might Well Met*, 257
———, *Twelve Considerable Cautions*, 143
Goodwin, Thomas, 321
Gorlois, 18, 23
Gorting, Mr., 132
Goths, 48
Gouda, 351
Gournay, Mlle. de, 74, 77
Graham, Sir Frederick, 4
Gray's Inn, 10, 341
Great Scotland Yard, 273
Great Turnstile, 200
Greece, 72, 75

Greek, 6, 8, 64, 112, 126, 130, 131, 175, 176, 202, 208
Gregory, Pope, 94
Greville, Robert, see Brooke
Grierson, Sir H. J. C., *Milton and Wordsworth*, 117
Grismond, John, printer, 276
Grolier Club Catalogue, 79
Gronovius, Frederick, 191
Grotius, Hugo, 70, 74, 87, 94, 285
Gualter of Zurich, 94
Gudii, Marquardi, *Epistolae*, 244
Guildhall, vi
Guimaraes, Don Joseph de, Ambassador from Portugal, 334, 349
Guiney, Louise Imogen, 172

H., C. J., 5
Haak, Theodore, 214, 215, 317
Haberdashers' Hall, 357, 358
Hackluyt, see Hakluyt
Hague, 241, 251, 258, 260, 264, 277, 288, 309, 348, 349, 352, 363, 364
Hakluyt (Hackluyt), John, 255
Halberstad, 94
Hales, J. W., *Folia Litteraria*, 47
Hales, James, 266
Hales, Sir James, judge, 52
Halkett, John, and Samuel Laing, *Dictionary of Anonymous and Pseudonymous English Literature*, 36, 40, 43, 69, 79, 84, 85, 318
Hall, Mr., printer, 62
Hall, John, 115, 116, 250, 312
———, *Humble Motion to the Parliament*, 224, 225
Hall, Joseph, Bishop of Exeter and Norwich, 11, 12, 41, 170
———, *Defence of the Humble Remonstrance*, 31, 32, 40, 41, 53, 54, 59
———, *Episcopacy by Divine Right*, 12, 13
———, *Humble Remonstrance*, 30-32, 40-42, 44, 59
———, *Letter lately sent by a Reverend Bishop from the Tower*, 55
———, *Modest Confutation*, 54, 55, 58
———, *Resolutions and Decisions of . . . Cases of Conscience*, 242
———, *Short Answer to . . . Smectymnuus*, 42 44, 53
Haller, William, 264
———, *Leveller Tracts*, 240

————, *Tracts on Liberty*, 96, 143, 174, 192

————, "Two Early Allusions to Milton's *Areopagitica*," 224, 225

Halliday, Bernard, bookseller, 87, 282

Halton, see Holton

Hamburg, 238-241, 258, 285, 286, 304, 305, 309

Hamilton, W. D., *Original Papers Illustrative of . . . John Milton*, 15, 16, 47, 60, 144-146, 150, 153, 155-159, 161-163, 173, 211, 241, 261, 272, 273, 276, 296, 306, 310, 313, 322-324, 326-329, 332-334, 336, 342, 344, 358, 359, 362

Hammond, Henry, 293

Hampson, Thomas, 163

Hampton, 334

Hancock, Daniel, 159

Hanford, James Holly, "Arrangement and Dates of Milton's Sonnets," 136

————, "Chronology of Milton's Private Studies," 4, 5

————, "Date of Milton's *De Doctrina Christiana*," 5

————, *Milton Handbook*, 268

Hanger, George, 218

Hansley, Mr., 31, 42

Harbardus, 94

Harby, Mr., 275

Harington, Sir John, 78, 79

Harleian Library, 236

Harleian Miscellany, 43, 294

Hart, W. H., *Index Expurgatorius Anglicanus*, 170, 240

Hartlib, Samuel, 99-102, 104, 105, 115, 116, 132, 168, 169, 219, 356

————, *Ephemerides*, 82, 214, 215, 278; see also Turnbull, G. H., *Hartlib, Dury and Comenius*

Hartlibe, Mr., 25

Harvard Studies and Notes in Philology and Literature, 193, 197

Harvard University (and College), 29, 36, 40, 69, 79, 84, 255, 259, 280, 281, 355, 356

Hassel, W., artist, 281

Hatton, Charles, 227

Hatton, Christopher, Lord, 333

Haug, Ralph A., "Milton and Sir John Harington," 79

Hearne, William, 45, 168, 180, 192-194, 361

Heath, James, *Chronicle of the Late Intestine War*, 312

Heath, Richard, 183

Heber, Richard, *Catalogue of the Library of*, 282

Hebrew, 7, 27, 64, 112

Hedio, 94

Heinsius, Daniel, 249

Heinsius, Nicholas, 191, 202, 208, 209, 223, 322

Hell, 43, 54

Hellespont, 204

Hemingius, 94

Henry VIII, King of England, 52

Henry, L. (N.) H., 317, 318

Heraclides Ponticus, 95

Herbert, George, 213

Herring, Michael, 158, 159

Hesiod, 6, 8

Heston, 13

Hetruria, see Tuscan

Heveningham, Mr., 291

Heylyn, Peter (Theophilus Churchman), *History of Episcopacy*, 53

Hibernia, see Ireland

High Holborn, 199, 200, 273

Hill, Henry, printer, 226-228

Hippisley, Sir John, 273

Hircanian, 206

Histoire entière et veritable du Proces de Charles Stuart, 276, 302

Historical Manuscripts Commission reports, 81

Historical Society of Pennsylvania, vi, 299

Hobson, Captain John, 69, 70

Hobson, Lady Margaret (Ley), 69, 70, 121

Hobson, Thomas, 11, 12, 96

Holborn, 129

Holcroft, Sir Henry, 272

Holland, 202, 208, 251, 275, 277, 299, 339, 345, 348

Holland, Cornelius, 240, 254, 255

Hollandsche Mercurius, 340

Hollis, Thomas, 283, 337, 338

Holton (Halton), co. Oxon, 65

Homer, 6, 48

————, *Iliad*, 51, 206

————, *Odyssey*, 51

Hooker, Edward, 301

Hooker, Richard, 28, 83, 99

Hoppe, Mr., 32; see also Hopper

Hopper, Mr., 29; see also Hoppe

Horace, 205, 206
———, *Art of Poetry*, 205
———, *Odes*, 203
Hore, Thomas, 195, 197
Horing, William, 32; see also Loring
Horne, Thomas (?), 169
Horsepath Copse, 261, 262
Horton, co. Bucks, 25, 233, 268
Horwood, Alfred J., 4
Hoskins, Mr., 305
Hotham, Charles, *Introduction to the Teutonic Philosophy*, 285
Houghton Library (Harvard), 255; see also Harvard University
Hours at Home, 44, 84, 85
House of Commons, see Commons
House of Lords, see Lords
Howard, Charles W. G., 114
Hoym, Count, 356
Hughes, G. R., vi, 245, 319
Hughes, Merritt Y., "Historical Setting of Milton's *Observations on the Articles of Peace*," 250
———, ed., *Paradise Regained*, see Milton
Humber (Abra) River, 18, 23
Humble Proposals of sundry Learned Divines, 285
Hunnius, 94
Hunt, John, 195, 197
Hunt, R. W., 213
Hunter, Joseph, *Milton*, 66, 153, 261; see also MS. 24,487 and MS. 24,501
Huntington Library, 225
Huntington Library Quarterly, 224, 311
Hunton, Philip, *Treatise of Monarchy*, 86
Hurst, John, 272
Husband, Edward, publisher, 240
Hutchins, John, 111
Hutchinson, Anne, 132
Hyas, 17, 21
Hyde, Edward, see Clarendon
Hyde, Sir Nicholas, 192, 193, 361

Idumanian, see Chelmer
Iffley, 261, 262
Ignatius, 95
Igraine (Iögernen), 18, 23
Illinois, University of, 352
Illustrated London News, 128
Imogen (Inogen), 18, 23
Independents, 132, 230, 294

Inderwick, F. A., ed., *Calendar of the Inner Temple Records*, 12
Inner Temple, 12
Inns of Court, 43, 54, 145
Inogen, see Imogen
Ion, 172, 173
Ipswich, 177
Ireland (Hibernia), 66, 192, 193, 195, 197, 240, 286, 292, 341
Irenaeus, 39
Irish, 66, 250
Irrevocabilité du Test . . . Charles Stuart, 302
Irvine, Presbytery of, 31
Ishbosheth, 312
Israel, 105
Italian (Tuscan, Etrurian, Hetrurian), 7, 202, 207, 209, 221
Italy, v, 2, 3, 5, 6, 19, 24, 27, 34, 48, 51, 70-78

Jackson, Henry, 99
Jackson, J. E., 70
Jackson, William A., vi, 255
James II, King of England, earlier Duke of York, 225, 228
James, Mr., 187, 191
Jane (Janes), Joseph, 341
———, *Eikon Aklastos*, 333, 336
———, *Salmasius his Dissection*, 336
Jansson, Mr., 351
Janus, see Jane
Jeaffreson, J. C., *Middlesex County Records*, 13
Jeanes, Henry, 336
Jeffrey, John, 127
Jenkins, Reverend R. C., 281
Jenney, William, 145
Jericho, 145
Jerome, St., 93
Jersey, 185
Jerusalem, 145
Jesuits, 57, 67
Jesus, see Christ
Jews, 90
Job, 48
Jögerne, see Igraine
John IV, King of Portugal, 297, 298, 300, 306
John, St., 45, 46, 48
John, St., epistle of, 105
John the Baptist, 84, 85, 192, 193
Johnson, C. S., 81
Johnson, Samuel, 137

————, *Prefaces, Biographical and Critical, To The Works of the English Poets*, 279
Jones, Michael, 250
Jones, Richard, see Ranelagh
Jones, Sir William, 63
Journals of the House of Commons, 107, 153, 170, 200, 252, 321, 334, 350
Journals of the House of Lords, 86, 116, 153, 200, 218
Jove, see Jupiter
Jovius, Paulus, 267
Joy, Frederick W., 95
Joyce, George, 307
Junius, Patricius, see Young
Jupiter (Jove), 141, 142, 175, 176
Justice Advanced, 257
Justin Martyr, St., 93
Justinian, 94
Juxon, William, Archbishop of Canterbury, 293

Keat, Gilbert, 218
Keech (Keeth), William, 159
Keeth, William, see Keech
"Kel: sen.," 179
Kelley, Maurice, vi, 95, 244
————, "Note on Milton's *Pro Populo Anglicano Defensio*," 351, 352
Kennedy, Mr., 281
Kennet, White, *Register and Chronicle*, 284
Kensington, 269
Kent, 52, 314, 315
Kerslake, Thomas, bookseller, 1
Killigrew, Lady, 274
King, Edward, 137, 149
King, John, 331
Kingdom's Faithful and Impartial Scout, 253
King's College, Oxford, 261, 262
Kingsgate, 200
King's Head, bookshop, 127
Knowles, Sir Francis, 37
Knox, John, 285

L., J. M. C., 79
Lactantius, 93
Laherne, see Laugharne
Laing, Samuel, see Halkett
Lambech, Peter, 191
Lambeth Palace, 79, 85, 108

Lambinus, 205
Lancashire, 285
Lane, Mr., see Jane
Langbaine, Gerard, *Account of the English Dramatic Poets*, 236
Langley, John, 218
Languedoc, 253
Latham, Mr., 216
Latian music, 23
Latimer, Hugh, Bishop of Worcester, 52, 83
Latin, 6, 8, 57, 64, 65, 78, 112, 137, 140, 168, 175, 176, 187, 190, 202, 207, 208, 238, 241, 246, 288, 318
Laud, William, Archbishop of Canterbury, 36, 43
Laugharne (Laherne?), 282, 283
Laurence, Mr. (Academy of), 168
Lausanne, 115
Lawes, Henry, 136, 142, 215
————, *Second Book of Airs*, 12
————, and William Lawes, *Choice Psalms*, 142, 215
Lawrence, Henry, 183
Lawson, Mr., 32; see also Dawson
Lee, Mr., printer, 108
Lee, Isaac, 239, 241
Lee, John, 254, 255
Lee, Lady Margaret, see Hobson
Lee, William, printer, 112
Leech, John, 323, 326
Legatt, Mr., 216
Leghorn (Lyvorne), 87
Legouis, Pierre, *Andre Marvell*, 121, 135
Leicester, 87
Lenthall, P., 193
Lenthall, William, 241, 345
Leo, 94
Leonora, see Baroni
Leopold, Prince, Archduke of Austria, 303
Lethe, 141, 142, 175, 176
Levellers, 239, 240
Lever, J. W., 322
Lewis, Anthony John, see Medina Celi
Lewis, Clarissa O., "Further Note on Milton's *Pro Populo Anglicano Defensio*," 352
Lex, Rex, 285
Ley, James, see Marlborough
Ley, Lady Margaret, see Hobson
Ley, Lady Mary (Petty), see Marlborough

Leyden, 249, 275, 299, 345, 348, 349
Libbe, Richard, 261, 262
Libbie, auctioneer, 356
Library, 41, 246, 347, 351, 352, 355
Lilburne, John, 185, 240
———, *England's New Chains Discovered*, 239, 240, 257
———, *Second Part of England's New Chains Discovered*, 239, 240
Liljegren, S. B., *Studies in Milton*, 227
Lilly, William, *Several Observations on the Life and Death of King Charles I*, 320
Lincoln's Inn, 315, 317
Lincoln's Inn Fields, 129, 199, 200
Lisle, John, 234, 304
Lisle, Philip Sidney, Viscount, 234
Liston, co. Middlesex, 10
Lithuania, 321
Little Turnstile, 200
Liverpool, 82
Livingston, Luther S., *Auction Prices of Books*, 138, 356, 357
Livy, 35, 230
Lloyd, James, 166
Lodge Copse, 261, 262
Lombards, 48
Loménie, Louis Henry, Comte de, 356
London *Times*, 7, 201, 276, 281, 302
London *Times Literary Supplement*, 32, 44, 179, 181, 216, 244, 250, 256, 317, 318
London Topographical Record, 245
Looten, C., "Les débuts de Milton pamphletaire," 30, 44
Lords, House of, 116, 117, 122
Lorenzo, Prince of Tuscany, 222, 223
Loring, Mr., 29; see also Horing
Los Angeles *Examiner*, 1
Louis XIV, King of France, 57, 70-78, 170, 171, 185, 187, 190
Love, Christopher, 212
Lowndes, William Thomas, 318
———, *Bibliographer's Manual*, 98, 282
Luca, see Lucca
Lucas, Perceval, 177
Lucca (Luca), 16, 19
Lucretius, 6, 8
Ludgate, 156, 157
Ludgate Hill, 103, 108
Ludlow Castle, 348
Luke, St., gospel of, 93, 94
Lund, 227

Lusher, Mr., 147
Luther, 94
Lydia, 28
Lyons, 253
Lyvorne, see Leghorn

M., G., printer, 112
M., I., 12
M., J. G., 250
M., R., 150, 336, 359
M., S., 334
Mabbott, Gilbert, 251-253, 276
Mabbott, Thomas O., vi, 52, 237
———, and J. Milton French, " 'The Grand Case of Conscience,' Wrongly Attributed to Milton," 291
Mabol, see Mabbott, Gilbert
McColley, Grant, "Milton's Lost Tragedy," 50
Macedo, 94
MacKellar, Walter, see Milton, *Latin Poems*, ed. W. MacKellar
McMurray, William, *Records of Two City Parishes*, 147
Macock, John, printer, 291
Macray, W. D., *Annals of the Bodleian Library*, 128
———, ed., *Calendar of the Clarendon Papers Preserved in the Bodleian Library*, 275
———, *Forty-Fifth Report of the Deputy Keeper of the Public Records*, 320
Madan, F. F., "Milton, Salmasius, and Dugard," 246, 338, 341, 351, 352, 355
Madrid, 330-332
Maggs Brothers, booksellers, vi, 25, 115
———, *Mercurius Britannicus*, 59
Maidenhead Court, London, 9
Malatesta, Antonio, 187, 191
Maldon, co. Essex, 127
Malone, Edmund, 96
Malvezzi, Virgilio, *Discourses Upon Tacitus*, 52
Man, Mr., 37
Man, John, *History and Antiquities of the Borough of Reading*, 157
Manchester, Edward Montagu, second Earl of, 116
Manchester, co. Lancashire, 236
Manilius, 6, 8
Man's Mortality, see Overton
Mansfield, A. S., 281
Mansfield, Arthur, 99

Manso, Giovanni Baptista, Marquis of Villa, 71, 75

Manwarden, Mr., 101

Marcion, 93

Margoliouth, H. M., see Marvell, Andrew

Marlborough, James Ley, Earl of, 69, 70, 121

Marlborough, Lady Mary (Petty) Lee, Countess of, 70

Marmoleso, Don Francisco Fernandez de, 330, 331

Mars, 64

Marsh, John, 79

Marsh, John Fitchett, *Papers connected with the Affairs of Milton and his Family*, 188, 207, 294, 337, 338

Marshall, William, artist, 130, 131

Marsyas, 258

Marten, Henry, 234

Martin, Burns, "Date of Milton's First Marriage," 62

Martin, L. C., 172

Martindale, Adam, *Life . . . written by Himself*, ed. Richard Parkinson, 285

Marvell, Andrew, 87

———, "Fleckno, an English Priest at Rome," 121

———, "Garden," 135

———, *Poems and Letters*, ed. H. M. Margoliouth, 121

Mary, Virgin, 212, 213

Mary I, Queen of England, 52, 236

Mary, daughter of Charles I, Princess of Orange, 244

Maseres, Francis, ed., *Select Tracts Relating to the Civil Wars in England*, 320

Masham, Sir William, 308

Masked, Richard, 32

Mason, Edmund, 327

Massey, Sir Edward, 199

Masson, David, 128

———, *Life of John Milton*, 3 et seq.

———, "Local Memories of Milton," 9, 273, 312

Mathews, Mr., 29, 66, 67

Matthaeus, Monachus, 94

Matthew, St., gospel of, 7, 87, 93, 94, 123, 124; in Syriac, 7

Matthews, J. and G. F., *Abstracts of the Probate Acts of the Prerogative Court of Canterbury*, 147

———, *Year Books of Probate*, 171, 184, 280

Maurice, Prince, 242, 243, 251

Maurice (Mauritius), John, 355

Mauritius, see Maurice

Maximian, *Elegy*, 205

May, Thomas, 317, 318

———, *Breviary of History of Parliament*, 318

———, *Historiae Parliamenti Angliae Breviarum*, 318

Maydwell, Mr., 177, 215, 216

Medina Celi, Anthony John Lewis, Duke of, 330

Melanchthon, 94

Melpomene, muse, 130

Menage, Giles, *Mescolanze* (*Miscellanies*), 191, 207

Merchant Adventurers, Company of, 238, 239

Merchant Taylors' School, 301

Mercurius Britannicus, 278

Mercurius Militaris, 255

Mercurius Politicus, 278, 309-312, 329, 345, 348-350

Mercurius Pragmaticus, 256, 257, 278, 292

Merlin, 18, 23

Metropolitan Nuncio, 255

Metropolitan Railway, 128

Meysey Hampton, co. Gloucestershire, 99

Michael, St., 193, 194

Michell, William, 195, 197

Middlesex Sessions Rolls, 13

Milan, 51, 72, 76, 94

Mildmay, Sir Henry, 254, 308

Miller, Mr., 10

Miller, Ella, ed., *Forest Hill with Shotover 1933 The Village Book*, 62

Miller, John, 10

Miller, Richard, 10

Millington, Edward, 226

Milton, Anne, brother's daughter, 29, 43

Milton, Anne, daughter, 134, 154

Milton, Anne, sister, see Phillips, Anne

Milton, Anne (?), sister's daughter, 7

Milton, Christopher, brother, 10, 12, 13, 25, 29, 43, 81, 85, 92, 99, 103, 104, 108-111, 115, 120, 130, 133, 144, 145, 155-159, 164, 177, 277, 278

Milton, Deborah, daughter, see Clarke

Milton, Elizabeth (Minshull), third wife, 278

Milton, John, father, 1, 2, 6, 13, 14, 29, 69, 83, 85, 86, 118, 126, 127, 129, 134, 182, 183, 361

MILTON, JOHN, poet

I. LIFE

and army, 47, 48, 122
and Miss Davis, 117, 118
blindness, 107, 290, 338, 339
change from poetry to prose, 26, 33
choice of English or Latin for writings, 27
cipher, 236, 237
confidence in own genius, 2, 3
contribution to Irish Protestants, 66
conversation, 8
distinguished visitors, 339
extent (seizure) of Wheatley, 13-16, 209, 210
eyesight, 6
friends, 2; see also Italian friends
"gawdy day," 10
help to brother Christopher in composition for estate, 158
Italian friends, 24
Italian journey, v, 2, 70-77
legal proceedings, see (1) Ashworth, (2) Cope, (3) Pye
licensing, 276, 311
loan (bond) to Sir John Cope, 2, 13, 25, 36, 46
loan (bond) to Richard Powell, 2, 25, 46, 82, 93, 103, 104, 160, 163, 167, 168, 178, 180, 181, 192-199, 210, 323, 360-362
loan (bond) to Robert Warcupp, 298
marriage to Mary Powell, 61-69
papers at Forest Hill (?), 63
petition to compound, 321, 322
poetic names, see (1) David, (2) Thyrsis
residences, see (1) Aldersgate, (2) Barbican, (3) Charing Cross, (4) High Holborn, (5) St. Bride's Churchyard, (6) Scotland Yard, (7) Whitehall, (8) York Street
rustication, 55
Secretary for the Foreign Tongues, 234-236, 238
servant, 43, 80; see also Yates, Jane

sickness, 290, 338, 339
study, 26, 27
summons to House of Lords, 116, 117
taxes, 29, 30, 32, 40, 42-45, 232
tutoring, 5-11, 69, 86, 128, 129, 132, 168, 169, 183, 289, 290
witnessing of will of Richard Powell, 164, 166; of William Blackborow, 147

II. WRITINGS

(see also presentation copies below)

"Abram from Morea," 4
"Ad Joannem Rousium," 140-142, 172-176
"Ad Leonoram," 71, 75
Animadversions, 38, 40-42, 54, 58, 59, 125, 140
Apology, 11, 38, 50, 58-60, 125, 140
"Arcades," 3
Areopagitica, 79, 113-115, 126, 128, 140, 224, 225, 251-253, 266, 278
"At a Solemn Music," 3
"At a Vacation Exercise," 28
"Baptistes," 4
Brief History of Moscovia, vi, 215, 267, 268
Cambridge Manuscript, see MS. Milton's Minor Poems
Character of the Long Parliament, 279
"Christus patiens," 4
Colasterion, 90, 112, 124-126, 139, 140, 169, 266, 337
Columbia Manuscript, see MS. Columbia
Commonplace Book, see MS. Add. 36,354; *Commonplace Book*, ed. A. J. Horwood, 4, 215
Complete Collection of the . . . Works, ed. Thomas Birch, 154, 279, 291
Complete Collection of the . . . Works, with prefatory life by John Toland (1698), 70, 226, 252, 339, 341, 363
Complete Poetical Works (not facsimile), ed. Harris F. Fletcher (1941), 8
Complete Poetical Works (facsimile),

MILTON, JOHN, poet (cont.)
ed. Harris F. Fletcher, 3, 130, 137, 142, 163, 175, 176, 215, 217
Comus, 3, 79, 137, 259, 283, 348, 356
Considerations touching . . . Hirelings, 353
De Doctrina Christiana, 5
Defensio pro Populo Anglicano, v, 244, 248, 249, 275, 281, 284, 286-290, 294, 302, 334, 335, 337-341, 345, 347-357, 360, 362-364
Defensio Pro Se, 131, 246
Defensio Secunda, 9, 30, 33, 38, 41, 47, 53, 54, 56, 57, 59, 78, 88, 89, 101, 113, 232-234, 246, 265, 287, 288, 290, 352, 363, 364
Doctrine and Discipline of Divorce, 65, 87-92, 94-100, 104, 106-108, 111, 112, 122-125, 127, 128, 132, 133, 140, 143-145, 169, 171, 185 (?), 211, 218, 242, 255, 266, 337, 352
Eikonoklastes, 226-228, 237, 248, 263-267, 275, 282-284, 292, 306, 333, 336, 352; translated into Latin by Lewis du Moulin (?), 284
Epistolarum Familiarium Liber Unus, 24, 107, 123, 125, 188, 339
"Epitaphium Damonis," 5, 6, 16-25, 28; ed. Walter W. Skeat, 19; ed. E. H. Visiak, 19
"Fable of the Head and the Wen," 35
Facsimile of the Manuscript of Milton's Minor Poems, ed. W. A. Wright, 3; see also MS. Milton's Minor Poems
"Here Hobson lies," 11, 12, 96
History of Britain, 214, 233, 234
"Il Penseroso," 135, 184
"In Effigei ejus Sculptorem," 130, 131
"Index Ethicus," 4
"Index Oeconomicus," 4
"Index Politicus," 4
Judgment of Martin Bucer, 88, 91, 92, 97, 100, 104-106, 109, 125, 126, 140, 266
"L'Allegro," 63, 184
Lament for Damon, see "Epitaphium Damonis"

Latin Poems, ed. Walter MacKellar, 19
Letters of State, edited with life of Milton by Edward Phillips, 2 *et seq.* (especially 258-259); see also Milton, *Literæ Pseudo-Senatûs*
Literæ Pseudo-Senatûs, 241, 258, 259, 285, 297, 300, 303, 304, 306, 309, 318, 330, 334, 345, 348
"Lycidas," 3, 121, 137, 184
Mask, see *Comus*
"Moabitides or Phineas," 4
notes from early English history, 4
notes from Old Testament history, 4
Observations upon the Articles of Peace, 250
Of Education, 100-102, 104, 105, 115, 116, 132, 140, 266, 305
Of Prelatical Episcopacy, 37-39, 45, 46, 56, 125, 139, 140
Of Reformation, 32-36, 39, 52, 53, 79, 83, 125, 139, 140
"On Shakespeare," 11, 12
"On the Death of a Fair Infant," 7
"On the Morning of Christ's Nativity," 184, 212-214
"On the New Forcers of Conscience," 4, 135, 136
"On Time," 3
Original Letters and Papers of State, ed. John Nickolls, 295, 296
Paradise Lost, 4, 24, 33, 158; ed. Thomas Newton, 70, 158
Paradise Regained, etc., ed. Merritt Y. Hughes, 19, 70, 82, 121, 136
"Perfect System of Divinity," 5, 7; see also *De Doctrina Christiana*
"Philosophus ad Regem," 121
"Phineas," 4
plans for poems and other writings, 3, 4, 16, 33, 42, 48-51
Poems (1645), 5, 18, 24, 50, 51, 82, 118, 120, 121, 129-131, 136-140, 172, 173, 201, 213-215, 315
Poems (1673), 69 (?), 135, 136, 142, 163, 214, 217
Poems, ed. Thomas Warton (1791), 142, 150, 184, 213, 214, 337, 338
Poetical Works, ed. Henry J. Todd (1826), 3, 79, 84, 85, 108, 150, 184, 218, 242, 248, 272, 296, 304, 317, 337, 338, 356, 358, 359, 362
Pro Se Defensio, see *Defensio Pro Se*

MILTON, JOHN, poet (cont.)
Prose Works, ed. J. A. St. John (Bohn edition, 1867-68), 54, 230, 232, 287
"Psalm 136," 212-214
Psalms 80-88, 217
Ready and Easy Way, 364
Reason of Church Government, 3, 26, 28, 38, 49-51, 55, 56, 59, 125, 139, 140
Samson Agonistes, 133
"Scotch Stories," 4
Skinner Manuscript, see MS. SP 9/61 [or 194]
"Sodom Burning," 4
Sonnet VII ("How soon hath Time"), 3
Sonnet VIII ("Captain or Colonel"), 3, 82
Sonnet IX ("Lady that in the prime"), 3, 69, 70, 118, 121
Sonnet X ("Daughter to that good Earl"), 121
Sonnet XI ("A book was writ of late called *Tetrachordon*"), 3, 136
Sonnet XII ("I did but prompt the age"), 136
Sonnet XIII ("Harry, whose tuneful and well measured song"), 3, 142, 215
Sonnet XIV ("When Faith and Love"), 3, 163
Sonnet XVIII ("Cyriack, whose grandsire"), 4
Sonnet XIX ("Methought I saw my late espoused saint"), 4
Sonnet [XX] ("Fairfax, whose name in arms"), 3, 218, 219
Sonnet [XXI] ("Cromwell, our chief of men"), 4, 219
Sonnet [XXII] ("Cyriack, this three years' day"), 4
Sonnet [XXIII] ("Vane, young in years"), 4
Sonnets, ed. John S. Smart, 19, 82, 118, 136, 163
"Speech for Unlicensed Printing," see *Areopagitica*
Tenure of Kings, 95, 228-235, 253, 254, 257, 260, 266, 298
Tetrachordon, 64, 90, 94, 95, 105, 109, 126, 136, 139, 140, 169, 266, 337

"Theological Index," 4
translations: (1) letters about Holland, 251; (2) letters from Spain, 330-332; (3) letter from Tetuan, 292; (4) letters of Princess Sophie, 242-244
Treatise of Civil Power, 288
Trinity Manuscript, see MS. Milton's Minor Poems
"Upon the Circumcision," 3
verses on or to Francesco Rovai (lost, if ever written), 207
Vindication, see *Colasterion*
Works, Columbia edition, 1 *et seq.*
Works, Pickering edition, 222, 336

III. FAMILIAR LETTERS TO AND FROM:

Aizema, 98, 123
Cromwell (attributed, but lost), 281
Dati, 24, 27, 134, 170, 171, 184-191, 188-189 (lost), 201-209, 215, 221-223
Louis XIV (?), 57, 70-78
Marvell, 87
Milton, Mary (Powell), 79-81 (lost)
Molière (?), 56-58, 67
monks at Vallombrosa (?), 5
Pauw, 339
Philaras, 107, 339
unknown addressee, 4
Voiture (?), 57, 60, 61
Wotton, 348

IV. LETTERS OF STATE TO:

Algiers, 281, 282
Cardenas of Spain, 346
Danzig, 348
Guimaraes of Portugal, 334
Hamburg, 238-241, 258, 285, 286, 304, 309
John VI of Portugal, 297, 300, 306
Leopold of Austria, 303
Lewis of Andalusia, 330
Philip IV of Spain, 297, 306, 318
Spain, 345, 346
Tetuan, 282, 293

V. ATTRIBUTED WRITINGS

"Alfred," 51
Answer to . . . Humble Remonstrance (share in), see Smectymnuus

MILTON, JOHN, poet (cont.)
Argument or Debate in Law, 79
"Arthur," 51
Canterbury's Dream, 36
Discourse Showing . . . Three Kingdoms, 40
epitome of Purchas, 214, 215
Grand Case of Conscience, 285, 291
Great Britain's Ruin Plotted, 33, 44
"He whom Heaven did call away," 200, 201
Historiæ Parliamenti, 318
Jus Populi, 96, 108
King's Cabinet Opened, 127, 128
"Lavinia Walking," 12
Lords Bishops none of the Lord's Bishops, 25
Man's Mortality (share in), 96
Mercurius Politicus, 329
News from Hell, Rome, and Inns of Court, 43, 44, 54
Novæ Solymæ, 216
Observations upon his Majesty's Late Answers, 69
Pious Annotations upon the Holy Bible (preface), 83
Plot Discovered, 44
Pro Populo Adversus Tyrannos, 95, 96
Psalm 11 (translation), 83
"Quod cum coelicolis habitus" (on William Staple), 279, 280
Reply to the Answer to . . . Observations upon some of his Majesty's late Answers and Expresses, 84
Responsio ad Apologiam, see Phillips, John
Rights of the People over Tyrants, 95, 96
School Laws, 280
Short View of the Prelatical Church, 30
Sovereign Salve to Cure the Blind, 85
"These shapes, of old transfigured by the charms," 135
Treatise of Monarchy, 86
True Character of an Untrue Bishop, 45
True Description . . . Cardinal Wolsey . . . and William Laud, 43
Tyrannical Government Anatomized (translation of Buchanan's *Baptistes*), 84, 85

VI. PRESENTATION COPIES
OF OWN BOOKS

Apology, 59, 60
Areopagitica, 113-115
Defensio pro Populo Anglicano, 355-357
Doctrine and Discipline of Divorce, 98, 99
Eikonoklastes, 282, 283
"Epitaphium Damonis," 24, 186, 187, 189
Of Education, 102
Poems (1645), 138, 174-176, 190, 222, 223
prose works, 36, 125, 126, 139-142, 176
Reason of Church Government, 56

VII. ASSOCIATION BOOKS
(see also names of individual authors)

Aratus, 95
Ariosto, 78, 79
Best, 170 (?)
Bibles: (1) of 1599, 1, 2; (2) of 1637 (?), 1, 25; (3) Milton family, 65; see also MS. Add. 32,310; (4) Powell family, 65; see also MS. Add. 4,244
Boiardo, 86, 87
concordance (?), 2
della Casa, 95
Dion Chrysostom, 95
Eikon Alethine, 259
Euripides, 95
Farnaby, 29
Heraclides Ponticus, 95
Malvezzi, 52
Polycarp and Ignatius, 95
prayer book (?), 2
Psalms (?), 2
Salmasius, 248
sermons (?), 2

VIII. PORTRAITS
(see also under names of individual artists)

Faithorne, 131, 281
Hassel, 281
himself (?), 134
Marshall, 130
Onslow (owner), 130

MILTON, JOHN, poet (cont.)
Petitot, 92, 93
Pierce (?), 337, 338
puncheon, 337
Richardson, 135, 280
seal, 337, 338
Simon (?), 337, 338
unknown, 281

IX. ALLUSIONS BY CONTEMPORARIES
(see also individual names)

Answer to . . . Doctrine and Discipline of Divorce, 108
Bachiler, 142, 143
Baillie, 132, 142
Baron, 315
Bramhall, 82
C., T., 218
Canne, 257
Catalogue of the Several Sects, 174
Edwards, 143, 144
Featley, 136, 337
Fuller, 52, 53
Goodwin, 253, 254
Hall, John, 224, 225
Hall, Joseph, 54, 55, 242
Hartlib, 82
Heylyn, 53
Hotham, 285
Hyde, 185
Mercurius Pragmaticus, 292
Pagitt, 127, 171
Palmer, 105, 106, 109
Plea for Non-Subscribers, 285
Prynne, 108
Rowland, 340-342
Smith, 305
Testimony to the Truth of Jesus Christ, 211, 216
These Tradesmen are Preachers, 191
unnamed, 91, 92
Vaughan, 171, 172
Wasse, 241, 242
Wilkins, 337

Milton, John, son, 273, 274
Milton, John, others, 86, 200, 218
Milton, Martha (Fleetwood, later Coward), wife of nephew Thomas, 177
Milton, Mary (Powell), first wife, 58, 61-70, 79-81, 84, 86, 91, 118-120, 122, 128, 129, 133, 134, 166, 220, 329

Milton, Mary, daughter, 220
Milton, Richard, father's father, 182
Milton, Sarah, brother's daughter, 25
Milton, Thomas, brother's son, 177
Milton, Thomasine (Webber), brother's wife, 25, 120, 177
"Milton Books," 2
"Milton gateway" (Forest Hill), 62
"Milton stone" (Forest Hill), 62
"Miltonic controversy," 201
Miltonist, 241, 242
"Milton's Cipher and the Harleian Library," 236
Miter Tavern, 112
Modern Language Notes, 46, 220
Modern Language Quarterly, 79, 95, 200
Modern Language Review, 11, 12, 29, 32, 44, 62, 96
Modern Philology, 50, 136
Molière, 56-58, 67
Molins, W., 334
Moon, Washington, 29
Moore, Rev. E. R., 220
Moorfields (Morefields), 294
Mopsus, 17, 21
More, Alexander, 131, 191, 288
Morefields, see Moorfields
Morgan Library, 355, 357
Morley, Henry, 201
Morley, William, 248, 249
Morley, William D., vi
Morocco, 293
Morrison, Mrs., 135
Mosaic law, 89, 90
Moseley, Humphrey, printer, 120, 129, 136
Moses, 7
Moule, G., bookseller, 282
Moulin, Lewis du (translated *Eikonoklastes* into Latin?), 284
Moulin, Pierre du, *Regii Sanguinis Clamor*, 88, 264, 265, 284, 288, 309, 320, 352
MS. III.E.9.15 (Universiteits Bibliotheek, Amsterdam), 322
MS. 1503/5-7 (Guildhall), 29, 32, 44
MS. Add. 4,244 (British Museum), 65, 66, 154, 220
MS. Add. 5,016* (British Museum), 222
MS. Add. 15,227 (British Museum), 12

MS. Add. 19,142 (British Museum), 111

MS. Add. 24,487-92 (British Museum), 40, 63, 220

MS. Add. 24,501 (British Museum), 40, 43, 66, 92, 99, 103, 104, 108, 109, 115, 130

MS. Add. 32,310 (British Museum), 65, 154, 220

MS. Add. 34,326 (British Museum), 314

MS. Add. 36,354 (British Museum), 4, 87, 233

MS. Assessment Roll of Oxfordshire (Public Record Office), 201

MS. Aubrey 8 (Bodleian), 8 *et seq.*

MS. C2 Charles I/P10/15 (Public Record Office), 179, 181

MS. C2 Charles I/P98/30 (Public Record Office), 216

MS. C5/2/65 (Public Record Office), 45, 47

MS. C33/173 (Public Record Office), 14

MS. C33/192 (Public Record Office), 256

MS. C228/6 (Public Record Office), 193, 197

MS. Clarendon 29 (Bodleian), 185

MS. Columbia (Milton's letters of state, Columbia University, call number X823M64/S62), 4, 239, 258, 281, 282, 297, 300, 303, 304, 306, 309, 318, 330-332, 334, 345, 348

MS. Court Book of the Worshipful Company of Goldsmiths (Goldsmiths' Company), 263, 270, 277, 302, 303

MS. Dati's letter to Milton (New York Public Library), 207

MS. E179/252 (Public Record Office), 40, 43, 66

MS. E372/493 (Public Record Office), 261

MS. Eg. 2,539 (British Museum), 84

MS. Eg. 2,547 (British Museum), 258

MS. Fines 52 (Prerogative Court of Canterbury), 166, 184

MS. Fines 92 (Prerogative Court of Canterbury), 171

MS. Harleian 6,802 (British Museum), 111

MS. Hist. 4to. 39 (University Library, Copenhagen), 320

MS. L.C. 4/200 (Public Record Office), 163

MS. Lat. Misc. (Bodleian), 138, 175

MS. Letters of State collected by Milton (Society of Antiquaries), 296

MS. Library Papers, Bills to 1763 (Bodleian), 128

MS. Malone 21 (Bodleian), 96

MS. Milton's letter to Dati (New York Public Library), 188

MS. Milton's Minor Poems (Trinity College, Cambridge, known as Trinity or Cambridge MS.), 3, 4, 82, 118, 121, 135, 136, 142, 163, 218, 219

MS. Minute Book of the Company of Goldsmiths (Goldsmiths' Company), 319

MS. Muster Roll (Town Hall, Reading), 81

MS. Old Royal, 8vo, 3,579 (Royal Library, Copenhagen), 354

MS. Parish Register (Horton), 25

MS. Parish Register (St. Clement Danes), 177

MS. Parish Register (St. Giles' Cripplegate), 182

MS. Parish Register (St. Giles in the Fields), 220

MS. Parish Register (St. Laurence, Reading), 43

MS. Pembroke 149 (Prerogative Court of Canterbury), 280

MS. Rawl. Misc. [or D] 230 (Bodleian), 354

MS. Sloane 542 (British Museum), 12

MS. Sloane 1,325 (British Museum), 285

MS. SP 9/61 [or 194] (Public Record Office), 239, 258, 285, 297, 300, 303, 304, 306, 309, 318, 330, 334, 345, 348

MS. SP Dom 16/517 (Public Record Office), 276

MS. SP Dom 18/1 (Public Record Office), 243, 244

MS. SP Dom 18/6 (Public Record Office), 269

MS. SP Dom 23/3 (Public Record Office), 158, 164

MS. SP Dom 23/6 (Public Record Office), 276

MS. SP Dom 23/11 (Public Record Office), 324, 326

MS. SP Dom 23/24 (Public Record Office), 158

MS. SP Dom 23/39 (Public Record Office), 263, 278

MS. SP Dom 23/43 (Public Record Office), 159

MS. SP Dom 23/54 (Public Record Office), 163

MS. SP Dom 23/64 (Public Record Office), 328

MS. SP Dom 23/82 (Public Record Office), 159

MS. SP Dom 23/101 (Public Record Office), 322, 358, 359, 362

MS. SP Dom 23/109 (Public Record Office), 15, 60, 146, 211, 326, 327, 333, 334, 336, 342, 344

MS. SP Dom 23/110 (Public Record Office), 15, 16, 47, 150, 161, 173, 313, 323, 329, 332, 359

MS. SP Dom 23/187 (Public Record Office), 144, 145, 156, 157

MS. SP Dom 23/193 (Public Record Office), 144

MS. SP Dom 23/194 (Public Record Office), 153, 155, 161-163, 272, 273

MS. SP Dom 23/251 (Public Record Office), 310

MS. SP Dom 25/2 (Public Record Office), 259

MS. SP Dom 25/5 (Public Record Office), 304

MS. SP Dom 25/6 (Public Record Office), 307

MS. SP Dom 25/8 (Public Record Office), 321

MS. SP Dom 25/15 (Public Record Office), 335

MS. SP Dom 25/16 (Public Record Office), 344

MS. SP Dom 25/17 (Public Record Office), 349

MS. SP Dom 25/18 (Public Record Office), 349

MS. SP Dom 25/62 (Public Record Office), 234, 236, 238-240, 245, 250, 251, 255-257

MS. SP Dom 25/63 (Public Record Office), 269, 270, 273-275, 286, 292, 293, 295

MS. SP Dom 25/64 (Public Record Office), 299, 300, 304, 307-309, 314, 315, 317, 318

MS. SP Dom 25/65 (Public Record Office), 349

MS. SP Dom 25/95 (Public Record Office), 299

MS. SP Dom 45/20 (Public Record Office), 296

MS. SP Dom 46/95 (Public Record Office), 311

MS. SP For 82/7 (Public Record Office), 241

MS. Stowe 305 (British Museum), 264

MS. Tanner 465 (Bodleian), 12, 213, 214

MS. Tanner 466 (Bodleian), 213, 214

MS. Twisse 82 (Prerogative Court of Canterbury), 127, 147

MS. Warcupp-Milton bond (Historical Society of Pennsylvania), 299

MS. Wood 515 (Bodleian), 45, 47

MS. Wood D 4 (Bodleian), 8 *et seq.*

MS. Wood F 39 (Bodleian), 219

Much's Land, 327

Muckingford, co. Essex, 126

Muddiman, J. G., *Trial of King Charles the First*, 302

Munger, Harold N., Jr., vi

Murcia, 331

Muscle, Mr., 29

Muscovy, see Russia

Musculus, 94

Muses, 141, 187, 190

Mutschmann, Heinrich, *Milton's Projected Epic*, 33

N., T., printer, 282

Nantes, Council of, 93

Naples, 71, 75

Narcissus, 131

Naseby, 127

National Portrait Gallery, vi, 338

Needham, Marchamont, 169, 257, 259, 270, 278, 309, 311, 312

————, *The Case of the Commonwealth of England Stated*, 329

————, *The Excellency of a Free State*, 329

Neocaesarea, Council of, 93

Neptune, 204, 205

Nero, 254

Netherlands, 274, 275

Nettleton, Christopher, 43

New England, 132

New English Dictionary, 224, 242

New Orleans, 281

New Statesman and Nation, 316
New York Public Library, 52, 135, 137, 188, 207, 226, 317, 347
New York *Times Book Review*, 137
Newgate, 259, 270
Newton, Thomas, see Milton, John, *Paradise Lost*
Nicene Council, 29
Nicholas, Sir Edward, 84, 185, 333, 336
Nicholas Papers, see Warner, G. F.
Nichols, John, *Literary Anecdotes of the Eighteenth Century*, 137
Nickolls, John, see Milton, John, *Original Letters*
Norman conquest, 233
Northampton, 177
Northumberland, Henry Percy, Earl of, 52
Notes and Queries, 5, 9, 29, 43, 92, 95, 127, 177, 201, 237, 247, 280, 291, 294, 318, 324
Nouvelles Ordinaires de Londres, 347, 351
Nye, Philip (?), 321

O., R., printer, 37
Observations upon some of his Majesty's late Answers and Expresses, 84
Ochtertyne, 114
Olai, Wilhelmus Worm, "Iter Anglicum anno MDCLII," 320
Old Exchange, 319, 320
Oldys, William, 79, 95, 236
Onslow, Arthur, Speaker of House of Commons, portrait of Milton, 130
Oppian, 8
———, *Cynegetica* and *Halieutica*, 6
Orcades, see Orkney Islands
Origen, 48, 93
Orkney Islands (Orcades), 18, 24
Ormond, James Butler, Duke of, 250
———, *Articles of Peace*, 250
Orpheus, 205
Ouse (Usa) River, 18, 23
Overton, Richard, 54, 96, 240
———, *Man's Mortality*, 96, 123, 171
Ovid, 206
Oxenbridge, Daniel, 86, 87
Oxford, Edward (?) Harley, Earl of, 236
Oxford, 1, 28, 64, 65, 68, 80, 84, 118, 120, 134, 145, 151-153, 155, 157, 162, 192, 193, 195, 197, 199, 261, 262, 312
Oxford and Cambridge Review, 250
Oxford University, 138-140, 174-176
Oxfordshire, 15, 153, 154, 209, 210

P., T., printer, 87
PMLA, 5, 38, 39, 250
Packer, Mr., 183
Page, Mr., 81
Page, Graland, 217
Page, John, 162
Pagitt, Ephraim, *Heresiography*, 127, 129, 171
Paine, Thomas, printer, 37, 259
Palladius, 6
Pallavicine, Mr., 29, 32
Palmer, Herbert, *Glass of God's Providence*, 92, 105, 106, 109
Pamela, 226, 227, 259, 301
Pandras, 18, 23
Pane, Remigio U., vi, 207
Pareus, 48
Paris, 60, 70, 71, 74, 308, 347
Parker, Mr., 42, 105
Parker, Henry, 108
———, *Observations upon his Majesty's late Answers*, 69
Parker, William R., 41
———, "Date of *Samson Agonistes*," 133
———, "Milton on King James the Second," 95
———, *Milton's Contemporary Reputation*, 12, 30-32, 39, 41, 53, 55, 58, 83, 87, 97, 108, 111, 112, 122, 123, 127, 129, 133, 143, 145, 160, 169, 171, 174, 184, 192, 211, 214, 218, 241, 242, 253-255, 260, 285, 292, 336, 337, 340, 341, 345, 348, 350
———, "Milton's Hobson Poems," 11, 12, 96
———, "On Milton's Early Literary Program," 50
Parkinson, Richard, see Martindale, Adam, *Life*
Parks, George B., "The Occasion of Milton's *Moscovia*," 268
Parliament, 33, 85, 114, 123, 124, 134, 145, 151-155, 157, 162, 218, 225, 229, 234, 235, 260, 265, 269, 271, 282-284, 291, 300, 304, 310, 317, 318, 334, 345, 350, 363

Parnassus, 175, 176
Pascal, M., 74, 77
Patin, Gui, *Lettres*, 308, 309
Paul, St., 46
Paul's Cross, 37
Pauncefoot (Pauncefote), Tracy, 150, 161, 271, 273, 313, 314, 332, 360
Pauw, Adrian de, 339
Payne, John, 338
Peach, Mr., 282
Pearse, Mr., 29
Pearson, Edward, 32
Peck, Francis, *New Memoirs*, 35, 36, 43, 51, 85, 134
Pell, John (?), 169
Pennsylvania, Historical Society of, see Historical
Pentateuch, 7
Pepys, Samuel, 138
Percy, Earl of, 244
Percy, Henry, see Northumberland
Perfect Diurnall, 252, 253
Perfect Narrative of the . . . High Court of Justice, 276
Peter, St., 45, 46
Peter Martyr, St., 94
Petiscus, 7
Petitot, Jean, painter, 92, 93
Petrarch, Francis, 73, 77, 187, 190
———, *Trionf. d'Amor*, 203, 208
Petty, John, 70
Petty, Mary, see Marlborough
Petty, Sir William, *Advice to Mr. S. Hartlib*, 100
Petty France, 274
Pforzheimer, Carl H., Library, see Unger, Emma, and W. A. Jackson
Philaras, Leonard, 107, 339
Philip IV, King of Spain, 297, 303, 306, 318, 345
Phillipps, Sir Thomas, 281
Phillips, Anne (Milton, later Agar), sister, 6-8
Phillips, Edward, brother-in-law, 8
Phillips, Edward, nephew, 6, 8-10, 51, 64, 183, 219
———, editor of Milton's *Letters of State*, see Milton
Phillips, John, nephew, 6-10, 64, 69, 183, 283
———, *Responsio ad Apologiam*, 237, 273, 274, 341
Phillips, Richard, 195, 197

Philological Quarterly, 50, 133
Phimostomus, 94
Phoebus, see Apollo
Photius, 94
Pickering, Sir Gilbert, 240
Pickering, publisher, see Milton, *Works*
Pierce, Mr., sculptor, 337
Pilfrance, 147
Pindar, 49, 203
Pisa, 191, 207, 222, 224
Pitt, Mr., clothier, 110
Pittheus, 206
Pitts, Philip, 261, 262
Platt, William, 196, 198
Plea for Non-Subscribers [*Non-scribers*], 285
Pliny the elder, *Natural History*, 6
Plutarch, *Placita Philosophorum* and *Peri Paidon Agogias*, 6
Poland, 243, 321
Poliziano, Mr., 222, 223
Pollentius, 93
Polyaenus, *Stratagemata*, 6
Polycarp, St., 45, 46, 95
Pope, the, 43, 54, 71, 74, 75, 187, 190
Pope, Arthur, 281
Popham, Edward, 306
Portugal, 306, 334, 349; see also John IV, King of Portugal
Povey, Mr., 66, 67
Powell, Anne, mother-in-law, 15, 16, 58, 61, 64, 65, 67, 68, 118-120, 134, 146, 149, 154, 165, 166, 173, 184, 195, 196, 198, 199, 201, 210, 217, 221, 246, 268, 270-273, 275, 276, 305, 312-314, 322-324, 330-332, 335, 343, 357, 359, 360
Powell, Sir Edward, 45-47, 174, 328, 329
Powell, Mary, see Milton, Mary
Powell, Richard, father-in-law, 2, 14, 15, 25, 45-47, 60, 61, 63-66, 82, 93, 103, 104, 118-120, 134, 146-155, 160-168, 173, 174, 177-180, 184, 192-199, 217, 221, 261-263, 271, 272, 275, 276, 306, 310, 312, 313, 322-329, 331-336, 342-344, 347, 357-361
Powell, Richard, brother-in-law, 84, 165, 166
Powell *alias* Hinman, William, 45, 47
Powell family, 62-66, 68, 80, 86, 91, 129, 133, 134, 165, 166, 183

Pragmaticus, see Needham, Marchamont

Prerogative Court of Canterbury, vi

Presbyterian, 35, 230, 231, 244, 260, 266, 294

Preston, 219

Prideaux, 245

Prince, Thomas, 240

Prince's Arms, bookshop, 136

Princeton University, 95, 351, 352

Privy Council, 69

Procopius, 94

Protestants, 83

Proverbs, 263

Prynne, William, 25, 112, 128, 185, 315-317

————, *Twelve Considerable Serious Questions*, 108

Public Record Office, 241

Puckering, Sir Henry Newton, 3

Purchas, Samuel, *Pilgrimage*, 215

Puritans, 34, 35

Pye, John, 15, 16, 211, 324-327, 342-344

Pye, Sir Robert, 14-16, 60, 103, 146, 166, 167, 177-181, 201, 211, 215, 216, 256, 310, 324, 325, 332-336, 342, 343, 347

Pythagoras, 73, 77

Quaritch, bookdealer, 280

Quarry Copse, 261, 262

Quarterly Review, 172

Racovian catechism, 321

Rainolds, Dr., 37, 94

Rainolds, John, 28

Rand, William (?), 169

Randolph, Mr., 257

Ranelagh, Lady, 9, 10

Ranelagh, Richard Jones, Earl of, 183

Ratchford, Fannie, 355

Ratzevil, Prince, 243

Raworth, Ruth, printer, 136

Raymond, Dora Neill, vi, 174, 255, 292

Reade, Thomas, 236

Reading, John, 15, 211, 326, 328, 343, 344

Reading, co. Berks, 29, 43, 81, 82, 85, 86, 92, 144, 155-159, 277

Redding (Ridding) Copse, 261, 262

Reeves, Mr., Justice, 116

Revelation (Apocalypse), 48

Review of English Studies, 114, 115, 322

Revue de Synthèse Historique, 347, 351

Reynolds, Dr., see Rainolds

Reynolds, Sir Joshua, 337

Ricci, Seymour de, *Book Collector's Guide*, 356

Richard, Andrew, 218

Richardson, Jonathan, painter and biographer of Milton, 135, 280, 337

————, *Explanatory Notes . . . on Milton's Paradise Lost*, 363

Ridding, see Redding

Ridley, Nicholas, Bishop of Rochester and London, 52, 83

Riff, 7

Rivet, Andrew, 249

Rivington, see *Stationers' Registers*

Robinson, bookseller, 102

Robinson, John, 217

Robinson, Luke, 291, 292

Robinson, Thomas, 128

Roe Copse, 261, 262

Rogers, Kenneth, "Bread Street," 245

Roman(s), 6, 35, 230

Rome, 17, 22, 27-29, 43, 45, 46, 54, 71, 72, 75, 76, 187, 190

Rose, Milton's house, 245, 246, 263, 270, 277, 302, 303, 319

Rosenbach Company, 98, 99

Ross, Alexander, 128

————, *Mel Heliconium*, 135

Rothwell, John, printer, 31, 40, 55, 59

Rotrou, M., 56, 74, 77

Rotterdam, 191

Rous, John, 128, 138-142, 172-176, 355

Rovai, Francesco, 202, 207, 208

————, *Poesie*, 209

Rowe, Sir Nicholas, 32

Rowe, Owen, 272

Rowe, Sir William, 272

Rowland, John, *Apologia*, 340-342

————, *Polemica Sive Supplementum*, 341

Royal Society of Literature, 281

Royalists, 84

Royston, Richard, printer, 227, 228

Rupert, Prince, Count Palatine, 242-244

Rushworth, John, *Historical Collections*, 152

Russell, Mr., tailor, 6, 8, 64

Russia (Moscovia, Muscovy), vi, 267, 268
Rutgers University Press, vi
Rutupian Sea, 18, 23
Rylands, W. W., engraver, 338

S., H., 358
S., M., printer, 87
Sacro Bosco, Joannes de, *De Sphaera*, 7
Sadleir, Mrs., 219
Sadler, Mr., 272
Sadler, John, 219
Sadler, William, 195, 197
St. Anne's parish, 126
St. Botolph's (Buttols, Buttolphes) Parish and Street, 29, 32, 40, 43, 44, 66
St. Bride's Churchyard, 6-10, 64
St. Buttals, see St. Botolph's
St. Buttolphes, see St. Botolph's
St. Clement Danes Church, 177
St. Clement's Churchyard, 119
St. David's, 283
St. Dunstan's in the West, 177
St. Giles Cripplegate, 182, 280
St. Giles in the Fields, 220
St. John Zachary's (Zecharies) Church, London, 144, 157, 161, 162
St. John's, 115
St. Lawrence parish and church, Reading, 43, 81
St. Margaret's Church, Westminster, 106, 109
St. Martin's le Grand, 119
St. Martin's parish, Ludgate, 156, 157
St. Paul, Triumph de, 195, 197
St. Paul's Churchyard, 55, 59, 127, 136, 282
St. Thomas Apostles Church, 86
Sallust, 263
Salmasius (Saumaise), Claudius, 244-246, 322, 336, 338, 341, 345, 347-350, 352, 353, 356
———, *Ad Johannem Miltonum Responsio, Opus Posthumum*, 68, 247, 249, 289, 362, 363
———, *Defensio Regia*, 244-250, 260, 274, 275, 277, 286-290, 299, 308, 334, 335, 340, 341, 347, 350, 351, 354, 360
———, *Plinian Exercitations*, 248
Saltmarsh, John, 145
Salvini, Salvino, *Fasti Consolari dell' Accademia Fiorentina*, 223

San Francisco, 127
Sancroft, William, Archbishop of Canterbury, 212-214
Sanderson, Robert, Bishop of Lincoln, 293
Sarravius, Claudius, 244
Satan, 24, 51
Saturday Review of Literature, 5
Saturn (planet), 17, 21, 71, 72, 74, 76
Saurat, Denis, *Milton Man and Thinker*, 96
Say, William (?), 275
Scaliger, 204, 357
Scherpbier, H., *Milton in Holland*, 340
Scotch (Scots), 219, 243
Scotch War, 40
Scotland, 192, 193, 195, 197, 318
Scotland Yard, 237, 273, 274
Scott, Mr., 291
Scott, Edward, 84
Scylla, 204, 311
Selden, John, 128, 237, 308, 309
———, *Opera Omnia*, ed. D. Wilkins, 237, 308
———, *Uxor Hebraea*, 89-91
Self-denying Ordinance, 122
Seneca, 83
———, *Hercules Oetacus*, 204, 206
———, *Hippolytus*, 204, 205
Sensabaugh, George F., "Milton Ascription," 127
Septuagint, 126
Sequestration, Committee for, 92, 104, 130
Sequestration of Delinquents' Books, 104, 109, 130; see also MS. SP Dom. 23, etc.
Seventeenth-Century News-Letter, 113, 114
Several Proceedings in Parliament, 277
Severus, Cornelius, *Aetna*, 204
Sewell, Arthur, *Study in Milton's Christian Doctrine*, 5
Shaftesbury Place, London, 9
Shakespeare, William, 11, 12, 315
———, *Poems*, 1640, 11, 12
Sharp, John, 137
Shaw, Dr., 52
Sherwyn, Richard, 14, 333, 334, 343, 347
Shotover, co. Oxon, 63, 64, 150, 261, 262
Sicily, 72, 75

Sidney, Sir Philip, *Arcadia*, 226-228, 301

Siena, 71, 75

Silius Italicus, 204

Simancos, 345

Simmons (Symmons), Matthew, printer, 105, 228, 238, 263, 298, 301

Simon, Abraham, sculptor, 337, 338

Sion College, 211, 212, 216

Skeat, Walter W., see Milton, *Epitaphium Damonis*, ed. W. W. Skeat

Skinner, Cyriack, 183

Slatford, John, 195, 197

Slatter, Anthony, 195, 197

Slatyer, William, *Psalms of David*, 83

Small, Mr., 256

Smart, John S., see Milton, *Sonnets*

Smectymnuus, 13, 30, 40, 59, 117, 169, 170

————, *Answer to . . . Humble Remonstrance*, 31, 32

————, *Vindication of the Answer*, 40-42, 44, 53

Smith (Smythe), Mr., 179, 216, 303, 333

Smith, George, vi

Smith, Peter, 305

Smith, Richard (?), 53

Smith, Sir Thomas, 236

Smyrna, 45, 46

Smythe, Mr., see Smith

Socinus, Faustus, 321

Sofia, 206

Song of Solomon, 48

Sophie, Princess, 242-244, 251

Sophocles, 48

Sorani, Aldo, 5

Sotheby, Samuel, *Ramblings in the Elucidation of the Autograph of Milton*, 3, 125, 135, 140, 175, 188, 299, 337, 358

Sotheby's auction rooms, 85, 138, 259, 280, 357

South Kensington Museum, 92, 93, 281

Southern California, University of, 1

Spain, 93, 297, 306, 330-332, 345; see also Philip IV, King of Spain

Spang, William, 164

Spencer, Lady, 63

Spencer, Mr., 259

Spenser, Edmund, 120

Spon, Dr. Charles, 308

Spread Eagle, Milton's house, 246

Spring Garden, Milton's residence, 237, 273

Stafford, Marquis of, 356

Stafford Close, 261, 262

Stanton St. John, 261, 262

Staple, Sarah, 279, 280

Staple, William, 279, 280

Stapleton, Sir Philip, 107

Star Chamber, 261, 262

Starke, John, 32

Stationers, Company of, 106, 107, 116

Stationers' Registers, ed. Arber to 1640 and Eyre and Rivington from 1641, 12, 30-32, 37, 40, 42, 101, 105, 108, 109, 127, 130, 216, 238, 252, 276, 335

Steeplehill Copse, 261, 262

Stephens, Mr., 107

Sterling Library, 283

Stern, Alfred, *Milton und seine Zeit*, 12, 36, 53, 55, 56, 92, 122, 153, 154, 185, 220, 243, 329

Stevens, David H., *Milton Papers*, 45, 47, 166, 174, 329

————, "Order of Milton's Sonnets," 136

————, *Reference Guide to Milton*, 54, 201

Stilpo, 55

Stock Talmadge, co. Oxon., 70

Stockholm, 322

Stow, John, *Survey of London*, 200

Stowood, 261, 262

Strafford, Thomas Wentworth, Earl of, 40

Strasburgh, 94

Strickland, Walter, 260, 275

Stuart, Dorothy Margaret, v, 316

Studies in Philology, 5, 62, 268, 311, 329

Sturmius, 94

Sun, bookshop, 55, 59

Surridge, Rev. H. A. D., 79

Surridge, Miss M. K., 79

Sutro Library, vi, 127, 128

Sweden, 245, 364, 365

Sweet, Henry, 218

Symmons, Matthew, see Simmons

Symons, Walter, 196, 198

Syriac, 7

Tacitus, Cornelius, 52

Tamar River, 18, 24

Tangye, Sir Richard, 138, 355

Targum, 7
Tartu, 33
Tasso, Torquato, 48, 71, 73, 75, 77
———, *Jerusalem Delivered*, 206
Taunton, 110, 111
Taylor, Colonel, 272
Taylor, John, 40
Teignmouth, Lord, *Memoirs of . . . Sir William Jones*, 63
Tertullian, 45, 46, 93
Testament, Greek, 7
Testimony to the Truth of Jesus Christ, 211, 216
Tetuan (Tituan), 282, 292, 293
Texas, University of, 355
Thackam, Thomas, 81
Thame, co. Oxon, 201
Thames River, 18, 24, 138, 139, 141
Theocritus, 222, 223
Theoctista, 94
Theodosius, 93
These Tradesmen are Preachers in and about the City of London, 191, 192
Theseus, 206
Thomas, St., see Aquinas
Thomas, William, 282
Thomas, William, Bishop of Worcester, 283
Thomas, William, M. P., 283
Thomason, George (including his collection in the British Museum and the catalogue of it by G. K. Fortescue), 13, 30-33, 35-38, 40, 43-46, 54-56, 59, 60, 69, 79, 84-87, 96-98, 105, 108, 109, 112, 113, 115, 116, 118, 122-124, 127, 133, 137, 142, 143, 145, 160, 163, 169, 172, 174, 184, 192, 218, 225, 228, 229, 239, 240, 242, 246, 250, 254, 257, 258, 260, 263, 264, 276, 286, 291, 298, 302, 317, 318, 321, 348
Thomason, Katharine (Mrs. George), 118, 163
Thompson, Francis, D.D., 225
Thomson, Mr., 237, 273
Thornbury, Walter, see Walford, Edward
Thornehill Copse, 261, 262
Three Bibles, bookshop, 282
Thurloe, John, *Collection of the State Papers*, 260
Thusca (Thuscia), see Tuscan
Thyrsis (*i.e.*, Milton), 16-24
Tibullus, 204

———, *Elegies*, 203, 205
Tilbury, 126
Tituan, see Tetuan
Tityrus, 17, 20, 22
Todd, H. J., see Milton, John, *Poetical Works*, ed. H. J. Todd
Toland, John, see Milton, John, *Complete Collection of the . . . Works*, with prefatory life of Milton by John Toland
———, *Amyntor*, 225, 228
Toledo, Ohio, 129
Tomlins, Henry, 327
Tonge, Eres, 169
Torricelli, Mr., 60, 61
Toulouse, 94
Tower of London, 55, 240
Tower Ward, 218
Tregaskis, bookseller, 52
Trenchard, John (?), 275
Trent, Council of, 353
Trent (Treanta) River, 18, 23
Trinity College, Cambridge, vi, 3
Trinity College, Dublin, 36, 115, 125
Trinity Manuscript, see MS. Milton's Minor Poems
Trobridge, John, 32
Trojan (Dardanian), 17, 18, 23
Trustees for sale of King's Goods, 314
Tudman, Mr., 29
Tunis, 282
Turk's Head, bookshop, 112
Turnbull, G. H., vi
———, *Hartlib, Dury and Comenius*, 82, 100, 104, 105, 116, 132, 169, 214, 219, 278, 306
Turnham Green, 82
Tuscan (Hetrurian, Thuscan), 1, 16, 19, 20, 202; see also Italian
Tuscany, 222, 223
Tyler, Moses C., 129
Tyton, Francis, printer, 291

Underhill, Thomas, printer, 32, 37, 40, 101, 109
Unger, Emma, and W. A. Jackson, *Carl H. Pforzheimer Library*, 264
Union List of Serials, 347
Union Theological Seminary, vi
Urania, muse, 130
Urstisius, 7
Usa, see Ouse River
Ussher, James, Archbishop of Armagh, 308, 341

————, "Geographical and Historical Disquisition, touching the *Lydian* or *Proconsular* Asia," 28
————, *Judgment of Dr. Reynolds*, 37-39
Uther, 23
Utrecht, 351

Valentinian, 94
Vallombrosa, 5
Van Sinderen, Mr. and Mrs. Adrian, 98, 115, 356
Vane, Charles, 349, 355
Vane, Sir Henry, 234
Varro, 6, 8
Vatican, 73, 77
Vaughan, Henry, "King Disguised," 171, 172
————, *Thalia Rediviva*, 172
————, *Works*, ed. L. C. Martin, 172
Vaughan, Richard, see Carbery
Venice, 86, 87, 191, 207
Venus (Cytherea), 203, 204, 206
Verax, Theodorus, see Walker, Clement
Verdussen, Jerome, Dutch publisher, 341, 342
Vertue, George, artist, 280, 337
Verwey, H. de la Fontaine, 322
Vesing, Mr., 149
Vettori, Mr., 222, 223
Villa, Marquis of, see Manso
Villani, Giovanni, 7
Vincent, Thomas, 144, 156, 161
Vindiciae Carolinae, 225
Violet, Thomas, *Advancement of Merchandise*, 335
Virgil, 48, 136
————, *Aeneid*, 204, 320
————, *Georgics*, 205
Visiak, E. H., see Milton, *Lament for Damon*, ed. E. H. Visiak
Visteni, Nicholas, 191
Vitruvius, 6
Vivers, Richard, 149
Viviani, Mr., 60, 61
Vlacq, Dutch printer, 264, 288, 309, 352, 363, 364
Voiture, Mr., 57, 60, 61
Voltaire, *Epic Poetry of the European Nations*, 51
————, "Essai sur la Poésie Epique," 51
————, *Oeuvres Complètes*, 51
Vossius, Isaac, 202, 208, 209, 223, 322

W., E., 358
Wagstaffe, Thomas, *Vindication of King Charles the Martyr*, 227, 301
Walbancke, Matthew, printer, 84
Waldenses, 253
Walford, Edward, "Unknown Portrait of John Milton," 134, 135
Walford, Edward, and Walter Thornbury, *Old and New London*, 200, 273, 294
Walker, Clement, 268, 269
————, *Anarchia Anglicana*, 260, 269
Wall, Heyling (?), 169
Wall, John, 212
Waller, Edmund, 219
Waller, Sir William, 122, 168
Walsall, Dr., 307
Walwyn, William, 240
Warcupp, Robert, 298
Warcupp, Rodolph, 298
Warcutt (Warrutt), Thomas, 32
Ward, Edward, *Secret History of the Calves-Head Club*, 294
Waring, Richard, 158, 169
Waring, Thomas, *Brief Narration of the Rebellion in Ireland*, 286
Warner, G. F., ed., *Nicholas Papers*, 333, 337
Warrutt, see Warcutt
Warton, Thomas, ed., *Milton's Poems upon Several Occasions*, see Milton, John, *Poems*
Washington, Mr., 351
Wasse, Christopher, *Electra of Sophocles*, 241, 242
Watkins, Mr., 245
Watkins, D., 163
Watson, Richard, 275
Way, Albert, 337, 338
Webb, John, 149, 331
Webber, Mrs. 119
Webster, Elizabeth (Mrs. Elijah), 104, 115, 130
Weckherlin, George, 236, 295
Wells, 110, 111
Wentworth, Thomas, see Strafford
Wesembechius, 94
West, Captain, 111
Westbury, co. Wilts, 70
Westminster, 117, 146, 168, 177, 193, 194, 241, 258, 263, 269, 271, 272, 277, 281, 285, 297, 298, 300, 303-306, 309, 310, 312, 318, 330, 332, 333, 335, 345, 348, 361

Westminster Abbey, 278, 279
Whalley, Colonel Edward, 272
Wheatley, co. Oxon., 15, 45-47, 148, 160, 162, 166, 174, 195-199, 201, 209, 210, 212, 217, 220, 239, 261, 303, 327-329, 357, 358
Wheatley Copse, 261, 262
Whitaker, Mr., 108
Whitaker, Richard, printer, 39
White, A. T., 356
White, Jeremiah, 294
White, John, 85
White Bear, 246
Whitehall, 257, 273, 281, 296, 299, 314, 316, 317, 344, 345
Whitehead, T. M., 93
Whitelocke, Bulstrode, 179, 234, 304
———, *Memorials of the English Affairs*, 152
Whiting, George W., 32, 38, 46
Whiting, Thomas, 87
Whittington, George, bookseller, 259
Widdrington, Sir Thomas, 107
"widow, rich," 58
Wigandus, Johann (?), 94, 169
Wike Copse, 261, 262
Wilcox, Mr., 256
Wild, John, 195, 197
Wilford, John, 32; see also Wilsford
Wilkins, David, 237, 308, 309
Wilkins, John, *Ecclesiastes*, 160, 169, 337
William III, King of England, 293
Williams, J., printer, 258
Williams, J. B., 250
———, *History of English Journalism*, 253, 255, 311, 329
Williams, Roger, *Bloody Tenent*, 123, 127, 143, 171
Williamson, George C., *Milton Tercentenary*, 93, 135, 138, 220, 280, 337, 338, 355
Williamson, Sir Joseph, 84
Williamson, William, 104
Willingham, Mr., 295, 296
Willmot, Richard, 327
Wilsford, Mr., 29; see also Wilford
Wilson, John, *Treatise of Monarchy*, 225
———, *Vindication of Eikon Basilike*, 225
Winchester College (?), 168
Windham, Mr., 110

Wing, Donald, *Short-Title Catalogue, 1641-1700*, 336
Winslow, E., 362
Wit Restored, 12
Wolfe, Edward, 144
Wollebius (Wolleb), Joannes, 5, 7
Wolsey, Thomas, Cardinal and Archbishop of York, 36, 43
Wood, Anthony, 219
———, *Athenae* (and *Fasti*) *Oxonienses*, 8 et seq.; ed. Philip Bliss, 284, 336
Wood Street, 37, 40
Woodington, Mr., 29; see also Woodrington
Woodrington, John 32; see also Woodington
Woodward, Hezekiah, 116, 117
Worcester, 283, 312
Wordsworth, Christopher, *Who Wrote Eikon Basilike?*, 225-227, 237, 254, 275, 301, 308
Worffeild, Mr., 32
Worsley, Benjamin, 214
Wotton, Sir Henry, 120, 213, 305, 348
———, *Reliquiae Wottonianae*, 348
Wright, B. A., "Milton's First Marriage," 62
Wright, Edward, 127
Wright, Nathaniel, 218
Wright, W. A., ed., Milton's Trinity Manuscript, see Milton, John, *Facsimile*
Wrighter, Clement, 96
Wycliffe, John, 94
Wyeth, Joseph, 295
Wykes, Dr., 30, 37

Xenophon, *Anabasis*, 6
———, *Cyri Institutio*, 6

Yale University (College), 39, 98, 113, 114, 129, 220, 228, 264, 283, 336
Yanning, William, 195, 197
Yates, Jane, 40
Yewelme, see Ewelme
York Street, 281
Young, Mr., printer, 301
Young, Patrick, 36, 115, 125, 126
Young, Thomas, 32

Zellius, 94
Zephyr, 17, 20
Zion, 145
Zurich, 94

DATE DUE

GAYLORD			PRINTED IN U.S.A.